SECOND EDITION

BREAKING GROUND

KEYS FOR SUCCESSFUL ONLINE LEARNING

AMY SCOTT HASSENPFLUG | AARON D. TRAPHAGEN | JAMAICA JOHNSON CONNER

Liberty University

Kendall Hunt
publishing company

D1708972

All Bible verses from the New International Version unless otherwise noted.

Cover images provided by the following:

Photo courtesy of Cali Lowdermilk
(Liberty University).
Artwork by Klaus Shmidheiser.

Kendall Hunt
publishing company

www.kendallhunt.com
Send all inquiries to:
4050 Westmark Drive
Dubuque, IA 52004-1840

CONTENTS

PREFACE

The development of your academic career is a lot like the construction of a building—you must build your education on a solid foundation. Upon this premise, we constructed the text, *Breaking Ground: Keys for Successful Online Learning*. This notion is nothing new. If you want to be successful in anything in life, you must begin with a purpose, building upon a firm foundation. Jesus related this very principle to our spiritual walk with Him in Luke 6:48–49,

> *Why do you call me, 'Lord, Lord,' and do not do what I say? As for everyone who comes to me and hears my words and puts them into practice, I will show you what they are like. They are like a man building a house, who dug down deep and laid the foundation on rock. When a fl ood came, the torrent struck that house but could not shake it, because it was well built. But the one who hears my words and does not put them into practice is like a man who built a house on the ground without a foundation. The moment the tor-rent struck that house, it collapsed and its destruction was complete". (NIV)*

Jesus' message is clear throughout the simile: listen to His instruction and apply it if you want to have a lasting, strong relationship with Him. The same is true for your education; you must apply the guidance, instruction, and advice of your professors and those who have gone before you to achieve success in your academics.

Though there is nothing glamorous about forming the foundation because of the gritty, dirty nature of the work, the preparation and perspiration is critical so that the beautiful features of the structure last. Once a builder establishes that foundation, choosing the best materials and the most experienced team of builders makes all the difference in the strength and magnificence of the building. In I Corinthians 3:9–13, Paul explains this further,

> *For we are co-workers in God's service; you are God's fi eld, God's building. By the grace God has given me, I laid a foundation as a wise builder, and someone else is building on it. But each one should build with care. For no one can lay any foundation other than the one already laid, which is Jesus Christ. If anyone builds on this foundation using gold, silver, costly stones, wood, hay or straw, their work will be shown for what it is, because the Day will bring it to light. (NIV)*

As you "build with care," dig into the course materials, lessons, and resources that have been carefully selected for you. Enjoy collaborating with your classmates and your professor and share your own prayer requests and encouragement in the discussion board forums. Take advantage of every opportunity designed to make your academic experience and development rich and robust.

In this textbook, our analogy begins by comparing your school selection process to the beginning phase of a construction project when clients peruse model homes to find the perfect fit, and we conclude by celebrating the day you earn your degree, just like a client celebrates the day he accepts the keys from the builder. Each chapter contains four essential elements: a devotional, known as The Cornerstone; Key Concepts that highlight the academic objectives and instruction; a review and application section called Building Blocks; and finally, an explanation and offering of resources, the Tool Box. Additionally, there are tips from former students, professors, and key leaders at Liberty University in the margins of each chapter. As you read each element of the text, our hope is that you recognize that not only is your academic career like a construction project, but your spiritual development is, as well. Ephesians 2:19–22 explains,

> *Consequently, you are no longer foreigners and strangers, but fellow citizens with God's people and also members of His household, built on the founda-tion of the apostles and prophets, with Christ Jesus Himself as the chief cor-nerstone. In Him the whole building is joined together and rises to become a holy temple in the Lord. And in Him you too are being built together to become a dwelling in which God lives by his Spirit. (NIV)*

Once a building is constructed, it must be maintained, and though you may need to renovate or add-on down the road, the structure you began with is going to be the basis and main support in each of those scenarios. If your foundation is rooted in a faith in Jesus Christ and His teachings, your building will be resilient, as it undergoes spiritual growth and improvement. If your academic foundation is rooted in the lessons you will learn and apply throughout *Breaking Ground: Keys for Successful Online Learning*, you will be set up for academic success. With these principles in mind, we look forward to the day we will celebrate with you as you finally accept your key from the builder and earn your college degree.

Your authors,

Amy Scott Hassenpflug
Aaron D. Traphagen
Jamaica Johnson Conner

CONSTRUCTION KEY

Throughout this textbook, you will see symbols that represent different pieces of information, like student testimonials or professor tips. Use this legend as a visual guide to connect you to these valuable pieces of information.

IMAGE	TEXTUAL COMPONENT
	THE CORNERSTONE A brief devotional to begin each chapter, written by Jamaica Johnson Conner, in partnership with Liberty University alumni and professors
	KEY CONCEPT The main objectives of each chapter
	THE LEVEL An opportunity to measure and apply what God's Word says about the information within the chapter
	PROFESSOR TIP Helpful tips from seasoned LUO faculty
	THE SHOVEL An opportunity to think critically and dig deeper into the content
	STUDENT TESTIMONIALS Current and former LUO students share their tips for success
	BUILDING BLOCKS A summary of each chapter

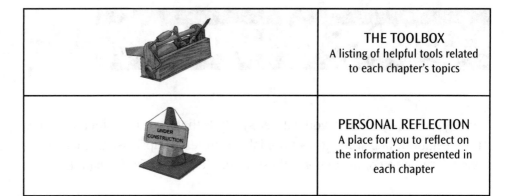	**THE TOOLBOX** A listing of helpful tools related to each chapter's topics
	PERSONAL REFLECTION A place for you to reflect on the information presented in each chapter

AUTHOR BIOS AND ACKNOWLEDGMENTS

Together, Amy, Aaron, and Jamaica would like to thank the following people for their invaluable contributions to the first and second editions of this textbook:

Amanda Smith	Jennifer Griffin	Nathaniel Valle
Brad Burgess	John E. Johnson, Sr.	Paul Gormley
Cami Smith	(1949–2014)	Paula Oldham Johnson
Cari Smith	Klaus Shmidheiser	Dr. Ron Godwin
College of General	Lisa Stephens Taylor	Dr. Ron Hawkins
Studies faculty	T. Marcus Christian	Tracey Good
Curtis Ross	Mark Heideman	Dr. Wayne Patton
Emily Foutz	Dr. Mark Tinsley	
Dr. Emily Heady	Mollie Yoder	

Psalm 127:1, "Unless the LORD builds the house, the builders labor in vain. Unless the LORD watches over the city, the guards stand watch in vain" (NIV).

Amy, Aaron, and Jamaica thank the Lord for his protection, provision, and guidance throughout the construction of this textbook. Thank you, Lord Jesus, for being the Cornerstone of this project and the Cornerstone of our lives. We love you!

Amy:

Amy Scott Hassenpflug, M.Ed.
Department Chair
Assistant Professor of General Education
College of General Studies

Amy Scott Hassenpflug, M.Ed., serves as the General Studies Department Chair in the College of General Studies. She enjoys working as an Assistant Professor of General Studies and has a variety of teaching experiences, both public and private. Her teaching posts have included students who excel, as well as those who struggle.

Amy Scott Hassenpflug is a product of public education, but she is nevertheless grateful for Christian education. Raised through high school in public schools, she is a graduate of the College of William and Mary and the University of Virginia, both public universities in Virginia. Having seen the best of public education as a student, she is delighted to be able to offer her skills in the online Christian arena.

Married for more than three decades to her Mary Baldwin College Governor's School sweetheart, she is the mother of two LU alumnae, Rachel and Madeline. Living in Central Virginia, yet longing to travel *everywhere*, she believes each day should be celebrated for the adventures it brings.

Amy wishes to thank . . .

You, family, for your steadfast encouragement and love in this new endurance event!

My gratitude goes to the dozens and dozens of Liberty University faculty who regularly inform my thinking on what and how we should be teaching our newest online college learners. Previous students, whose comments, suggestions, and feedback we treasure, should be mentioned here with thanks as well.

No new version of this textbook would be complete without the daily intentional leadership of Vice Provost and College of General Studies Dean Emily Heady and AD Wayne Patton. Thank you both for making the College of General Studies a fun place to contribute our skills. To Jamaica and Aaron, thank you both for laughing when we could have cried! I love working with both of you. Creating the second edition is certainly much different than stitching together the original, isn't it?

Thank you to my wonderful family: Leon, Madeline, Rachel, Beau, Mom, and Bill. You each contributed to my ability to get this done and to my belief that it WOULD be possible, in due time!

Aaron:

Aaron D. Traphagen, M.Ed.
Assistant Professor of General Education
College of General Studies, Liberty University

Aaron D. Traphagen began his work in academics when he joined Liberty University's staff in 2008. Since that time, he has served as an

Academic Advisor, Academic Progress Analyst, and Faculty Support Coordinator. Mr. Traphagen works as a residential faculty member for the College of General Studies, primarily focusing on assessment and reporting.

Aaron spent 12 years in the United States Marine Corps, where he served as a Communications Specialist, Close Combat Instructor, and Recruiter. Upon medical retirement from the Marines in 2005, he earned a Bachelor of Science in Biblical Studies and a Master of Education in Teaching and Learning, both from Liberty University.

Aaron is passionate about educational technology, online learning, and adult education. In his free time, he enjoys kayaking, woodworking, and spending time with his family. Aaron resides in Lynchburg, VA, with his wife Lauren and their two teenage daughters, Calista and Olivia.

Aaron wishes to thank . . .

Mark T., you have been a friend and mentor. Your support and wise counsel have meant the world to me.

Wayne, I have valued all of your advice and support. Stay humble.

Dr. Heady, your leadership and support make all that we do in CGS possible. You are appreciated beyond words.

Amy and Jamaica, I could not have asked to work with two more amazing people. Thank you for every minute of this experience.

Mom and Grandma, I thank you, both, for everything you did to help make me who I am today. You are loved and missed every day.

Calista and Olivia, thank you for challenging me each day and for making me the proudest dad around. I love you both!

Lauren, You are my wife, partner, and dearest friend. Thank you for being you and for loving and supporting me.

Jamaica:

Jamaica Johnson Conner, M.Ed.
Department Chair for the College of
General Studies, Liberty University
Assistant Professor of English, Liberty
University

Jamaica Johnson Conner lives on a family farm in Amherst, Virginia with her husband Terry, and their two young daughters, Laura Grace and Marianna Cadence. As a family, the Conners love doing things together, especially laser tag, skating, hiking, painting, singing, dancing, and playing with their pets: a dog named, "Suki," a cat named "Daisy," and a white, fluffy bunny called "Nibbles."

Jamaica has served as a professor for LUO since 2007, after she received her Masters of Education in Teaching and Learning from Liberty University. In 2011, she wrote the book *Sparky's ABC Adventure*, a children's ABC book that celebrates Liberty University and its energetic and fun eagle mascot. In 2012, Jamaica began serving in her current role as Department Chair for the College of General Studies. Prior to her work at LU with students, faculty, and administration, Jamaica taught English to middle and high school students in both private and public institutions.

Liberty University's school and ministry heavily influenced Jamaica's life, even before she was born. Her mom and dad, Paula and John Johnson (1949–2014), met at Liberty. Her mom was one of the first students in 1971, and her dad was in the first graduating class. (You will get a chance to read their stories within two of the Cornerstone devotionals in this textbook.) Her grandfather, Doug Oldham, sang for the Liberty and TRBC ministries from the 1970s until his homegoing in 2010. Jamaica feels very blessed that God brought her family to Liberty ages ago to learn and to serve and to pass that legacy on to her, as she shares it with her students, her own children, and with you through *Breaking Ground*.

Jamaica wishes to thank . . .

Terry, thank you for your unfailing love, support, and goodness to me every day of our life together. Without you, I could not do what I do! I love you more than words can express, but I'll endeavor every day to find the words. I love you! Thank you for everything!

Laura Grace and Marianna, thank you for inspiring me with your contagious giggles and addictive cuddles. Every day is a story-writing adventure with you two! I love you both so much!

Mom and Dad, thank you for your insightful contributions to this textbook and the wealth of knowledge that you brought to this project. Thank you for spending time with your grandbabies, so I could finish it! Thank you for falling in love with each other, with Liberty, and with the Lord, and for passing that legacy on to me. I love you both! Daddy, I can't wait to see you again in heaven! I miss you so much here on earth. Mom, thank you for taking such good care of Dad and for all you do for us. You are a guiding light in my life, and I thank God that you are my mom!

John, you are an inspirational and remarkable brother! Thank you for all you have done for our family. Thank you for supporting us all from miles away. I love you, and I'm so proud of you!

Lynn, thank you for living every day with a "never ever quit" attitude and for all of your help taking care of our girls! I love you!

Dr. Yaw, thank you for recommending me to be a part of this wonderful team. God blessed me abundantly through you!

Emily and Wayne, thanks for leading our team with compassion and understanding, while holding us all to standard of excellence—all while having fun! What a balancing act that is! It is a privilege to serve under your leadership. Thank you, both, for everything!

Marcus, it takes a lot of talent and guts to write a really awful rough draft when you are such a great writer! Thank you for being willing to do that! Nate, thank you for sharing your heart with us through your devotional. It holds such a powerful message.

Amy and Aaron, thank you for allowing me to work with you on this amazing project. I have loved collaborating with both of you!

For the Conner, Harmon, and Tomlin families; for the Cox, Johnson, Nicholson, Offenbacker, and Oldham families; for my dear friends Patricia and David Emmert, Emily Foutz, and Stacey Hester; for my team of babysitters: Jenny Harris, Emily Hine Elrod, Emily Cox, Rebekah Cox (aka Aunt Dee Dee), and Thais Jardim; for Michelle Martilla and your artistic advice; for my colleagues and friends in the College of General Studies; for my incredible team of professors, led by their incredible instructional mentors: Heather Burgess, Mary Dixon, Alissa Keith, and Katie Robinson; for my students, past and present—thank you all for all you do! You are a blessing to me!

Article Contributors

Alicia Castaneda
Brad Burgess
Emily Foutz
Emily Heady
John E. Johnson, Sr. (1949–2014)
T. Marcus Christian
Nathaniel Valle
Lisa Stephens Taylor
Mark Tinsley

Paula Oldham Johnson
Tracey Good
Wayne Patton

Student Contributors

Terry Conner
Emily Cox
Ruth Ferrell
Tim Harpe
Maddy Hassenpflug
Roger Nauss
Cheryl Palmer

Tip Contributors

Alexandra Barnett
Hanna Bruce
Betsey Caballero
T. Marcus Christian
Terry Conner
Jessica Cromley
Shaun Curran
Sherry Dickerson
Mary Marie Dixon
Lisa Eppard
Josh Gerstner
Tracey Good
Silvia Graham
Jennifer Griffin
David Hart
Mark Heideman
Stephanie Hobson
Kirsten Hoegh
Alissa Keith
Nicole Lowes
Debra Magnuson
Michael Marrano
Kristy Motte
Lucy Montalvo
Ramona Myers
Sue Ocealis
Heather Patterson

Katie Robinson
Michael Shenkle
Barbara Sherman
Cari Smith
Katie Stewart
Joe Super
Nathaniel Valle
Jenny Walter
Terri Washer
Sherrie Welfel
Dustin Williams

Photography Contributors

Jamaica Johnson Conner
Paula Johnson
Dave Moquin
Faith Perry
Aaron D. Traphagen

Liberty University Photographers

Bob Duval
Cali Lowdermilk
David Duncan
Joel Coleman
Kevin Maguiob
Les Schofer
LU Marketing
Rachel Dugan
Ty Hester

FOREWORD

Solutions . . .

Ironically, and perhaps providentially, as I sit to prepare the foreword for this edition of *Breaking Ground,* I am at a conference of university deans and directors in San Diego, California. Now my home is in Lynchburg, Virginia, where for the past three weeks we have been hit with as hard of a winter as I can recall. In San Diego, on the other hand, it is 75 degrees and sunny today.

Ask anyone, I am as devout a Virginian as there can be, but the timing to be far away from my beloved home and at this particular event, is quite good on several levels. For one, as noted, the weather is beautiful here! Also, because I have struggled in my efforts to craft a follow-up foreword to the previous edition of this textbook, and the conference has been inspiring on that front.

To clarify the focus of the conference is, in sum, a dialogue on:

> How academic leadership, whose areas of oversight is on new and returning college students, can best address the needs of such students, strategies to retain such students, and set these students up for long term academic success.

This could almost be the mission statement of *Breaking Ground.* In actuality, this topic is a very big focus in higher education across the spectrum of institutions for both residential and online programs. It is, in a word, a battle, a strategic battle for your success. So yes, this arena is an important and an intentional part of the mission for at least one or more academic divisions within most all colleges and universities.

What has struck me the most from the conference sessions so far is how much people care. Perhaps you have never thought and imagined that university administrators, faculty, and advisors are actually gathered around tables in conference centers, leaning in, listening hard, passionately dialoging, and diligently seeking a solution, THE solution, many SOLUTIONS to the vast array of targets in the battle for your academic success and survival. Why?

There are numerous answers to that question. Some of the answers are related to the solvency of an institution, that is the university's economic survival, various regulations, complex financial aid stipulations, and other issues that in some way tie back to economics and policies. These may seem shallow or ominous, but it is just reality, most of the world works this way.

Still, many people in higher education, those who have a vocational calling to this work, seek solutions to these student-based issues, because they simply have a burden to do all they can to put strategies, processes, resources, knowledge, the right people, the right curriculum, and the right advice into your hands. Perhaps it is cheesy, but the phrase is, "we care."

I personally know the team that put this textbook and the corresponding course together and let me tell you: they really do care. Not only do they care, they also know students and the variety of needs that, if addressed, will optimize their experience and success. They also know the pitfalls we have seen time and time again that slow down, discourage, or even derail students. This textbook seeks to instruct and inform in such a way as to minimize or eradicate those pitfalls.

It is based upon years of observation, a range of online student demographics, and student record data. So, its contents are not just based upon some crunching of statistics. Granted that is good information, but it is also based upon years of personal interaction with students, professors, and administrators across the spectrum of online higher education and across numerous online course offerings, that is math, english, history, science, information technology, information literacy, and so on. It is based upon the science of learning and yet includes the soft sciences of relationships, community, compassion, and meeting students where they are in their level of preparedness. No small task.

So, it is not enough that we simply care. We must also put careful planning and action into play. The heart and mind need the hands and the feet, eh? But that is not just a maxim for administrators, faculty, and advisors. You, as students, need to plan and move wisely, as well.

I will close this foreword where I began the last version, since the scripture's utility is timeless.

Proverbs 15:22, *"Plans fail for lack of counsel, but with many advisers they succeed"* (NIV).

Wisdom literature, such as Proverbs and Ecclesiastes, is not meant to be lofty, but rather it is practical and seeks to show us how to best live our lives. If you look carefully at the verse, it presupposes a key aspect, that is, that a plan is in place. Without a plan, a hope, a vision, a dream, a mission, we are just arbitrarily going through the motions of existence. The good news is we all tend to have a plan or plans. These ventures may just be laid out as vague goals or concepts. They may be well-thought-out objectives with each step of the agenda meticulously thought through, a timetable established, and action points clarified.

Our personalities, strengths, and weaknesses all play into how we proceed with such tasks. Within the context of this study, the plan is for you to engage your educational goals, seek knowledge, earn your degree, improve your standing, and use your skills and gifts in your field. Clearly, such a mission requires a lot of thought and planning. If you are engaging this text-book, you are about to, or are currently, undertaking that mission. So, what is your plan? Why are you here? What is the goal? How will you get there?

Often, we set out to do something and may not be fully prepared. We may have pondered it greatly and committed to it, yet our levels of read-iness and ability to complete the task were not quite up to the challenge. That reality either made for a difficult journey or found us failing altogether. In our preparation of the plan, did we ask the right questions? Did we talk to the right people? Did we set ourselves up for success? Did we get a lay of the land? Yes, the counsel of others, who have been there before us and know the road ahead of us, is of great benefit.

Breaking Ground seeks to be a part of that wise council. It was crafted in the same spirit of the aforementioned verse and within the context of the passion and care I saw here in San Diego. We will do our best to continue to equip and edify you. We will continue to be inspired by our peers and students—just like you! May we all find the solutions we need.

In the spirit of the aforementioned verse, may you plan well, find and listen to wise counsel, and may you succeed!

Blessings . . .

Wayne A. Patton, D.Min.
Associate Dean
College of General Studies
Liberty University, Lynchburg, Virginia
March 2015

STUDENT TESTIMONIALS

These students have gone before you at Liberty University Online. Read their brief biographies below to find one that you most closely relate to as a student. Keep an eye out for that former student's comments throughout the textbook to guide you.

Cheryl, 30-something, graduate

Cheryl's Story:

"I am a single mother of two, a caregiver for my Mom (who is disabled), and I homeschool my son. Time is the hugest challenge that my situation has brought to my personal educational goals. I do not resent this. 'It is what it is.' However, someone always needs my attention and care. It is not usually small tasks either, as the 'time' thing in my situation has usually included doctor appointments, emergency room trips (sometimes all-nighters), or doctor follow-up appointments."

Emily, 19-year-old, freshman at Liberty University

Emily's Story:

"My name is Emily. I am an only child, and my parents are divorced. However, they would not be the same people together, and I have a great step family . . . I never had much discipline growing up, and I was never really good at disciplining myself so my first semester was rough trying to balance activities with school work. Honestly, I didn't do that well academically, so it was a hard lesson learned."

Maddy, 20-something, Liberty student

Maddy's Story:

"I am a 22-year-old 'traditional' college student, in my final year on campus. I have changed my major more than once, and have begun to take advantage of online classes in order to graduate in a more timely fashion. My main concern starting online classes was that I would completely forget about them, just because they would be unlike anything I had done before.

I mainly came to Liberty because of my scholarship from attending Liberty Christian Academy (LCA). There was also the comfort of not leaving home yet. Having been a student at LCA for most of my schooling, I was able to hear Dr. Falwell speak on multiple occasions. My favorite quote of his was one I heard often. When telling the story of how Thomas Road Baptist Church, LU, and LCA came to be, he would tell the students 'I walked this mountain; I claimed this land.'" I'm grateful that he did!

Roger, 50-something graduate of Liberty University with a MAT, 2011

Roger's Story:

"I was raised in New York to Christian parents and came to faith in Jesus Christ at an early age. Our church had many good role models and I felt truly blessed to enjoy a good relationship with them. Although neither of my parents had a high school education, they strongly believed their children should have a good education.

Dad was a bricklayer and the only breadwinner in the family. He worked very hard but he could only work if the weather cooperated or if there was a job. I remember one time when the construction trade collapsed and he was without work for nine months. He reminded us that God would take care of us and keep food on the table. In all that time, he never failed to tithe unto the Lord, even his unemployment check. Dad didn't want me to follow in his trade. He wanted me to develop talents in serving the Lord, so he didn't teach me the masonry skills.

After high school, I really didn't know what I wanted to do with my life. I wanted to go to college, but my family couldn't afford to send me. I worked for about a year and then was laid off on Christmas Eve. "What should I do now?" I prayed. I felt the urge to apply to a Christian college about a half-hour from home. What did I have to lose? Shortly thereafter, I received an acceptance letter. God provided state and federal tuition grants, part-time jobs, and I made it through school without owing any money.

My educational journey had only begun. Within two years I was married and off to seminary for a Master of Divinity degree. Again God had provided and I graduated debt free.

Over 20 years of pastoral ministry had passed and I was becoming tired out; I needed a ministry change. So I asked the Lord, how can I use my ministry gifts to serve people? Teaching was always a strong point in my life. Both major and minor concentrations were in religious education; and in pastoral ministry, opportunities abound for teaching all educational levels. So, I applied to Liberty University

I had heard about Liberty University for many years. Dr. Falwell often invited pastors to refer qualified students to the college with reduced tuition incentives. Furthermore, LU had a great education department that was certified by several accrediting agencies. So, I applied and was accepted into the MAT program (Master of Arts in Teaching and Learning). I believed that I could use my gifts and abilities to positively influence young people in a public education setting as a licensed and certified teacher.

In May 2011, I graduated with a dual endorsement in Secondary Education—History and Special Education K–12 General Curriculum. One week before the fall term began, I was hired as a special education teacher for Pittsylvania County, VA. That's not bad for a 52-year-old career changer."

Ruth, LU employee, completing her degree after raising children

Ruth's Story:

"Because I was a single mom with three children to raise, I did not have the opportunity to get a college education until they were older, and I accomplished an associate's degree from Central Virginia Community College, one class at a time for a few years. Once I became employed with Liberty and my children were grown, my personal goal was to work toward a bachelor's degree. If it wasn't for online courses and being able to take them from home, I never would have been able to accomplish this goal. During the time I was taking online courses, my father became ill, and I had to skip a term, sometimes two, but I was able to get back on track when I could return."

Terry, 30-something graduate of Liberty University with an M.A., 2007

Terry's Story:

"My situation is not unique; before I went to LU, I was in a company that I loved. The environment was great, I was able to have good balance with work and family, and I genuinely liked what I was doing. However, I had been at the company for many years, and it appeared that I'd hit a ceiling as far as my advancement went. I came to Liberty to get input from experts outside of my company to expand my understanding of business. I could have certainly gone to any other university, but Liberty's mission aligned with my Christian beliefs, so I came here and haven't regretted the choice."

Tim, 20-something, Active Duty Marine

Tim's Story:

"My name is Corporal Timothy W. Harpe, II. I am a married, active duty Marine finishing my last few classes before I graduate. Some of the biggest challenges with taking college courses and being active duty is field duty and deployment. It was definitely difficult to submit course work when I was in the field without internet or cell phone service for days and sometimes weeks. It can also be difficult to do course work when you are in a different time zone. The difficulty is that when I get off work, I have maybe an hour to submit homework because of the time zone difference. . . Being married and completing course work can also have its own set of challenges. Typically, when my wife wanted to do something, I had to do course work, but when I had completed all of my course work, she did not want to do anything."

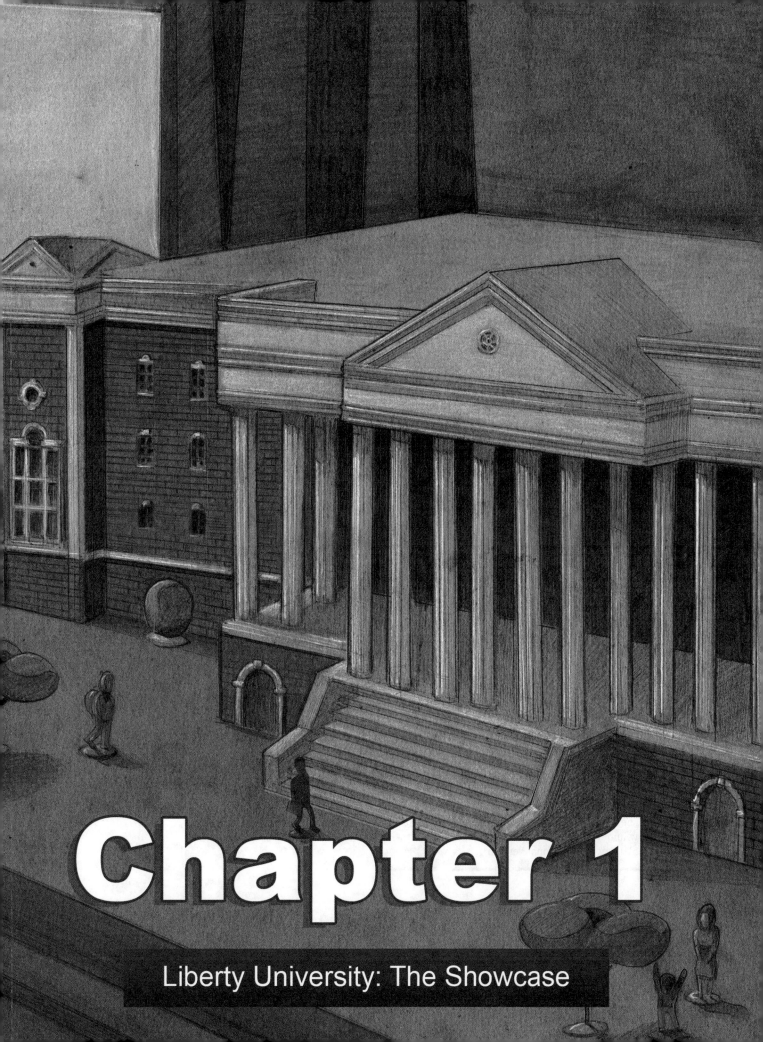

Chapter 1

Liberty University: The Showcase

In this chapter, you will:

- ◼ Acquaint yourself with Liberty University's history.
- ◼ Review Liberty University's Mission Statement.

SHOWCASE HOME

As Matthew 7:24–27 explains, a home must be built on a firm foundation to withstand the elements. Before the construction process starts, however, builders often recommend that their clients tour showcase homes to discover what they like best. As you pursue your college education, you must also build on a solid foundation, and finding the perfect school is the best place to start. We believe Liberty University Online is the best place for you! Liberty University Online offers a Christ-centered, liberal arts education in a flexible, engaging, and interactive format. We welcome you to our showcase as you begin the building process of your academic career.

© 2013 by Lightspring. Used under license of Shutterstock, Inc.

Matthew 7:24–27,
"Therefore everyone who hears these words of mine and puts them into practice is like a wise man who built his house on the rock. The rain came down, the streams rose, and the winds blew and beat against that house; yet it did not fall, because it had its foundation on the rock. But everyone who hears these words of mine and does not put them into practice is like a foolish man who built his house on sand. The rain came down, the streams rose, and the winds blew and beat against that house, and it fell with a great crash" (New International Version).

THE CORNERSTONE

The Vision: Year One

> Habakuk 2:2–3, "And the Lord answered me, and said, Write the vision, and make it plain upon tables, that he may run that readeth it. For the vision is yet for an appointed time, but at the end it shall speak, and not lie: though it tarry, wait for it; because it will surely come, it will not tarry" (King James Version).

In 1971, Dr. Jerry Falwell Sr. spread his vision of a Christian college to "train young champions for Christ" across the East Coast of the United States. During that first year, Paula Johnson was one of the first 235 students who came to the Lynchburg Baptist College to share in the humble inception of Falwell's vision. In the following narrative, she shares how the Lord led her to Lynchburg Baptist College, now Liberty University, and how that vision impacted her life.

Having made new friends in my freshman year at a college in the Midwest, I was not very excited to hit the road with my family for summer travels. I wanted to stay in town and hang out with my new college buddies.

But, as usual, the whole family was expected to go along in my Dad's bus for his summer tour. Being the child of a gospel singer had its perks and its drawbacks. Leaving town this particular summer seemed like a drawback to me.

One of our first stops this summer of 1971 was in a little town in the foothills of Virginia's Blue Ridge Mountains. I was familiar with several little towns in Virginia as we had spent other summers in the area, but I had never been to Lynchburg. I was impressed with its charming neighborhoods with homes fronted by amazing electric blue hydrangeas and pink-red climbing roses.

Photo courtesy of Les Schofer and courtesy of Liberty University.

Aerial view of the original Thomas Road Baptist Church on Thomas Road in Lynchburg, VA.

Dad pulled our big bus up in front of Thomas Road Baptist Church. I jumped down the bus steps and onto the heat of the blacktop on the parking lot. Dad took me through a side door into the sanctuary of the church where we were welcomed by a gust of air conditioning. And there, my Dad, Doug Oldham, introduced me to pastor Jerry Falwell. Dad said, "Jerry, this is my daughter, Paula," and Dr. Jerry stretched out his big paw for a handshake.

Paula Johnson and Jerry Falwell, Sr. at the Jerry Falwell Museum opening in 2003.

Unbeknownst to me, at the same time, he placed his hand near my back, so that when he kicked my feet out from under me during the handshake, he could catch me and help me gently fall to the floor.

Needless to say, this was the most unusual handshake from a preacher I had ever received! There I was, laying on the floor of the sanctuary with my dad and Jerry Falwell laughing and looking at me. I said, "So! This is how it is going to be?" Still laughing, Dr. Jerry reached down and pulled me to my feet and gave me a big bear hug. As I look back over the 42 years since that moment, that is how our friendship was . . . full of the unexpected, slightly scary moments and an affectionate helping hand.

As we traveled the summer months with Dr. Falwell, Dr. Elmer Towns, and others, Dad would sing in the rallies or services and Dr. Falwell would preach and share his vision of starting a new Bible college in Lynchburg. As a 17-year-old girl, I spent a lot of time rolling my eyes at my mother with my cynical attitude. Who would want to go to a college with no professors, no classrooms, no campus, no traditions, nothing?

Near the end of the summer, the last rally to raise money and recruit students for the new Lynchburg Baptist College was held at the Pate Chapel at the Thomas Road Baptist Church in Lynchburg. Having heard the spiel many times over the summer, I paid little attention as Dr. Towns explained the academic goals of the new college. Dad sang another song and then Dr. Falwell took the pulpit. He spoke of his vision for the college . . . to train young champions for Christ, to change the world by educating young Christians to go into every conceivable field of endeavor ... lawyers, doctors, teachers, preachers, mechanics, entertainers, missionaries, pilots, artists, musicians . . . the list went on and on.

I had zoned out a bit thinking of my own life . . . where was I headed? What would I do for Christ in my lifetime? At just about that time I heard the voice of God . . . (no kidding) . . . say, "Go."

I knew without a shadow of a doubt God wanted to me to come to the "nothing college" I had ranted about all summer long. And so, I came to this new school. And we did have nothing. Dr. Towns managed to convince a few quality professors to teach. Our classes met in the Sunday school rooms of Thomas Road Baptist Church. The "campus" was the parking lot and hallways of the church. We had no cafeteria, so some of us walked more than a mile in the evenings up the steep Thomas Road hill to Burger King or Pizza Hut. We even did our laundry at the local laundromat.

My first "dorm room" (I use that term loosely) was in the basement of the oldest part of the church facility. It had a cement floor, a cot, a brown metal folding chair, a used dresser, and a closet. Or, at least I thought it was a closet. When I opened the "closet" door, before me stood the building's old boiler. I looked around for the bathroom and was told it was out the door, up the outside steps, through the courtyard, into another building, up the steps, and down the hall. Convenient.

As little as we had in the way of a campus or dorms, we more than made up in a passionate approach to living for Christ. Everyone who came was at the new college because God had led him or her there. We were a motley bunch, but we loved the Lord more than fancy college facilities. And we were given hands-on experience. If a student was there for a communications diploma, they were put in front of the camera in the church services or behind the camera or up in the control room or in the editing suite. If you were there to become a missionary, you were spending breaks in foreign lands reaching souls for Christ and building churches. If you were going to be a preacher or singer, you were traveling to other churches on the weekends, singing and preaching.

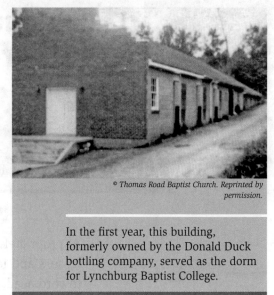

© *Thomas Road Baptist Church. Reprinted by permission.*

In the first year, this building, formerly owned by the Donald Duck bottling company, served as the dorm for Lynchburg Baptist College.

Dr. Falwell urged us on, prayed with us, encouraged us, opened doors of opportunity for us; he personally paid for our trips overseas, paid for our lunches. He poured his life into us and pulled us along to help make the vision of this new school a reality.

Now, 43 years later, sometimes after work, I leave the beautiful campus of Liberty University where I work as the curator for the Jerry Falwell Museum and drive up the mountain to an overlook. As the sun sets over the 6,000-acre campus of Liberty University, I look over what God has done through the life of Jerry Falwell, and I thank God for His blessings. And I thank Him for giving Jerry Falwell the vision of Liberty University.

I pray your life will be changed by your experience with Liberty University as dramatically and powerfully as mine was years ago. And, if God said, "Go" to you, I am sure it will be!

Photo courtesy of Kevin Manguiob and Liberty University.

"As the sun sets over the 6,000-acre campus of Liberty University, I look over what God has done through the life of Jerry Falwell, and I thank God for His blessings."

As Paula Johnson shared, Dr. Falwell's vision for Liberty University has come to fruition in the beautiful campus, the competitive residential and online academic programs, the qualified and Spirit-filled faculty and administration, and the remarkable body of students training to be effective "Champions for Christ." Just as the Lord led Paula to Liberty University those many years ago, He has also led you to take part in the vision, and God's best is yet to come! ". . . as it is written: 'What no eye has seen, what no ear has heard, and what no human mind has conceived'—the things God has prepared for those who love him" (I Corinthians 2:9, NIV).

Acquaint Yourself with Liberty University's History

II Corinthians 3:17,
". . . where the Spirit of the Lord is, there is Liberty" (KJV).

Dr. Jerry Falwell, Sr., founder

"If America is to remain free, we must raise up a generation of young people who are trained as witnesses for Christ and voices for righteousness who can call this nation back to God and back to the principles upon which it was built. We must bring America back to God and back to greatness. We can only do it by helping young people find purpose in life in Christ" (Falwell, 2008, p. 145).

Appropriately nicknamed "the World's Most Exciting University," the professors and leadership of Liberty University have trained men and women toward academic excellence since 1971. At the school's inception, Dr. Jerry Falwell, Sr. and Dr. Elmer Towns determined that this college would be different than any other; this college would prepare young Christians to be successful and to make a difference in their chosen professions. They determined that Lynchburg Baptist College would be a place where the Spirit of the Lord would dwell, and the Spirit of the Lord is "alive and well here at Liberty University" all these years later (Falwell, 2007). Along with a variety of academic, athletic, and spiritual programs, Liberty University offers support to students through first-class facilities and valuable resources.

Photo by Kevin Manguiob. Courtesy of Liberty University.

Liberty University's Hancock Welcome Center and Williams Stadium aglow as the sun sets over the Blue Ridge Mountains.

Notable Academic and Institutional Advances

Then . . .	Now . . .
In 1971, 235 residential students attended Lynchburg Baptist College.	Over 100,000 residential and online students attend Liberty University.
In that first year, co-founder, Dr. Elmer Towns, was the only full-time professor.	About 3,000 full-time and part-time professors teach for Liberty University.
In the 1970s, Lynchburg Baptist College offered students many opportunities to use what they had learned in their field in a meaningful way: communications (camera crew), hospitality (flight attendants), recruitment (singing teams), and evangelism experiences.	Relevant learning experiences have continued today at Liberty University, with internship programs in various fields, student teaching placements, medical and mission outreach experiences, cinematic and theatre arts opportunities, and much, much more!
During 1971–1973, students were awarded certificates of completion instead of degrees. Lynchburg Baptist College began conferring degrees in 1974.	In 1980, Liberty University earned accreditation from the Southern Association of Colleges and Schools (SACS).
	Liberty University now offers over 450 degree programs. This number is constantly growing!
In 1975, the school changed its name to Liberty Baptist College.	In 1984, the school changed its name to Liberty University.
Liberty University School of Lifelong Learning (LUSLL) began in 1985. This correspondence program offered students the opportunity to earn a degree at a distance. Students could choose from three different degree options.	Liberty University Online now offers over 250 degree programs! This number continues to grow!
In Liberty University's short life, there have been four presidents, including Dr. A. Pierre Guillermin, Dr. John M. Borek, and Dr. Jerry Falwell, Sr.	Today, Jerry Falwell, proudly serves as Liberty University's president.

Dr. Jerry Falwell, Sr.

"I am convinced that if we will attend to the depth of our ministry, God will attend to its breadth" (Falwell, 1997, p. 265).

Rev. Jonathan Falwell, Pastor of Thomas Road Baptist Church

"Whenever he [Dr. Jerry Falwell, Sr.] mentioned the words 'Liberty University,' somewhere in that conversation was 'training young champions for Christ.' It wasn't a flippant phrase that he just happened to come up with—it's something that was purposeful, intentional and it was often" (Bible, 2009, Training champions for Christ section).

Athletic Programs

Liberty's fans pack Williams Stadium for a night of football and fireworks.

Dr. Elmer Towns, Co-Founder

"I was excited about what we could do to reach the world for Jesus Christ, and because of Dr. Falwell and his vision, I got excited about what we have done in the past and what we can do in the future, and I am so thrilled to have been a part of Liberty University and what God has done here" (Liberty University News Service, 2014).

LU's Mascot "Sparky fiercely supports the Flames at each athletic event and welcomes a hi-five, a picture snapshot, or a hug when walking throughout campus."

Then . . .	Now . . .
In 1971, the school colors were green and gold.	In 1975, the school colors changed to the ones students wear today to show their school spirit: red, white, and blue.
Basketball was Lynchburg Baptist College's first sports team.	Liberty University's sports teams include basketball, football, softball, baseball, soccer, hockey, volleyball, track, rowing, swimming, tennis, and more. 20 different teams are a part of the NCAA Division I program. There are 32 Club Sports teams and an intra-mural program (Liberty University, 2014).
"Knowledge Aflame" is the school's motto, and that is how Liberty University's sports teams became known as the Flames. The eagle mascot of the Liberty University Flames, Sparky, was born on August 20, 1971.	Sparky fiercely supports the Flames at each athletic event and welcomes a hi-five, a picture snapshot, or a hug when walking throughout campus. Sparky is even the star of his own children's book, *Sparky's ABC Adventure*.
At the first basketball game, only 20 people cheered the Flames.	Flames fans pack each sport facility to support the different teams. On September 19, 2015, the Liberty Flames football team defeated University of Montana's Grizzlies with a final score of 31-21. This historic Flames' victory in Williams Stadium showcased "a record crowd of 22,551 fans . . .The contest also marked the first-ever Top 15 matchup in stadium history" (Liberty University Athletics, 2015).
In 1973, Chip Smith made the first touchdown on the football team coached by Rock Royer.	The Jerry Falwell Museum in DeMoss Hall showcases the football that began a long history of touchdowns. Currently, Turner Gill leads Liberty University's fierce football team.

Spiritual Programs

Then . . .	Now . . .
Dr. Falwell's vision for a Christian college committed to a Christ-centered education began in 1971.	Dr. Falwell's vision continues in each residential and online classroom as professors share with their students their love for the Lord and each subject they teach.
Students attended Thomas Road Baptist Church for Sunday services, including Dr. Elmer Towns' Sunday school class.	Liberty University students worship the Lord at Thomas Road Baptist Church, Liberty University's Campus Church, and many local churches in the Lynchburg area.
Students attended Thomas Road Baptist Church for all chapels and assemblies.	Liberty University hosts convocation on Mondays, Wednesdays, and Fridays at the Vines Center. Online students can view the services through streaming or recorded format on LU's website. Another way for online students to stay connected to the physical campus and to receive spiritual encouragement is through Liberty Online Communities.
On January 21, 1977, the students attended a prayer meeting in the snow on what is now Liberty Mountain. Robbie Hiner sang the song, "I Want that Mountain."	In 2012, over 5,000 Liberty University students, faculty, and staff gathered at the groundbreaking site for the Jerry Falwell Library to pray over the new construction and to reflect on God's blessings and provision over the years at Liberty University. In January 2014, Liberty University held a dedication service for the new Jerry Falwell Library (Bible & Liberty University News Service, 2012).

Photo courtesy Bob Duval. © Liberty University.

© *Thomas Road Baptist Church. Reprinted by permission.*

In the early days, students met in a tent to attend worship services and convocation.

Ruth, LU employee, completing her degree after raising children

Ruth's Story:

Q: *What brought you to Liberty University?*

A: "I had an application with Liberty for two years before they called me. It was a God thing because the company I had previous worked for was closing, and I would have been without a job. I had always wanted to be a teacher, but because I had a family to raise and educate, there was no time or money for me to do so. Liberty was the closest to being a teacher I would ever get, and it has been a blessing being a servant to the faculty and students since I have been here for 25 years."

Student Facilities

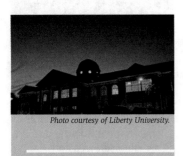

Photo courtesy of Liberty University.

Students enjoy study or fellowship time in the Hancock Welcome Center.

Then . . .	Now . . .
In 1971, the dorm rooms were in different houses on Thomas Road in Lynchburg, VA, as well as in the basement of the Donald Duck Bottling Company building that was the first Thomas Road Baptist Church sanctuary.	On Liberty Mountain, beautiful brick dorms, along with the newly constructed, nine-story Residential Commons, house students comfortably.
In the second year, the dorms were housed on Treasure Island on the James River in Lynchburg, VA, and in the Old Virginian Hotel.	
In 1971, Elmer Towns held a journalism class in his office. Eight students brought in folding metal chairs to make themselves comfortable in the makeshift classroom.	Liberty University's classes are now held in various buildings, such as Arthur S. DeMoss Learning Center, Elmer L. Towns Religion Hall, and Green Hall. Smart Classrooms in each building are constantly updated with the latest technologies to allow for interactive learning experiences.
Dr. Jerry Falwell, Sr. loved Thomas Jefferson's architecture and wanted to infuse that into the style of all of Liberty University's buildings. He started by having an architect use one of Jefferson's designs to develop the octagon-shaped building that served as the home for Thomas Road Baptist Church from 1969 to 2006.	Jeffersonian inspired architecture can be found in various buildings across campus, such as the Arthur S. DeMoss Learning Center, the Towns Alumni Lecture Hall, the Hancock Welcome Center, the Center for Medical and Health Sciences, and the LaHaye Student Union. The architecture in these red-brick buildings feature elements unique to the third U.S. President's own neoclassical-style: ivory columns, pediments, and exterior moulding; copper roof domes; rotundas.
In 1971, Dr. Falwell flew over Candlers Mountain Road (the site of what is now Liberty University's campus) in a helicopter. At the time, he was just interested in 60 acres of timbering land. He asked the real estate agent accompanying him if the owners of the property would be willing to sell it.	Liberty University now owns over 7,000 acres of land and has built many first-class facilities to generate a comfortable and recreational home away from home for Liberty University's residential students: Liberty Mountain Snowflex Center, Barrick-Falwell Lodge, Williams Stadium, the Vines Center,

Then . . .	Now . . .
When the owners were ready to part with the land, Dr. Jerry wrote a personal check of $10,000 earnest money and asked them to wait until the end of the week to cash the check. By the end of the week, the check was good!	LaHaye Ice Rink, David's Place, Tower Theatre, LaHaye Student Union, Jerry Falwell Library, and many more (Liberty University, 2014).
Fundraising built Liberty University.	Donors such as A. L. Williams, Jerry Vines, Dan Reber, Jimmy Thomas, Tim LaHaye, Arthur S. DeMoss, Jerry Falwell, the Tilley family, David Green, and many others, along with alumni and ministry supporters, have made each construction project possible.

Leadership Legacy

Since 1971, Liberty University's resources, facilities, academic, athletic, and spiritual programs have benefited each student's academic experience, bringing Dr. Jerry Falwell, Sr.'s vision to fruition. In order to appreciate the remarkable achievements and growth of Liberty University, it is important to recognize the life and legacy of its founder, Dr. Jerry Falwell, Sr. and its current president, Jerry Falwell. Friend and former LU Provost, Dr. Ronald S. Godwin elaborates further regarding this legacy:

> Liberty University exists today because of one of the most gifted and talented pastors and leaders of our generation. During his entire ministry, Dr. Jerry Falwell demonstrated the heart of a pastor, the keen mind of a world-class educator, and the courage and vision of a great citizen statesman. His greatest passion was to establish a Christian university that would be for protestant Christians what Brigham Young is for Mormons and Notre Dame is for the Roman Catholics. Today, America, the world, and Christians everywhere are the beneficiaries of his vision and incredibly tenacious faith.

> Safely beyond its struggles to survive during its pioneer years, and now enjoying the visionary and yet prudent leadership of Chancellor Jerry Falwell, Jr., Liberty is continuing to dramatically expand its facilities, programs, and enrollments. Already it has become the largest private Christian University in the world. (Falwell & Godwin 2014)

Take some time to get to know Liberty University's founder, Dr. Jerry Falwell, Sr. and his son, President Jerry Falwell. These men have invested their lives, wisdom, and experience to ensure that students of all ages have a quality Christian education.

Dr. Elmer Towns

"Some of the greatest spiritual leaders have been motivated by a great vision" (McKay, 2009).

President Jerry Falwell

"Liberty was a school that wasn't supposed to happen. Everybody said a conservative Christian school could not survive—but we did" (Falwell, 2014).

President Jerry Falwell

"As part of Liberty's Christian mission, we have always sought to make Christian education as affordable and as accessible for as many individuals as possible . . . Liberty University Online is achieving this objective every day, making the dreams of tens of thousands of men and women come true" (Menard, 2013).

Photo courtesy of Liberty University

Jerry Falwell, Sr. passed away on May 15, 2007, at age 73. He was married to Macel Pate Falwell for 49 years. They had three children: Jerry, Jr., now President of Liberty University; Jeannie, Chief of Surgery at Hunter Holmes McGuire, VA Medical Center in Richmond, Virginia; and Jonathan, senior pastor of Thomas Road Baptist Church; and eight grandchildren.

Emily, 19-year-old freshman at Liberty University

Q: *What brought you to Liberty University?*

A: "Liberty was always in my mind . . . I knew God was calling me to Liberty and I had to follow . . . Once coming to Liberty, I realized it was the best decision I could have made, and obviously, it was since God led me here."

Jerry Falwell, Sr. . . . a legacy of faith.

Then . . .

Falwells have lived in Virginia since the first "Fallwell" ancestors arrived on the shores of Chesapeake Bay in the early 1600s. Over the centuries, they made their way up the mighty James River through Goochland County and on to Buckingham County, where an ancestor who lived there served in the Revolutionary War.

The Falwells were of sturdy stock and their personalities were as strong as the great hickory trees that forest the Blue Ridge Mountains of Virginia. Tough and resilient, the family prospered in the New World.

In 1850, Jerry Falwell's great-grandfather, Hezekiah Carey Falwell, moved up the James and bought 1,000 acres of land in Campbell County. True Southerners at heart, Hezekiah used his farm's bounty to feed Confederate soldiers and his skills as a wheelwright to fix their wagons and shoe their horses. His son, Charles William (Charlie) Falwell, built a large dairy farm on his portion of the family land.

Charlie was married to the very beautiful Martha Catherine Bell Falwell. Photographs of her show a slim, dark-haired beauty, dressed in a very fashionable white Victorian dress. When she died of cancer at an early age, Charlie turned his back on God forever.

Their son, Carey Hezekiah, must have sensed his father's anger and bitterness toward the Lord. Carey was high-spirited, talented, and energetic. He was not a church-going man, but he married the beautiful and gentle Helen Beasley, who had been raised by her parents, King David and Sallie Beasley, in the ways of the Lord. King David saw to it that his 14 children were in the Baptist church in the tiny town of Hollywood, Virginia, every Sunday morning.

Carey began to build a business empire in Campbell County and a reputation as a tough entrepreneur, who worked tirelessly to provide the best of the best for his young family. Helen presented Carey with a son and two girls. Rosha, the youngest girl, was the apple of her father's eye. When she died at age ten from appendicitis, Carey, no doubt remembering the loss of his mother and his own father's reaction, turned his heart away from the Lord. Two years after Rosha's death in 1933, Carey and Helen welcomed twins into their home. Jerry and Gene Falwell brought joy back into the Falwell household.

Carey doted on his twin boys while overseeing his many business ventures. He sold bootleg whiskey during the Prohibition years from his many Falwell service stations to raise working capital. He built and operated the popular Merry Garden Dance Hall. He brought big name celebrities into town for the entertainment of the community, such as the Tommy Dorsey Orchestra, Houdini, Claude Thornhill, and Jack Teagarden.

(continues)

(continued)

So, when Jerry Falwell, son of Carey, was saved in 1952 at the Park Avenue Baptist Church, is it any wonder that the people of Lynchburg, Virginia, had a difficult time believing that a preacher could come from such a family?

As a young teenager, Jerry Falwell saw a real change in his father after Carey accepted Christ on his deathbed. This transformation had an impact on the young man, as did his mother's faithful Christian life. Each Sunday morning, as she served big Southern breakfasts to her twins, Helen was sure to have the family radio playing Charles Fuller's "The Old-Fashioned Revival Hour." Those songs and sermons laid the foundation for Jerry's salvation.

Following his years at Baptist Bible College, Jerry returned to Lynchburg and founded the Thomas Road Baptist Church in 1956. Starting with just 35 adults and their children, Thomas Road Baptist Church grew by leaps and bounds. Jerry Falwell was not only a man of prayer—he was also a man of action. He determined to knock on 100 doors a day to meet new families, to pray for their needs, and to invite them to church. Like his father, Jerry did things in a big way.

In 1956, just months after founding the church, Jerry began a radio and television ministry. His "Old Time Gospel Hour" program, which was the broadcast of the Sunday morning services of the Thomas Road Baptist Church, has led millions to Christ and became the longest continually running televised religious program in America.

Jerry Falwell began to build ministries. The first was the Elim Home for Alcoholics, which he built in memory of his father who had died of alcoholism. From there he built the Treasure Island summer youth camp and reached thousands of children for Christ. Then, seeing a need for Christian education, he founded Lynchburg Christian Academy (now Liberty Christian Academy), and in 1971, he founded Lynchburg Baptist College, now known as Liberty University. He would go on to establish the Liberty Godparent Home and Adoption Agency to help unwed mothers.

In the 1980s, Jerry Falwell, influenced by the great Christian apologist, Francis Schaeffer, entered the political arena by establishing, with other Christian leaders, the Moral Majority. Their fervent endeavors ultimately led to the election of Ronald Reagan as President of the United States.

Jerry left politics and returned his attention full time to Thomas Road Baptist Church and her ministries. Liberty University had grown from 235 students in 1971 to tens of thousands. His strong, godly leadership led the university to become the largest Christian university in the world. Jerry bought land on the other side of the mountain where he grew up and where his great-grandfather, Hezekiah Falwell, had purchased 1,000 acres in 1850, to build the campus of Liberty University.

Jerry Falwell became a national leader, seen by millions weekly on television talk shows, but his real passion was being pastor of Thomas Road Baptist Church and "training young Champions for Christ" as a Christian educator.

Written by Paula Johnson, Curator of the Jerry Falwell Museum.

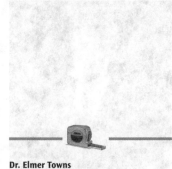

Dr. Elmer Towns

"Vision is for an appointed time . . . wait for it because it will surely come" (McKay, 2009).

Dr. Jerry Falwell, Sr.

"You are never really fulfilled in life until you recognize your vision and fulfill it" (Falwell, 1997, p. 480).

Photo courtesy of Kevin Manguiob.
© Liberty University.

On October 3, 1987, Jerry Falwell married Becki Tilley in the little white Prayer Chapel on the campus of Liberty University. Together, over the years, they have renovated a charming farmhouse in the countryside outside of Lynchburg, Virginia. They have three children, Trey (Jerry Falwell, III), Wesley, and Caroline. The Falwells are generous and loving people, who opened their home for the Senior Class Picnic for many years before the number of seniors outgrew their home's capacity. Their investment in students' lives can also be witnessed as they share in enthusiasm and school spirit while attending sport events, faithfully cheering on the Flames!

Jerry Falwell . . . realizing the vision.

Now . . .

Liberty University President, Jerry Falwell, has taken on the task of transforming the Liberty campus above and beyond anything previously envisioned. To see the fast-paced building program that is now underway is nothing short of amazing and a credit to the vision of Liberty's founder, Dr. Jerry Falwell, Sr.

President Falwell grew up in the home of Liberty's founder, Dr. Jerry Falwell, Sr., and saw firsthand the growth of the university from a tiny Baptist Bible college founded in 1971 to the largest Christian university in the world. From the time he was a young boy, Jerry Jr. soaked up the wisdom and business sense he would need to run a university with more than 100,000 residential and online students.

President Jerry Falwell attended Liberty Christian Academy and Liberty University, graduating with a Bachelor of Arts in Religious Studies in 1984. He then went on to attend the University of Virginia School of Law, and in 1987, he obtained a Juris Doctor degree and became licensed to practice law that same year. Jerry began to work closely with his father to help develop and manage the university.

Following his father's passing, Jerry became deeply involved in the planning and construction of improvements on campus, explaining that "All of these buildings and programs are ultimately and primarily about building lives—the lives of our students and the lives of those they will impact."

When you walk across campus, there is a sense that this place is different. It is alive with the hum of construction equipment working on more than 20 major construction projects currently underway. It is also alive with the excitement of thousands of Christian students attending classes, meeting and studying together . . . making plans to change their world.

Often labeled "the world's most exciting Christian university," one cannot visit the campus without sensing that something big, something ordained, and something blessed by God is happening in Lynchburg, Virginia.

One of the largest and newly completed construction projects is the Jerry Falwell Library. Named for the founder, Dr. Jerry Falwell, Sr. this new state-of-the-art facility features an automated robotic retrieval system for the catalogue of books, conventional stacks of books, reading rooms, study rooms, and a food court.

Other projects being completed in the months to come include the new Science Hall, improvements to the Equestrian Center, ten-story residence halls, a 17-level tower (once completed it will be the tallest building in Lynchburg and will serve as an academic building), a new softball facility, and improvements to

(continues)

(continued)

the hiking and biking trails on the mountain. The projects, too many to list, are adding to the rich collegiate experience offered at Liberty University.

Convocation speakers challenge and motivate Liberty University students. Convocation guest speakers have included President and CEO of Samaritan's Purse Franklin Graham, football standout Tim Tebow, Kay Arthur, former House Speaker Newt Gingrich, inspirational speaker Joni Eareckson Tada, Donald Trump, U.S. Rep. Michelle Bachmann, neurosurgeon Dr. Ben Carson, former Governor Mike Huckabee . . . the list goes on and on. Students are challenged on a weekly basis by successful Christian and world leaders to become the best they can be with the help of the Lord.

President Falwell understands that every aspect of a student's life is important, from academic classes to recreational facilities. Each aspect of student life is being enriched, with spiritual leadership chosen carefully, buildings erected and improved, convocation and commencement speakers chosen with today's challenges in mind, and new physical and recreational facilities being added. The student who attends Liberty will leave not only with a first-class education, but also with a rich and varied experience that gives the student a foundation for the future.

When Liberty's founder, Dr. Jerry Falwell, Sr. passed away just a week before commencement exercises were held in May of 2007, the first words his son, President Jerry Falwell, spoke to the thousands upon thousands of people gathered at that momentous occasion were, "Liberty University is alive and well!"

Today, Liberty is more alive than any time in its brief history. President Falwell is leading Liberty into a bright and amazing future. We are excited to have you as a part of Liberty University!

Written by Paula Johnson, Curator of the Jerry Falwell Museum.

Terry, 30-something graduate of Liberty University with an M.A., 2007

My favorite quote from Dr. Falwell is "Sometimes the rabbit has to climb the tree." This is a quote that was used a lot in the early years of Liberty as a metaphor for having to do a task, regardless of our own limitations. The university accomplished many things through the grace of God, so that rabbit climbed the tree.

Personal Reflection

Assess your previous knowledge of Liberty University. Why did you choose to take classes with Liberty University Online? What factors influenced this decision? After reading about Liberty's history, founder, developments, and current President, what facts came as a surprise to you? What would you like to investigate further?

entrepeaneurship   history of Falwells during war

choose for staunch conservative Christian education

Review Liberty University's Mission Statement

> I Timothy 4:7–9,
> "Have nothing to do with godless myths and old wives' tales; rather, train yourself to be godly. For physical training is of some value, but godliness has value for all things, holding promise for both the present life and the life to come. This is a trustworthy saying that deserves full acceptance" (NIV).

Dr. Ron Hawkins, Provost of Liberty University

"Liberty is about impacting the culture. Equipping men and women with the knowledge, values, and skills to impact the culture for Jesus Christ" (Menard & Liberty University News Service, 2012).

As Timothy 4:7–9 explains, Christians should strive for godliness in every area of their lives. Liberty University's core values reflect the truth of God's Word. These reflections of God's truth can be found in Liberty's Mission Statement, which includes the Philosophy of Education, the Statement of Mission and Purpose, and the Doctrinal Statement. (We will review the Doctrinal Statement in Chapter 4.) Take some time to familiarize yourself with Liberty's value system and consider how it lines up with your own.

Terry

Q: *What brought you to Liberty University?*

A: "I was looking for a school that not only taught up-to-date information in my field of study, but also taught it from a Christian perspective. Ethics is a hot topic in the realm of business now, and I wanted to complete a degree at a university that was rooted in longstanding biblical beliefs."

Mission Statement

Philosophy of Education

Liberty University is a Christian academic community in the tradition of evangelical institutions of higher education. As such, Liberty continues the philosophy of education that first gave rise to the university, and that is summarized in the following propositions.

God, the infinite source of all things, has shown us truth through scripture, nature, history, and above all, in Christ.

Persons are spiritual, rational, moral, social, and physical, created in the image of God. They are, therefore, able to know and to value themselves and other persons, the universe, and God.

Education, as the process of teaching and learning, involves the whole person, by developing the knowledge, values, and skills that enable each individual to change freely. Thus it occurs most effectively when both instructor and student are properly related to God and each other through Christ.

Statement of Mission and Purpose

Maintaining the vision of the founder, Dr. Jerry Falwell, Liberty University develops Christ-centered men and women with the values, knowledge, and skills essential to impact the world.

Through its residential and online programs, the university educates men and women who will make important contributions to their workplaces and communities, follow their chosen vocations as callings glorify God, and fulfill the Great Commission.

Liberty University will:

1. Emphasize excellence in teaching and learning.

2. Foster university-level competencies in communication, critical thinking, information literacy, and mathematics in all undergraduate programs.

3. Ensure competency in scholarship, research, and professional communication in all graduate programs.

4. Promote the synthesis of academic knowledge and Christian worldview in order that there might be a maturing of spiritual, intellectual, social and physical value-driven behavior.

5. Enable students to engage in a major field of study in career-focused disciplines built on a solid foundation in the liberal arts.

6. Promote an understanding of the Western tradition and the diverse elements of American cultural history, especially the importance of the individual in maintaining democratic and free market processes.

7. Contribute to a knowledge and understanding of other cultures and of international events.

8. Encourage a commitment to the Christian life, one of personal integrity, sensitivity to the needs of others, social responsibility and active communication of the Christian faith, and, as it is lived out, a life that leads people to Jesus Christ as the Lord of the universe and their own personal Savior. (Liberty University Board of Trustees, 2010)

Approved by the Liberty University Board of Trustees, November 12, 2010

Ruth

Q: *What is your favorite Dr. Falwell quote?*

A: "'Don't quit!' What a testimony that was for me during the 4–5 years I took online courses."

Roger, 50-something graduate of Liberty University with a MAT, 2011

Why attend Liberty University?

"I received a world-class education from qualified faculty. Online classes provided flexibility, affordability, and convenience. The school had my major and helped me to achieve my goals. And most importantly, it approached my major from a biblical worldview."

Liberty's Mission Statement clearly outlines a value system that embraces a biblical worldview. (Chapter 4 in the text will elaborate on the biblical worldview concept further.) The Philosophy of Education and the Statement of Mission and Purpose both reinforce an allegiance and commitment to Jesus Christ in all arenas of life. Our Provost, Dr. Ronald E. Hawkins, D. Min., Ed.D., echoes this as he explains:

As the largest Christian university in the world, Liberty University occupies a special space in university graduate and online education. In our graduate and online programs, we seek to assure the ongoing development of a curriculum and instructional environment where faith and scholarship are melded together. The result we desire most is producing a trained body of professionals who possess the knowledge, values, and skills to make significant contributions to their chosen professionals and to impact their culture for the glory of God. (Hawkins, 2015)

Personal Reflection

In the space provided, list the "significant contributions" you want to make in life. How does Liberty's philosophy of education, mission, and purpose line up with these aspirations?

BUILDING BLOCKS

As you look back on your decision to begin online education with Liberty University, what factors did you consider? Were you looking forward to the final outcome or considering the milestones of personal growth along the way? Did you consider the investment of time, money, and family resources, and weigh them against the long-term benefits? Perhaps you looked at how you would work out the details of tuition and financial aid, books, and course offerings.

Dr. Falwell often described his "BHAGs," or big, hairy, audacious goals. He felt that God was leading him, and he simply pursued the path laid out ahead of him. Those goals were ones that he never swerved from, once they were crystallized, and he was galvanized into action to pursue them. Reviewing what you read in this chapter about the founding of what would become Liberty University, would you expect what you see when you evaluate the school today? Many people have big dreams, but few live out the accomplishments that Dr. Falwell was able to realize. Thinking about where you are in life, do you have audacious goals? Are you sensitive to God's leading in your life?

Liberty University does not have a hundred-plus year history like many of the prestigious universities around the United States or around the world. This university has developed only since 1971. That is a relatively brief period for such incredible growth, but God has had His hand on our university. We know that many students come to Liberty University *because* they want an education that is distinctively Christian. We also understand that some students come to us despite the fact that we are founded and guided by God's design and direction. What factors did you consider when you decided to attend Liberty University? It may be that you have never thought about this to this degree before, but we believe you are learning here with us as part of God's design.

On what foundations have you built your life to date? Read the following verse. Psalm 19:14 "Let the words of my mouth, and the meditation of my heart, be acceptable in thy sight, O Lord, my strength, and my redeemer" (KJV). Is this a verse that you can pray?

In the New Testament book of Romans, we read in 12:2, "Do not conform to the pattern of this world, but be transformed by the renewing of your mind. Then you will be able to test and approve what God's will is— his good, pleasing, and perfect will" (NIV). If we are pursuing God's will, described in that verse as "good" and "perfect," we will not necessarily be doing things that others expect. Just as Dr. Falwell frequently found himself outside of the expectations of others, what differences might that bring to your life? How will that influence your work as a college student?

Personal Reflection

Read the story of Joshua at the Battle of Jericho in Joshua 6:2–20. What evidence can you see of the Israelite's dependence on God to achieve what might be described as a "big, hairy, audacious goal?"

_____

_____

_____

_____

_____

_____

_____

_____

_____

_____

TOOL BOX

More about Liberty

- **About Liberty**—Only so much can be summed up in a single chapter, especially when you are talking about a campus where so much is continuously happening. To learn more about Liberty University and to keep up-to-date with the latest happenings, check out these resources (www. liberty.edu/aboutliberty/).

- **Social Media**—Keep up-to-date with all of the latest happenings at Liberty by liking us on Facebook, following us on Twitter, or connecting through a number of other social media outlets.

- **The Liberty Journal**—Liberty University's official journal, published each semester. As a student you can subscribe for free print copies or read online (www.liberty.edu/libertyjournal/).

- **Athletics Department**—Become a fan of your university's sports teams. Follow football, soccer, swimming, or tour the various athletic facilities on campus (www.liberty.edu/flames/).

Student Resources

- **Blackboard Tutorials**—The Center for Curriculum Development continuously develops new tutorials aimed at helping students navigate the Blackboard learning management system where all of Liberty's courses are housed. A link to these tutorials can be found on the Breaking Ground website.

- **Information Technology**—Liberty's IT department works continuously to maintain all of the technology with which students interface and also offers additional services. Through the IT department, you can access a personal help desk agent to troubleshoot problems with your computer, search for self-help topics on things like how to set up email on your smartphone, and even shop a virtual storefront where Liberty students can buy computers and software at significantly reduced prices (www. liberty.edu/helpdesk.

- **Academic Advising**—Liberty University employs an army of highly trained academic advisors to assist and guide you through your academic journey. You can reach an advisor by email, chat, or even a personal phone call (www.liberty.edu/online/academic-advisors/).

Additional resources and links to specific sites, worksheets, and apps can be located by accessing the Breaking Ground website:

www.breakinggroundlu.com

References

Bible, M. (2009). *Championing the vision: Jonathan Falwell leads TRBC into its second generation*. Retrieved from http://www.liberty.edu/libertyjournal/index.cfm?PID = 15758&section = 3&artid = 736

Bible, M. & Liberty University News Service. (2012). *Liberty University honors founder Dr. Jerry Falwell at library groundbreaking*. Retrieved from http://www.liberty.edu/index.cfm?PID = 18495&MID = 49773

Falwell, J. (1997). *Falwell: An autobiography*. Lynchburg, VA: Liberty House Publishers.

Falwell, J. (2007). *Liberty University commencement address*. Liberty University, Lynchburg, VA.

Falwell, J. (2014). *Press quotes*. Retrieved from http://www.liberty.edu/aboutliberty/index.cfm?PID = 26726

Falwell, J. & Godwin, R. (2014). *Message from the president and the provost*. Retrieved from http://www.liberty.edu/index.cfm?PID = 27045

Falwell, M. (2008). *Jerry Falwell: His life and legacy*. New York, NY: Howard Books.

Hawkins, R. (2015). *Office of the Provost: Welcome*. Retrieved from http://www.liberty.edu/index.cfm?PID = 20398

Liberty University. (2014). *About Liberty*. Retrieved from http://www.liberty.edu/aboutliberty/

Liberty University Athletics. (2015). *Flames down no. 8/7 Montana in front of record crowd*. Retrieved from http://www.liberty.edu/flames/index.cfm?PID = 10869&NewsID = 15245&TeamID = 9

Liberty University Board of Trustees. (2010). *Mission statement*. Retrieved from http://www.liberty.edu/aboutliberty/index.cfm?PID = 6899

Liberty University News Service. (2014). *Chancellor Falwell announces Towns will step down for sabbatical*. Retrieved from http://www.liberty.edu/news/index.cfm?PID = 18495&MID = 97080

McKay, D. (2009). *Dr. Elmer Towns speaks at convocation*. Retrieved from http://www.liberty.edu/news/index.cfm?PID = 18495&MID = 5840

Menard, D. (2012). *From vision to reality*. Retrieved from http://www.liberty.edu/libertyjournal/index.cfm?PID = 24995&MID = 56752

Menard, D. (2013). *40th commencement: Celebrating historic accomplishments, continuous growth*. Retrieved from http://www.liberty.edu/aboutliberty/index.cfm?PID = 24995&MID = 91512

Menard, D & Liberty University News Service. (2012). *Liberty online now 80,000 strong*. Retrieved from http://www.liberty.edu/news/index.cfm?PID = 18495&MID = 56836

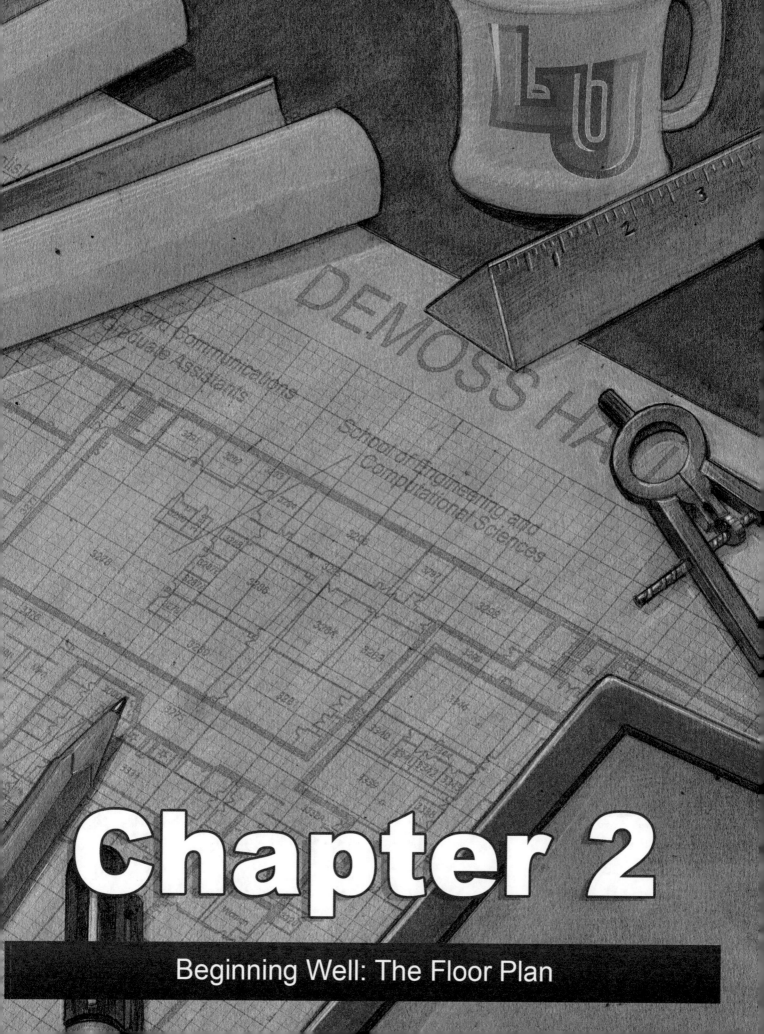

Chapter 2

Beginning Well: The Floor Plan

In this chapter you will:

■ Understand what is expected of you as an online college student.

■ Explore the Liberty University resources available to help you.

■ Practice self-reflection to fuel personal academic growth.

THE FLOOR PLAN

When designing the floor plans of a new home, a contractor must understand the parameters set for the home, and understand the expectations made by the potential homeowners. Once the contractor has established a floor plan, he is able to begin the construction project. Similarly, as a new student you must understand the tools, personnel, and constraints set for your college career. A strong beginning is a critical step toward college success, but is only possible once you understand the basic parameters under which you will be learning. These would include the guiding documents, policies, and student expectations that Liberty University holds. In order to begin well, you need to know which offices and personnel can provide assistance to you, and determine the tasks, habits, and responsibilities you must meet to create your college learning success.

Beginning Well: The Floor Plan

CORNERSTONE

Proverbs 6:6–8, "Go to the ant, you sluggard; consider its ways and be wise! It has no commander, no overseer or ruler, yet it stores its provisions in summer and gathers its food at harvest" (NIV).

I love the fall in Virginia. In the early days of Virginia's autumn, the temperature settles in between 60° and 75°. The cooler temperatures produce a freshness to the air that compels Virginians, and visitors alike, to draw in a deep breath and exhale, releasing the stresses of the day. Later in the fall comes the change in the leaves. Our mountains transform from a lovely blanket of green to a patchwork quilt boasting hues of orange, red, and gold—until at last, the leaves of the trees fall to the ground ushering in the early days of winter. In the fall, my husband's grandparents, Nanny and PaPa Tomlin, faithfully remind me, "You can always tell what kind of winter you are going to have, depending on the amount of nuts that fall from the trees onto the ground." PaPa always explains, just in case I've forgotten, "God is going to take care of His animals, so if there are a lot of nuts, you know it's gonna be a hard winter."

On a beautiful fall day, I decided to hike up our hill at the foot of Bear Mountain for exercise. While drawing in my favorite breaths of the cool autumn air, I noticed the squirrels busying about our house underneath a grand hickory tree. They darted up and down the tree, crossed over our yard from one forest of trees to the next, skipped, jumped, and swiveled about in mid-air. Their acrobatics impressed me! As they'd run up our hickory tree, I'd hear clickety-clacking noises and see the shells of hickory nuts

Photo by Jamaica Johnson Conner.

In the autumn of Virginia, the Blue Ridge Mountains transform from a lovely blanket of green to a patchwork quilt boasting hues of orange, red, and gold.

fall onto our sidewalk. Below the grand old tree, I noticed a generous covering of hickory nuts and realized that this winter was going to be a bear.

The Lord brought Proverbs 6:6–8 to mind as I watched the industrious squirrels, "Go to the ant, you sluggard; consider its ways and be wise! It has no commander, no overseer or ruler, yet it stores its provisions in summer and gathers its food at harvest" (NIV). Humbly, I realized that I had better prepare our home and family for the cold days ahead, for though that crisp, clean, and cool air cleanses my lungs, it also signifies the beginning of harsh weather. In order to begin the winter well, I need to gather food, blankets, candles, kerosene for lanterns, batteries for flashlights, and bottles of water. I must be as industrious as the squirrel.

In your college career, the same is true; you must be as industrious as the squirrel to begin well. God is going to take care of you; He's dropped little nuts of information throughout this textbook and throughout your course to prepare you. These nuts come in the form of facts relating to navigation of your online course and campus, the student honor code and code of conduct, student expectations, and proper communication. By collecting this information, you will store up a healthy supply of information to help you survive and thrive in the days ahead, "May the favor of the Lord our God rest on us; establish the work of our hands for us—yes, establish the work of our hands" (Psalms 90:17, ESV).

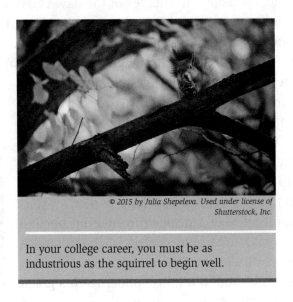

© 2015 by Julia Shepeleva. Used under license of Shutterstock, Inc.

In your college career, you must be as industrious as the squirrel to begin well.

Understand What Is Expected of You

Psalm 51:10,
"Create in me a clean heart, O God; and renew a right spirit within me" (KJV).

At the beginning of a student's experiences with Liberty University, there are many things to learn in the first term that are not necessarily related to course content. Students learn how to meet basic expectations for course behavior, communication, submission of work, and much more. Once you understand the basic expectations, it is easy to create your academic success. Let's look at some of the early, nonacademic lessons that new online students must master.

Course Requirements Checklist

The first task of each term is to complete what we call the **Course Requirements Checklist (CRC)**. This brief checklist ensures that students are aware of some basic expectations and is the tool we use to record initial attendance. For federal financial aid reporting, it is our roll-taking tool. Students may access this first "assignment" no sooner than midnight on the first Monday morning of the course. Those who fail to complete the CRC risk being dropped from the course for non-participation.

Course Guides

Each course has a syllabus and course schedule, which are the blueprints for expectations and how they will play out during the course. The **course schedule** specifies what reading and study assignments are to be done for each module/week of the term. The assignment expectations are detailed by week, as well. The **course syllabus** includes a description of

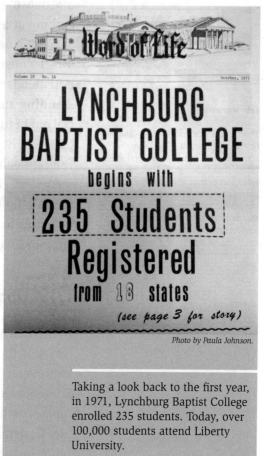

Taking a look back to the first year, in 1971, Lynchburg Baptist College enrolled 235 students. Today, over 100,000 students attend Liberty University.

the course content, rationale, **prerequisite courses**, required course materials, and expected **learning outcomes**. Details of expectations for required assignments, evaluation, and grading are included. The policy regarding late work is detailed in the course syllabus, as well. Each course syllabus includes information for those students who have a disability that may require **academic accommodations**. The course syllabus is the guiding policy document, while the course schedule lays out how assignment expectations will be met over the weeks of the course term.

Timely Work

While the beauty of online education is that students may complete their assignments online at their leisure, there are routine deadlines to be met in each course each week. Some students are surprised to learn that we expect regular **"attendance"** in our online program through work on various assignments. In other words, we mark your routine weekly attendance by noting the assignments that you complete in each module/week. You are required to keep up with weekly assignments, submitting each no later than the required due date in order to earn full credit for the work. Just checking into the course, looking at assignments, or viewing a presentation does not count as "attendance." Students who do not attend the course (by submitting assignments) for 21 consecutive days receive a final grade of **FN**, which means "failure, nonattendance." The FN grade is not only a blow to the student's **academic standing** and **transcript**, but it may also limit the availability of federal financial aid in future terms. Regular attendance and submission of work is critical, particularly in courses (such as math) where concepts build on each other. Falling behind in reading, viewing presentations, and doing regular assignments can lead to very poor outcomes. Students find themselves struggling to catch up may rush through assignments or be tempted to cheat. There are penalties for late work in each course. For these reasons, timely work that complies with the attendance policy and course deadlines is essential!

Discussion Boards

In the first week, students can begin to get to know their peers and the professor as they engage in the **discussion board**. This is a form of online, ongoing (over a few days) conversation that allows students to "meet" each other. Students learn from the experiences and ideas shared in the forum, with a topic specified by the instructor, which highlights the instruction for the module. Generally speaking, undergraduate students post their "thread" (initial post) in the discussion board no later than midnight on the specified day of the module/week. Students answer the prompt question(s) in paragraph

Lucy Montalvo

"Review the rubric for each assignment before completing it. This can assist you when you do not understand the instructions thoroughly. Also, this way you know exactly what is requested to obtain a perfect score. After submitting your work and receiving a grade, take a few minutes to review the graded rubric and the instructor feedback."

format, expounding on what they have learned from the study material, which might include textbook reading, course presentations, and website links. They share ideas and interpretations of what they have learned so far. Then, students reply to a few of their peers' threads, responding to ideas presented. Sharing your thoughts, in response to others in the discussion board, can help develop and extend your ideas as you consider points provided by others that may not previously have occurred to you. This conversation will continue for a few days and usually closes when the module/week ends.

© 2015 by Rawpixel. Used under license of Shutterstock, Inc.

"Sharing your thoughts, in response to others in the discussion board, can help develop and extend your ideas as you consider points provided by others that may not previously have occurred to you."

Netiquette

Students who write their posts and replies in discussion board forums must adhere to a code of ethical behavior that permits the free flow of ideas while respecting the thoughts and words of other posters. Students must be careful to observe the rules of **"netiquette"** or network etiquette, which require that responses be respectful, using polite language to agree or disagree with the thoughts shared by others. Students are free to disagree without being disagreeable! Carefully responding with evidence to refute a claim with which you disagree is a skill that students learn and develop in their discussion board work. While it is important to be polite when disagreeing, it is also important to avoid simply agreeing with each post to which you respond. The point of the discussion board is to share ideas and develop your thinking. Agreeing with everyone you respond to does not allow you to demonstrate your understanding of deeper meaning in the topic. Try to ask a question to extend the discussion or bring up a different aspect of the topic, or disagree politely, but be sure to post in such a way as to carry the conversation forward.

Careful, Respectful Communication

The respectful tone required in the discussion board is to be observed in all Liberty University communication. It is important to frame communication, by email or phone, in polite speech, using correct grammar, punctuation, and proper terminology. A student should begin each message by identifying himself or herself fully, which means giving the full name (Jane T. Doe) and

Terri Washer

"Be sure to request extensions at least 24 hours ahead of time since faculty members are not always online."

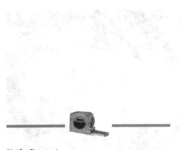

Katie Stewart

"The best thing you can do for yourself as a student and employee is to learn how to write a professional and courteous email. If you introduce yourself politely, state your concern as specifically as possible, and end with a courteous salutation, you will find that your instructor, boss, co-worker, etc. will take you more seriously and treat you with more respect."

Cari Smith

"Students may consider creating a signature within Microsoft Outlook, which will automatically populate every email with their name, student ID, etc."

Michael Marrano

"Take each set of assignment instructions and break down its requirements into its component pieces in bullet point fashion. Review the grading rubric also for possible additional details to include on your list. This way you do not miss the finer details of an assignment and lose points when it is graded."

student identification number (L00######). Letting the recipient know the name, number, and section of your course helps give context to what will follow. Only after identifying yourself and the course should you launch into what you are writing about. Choosing your words carefully, after gathering all appropriate facts for the inquiry you wish to pose, is critical for a quick response and resolution of the concern you are attempting to express. If you are writing to ask about a certain quiz item, it is best to identify the quiz, the topic, and the content of the question, rather than just asking "Why did I get #7 wrong?" especially since most quiz questions are **randomized** (meaning that the #7 for your quiz may be #3 for someone else's quiz). Providing as much information as possible is the key to having your inquiry answered quickly and correctly the first time.

While most professors are very responsive to student emails, remember that Liberty University expects faculty to respond to email messages within 48 hours of receiving them. In other words, if you have a question on Monday night at 10:00 p.m. and you write an email to your professor to ask for clarification, you should expect to have an answer no later than Wednesday night at 10:00 p.m. Again, many professors respond more quickly than that, but try to temper your expectations with the turnaround time in mind. Consider that questions asked just minutes before an assignment deadline will probably NOT receive a reply in time for you to submit your work on time. This is another reason not to wait until the last minute to begin your course work.

Weekly Deadlines

It is a wise student who consistently works ahead of routine deadlines. Balancing the life you already have before you decide to become a student with course work in college can be a challenge for many students. With work, church, family, and community commitments, many students are already fully engaged before trying to factor in college coursework. As mentioned earlier, while the beauty of online college work is that you have flexibility in how you complete your work, you still must meet regular deadlines. No one expects the unexpected events that happen, such as a loss of power, a balky computer, sudden illness, or any of the other "dog ate my homework" events in life that just happen! The way to avoid difficulties of this sort is to work a bit ahead of deadlines. Completing the module/ week's work on the weekend can help avoid the stress of frantic late-night Monday work . . . particularly when something goes wrong or assignments simply take longer to complete than you expect. Emailing the professor just minutes before the submission deadline to request an extension is *not* an acceptable way to end the week's work!

Ethical Behavior

Liberty University was founded in 1971 as a Christian university. Consequently, there is a basic expectation of **ethical behavior** in all work done for courses. Here is the Preamble to the Code of Honor:

> Liberty University students, faculty, administrators, and staff together form a Christian community based upon the values and goals of the Bible. These are defined in our foundational statements, including our Doctrinal Statement, our Philosophy of Education and Mission Statement, the Statement of Professional Ethics for the Faculty, and our Student Code. Together, these statements situate Liberty University within the long tradition of university culture, which in its beginnings was distinctively Christian, designed to preserve and advance truth.

> Anyone, whether Christian or non-Christian, who shares our values and goals, is both welcome and valued in our community. We want all students to feel comfortable in our community of learning, and we extend to all of our students our spiritual and academic resources, with the goal of fostering spiritual growth, character development, and academic maturity.

> Communities are based upon shared values and practices. This Code of Honor, an expression of the values inherent in our Doctrinal Statement, defines the rules and principles by which our community functions. At the core of this Code are two key concepts: a belief in the dignity of all persons and an insistence on the existence of objective truth.

> While we understand that everyone will not agree with the statements that follow, we do expect that our students respect and uphold these standards while registered at Liberty University. Abiding by the principles and behaviors established in this Code of Honor makes possible the success of our students and the strengthening of the Liberty community.

> Students who violate the Code of Honor, with either academic or personal offenses, are subject to sanctions as administered through the Graduate and Online Student Affairs Office. The Liberty University Code of Honor is a guiding document, which describes expectations for appropriate/acceptable student conduct, both on campus and online.

This preamble is followed by a detailed description of the academic code of honor, which identifies **academic misconduct** in three forms: **plagiarism, cheating,** and **falsification**. Definitions, consequences, and appeal procedures are described in full.

The personal code of honor for Liberty University Online is described, along with consequences and appeal procedures. The full Code of Honor for Liberty University Online students can be found on the Liberty University website (Liberty University Student Affairs, 2014).

Lucy Montalvo

"Consider the following when addressing your instructor for an extension:

1. Proactive steps consist of giving your instructor a time plan/goal allowing the instructor to see the intentions you have of completing the assignment you are requesting an extension for.

2. Properly identify yourself by including your full name followed by the course and section. This is necessary for when an instructor has several classes."

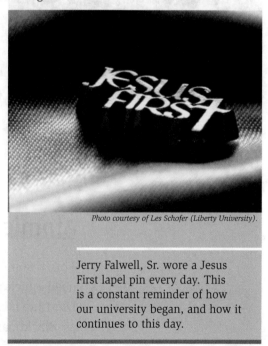

Photo courtesy of Les Schofer (Liberty University).

Jerry Falwell, Sr. wore a Jesus First lapel pin every day. This is a constant reminder of how our university began, and how it continues to this day.

Explore the Liberty University Resources Available to Help You

Jeremiah 3:15,
"Then I will give you shepherds after my own heart, who will lead you with knowledge and understanding" (NIV).

Your time in college learning can bring a bewildering array of information, choices, and tasks. Make sure you understand the opportunities that you have to ask for and receive guidance and support. Liberty University provides online students a wealth of campus-based online resources to smooth the path to online learning success.

Read the following to learn about opportunities for assistance from the offices and services designed to help you create your successful college learning experiences. The offices and resources are given in alphabetical order for easy future reference.

Photo by Kevin Manguiob, courtesy of Liberty University.

President Jerry Falwell reviewing plans for future developments on campus.

Academic Advising Department

Online learners may have a firm idea of the courses that are interesting, but the academic advisors can help you understand the correct course sequence to help you complete your program well and in the time frame you have in mind. Because online academic advising is done by major, you can be assured that the individual helping you is fully aware of the details of the degree that you are seeking.

Atomic Learning

This resource is not an office, but is a website you can access when you need quick information on software and related learning topics. Atomic Learning is a nearly boundless resource available to students and is as close as Blackboard. The Atomic Learning resources provide brief tutorials on every topic imaginable from Facebook to YouTube to all sorts of software tools. Access Atomic Learning to find exactly what you need, when you need it. Software and technology learning resources are available around the clock, on demand with this free service provided to all online learners.

Career Center

While you may not believe the Career Center has anything to offer a beginning student, that would be a mistake. Connect with the Advisors in the Career Center early in your college learning to explore careers, understand employment requirements, and begin to develop your personal career goals and plans. You can explore options for internships and externships, as well as potential jobs, too. The FOCUS two assessment, administered by the Career Center, can help you focus your thinking regarding your career options. Connect with the Career Center online or by telephone.

Financial Aid Office

The Financial Aid office is part of the Student Service Center. Financial Aid Officers can help you manage payment for your college career. You may be able to find scholarships or grants for which you are eligible, along with federally funded low interest loans. While the details of financial aid may seem overwhelming to new students, the professionals in the Financial Aid Office can smooth your way in arranging and understanding the details of financing your college education.

IT Help Desk/IT Marketplace

Did you know that students can purchase computer software at a discounted rate through the IT Marketplace? Most of the software required for courses is available for students at a specially arranged student price, when purchased through the University's IT Marketplace. In addition, there are software packages that are free of charge for students if downloaded through the IT Marketplace.

Roger

"Online students must realize that they are responsible for their online education. They are the best advocates for a good education. But they don't have to figure it all out on their own. There are resources such as degree completion plans. The school has invested heavily in training academic advisors.

Students must realize that they are expected to produce college level work. They need to learn how to write in Turabian, APA, and other formats. The school has entered into partnership with the Online Writing Center and Tutor.com to assist students with writing assignments.

Students do not have to feel that they are carrying heavy burdens alone. There is an entire online community to come alongside and bring encouragement and assistance. The LU Online Ministries department has advocates trained to provide prayerful support in time of need. Many classrooms have a community center (in the discussion board forums) where students can fellowship and pray with one another."

Betsey Caballero

"When in doubt . . . ASK!"

There are several free applications you can access.

- Blackboard Mobile Learn allows you to connect to Blackboard.

- MyLibertyU is a free suite of applications linking you to news of Liberty, athletic information, Blackboard, the LU Course Catalog, and more.

- LU Today is a free application that gives you immediate access to LU media and news, including Liberty Journal, Liberty News, Liberty TV, and more.

Another service that nearly every student will eventually become familiar with is the IT Help Desk. This is the resource to consult when you are having technical difficulty. Problems with Blackboard? Can't get the presentation to open? Your test "freezes" while you are in the middle of taking it? These issues, and others, can all be handled by submitting a HelpTicket to the IT Help Desk. The professionals at the IT Help Desk can assist you remotely or by phone to quickly resolve whatever technical issue is preventing your smooth progress.

Virus protection is essential for keeping your computer safe online. Liberty University provides antivirus protection to students, faculty, and staff at no cost.

Even before submitting a Help Ticket to resolve a problem, you may find that if you consult Ask LUKE, you can solve your own problem. Ask LUKE stands for "Ask Liberty University Knowledge Experts." There are quick tutorials that describe steps to set up your iPhone or Android smartphone and answer questions on applications, Blackboard, our webmail program, and so on.

Photo courtesy of Cali Lowdermilk (Liberty University).

Liberty University's school seal reveals the school motto: "Knowledge Aflame!" This floor mosaic can be found in the Hancock Welcome Center.

Jerry Falwell Library

The new state-of-the-art Jerry Falwell Library is your academic research resource. Combined with the assistance of the Online Librarians, you will find the library an invaluable resource for course research assignments, such as term papers and other writing and research projects. You can learn to search, locate, retrieve, and evaluate resources for any course you are taking. Online learners have access to the full range of scholarly materials and assistance through the Jerry Falwell Library.

Liberty Online Communities

Liberty University Online students can keep abreast of all that is happening on campus with the link to LU Communities. This site provides many ways for distant students to engage Liberty University through live streaming events, social media options, and links to the events and services of the university community. Requests for prayer can also be submitted through LU Communities, which is then shared with campus pastors as prayer partners.

MyLU Portal

The MyLU Portal offers a website link that you can customize. It offers you access to a wide variety of Liberty University information. It features **widgets** that show specific information such as Blackboard, Liberty news, class schedules, Liberty announcements, financial aid information, and more.

LU Flames Pass

The LU Flames Pass is your official Liberty University ID card. It can help you access student privileges off campus. It remains valid as long as you are actively enrolled. Students can receive a Flames Pass by visiting Card Services and providing a valid government-issued photo ID or by requesting online via the photo upload application.

Photo by Kevin Manguiob © Liberty University.

The Office of Military Affairs exists to support our service members, veterans, and military families with specific needs related to their education.

Office of Military Affairs

Excerpt provided by Emily Foutz, Director, Office of Military Affairs

Liberty University greatly appreciates the dedication and sacrifices made by our nation's Armed Forces, and we understand the needs of our service members, veterans, and military spouses and dependents. There are several resources and provisions provided for military students as they pursue their educational goals.

Alexandra Barnett

"Do not be afraid to let your instructor and ODAS (Office of Disability Academic Support) know if you have challenges that we can help you overcome by offering accommodations—we all have challenges in one area or another!"

The Office of Military Affairs exists to support our service members, veterans, and military families with specific needs related to their education, including military and veteran benefit counseling to help students navigate through the process for military Tuition Assistance and the GI Bill, and assistance when military duty occasionally impedes progress toward educational goals. Military Affairs acts as a liaison between the student, the Department of Veterans Affairs, and military branches to assist students with their financial needs so that they may focus on their educational pursuits. We encourage students to participate in our military student community online through social media and on-campus events to connect with fellow student veterans.

The Office of Online Disability Academic Support offers assistance for those veterans faced with challenges related to posttraumatic stress disorder (PTSD) and traumatic brain injury (TBI). Students who are facing these challenges are encouraged to contact this office for support.

Online Foreign Language Lab

Excerpt provided by Alisha Castaneda, Director, Online Foreign Language Lab

In August 2012, Liberty University's Center for Writing and Languages (CWL) opened the Online Foreign Language Lab (OFLL), which offers synchronous one-on-one tutoring sessions to distance learning students studying Chinese, English as a Second Language (ESL), French, German, and Spanish through Liberty University Online's conversational language courses, which are also offered for Liberty University en Español (LUE) students. These synchronous sessions occur via Skype and Google Hangouts and provide students with the opportunity to have an experienced tutor help them understand and learn more about the structure, grammar, interpretation, nuances, and cultural background of the target language, while also providing practical listening and speaking skills development.

Online Office of Disability Academic Support

Katie Stewart

"Reach out to your instructor! When you are confused about an assignment or unsure of your ability to write a college level summary, let your instructor know your concern as soon as possible. Instructors want to help their students succeed, but they can't offer the extra help you need unless they know how you are struggling specifically."

The Liberty University Online Office of Disability Academic Support (LUO ODAS) works with students and faculty to coordinate support services for online students with a documented disability. Under Section 504 of the Rehabilitation Act of 1973, this office provides "reasonable" accommodations and creates equal program access for all students. The online ODAS office works in conjunction with students and faculty to ensure that reasonable accommodations are made for students with documented disabilities. Once a student's disability is verified, this office notifies faculty members of the appropriate accommodations to make for students. These accommodations might include extended time on testing or other reasonable adjustments to ensure that the student receives appropriate support despite a disability.

Online Writing Center

Liberty University Online Writing Center is a resource that helps students evaluate and improve their college writing skills. As writing is a skill you will exercise often in college, it is wise to become the best writer you can be. Thus, we strongly encourage you to capitalize on this resource. To use the resources of the Online Writing Center, you will need to make an appointment. The service is free of charge, but the Online Writing Center will only review each writing assignment one time. Be sure to choose what stage of the work you wish to have help with and make your appointment for help with that in mind.

© 2015 by Odua Images. Used under license of Shutterstock, Inc.

Liberty University Online's Foreign Language Lab, Online Writing Center, and Spanish Writing Center are all designed to help students improve and enhance their communication and writing skills.

Registrar's Office

The **Registrar's Office** is the official custodian of all your academic records for the university. When you need to check your transcript or have a copy of it mailed to a potential employer or scholarship granter, the Registrar's Office is your contact point.

Spanish Writing Center

Excerpt provided by Alisha Castaneda, Director, Online Foreign Language Lab

The Spanish Writing Center (SWC), part of Liberty University's Center for Writing and Languages (CWL), provides writing tutoring services for Liberty University en Español (LUE) students. While other universities have Spanish writing centers geared toward tutoring students learning the Spanish language, Liberty University's SWC is a unique and innovative center that assists Spanish-speaking graduate and undergraduate students who are writing in their native language. Please visit www.liberty.edu/spanishwritingcenter for more information about this exciting new program.

Cari Smith

"When you are unsure of something or find yourself confused—ASK THE PROFESSOR. We are here to help you succeed."

Cari Smith

"When emailing your professor, ask specific questions and provide lots of detail."

Student Accounts

The Student Accounts Office keeps track of your financial obligations and payments to the university. The Student Accounts Office and the Financial Aid Office work together to manage and disburse your financial aid funds, whether from scholarships, military/veterans benefits, or outside sources.

Student Advocate Office

The Student Advocate Office is available to help online students dealing with obstacles to their academic progress. In order to accomplish this, the office acts as a liaison between a student and other university departments and helps students who face difficulties that affect their progress, such as emergencies or situations such as course problems, medical difficulties, or any situation involving academic warning or probation, and so on. The Student Advocate Office also assists in resolution of student appeals. In an effort to be proactive, the Student Advocate Office regularly polls students in order to discover ways to improve the experiences of online learners at Liberty University.

Tutor.com

Tutor.com is an individual tutoring service that online learners can access free of charge, if connected through Liberty University. Students can learn about a host of topics, with professionally trained tutors. Favorite tutors can be used repeatedly, and the service is available 24 hours per day. There is no need to make an appointment for tutoring. Students who struggle with difficult course concepts can make great progress with the help of a one-on-one tutor.

Many students assume that tutoring is only available for those who are not smart or who cannot learn. To the contrary, students who seek assistance are often able to make significant progress because of the help. If you are striving for academic success, consider what help the free services of Tutor.com might offer you.

Practice Self-Reflection to Fuel Personal Academic Growth

Job 34:4, "Let us discern for ourselves what is right; let us learn together what is good" (NLT).

2 Cor. 12:9a, "My grace is sufficient for you, for my power is made perfect in weakness" (ESV).

For many online learners, juggling responsibilities of family, work, and church can be nearly consuming. Adding in college coursework brings another layer of responsibility, but it does not really stop there, as there is more to be considered. Students need to be introspective, making a conscious effort to reflect on the choices made, the lessons learned, and how everything fits together to complete a cohesive plan of academic growth. Your times of introspection can be guided by the Holy Spirit, if you ask for wisdom and guidance.

Personal Reflection and Monitoring

An important step in academic growth that many students ignore is personal reflection. As you are learning, it is important to periodically take a moment (or more!) to consider what you are learning, how it fits into what you have already learned, and what this might indicate for the future. We can describe this type of thinking-about-thinking as **metacognition**. Metacognition allows you to open yourself to the deeper thinking we describe as critical thinking. Critical thinkers are able to evaluate what they have learned and are then open to creative thought. College-level learning demands that you take the steps you've used previously to memorize and understand, but also to consolidate what you understand so that you are able to move forward.

Two forms of personal reflection that you should engage as a college learner include self-assessment and self-monitoring. According to

Dr. Jerry Falwell, Sr., founder

"In the life of a believer, nothing happens by chance, fate or fortune" (Falwell, 1997, p. 428).

Cuseo, Thompson, Campagna, & Fecas (2013), self-assessment includes the following:

1. Looking at your personal interests and values

2. Understanding your personal aptitudes

3. Identifying your learning habits and style, as well as your personality traits.

4. Evaluating your academic self-concept, or what type of learner you are, whether confident or not, and whether self-directed or influenced by other factors.

When you have considered how all of these factors influence your learning, it is also important to monitor your learning. Successful students are able to determine:

- When they are effective in choosing learning strategies

- Whether or not they understand fully what they are reading and learning

- How to change gears to adjust learning strategies or practices to master the task at hand, such as reading more slowly, and so on.

Students who are good at monitoring their learning are able to determine if they are using effective strategies to read, understand, and make use of what they are learning. If you fail to take time to pause for metacognitive reflection, you miss the last important steps to ensure you are making adequate progress in using what you are learning. You must be able to apply new information to your knowledge base, make connections with other material, and evaluate the strength of your overall understanding.

Roger

"I can honestly say that I was not surprised by Liberty's expectations. I had experienced a rigorous education in both college and seminary. So I knew the level of work that I had to perform. I had forgotten the amount of reading required and at first was overwhelmed. Yet, I expected to be overwhelmed at first. But I knew the best thing to do is keep moving forward to accomplish projects a little at a time."

Photo courtesy of David Duncan (Liberty University).

Carving out a roadway on campus requires lots of planning and moving of mountains of dirt!

BUILDING BLOCKS

Summary and Conclusion

Information presented in this chapter points to the conclusion that successful students are:

1. **Engaged.** They seek to understand and meet the basic Liberty University expectations of students in the online community.

2. **Active.** They are careful to understand what is expected of them in the way of participation, communication, and timeliness of work.

3. **Resourceful.** They capitalize on resources offered, knowing who or which office can provide assistance in each situation encountered on the path to completing a college degree online.

4. **Reflective.** They are thoughtful students who assess and monitor their own learning processes in order to turn academic potential into positive outcomes.

Personal Reflection

Now that you have seen what it takes to begin well, consider areas that you think will require additional effort on your part. What surprises you in the expectations of students? Are there areas that you think will be difficult for you? Describe the difficulty and how you plan to mitigate it.

_____

_____

_____

_____

_____

_____

Personal Reflection

Now, as you consider the helpers in place on campus, determine which ones you think will be necessary for you to contact. List the contacts that you may need to make and jot down what you will need to have ready when you make the contact:

_____

_____

_____

_____

_____

_____

_____

Personal Reflection

Word Study

Using Biblegateway.com or Blueletterbible.com, do a word study on "plan" or "plans" to determine what God's Word has to say about making and carrying out plans.

_____

_____

_____

_____

How does God's plan for you include education here at Liberty University Online? Have you followed His guidance in your educational pursuits? Here is a verse to get you started. It is our wish for you as you begin well:

Psalm 20:4, "May he give you the desire of your heart and make all your plans succeed" (ESV).

_____

_____

_____

_____

_____

_____

TOOL BOX

- **Course Requirements Checklist (CRC):** As indicated in the chapter, the CRC is a crucial tool for taking attendance and for financial aid reporting. You can locate a tutorial on how to complete the CRC on the Breaking Ground website.

- **Syllabus and Course Schedule:** While the official syllabus and course schedule will not be available until your courses are available for the term, you may review the samples provided in the Course Guides section of the website (www.liberty.edu/online/course-guides).

- **Discussion Boards:** You will interact with faculty and students through Discussion Board forums in most of your courses. Review the tutorial on the Breaking Ground website to be sure you know how to use this critical tool.

- **Deadlines:** Deadlines for each course are unique; use the calendar feature on your smartphone or computer to track upcoming due dates and to stay on track.

- **Ethical Behavior:** As an online student with Liberty University, you are expected to uphold the online honor code. You can access a copy of the Liberty Online Honor Code through the Liberty University website or by navigating to the Breaking Ground website.

- **Interpersonal Communication**

  - *Student to Faculty*—To communicate with faculty, you will typically use your Liberty University email address. You can email your professor through the webmail tool or directly through the Blackboard Learning Management System. Some faculty may even offer optional live sessions or interaction through social media sites.

  - *Student to Advisor*—Advisors can be reached by phone, email, and live chat.

  - *Student to Student*—You can communicate with other students using the Discussion Boards in your courses, but you might also consider connecting through the Liberty University social media sites or by creating your own cohort of students in a social media group.

- **Student Support Offices:** For a full listing of links to the support offices referenced in the chapter, please navigate to the Breaking Ground website.

Additional resources and links to specific sites, worksheets, and apps can be located by accessing the Breaking Ground website:

www.breakinggroundlu.com

References

Cuseo, J. B., Thompson, A., Campagna, M., & Fecas, V. (2013). *Thriving in college and beyond*, 3rd edition. Dubuque, IA: Kendall Hunt Publishing.

Falwell, J. (1997). *Falwell: An autobiography.* Lynchburg, VA: Liberty House Publishers.

Liberty University Student Affairs. (2014). *Liberty University Online honor code: Preamble.* Retrieved from https://www.liberty.edu/index.cfm?PID=19155

Chapter 3

In this chapter, you will:

- Determine to be actively engaged in your courses.
- Develop an effective strategy for careful reading and text mastery.
- Select techniques to gain maximum benefit from lecture presentations.
- Choose an effective note-taking strategy to document important information.
- Select study skills to make wise use of study time.

THE BLUEPRINTS

Blueprints are the plans that guide a construction job. They provide a visual framework of the tasks to be done and provide the springboard from which the work proceeds. Imagine trying to build a house with no plans . . . the results would not be pleasing! Just as blueprints provide a guide for construction, study strategies are the guiding tools for creating academic success. Your college work requires a commitment to understanding and using good strategies to building your academic skills for college success.

© Solis Images.

Jeremiah 29:11, "For I know the plans I have for you," saith the Lord, "plans to prosper and not to harm you, plans to give you a hope and a future" (NIV).

THE CORNERSTONE

II Timothy 2:15, "Study to shew thyself approved unto God, a workman that needeth not to be ashamed, rightly dividing the word of truth" (KJV).

In life, there are many things that require careful study; while some of these things are academic in nature, many of them are not. Do you need to study to get better grades? Absolutely. However, you also need to study the cookbook to make sure that your dinner tastes delicious; for your plants, you need to study the elements that will make them thrive: partial sun or full sun, daily watering or occasional watering. Mark Tinsley, Army Chaplain (retired) and Associate Dean for the College of General Studies, explains this further in a story from his childhood regarding the skill of studying.

My father introduced me at a young age to the sport of shooting. Virtually every day during my childhood, I would grab the 12-gauge shotgun, the .38 caliber pistol, or one of the sundry hunting rifles my father owned, and I would shoot at cans, targets, bottles, trees, or whatever else I could find. Over the years, I became a pretty good shot and prided myself in taking out small targets at long distances. However, it didn't take me long in my shooting 'career' to realize that wind is the archenemy of any marksman, especially when firing at far-off targets. For instance, a swift breeze at a 100-meter target can be enough to blow a small caliber bullet slightly off course, resulting in a missed shot. As such, I learned early on to pay attention to the wind and adjust my point of aim. If the wind was blowing from the right, then I would aim a little bit to the right of my target. In this way, the bullet, as it was pushed left by the wind during flight, would ultimately impact the intended target. Those in the shooting 'business' will recognize this as the art of 'Kentucky windage.'

Our spiritual lives require a little bit of 'Kentucky windage' at times. Hebrews 2:1 states, "We must pay more careful attention . . . so that we do not drift away" (NIV). The winds of life—for example, stress, pride, loss, grief—can easily push us off course and cause us to drift away from God. Hitting the target—that is, maintaining a vibrant, fulfilling relationship with

"Hitting the target—that is, maintaining a vibrant, fulfilling relationship with God—requires a precision shot that takes into account the complexities of the environment in which we find ourselves." Mark Tinsley, Army Chaplain (retired)

God—requires a precision shot that takes into account the complexities of the environment in which we find ourselves. Those Christians who believe the life of faith should be easy and simple are deluding themselves. God never promised us a windless shot. To the contrary, we are told to expect pain, hardship, and suffering. During all this, however, we are admonished to pay close attention to what we are doing and what God would have us do, adjust our aim according to the conditions presented, and take the shot that is most pleasing to God. Of course, like any marksman, we'll miss the target sometimes. However, the more we practice, the better our aim will become.

Dr. Tinsley's story urges us to study all of the elements that impact our relationship with the Lord and with others, aiming carefully at the things that matter most. In our relationships with the Lord and with others, as well as our academic, personal, and professional responsibilities, let us do as Chaplain Tinsley and II Timothy 2:15 urge us, "Study to shew thyself approved unto God, a workman that needeth not to be ashamed, rightly dividing the word of truth" (KJV).

II Timothy 2:15 urges us, "Study to shew thyself approved unto God, a workman that needeth not to be ashamed, rightly dividing the word of truth" (KJV).

Determine to be Actively Engaged in Your Courses

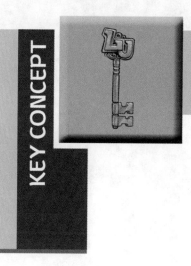

KEY CONCEPT

Micah 6:8,
"He has shown you, O mortal, what is good. And what does the Lord require of you? To act justly and to love mercy and to walk humbly with your God" (NIV).

The first principle of learning college material is that you have to be engaged with what you are doing. In other words, you simply must be completely involved: no second best efforts will serve your needs. If you are to succeed, you will need to actively read to get the "meat" of the content in your textbooks, articles, and so on, and you must devote yourself to significant time in the process. When we speak of the so-called "**active engagement**," we refer to the efforts you will put in to read, write, and think about what you are learning.

Time Spent On Coursework: What Are Your Expectations?

As you begin your college coursework, you should expect that you will spend plenty of time to gain mastery. Students who attend residential courses expect to spend, on average, 150 minutes per week in class, for a semester. Time spent outside of the lecture hall (classroom) includes reading, study, and organization of materials. A common metric for time outside class is approximately 2–3 hours outside class for each hour spent in class. So for a class that meets three times weekly, a student should expect to spend 2½ hours in class, and 5–7 hours out of class for each week, for a total of 7½–9½ hours per week. Consider that a semester is 14–15 weeks long, this will cumulate to 105–150 hours over an entire semester. Many students who begin online college work believe that the convenience of attending college online will limit the time needed to master the work. This is a mistaken assumption, as the time required for learning mastery is not very different between online learning and the residential college setting.

As you look at the time required for college study, you may be thinking that this is more time than you had planned to devote to your course. If so, please carefully consider what you are willing to do to become successful in your college work. If you wish to learn well from each course, you will need to devote significant time to earn your success. On the other hand, less than 40% of first-year college students report having spent more than 6 hours per week during their last year of high school. (Pryor, De Angelo, Palucki-Blake, Hurtado, & Tran, 2012). Try to think back to what your pattern of reading and study was in high school. Did you put in sufficient time to be successful? If you are a sports fan, you are probably familiar with the workout and training regimen of your favorite athletes. They devote time to their sport to gain the advantage at game time. If it helps you, consider how this may apply to you as you begin to "run the race" of your college courses.

Active Listening and Note-Taking

Residential college courses depend significantly on classroom lectures to deliver content to students. While there are some "lectures" in online learning, there are significant differences, too. Online learners do not attend hour-long lectures, as content is usually delivered in shorter presentations. What is the best way to take advantage of online lecture presentations? Just as a residential student might be taking notes, that is a wise action for online learners, too. Unlike lengthy lectures, however, online students usually discover that presentations are much briefer. The best thing about viewing lecture presentations online is that you can pause the presentation if you need to finish something in your notes, and then resume once you've caught up. You can also back up to review the material and repeat it as necessary. While you may be tempted to simply listen to the presentation, it is wise to take notes. This allows you to be actively engaged, and the more senses you engage in learning, the better. If you take notes while listening, you get the benefit of hearing the content, as well as the hands-on experience of note-taking.

© 2013 by Humannet Used under license of Shutterstock, Inc.

"Being able to read effectively is a critical skill."

Active Reading

For online students, the reading load matches that of the full semester, though the online term you are experiencing is only half as long. In other words, the reading intensity for online students is roughly double that of residential students working on the same course over the months of an entire semester. Being able to read effectively is a critical skill.

Are you a reader who just jumps in and plods along, dying to cross the finish line of the last page? Hopefully, not. However, if that does describe you, since the largest portion of your coursework will involve reading and learning from text materials, there are steps you can take to make your reading much more effective. Identifying, understanding, and using strategies and techniques to take advantage of good reading can equip you to read with excellent comprehension, so that you can retain what you have read and absorbed for practical application within the classroom and within your field. "Good readers connect their past experiences with the text: interpreting, evaluating, and considering alternative responses or interpretations." (Tomasek, 2009, p. 127). You may be pleasantly surprised at how much you gain from applying the following active reading techniques:

First, get ready to read:

© 2013 by razihusin. Used under license of Shutterstock, Inc.

"If you are a sports fan, you are probably familiar with the workout and training regimen of your favorite athletes. They devote time to their sport to gain the advantage at game time. If it helps you, consider how this may apply to you as you begin to 'run the race' of your college courses."

- Find a comfortable place to sit that will encourage good posture. Sitting at a desk to read facilitates note-taking and also puts you in a proper frame of mind for reading and study. (A comfortable chair may be so comfortable that you are soon distracted! Don't get too cozy!)

- Ensure that you have adequate lighting to avoid eye strain, which will be a distraction. This can cause you to prematurely stop reading and to be less effective while reading. Good lighting is a key to success. Ideally, you'll have natural light over your shoulder, but barring that, a good overhead light or lamp will help light your work area.

- Gather materials you may need: a pen/pencil for note-taking, paper or notepaper, a highlighter, and perhaps a dictionary.

- Consider adding headphones to enable you to avoid distractions from your environment.

- Put away other distractors. Turn off the television. Turn your phone to "silent" or leave it in another room while you are reading. Teach your family that unless the house is on fire while you are studying, you are not to be disturbed. Do not be tempted to have Facebook or chat features open while you are reading/studying. Consider downloading lectures, if possible, and turn off the Internet while you are listening.

- Say a brief prayer. Ask God to open your mind to the material you are about to encounter and to bless you with clear thought and easy comprehension.

- Begin by quickly reviewing notes taken in your last reading and study session. This activates your thinking, preparing you to build your learning with new information.

Develop an Effective Strategy for Careful Reading and Text Mastery

Acts 8:30–31,

"'Do you understand what you are reading?' 'How can I,' he said, 'unless someone explains it to me?' So he invited Philip to come up and sit with him" (NIV).

© 2013 by michaeljung. Used under license of Shutterstock, Inc.

"When we speak of so-called 'active engagement' we refer to the efforts you will put in to read, write, and think about what you are learning."

In the New Testament book of Acts, Chapter 8, we read the story of Philip and the Ethiopian man he met. Philip was walking on the road, and he met an important official in the Ethiopian kingdom. This man had been to Jerusalem to worship and was reading in the Old Testament book of Isaiah as he rode along in his chariot. Philip approached the man and asked, "'Do you understand what you are reading?' 'How can I,' he said, 'unless someone explains it to me?' So he invited Philip to come up and sit with him" (Acts 8:30–31, NIV). Philip was able to explain what the man was reading and was also able to tell him the good news of Jesus. Do you ever find that you have difficulty understanding what you are reading? What steps do you take to overcome this problem? Do you seek help, like the Ethiopian man did? Continue reading to find strategies to help you understand and remember what you read.

Pre-Reading Strategies

You have your textbook and you are ready to read, but don't just dive in! Before you begin to read the chapter, or whatever measure of reading is assigned, take a few minutes to "walk" through the reading. Previewing the main topics, the content, and the resources available to you within a chapter can help you remember more than you might expect.

- Review the notes you have from the previous session of reading. Activate your thinking on the topic before you begin to read.

- Examine the chapter and note any helpful features. Is there a glossary provided in the text? If so, locate it for easy reference.

- Look at the title. Can you see how this reading selection will relate to what you have learned already on the topic?

- Briefly look through the chapter and review the headings, subheadings, and bold words. Ask yourself a few questions, write them down, and look for the answers to your questions while reading.

- Locate the introductory paragraph and read it to develop an idea of what you will be learning in the chapter.

- Carefully examine the pictures, graphs, diagrams, maps, and other graphic material included in the book. These images are carefully selected to provide further information and illustration about what the author will be revealing.

- Locate the conclusion paragraph and read that. This synopsis generally covers what the author considers most important in the chapter.

- Are there end-of-chapter activities and questions? Look over those before you begin the reading. They will give you an idea of what you can expect to learn (and be able to answer) after reading the chapter. Later, when you are reading, keep them in mind as you discover answers.

© 2013 by InesBazdar. Used under license of Shutterstock, Inc.

Many students like to use sticky notes to mark their textbooks, but don't get carried away!

Cari Smith

"Determine the number of pages for each week's reading and break that into days. Example, you have 70 pages to read for week two—that requires 10 pages of reading a day. Set aside a specific time each day for reading and when you are done, reward yourself with something fun."

Now that you've previewed the material, you are ready to read. Don't regret the time you spent preparing to read, as it can help you understand what the chapter is about and what you will be expected to learn as you read. The time spent in pre-reading activities will be a worthwhile investment in your learning experience. Now you are ready to actively and critically read the text. The act of critical reading engages you in analysis and evaluation of the reading material (Paul & Elder, 2008).

During-Reading Strategies

As you read, do the following

- Read under a heading or subheading, thinking about the title and what you expect might be covered. As you are reading, think about how what you are reading connects to the heading or subheading and your prior knowledge of the topic. How does this fit in with what you know already, or how does this extend your knowledge?

Photo courtesy of Aaron Traphagen.

Intensive student, Lynn Rabun, works diligently during her course.

- Look for answers to the questions you identified already or those at the end of the chapter.

- Pay close attention to words that have been bolded, italicized, or underlined. If you encounter unfamiliar words, look them up, either in the text glossary or your dictionary. Note the definitions, as needed.

- Take notes. You can do this in several ways. You can make marginal notes if there is sufficient room in your textbook or you can write on notepaper or note-cards.

- Highlight as needed. Be careful to use the highlighter judiciously. Many students are tempted to highlight *everything* they see. When that happens, the text page just changes color, instead of allowing the highlighting to show what should stand out.

- Examine the accompanying pictures, diagrams, graphs, and so on, as you go, seeing how they fit into the "big picture" of what you are reading and learning.

- As you read, pay particular attention to the introductory and closing sentences of each paragraph, as they often introduce and then reiterate the main ideas of the paragraph.

Cari Smith

"Notecards can be used similar to the flashcards you had as a child; they are great for studying. Write the word or phrase on one side and on the other side, write out the definition."

Post-Reading Strategies

Once you have finished reading, you're finished, right? Not exactly. If you truly want to master the material you've read, there are additional important steps to take. Research shows that students who are good at mastering reading material engage in integrating the information they have learned with what they already understand, ask questions, interpret the text, reflect on what they have read, and monitor their comprehension (Yang, 2006).

- Take a few moments to think back over what you have read. Does it make sense to you? Are there gaps in your understanding? If so, look back to clear up any confusion.

- Look over the notes you have taken. Are they clear enough that they will provide a good set of study materials when you need to review them for a test? If not, now is the time to make corrections or additions.

- Go to the questions at the end of the reading/chapter. Can you provide good answers for each? If not, review to find adequate responses. Update your notes as needed.

- Think over what you have read, making connections between this new material and the understanding you had previously. Does this fit into your overall scheme of knowledge on this topic and extend it?

- If you have questions remaining, you can email your professor to indicate your confusion, and ask him/her to help clarify any confusion.

- You can also consult with the free tutors available to you, courtesy of Liberty University. Tutor.com is available on demand, around the clock. Talking with a tutor can help you see the big picture and help you prepare to take the next step in learning.

- Once you have completed your reading, be sure to review the notes you have taken regularly, so that you can retain and remember what you have read and learned.

Photo courtesy of Faith Perry.

The Jerry Falwell Library has many books which students can consult for further information on any class topic. Online librarians can assist students with access to these resources.

Personal Reflection

1. What strategies have you used to help you be an effective reader?

note taking

2. What strategies that you've read about here do you need to adopt?

pre-reading

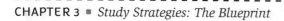

Select Techniques to Gain Maximum Benefit from Lecture Presentations

Proverbs 1:5,
"Let the wise listen and add to their learning, and let the discerning get guidance" (NLT).

© 2015 by Agenturfotografin. Used under license of Shutterstock, Inc.

"Ensure that you are distraction-free before you begin. Find a location that is quiet and put away distractors such as the phone and chat functions."

Much of the interaction you have with course materials in an online program of study is given to you in recorded presentations. Your professors have distilled critical information into presentations that last just a few minutes. Give yourself maximum benefit from the lecture presentations and PowerPoints by preparing ahead of time, taking good notes, and reviewing what you have heard and learned before moving on. Just like you prepared to read, it is a good idea to think ahead for best retention of information within course presentations. In order to accomplish this, follow these steps:

Pre-Viewing Strategies

Before you click to open the presentation:

- Choose a good time to view the presentation. Some students enjoy engaging course materials early in the morning before the family is up. Others like to watch presentations after the family is quiet for the night. You will quickly be able to establish a time that works best for you. Keep it in mind as you plan to watch your presentation.

- Review what you know about the material already. Predict how the topic of the presentation may fit into the overall scheme of the course.

Alexandra Barnett

"The difference between success and failure in an online class is focus. Avoid multi-tasking; focus on one task at a time until the work is completed."

- Look over your notes from the previous presentation, along with any notes you took during the reading assignment that correlates with this presentation. Gather note-taking materials, so that you can be an active participant during the presentation.

- Ensure that you are distraction-free before you begin. Find a location that is quiet and put away distractors such as the phone and chat functions.

During-Viewing Strategies

While you are listening to an audio presentation:

Corepics VOF

During the presentation, take notes!

- Use headphones to help you focus your attention on the content of the presentation.

- Take notes. You can listen all the way through, then come back for careful note-taking on the most important points of the presentation.

- Pause the presentation if you need to catch up in your note-taking. You can resume or repeat the presentation, as necessary.

- As you are watching, take note of anything the professor has shared in print on the lesson. It's a good bet that this is important information which you may see again later on a test!

- Watch the professor with an eye for verbal and nonverbal cues. Does the professor repeat something or raise his/her voice for emphasis? If so, what is emphasized and why?

- Give yourself plenty of "white space" on your note-taking page (or app) to fill in details later that you may have missed when first exposed to the information.

Post-Viewing Strategies

When you finish the presentation:

- You've read far enough in this chapter to know you are not really finished when you conclude viewing the presentation. Here are some tips to help you get the most out of the presentation.

- Review your notes. Do they seem complete, or are there gaps in either your notes or your understanding? If necessary, review the presentation to glean what you may have missed previously.

- Think about how what you just heard relates to the overall picture of what you are learning. How does this fit in? Does it mirror what you read, or does it go the next step in developing ideas?

- Be sure to find definitions of any words you did not understand or any technical jargon you may not have encountered previously.

- Finally, if you have questions after viewing the presentation, consult your professor or Tutor.com for more information.

Personal Reflection

1. Are you a good listener? YES/NO

2. What strategies have you used to help you be an effective listener/note-taker?

note taking being distraction free

3. What strategies that you've learned about here do you need to adopt?

watch for verbal cues

Choose an Effective Note-Taking Strategy to Document Important Information

KEY CONCEPT

Prov. 22:17,
"Pay attention and turn your ear to the sayings of the wise; apply your heart to what I teach" (NLT).

How good are you at taking notes? Do you have a strategy or method, or do you just try to pluck bits of information that you think may be important? Do you try to write down everything, capturing word-for-word what the professor shares in his or her presentation? Perhaps you write in sentences, making sure to use correct capitalization and punctuation. Do you often find that when you are finished taking notes, you have difficulty making sense of what you have written? Here are some note-taking strategies that can help you capture the essence of the important information you will need for later study.

Outline Notes

Outlining is a system of note-taking that follows a strict structure, but gives a clear organization to the material. A good outline is like a skeleton of the information. Roman numerals are used for major headings, and begin at the far left side of the page. Underneath that, capital letters are used for subheadings, indented. Beneath the capital letters, Arabic numerals appear, indented further in, which provide details. Other supporting details can be shown with lower-case letters, indented in still further.

Here is a sample of what an outline form looks like:

I. Roman numerals give the main ideas.
   A. Subheadings are indented beneath the main ideas.
      1. Arabic numerals give details.
         a. Finer levels of detail are shown with lower-case letters.

Note that in formal outlining, there should never be a "I" without a "II," no "A" without a corresponding "B," no "1" without a "2," and no "a" without a "b."

The benefit of outlining is that you can use the outline as a study guide, reciting information that you recall under each succeeding level of the outline. You can use an outline to write a summary of the information.

Cornell Note-Taking

The Cornell method of note-taking was developed at Cornell University Law School. The method relies on dividing the notepaper into a specific format to indicate the relative value of ideas and details. You can purchase "Cornell notepaper," also called "law-ruled paper," but it is easy to create your own. Here is how to use Cornell notes.

1. Draw a dark line across the bottom of the page, approximately five lines from the bottom.
2. Draw a similar dark line from top to bottom, two inches from the left side of the page.
3. Key points or main ideas, names, dates, and so on are written into the left column.
4. The right side is used for note-taking. Be careful to leave room to add information later, skipping lines between the notes you take.
5. When you finish the notes, be sure to put the date, course, and topic at the top right of the page.
6. The bottom portion of the page is left to create a summary/review of that page of notes.

Here is a sample of the Cornell format for note-taking.

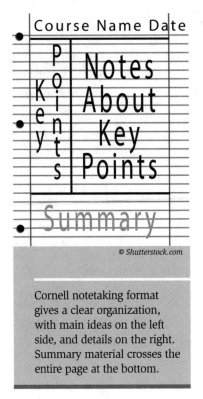

© Shutterstock.com

Cornell notetaking format gives a clear organization, with main ideas on the left side, and details on the right. Summary material crosses the entire page at the bottom.

You can review with the Cornell note-taking format by asking a family member or friend to quiz you, asking questions from the left column to see if you can recall the details from the right. You can also fold the paper along the line that separates the topics from the information and quiz yourself by asking questions you generate based on the topics. In the end, if you can give a good summary of the noted information, you are well on your way to mastery!

Concept Mapping

While the Cornell note-taking system is a powerful tool for some students, others prefer to create a concept map. Concept mapping allows you to see relationships between concepts easily, as you draw boxes or circles and insert information. Related concepts are joined by lines. This system of note-taking is excellent for learners who prefer to see things visually, as it allows you to "see the big picture" of how concepts fit together. Here is an example of a concept map:

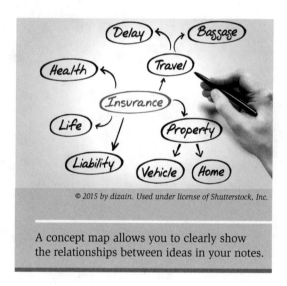

© 2015 by dizain. Used under license of Shutterstock, Inc.

A concept map allows you to clearly show the relationships between ideas in your notes.

Some students enjoy creating notes as concept maps. For others, taking notes in outline form is an easy way to establish the main ideas and supporting details of the information to be learned. Still other students gain mastery through the use of Cornell notes. It is a good idea to try several note-taking strategies, so you can determine which one works best with your learning preferences.

Personal Reflection

1. What method of note-taking have you used previously?

outline

2. What are the advantages that you enjoy with that method?

visual

3. What are the disadvantages you see for that method of note-taking?

adding later —

no space

4. Think of a course you're taking this term in which you are learning related pieces of information that could be joined together to form a concept map. In the given space, make a sketch of the concept map, indicating relationships between concepts with lines. Include all the information you would want to remember on the topic.

Select Study Skills to Make Wise Use of Study Time

Prov. 9:9,
"Instruct the wise and they will be wiser still; teach the righteous and they will add to their learning" (NIV).

Reading course textbooks and viewing presentations and PowerPoints are important to your online college learning success . . . but these are foundations upon which to build your learning. There are other strategies that can enhance your learning beyond the initial reading of your textbook and review of presentations. Which of the following strategies are you using now? Which do you need to add to your study "tool kit?"

Cari Smith

"Choose a study place with no distractions—turn your phone off, turn off Facebook chat."

Study Strategies for Successful Students

William Shakespeare is quoted as saying, "Study is like the heaven's glorious sun." Do you share that same enthusiasm? Many students do not. Yet, to be a successful student, it is essential to embrace and practice strategies that can improve your chances of performing well in your courses. Once you have read the textbook and viewed the presentations, what do you do next to lead to a good result when it is test-taking time? Here are some strategies you should consider as you work to create your success:

- Choose a site for study that is likely to help you avoid distraction, whether it's a corner in the basement or at a desk in the local public library.

- Begin the study session when you have time to give your undivided attention to study. Multitasking will *not* contribute to your success. You will need a reasonable period of time to study, rest, and review your materials.

- Make sure you are not hungry or thirsty, as these can be distractions, too.

- Choose to study at the time of day when you are at your best.

Photo courtesy of David Duncan (Liberty University).

Liberty University Hancock Visitor's Center provides a gracious welcome to visitors. Some students find this a quiet, welcoming place for study.

© 2015 by Dragon Images. Used under license of Shutterstock, Inc.

Test preparation begins when the course starts!

- Gather all your materials: notes, textbook, and computer.

- Plan to use all of your senses to engage the study material. In Chapter 7, you will learn about choosing strategies that serve you well based on your learning preferences.

- As you begin to study, ask God to clear your mind of other concerns, give you deep understanding, and allow you to master your work.

- To begin your study period, review your notes. This will begin to help you connect concepts, making associations to connect what you already know to what you are beginning to learn. This is the deep learning that you want to capitalize on when you are studying.

- See if you can write a summary document for the material you are studying. When you are finished, compare it to your notes. Are there any gaps you left out?

Test Preparation

As soon as you begin the course, you actually begin to prepare for your first test. All your work to read the textbook, view and listen to professor presentations, and think about the concepts you are learning contributes to your results on the test. However, when you see on the course chart that a test is imminent, there are some steps which you can take to help you prepare for the test.

- Make a test preparation schedule, so you are prepared to set aside sufficient time to prepare.

- **Memorization** is one of the key strategies to prepare for a test. You can use the following aids to help you memorize what you need:

  - **Acronyms** are memory aids composed of the first letter of the words you need to remember, formed into a word. For example, if you need to recall the names of the Great Lakes, the acronym "HOMES" can help you recall Huron, Ontario, Michigan, Erie, and Superior. You can create acronyms to relate to any list of words you need to recall, in order.

  - **Rhymes** and **songs** are excellent memory devices that prompt your recall. Do you remember when Christopher Columbus sailed from this old rhyme?

    "In fourteen hundred ninety-two,
    Columbus sailed the ocean blue."

Cari Smith

"Let your family and friends know the days and times you have set aside to study. This gives them the opportunity to support you by helping protect your school time."

Alexandra Barnett

"Review all assignment information early in the week and email your instructor with questions as many days before the assignment due date as possible."

- **Chaining** is a memorization device in which you build a sentence with the words you want to remember, in order. For example, <u>M</u>y <u>v</u>ery <u>e</u>xcellent <u>m</u>other just <u>s</u>erved <u>u</u>s <u>n</u>uts! (<u>M</u>ercury, <u>V</u>enus, <u>E</u>arth, <u>M</u>ars, <u>J</u>upiter, <u>S</u>aturn, <u>U</u>ranus, <u>N</u>eptune).

- **Flashcards** are easy to make and are great study tools. Moving while you review the flashcards, such as walking or pacing, can add power to your effort, as can reviewing the cards aloud. Each sense you add enhances your study effort. Carry your flashcards with you, and use them to study when the opportunity arises, such as standing in line or waiting in traffic.

- Summarize by writing the main points in one brief paragraph. While memorization is an important step in preparing for a test, there are more strategies you should consider as well. Think about what you have learned, and see if you can relate it all in one coherent whole. Can you summarize the material effectively?

- Look over any **study guides** that are provided in your course. Can you answer the questions? Write out the answers and review them in your study time.

- If no study guide is provided, make your own. Anticipate what questions you will be asked by reviewing broad concepts and important details, and then write out answers to demonstrate your knowledge. If you prepare potential essay questions before the test, you will consolidate your understanding of concepts as you put together your responses. Even if the professor does not ask what you were anticipating, your preparation will heighten your understanding of the material you are studying.

- Reviewing your notes is an obvious help, but don't forget to look back over the textbook. Have you highlighted information that you think will be important? Make sure you understand all the concepts you find underlined or in bold in the textbook. Outlining the textbook is an excellent way to solidify your understanding of the chapter.

- Teaching someone what you know can help you identify holes in your knowledge. If you get stuck as you are explaining something, you know you'll need to back up and review that information more thoroughly.

- **Overlearning** is a strategy in which you rehearse the study material past the point of mastery. This can be a powerful way to defeat test anxiety. Students who find that they typically "freeze" at test time can use this technique to help overcome test anxiety and get back on track to finish a test.

Alexandra Barnett

"Read the rubrics and use them as checklists to ensure all requirements are met prior to submitting assignments."

Cari Smith

"Take frequent study breaks—give yourself 5–15 minutes before returning to your studies."

Cari Smith

"Read the directions. Read the directions again. Complete your assignment. Read the directions one last time to confirm your work is correct."

© 2015 by Angela Waye. Used under license of Shutterstock, Inc.

Cramming to exhaustion is not a good study strategy!

Alexandra Barnett

"Complete small tasks and assignments first. The accomplishment you feel by completing these tasks will propel you forward to completing the bigger tasks."

Cari Smith

"Use the assignment rubric as a guideline, as it shows EXACTLY what you will be graded on."

- **Cramming**, though a strategy many students claim to employ at one time or another, is NOT a wise study practice. Plan time to master the information you need to learn gradually. Studying over two or more sessions yields better learning than spending an equal amount of time studying in a single study session (Carpenter, Cepeda, Rohrer, Kang, & Pashler, 2012).

Make sure that you are well-rested, both when you are studying and when it is time to take your test. Lack of sleep leaves you unable to focus and do your best thinking and responding. If you have to choose between staying up and cramming or getting adequate rest, you should opt for sleep, since you will not be able to perform your best if you have not given your body time to rest, and you will likely not remember what you tried to cram into your brain the night before. Your body uses sleep time to consolidate your learning. Failure to sleep means you will not be at your best for the test.

Test-Taking Strategies

Wise students prepare well for any testing situation. There are also strategies to apply once you are taking the test. Before you begin the test, ask God to calm your nerves, give you the ability to show what you know, and help do your very best work, based on the study preparation you have done. However, do not ask for a miracle if you didn't study!

When you first open the test, take a few moments to look it over. See what types of questions there are and how many. This allows you to budget the time available most effectively. As you are considering your budget of time, think about the relative value of the questions. For example, if ten True/False questions are one point each and the essay is worth 50 points, you can see that you should allow much more time for writing the essay response. Generally, it is best to answer easy questions first to build your confidence. Skip over the ones that you do not know how to answer and, if you are able to, come back to them later in the test. You may find hints in the rest of the test that will help you with questions you hesitated on at first.

Read the instructions for each portion carefully. Sometimes, there are surprises there. For example, on what may look like simple True/False questions, you may also need to correct a false question to make it true.

For example, if the question is "The first ten amendments to the U.S. Constitution are known as the Corrective Amendments," you might strike through "Corrective Amendments" and write "Bill of Rights." Overlooking part of the instructions can have disastrous consequences.

Keep in mind that for True/False questions, there are a few keys to help you:

1. If any part of a True/False question is False, the answer has to be False.

2. Look out for absolute words: "always," "never," "any," "only," "every," "no," "none of," "all," and so on. These words usually tend to appear in questions that are False.

3. On the other hand, qualifying words, such as "some," "many," "at times," "few," "frequently," "generally," and the like, usually tend to appear in questions that are True.

4. Watch out for negatives, such as "no," "not," "cannot." Read the item without the negative word; then decide if it is True or False. If it is True, its opposite, or negative, is usually False.

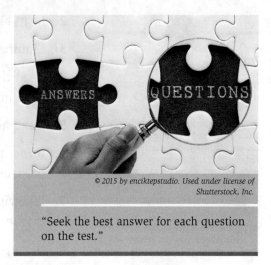

"Seek the best answer for each question on the test."

The following are some tips to help you with matching items:

1. Be sure to read all the matching items FIRST. Look at both columns of items to be matched.

2. Then match stems to ends that you are absolutely sure are correct.

3. Work your way through from the top of the first column. If you are not sure of an item, skip it.

4. Once you have reduced the choices of possible matches, it may be easier to find matches of items you were not sure of at first.

5. If an item seems to match more than one place, make a note of the two possible matches, so you can resolve it when there are fewer choices.

6. If you exhaust all of the responses you are not sure of, you'll have to guess. It is better to guess and perhaps get it correct than to leave it blank and have no chance of getting it correct.

Emily

"Flash cards are really helpful for me when studying. It may seem like more work, but having to write it all out then reading them over and over really helps."

If your test has multiple choice questions, employ these strategies for the best possible outcome:

1. Read through each stem without looking at the answer choices. See if a possible answer comes to your mind. If your answer is one of the choices, it's a good bet that's the correct answer.

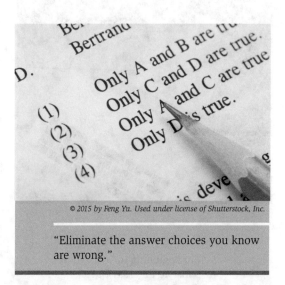

"Eliminate the answer choices you know are wrong."

Terry

Q: *What learning/test-taking strategies did you pick up in college that you did not use previously?*

A: "I always preferred the outline strategy. I would create an outline of the chapters that were being covered that included key topics/concepts, as well as page numbers where I could find that information later."

Q: *How can students overcome their test fears?*

A: "I believe most fear comes from lack of preparedness: prepare, prepare and prepare and you'll have nothing to fear."

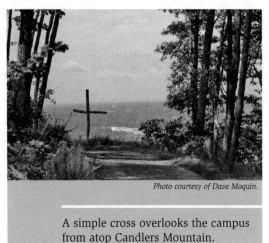

Photo courtesy of Dave Moquin.

A simple cross overlooks the campus from atop Candlers Mountain.

© 2015 by Kaylie_Kell. Used under license of Shutterstock, Inc.

"Take time to organize your thoughts before beginning to write your response to an essay question."

2. Read all of the answer choices before selecting one.

3. Eliminate the answer choices you know are wrong.

4. Read the stem and answer choice(s) aloud, noting whether or not the stem and end agree in verb tense and number.

5. Generally, the choice with more information is the correct one.

6. If the question includes "all of the above" but you are sure that one is not true, do not choose "all of the above."

7. Likewise, if "none of the above" is a choice, but you are sure that one is true, do not choose "none of the above."

8. If you are reduced to guessing, make sure you have eliminated all choices you can, and then make your best guess.

For tests that include essay questions, apply the following strategies:

1. Make sure that you have budgeted time to develop your answer. Don't spend too much time on the rest of the test and leave yourself little time to create a well-supported response.

2. If you have memorized information for the test, and you need it for the essay, go ahead and do a "brain dump." This is where you quickly write down all the relevant information that you have memorized, so you are not strained to keep it in memory. Once you've written, you can organize and refine your response. A brief period spent outlining your response is a good use of your time.

3. Note the parameters of the question. If it requires a response of three paragraphs, for example, ensure that you format your response that way. If it asks you to list seven items, make sure you include seven items in your response.

4. If the question asks you to list and define, or respond and defend your answer, be sure to include a response to each part of the question. Sometimes, underlining the verbs in the instructions can be helpful to ensure that you do all that is asked of you.

5. Begin each paragraph with an introductory sentence. Give a few points (one per sentence) and wrap up your paragraph with a concluding sentence. Continue in this manner until you finish the essay.

6. Use transitions to move your work along.

7. Review what you have written. It is usually difficult to proofread your own work, but it is necessary to ensure that you don't lose any points for careless errors. Work backward, so you can test each sentence individually for clarity, punctuation, spelling, and so on.

As you are working through the test, keep an eye on the time available. Take a deep breath each time you complete a section of the test. Don't stress much over any one question or answer.

Once you have completed the test, if time remains, go over the test. Look to ensure that you have responded to each question and that you have marked the answer that you chose. Don't second guess yourself: usually, your first response is more likely to be correct than one chosen on review, unless you simply marked a choice you did not intend to choose.

Photo courtesy of Dave Moquin.

Sharp Top and Flat Top, the Peaks of Otter, in nearby Bedford County, can be seen from the Liberty University campus.

Strategies to Use When the Test Is Over

When you finish the test and select "SUBMIT," you are finished, right? Not exactly! A wise student will use opportunities to keep learning, even when the test is over. If there is an area of testing that you feel you did poorly on, try to find information to complete your knowledge. Is there additional information in a course presentation or the textbook that can help you round out your knowledge? Much of what you learn in college is **scaffolded**, that is, one concept is built upon a previous one. Misunderstandings at a lower level can hurt your experience and understanding as you build through your curriculum unless you fill in any knowledge gaps you discover.

If you are allowed to review your graded test, take advantage of a good learning opportunity:

1. Read your professor's feedback. It can be very enlightening.

2. Look over the test questions. See what you missed.

3. Look for patterns: did you miss several questions on a certain concept, or

4. Did you do poorly on a certain type of question, or

A well-completed test is a good reason to celebrate!

© Andresr.

5. Were you unable to articulate an understanding of the "big picture?"

6. Did your essay responses earn high marks? If not, why not? What might you need to do differently next time in order to earn a higher score?

7. Be sure to use what you learned upon inspection of this test to inform your thinking for the next test. You can adjust both your study/preparation and your test-taking strategies based on what you discovered.

No matter what your college major or method of studying, there is always room for improvement. Applying good study habits and strategies systematically can help you learn well and demonstrate your understanding when it is time to "show what you know" on the test.

BUILDING BLOCKS

Though your objective in college is not necessarily to do well on tests and quizzes, those are two of the ways that we use to measure your learning. It is important to read well, with good comprehension, and to understand what is presented in course audio/video lectures and PowerPoints, in order to be able to demonstrate your knowledge. There are many ways to take advantage of textbook and course materials.

How do you approach a learning session? Do you do anything to prepare for viewing a lecture presentation or PowerPoint? What strategies do you apply when it is time to read the textbook?

Carefully review your reading and study habits, so you can incorporate wise practices.

Personal Reflection

Record some strategies here that you are not currently using and that you plan to put into practice.

Preparation for textbook reading

_____ outlining _____

_____

_____

_____

Preparation for course presentations

_____ active listening _____

_____

_____

_____

Study techniques and strategies

_____

_____

_____

_____

Test-taking strategies

_____

_____

_____

_____

In the Bible, we read about King Solomon, honored as the wisest man. The Old Testament book of I Kings, Chapter 2 relates that King David instructed his son Solomon to ". . . be strong, act like a man, and observe what the Lord your God requires: Walk in obedience to him, and keep his decrees and commands, his laws and regulations, as written in the Law of Moses. Do this so that you may prosper in all you do. . . ." (I Kings 2:2b–3a, NIV). Later, God told the young king to ask for whatever he wanted. Solomon answered, asking God to give him wisdom to rule His people. God was pleased by this request and granted it and much more. God replied,

> ". . . I will do what you have asked. I will give you a wise and discerning heart, so that there will never have been anyone like you, nor will there ever be. Moreover, I will give you what you have not asked for—both wealth and honor—so that in your lifetime you will have no equal among kings. And if you walk in obedience to me and keep my decrees and commands as David your father did, I will give you a long life" (I Kings 3:11–14, NIV).

Have you asked God to grant you wisdom as you pursue your college education? You will need to be wise in determining how to use your time and also how to devote yourself to careful reading, presentation review, and study practices. Pray with Solomon, that God will _give me {you} wisdom and knowledge_" (II Chronicles 1:10, NIV).

TOOL BOX

Reading

Reading Speed and Comprehension—Since much of the material in the online classroom is written, good reading speed and comprehension are critical. If you are among the many who are less than happy with the speed at which they read while simultaneously absorbing information, you might consider taking a speed reading course. Liberty University offers a for-credit class that is designed to increase both reading speed and comprehension (CLST 301).

Studying

Flashcards—An old standby in the realm of study tools, but you may be happy to hear that the concept has been updated for the 21st century. Instead of walking around with a deck of cards in your pocket, consider downloading a flashcard app for your mobile device. These apps allow you to create digital flashcards in much the same way that you would create physical flashcards, but also offer some additional features. Once you are through your stack of cards, the program will let you start again from the beginning, shuffle the deck, or even quiz you on just the items you got wrong the first time.

Note-Taking—Programs like Evernote allow you to take notes, organize information, and perform detailed searches of your notes, all while syncing them across multiple devices. This means you can take notes on your laptop while listening to a lecture and then review them on your phone while you wait in line at the doctor's office. Best of all, most of these types of applications are low cost or free, work across multiple operating systems, and are fairly intuitive.

Additional resources and links to specific sites, worksheets, and apps can be located by accessing the Breaking Ground website:

www.breakinggroundlu.com

References

Carpenter, S. K., Cepeda, N. J., Rohrer, D., Kang, S. H. K., & Pashler, H. (2012). Using spacing to enhance diverse forms of learning: Review of recent research and implications for instruction. *Educational Psychology Review*, 24, 369–378. DOI: 10.1007/s10648-012-9205-z

Paul, R. & Elder, L. (2008). *The miniature guide to critical thinking concepts and tools*. Dillon Beach, CA: Foundation for Critical Thinking Press.

Pryor, J. H., DeAngelo, L., Palucki Blake, L., Hurtado, S., & Tran, S. (2012). The *American freshman: National norms fall 2011*. Los Angeles: Higher Education Research Institute, UCLA.

Tomasek, T. (2009). Critical reading: Using reading prompts to promote active engagement with text. *International Journal of Teaching and Learning in Higher Education*, 21(1), 127–132.

Yang, Y. F. (2006). Reading strategies or comprehension monitoring strategies? *Reading Psychology*, 27, 313–343.

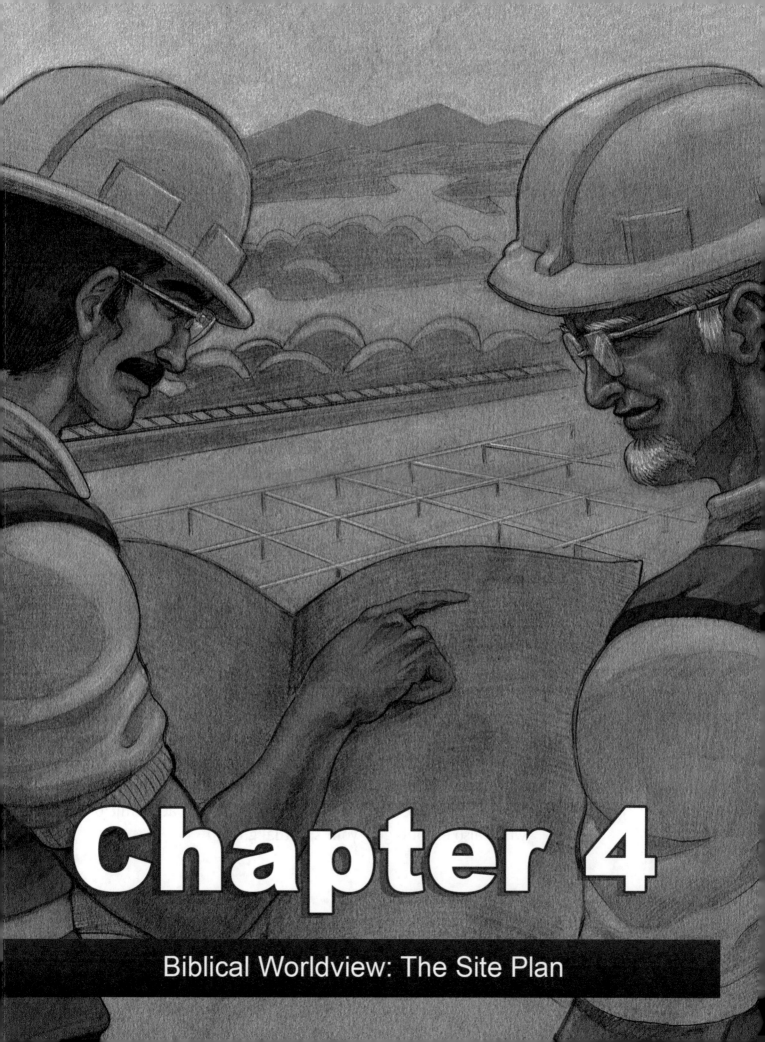

Chapter 4

Biblical Worldview: The Site Plan

In this chapter, you will:

- Define the concept of worldview.
- Examine the way you view the world.
- Identify the tenets of a Christian worldview.
- Identify Liberty University's core values.
- Generate ideas to implement a biblical worldview.

SITE PLAN

When you first dream of constructing a new building, you must complete many tasks to ensure that the dream transforms into reality. One of these tasks requires determining the best placement for your proposed building; in order to achieve this, your contractor will carefully develop a site plan, taking the existing landscape and infrastructure into consideration along the way. Your project may fit perfectly, or changes may need to be made to make the dream a reality. The same is true for your academic dreams. You must find the best school for you to pursue those dreams, and once you find it, you must evaluate existing values and philosophies taught there and determine how these fit in with the way you view the world. Since you are already a student at Liberty University, you must have determined that this is the best place to make your academic dreams come true. Here your professors will teach you subject matter infused with a Christian worldview that is rooted in biblical truth. You will be surrounded by godly counsel and advisers, who are invested in the success of your academic plans, while also encouraging your spiritual growth.

© 2013 by Lightspring. Used under license of Shutterstock, Inc.

Proverbs 15:22,
"Plans fail for lack of counsel, but with many advisers they succeed" (NIV).

THE CORNERSTONE

Through His Eyes and in His Steps

Micah 6:8, "He has told you, O man, what is good; and what does the LORD require of you but to do justice, and to love kindness, and to walk humbly with your God?" (ESV).

Colossians 2:6–10, "So then, just as you received Christ Jesus as Lord, continue to live your lives in him, rooted and built up in him, strengthened in the faith as you were taught, and overflowing with thankfulness. See to it that no one takes you captive through hollow and deceptive philosophy, which depends on human tradition and the elemental spiritual forces of this world rather than on Christ. For in Christ all the fullness of the Deity lives in bodily form, and in Christ you have been brought to fullness. He is the head over every power and authority" (NIV). As Colossians 2:6–10 explains, when you become a Christian, you begin a relationship with Jesus Christ, and as you get to know Jesus better, you begin to look at the world through His eyes; this relationship informs your worldview. Liberty University professor, Nathaniel Valle, elaborates further about what it means to have a Christian, biblical worldview.

© 2015 by Patrick Lynch Photography

WWJD: What Would Jesus do?

One of the most difficult tasks we face as Christians is trying to determine what exactly a biblical worldview looks like in a modern culture. It can be exhausting, especially when faced with so many voices claiming to know exactly why and how we should interpret the world. When I was a teenager, I was told that a biblical worldview was one thing: knowing what was wrong and right. Certainly, that is an important and essential part of what comprises a biblical worldview. Like 1 John 2:29 mentions, when we know Christ's righteousness, we will also recognize and know other Christians because we see the same righteousness within them.

But if we stop at that definition, it can seem like we favor our actions as the primary way to define a biblical worldview. If that happens, an inevitable

"When we are given the command to embrace a biblical worldview, it means we show humility and kindness while we engage the world to find the goodness, beauty, and truth of God in a way that glorifies Him."

result is that we instinctively compare our lives to others, attempting to make ourselves look better than we are because other people say, see, or do things that we do not.

When I was younger, one of my favorite books was Charles Sheldon's classic 1896 novel, In His Steps: What Would Jesus Do? In the story, a pastor asks his congregation to remember a simple question each time they are confronted with a problem or challenge, "What would Jesus do?" When I first read the book, a proverbial light bulb moment illuminated my understanding of what it meant to have a biblical worldview. Saying I was a Christian was not enough.

From my newfound book knowledge, a biblical worldview meant I needed to make decisions like Christ himself. Like me, other Christians my age were experiencing these same ideas. If you remember life during the 1990s, the phrase was seemingly everywhere in Christian churches and even in the conscience of American culture. I remember t-shirts, bracelets, youth groups, worships songs, and retreats themed around the phrase, and it was exciting to be part of that movement.

But as I returned to In His Steps and reread it, I found myself asking this question: what exactly would Jesus do? I was not sure. Would Jesus approve of a PG-13 movie or the National Football League? Would Jesus laugh with me while watching The Princess Bride, one of the greatest comedies in cinematic history? Should I listen to U2's music? Perhaps the most important question: would Jesus go on a date?

As you may have guessed, I quickly burned out. I was overwhelmed by the uncertainty that comes with not knowing if God was happy with me, and I spent hours reviewing and critiquing my days in an attempt to try and master what it meant to be like Christ. But no matter how many times I read In His Steps or tried to act a certain way, the answer to these questions eluded me.

It was later in life when I realized God wanted me to see **everything through His Son and Scripture**, meaning my life needed to be spent in pursuit of understanding God's truths, while I attempted to engage with those around me. Essentially, I needed to stop thinking of a biblical worldview as only a strategy to avoid sin; instead, I needed to become the kind of person that values the wisdom of Philippians 4:8: "Finally, brothers, whatever is true, whatever is honorable, whatever is just, whatever is pure, whatever is lovely, whatever is commendable, if there is any excellence, if there is anything worthy of praise, think about these things" (ESV).

That verse commands us to desire goodness in every part of our lives, regardless of where we live or the people with whom we interact. Accordingly, when we look at Christ's life, we see He spent His time not only helping people, but discussing truth and revealing it in every part of their world. Though impossible to replicate His life, we should remember the words of Micah 6:8, where the foundations of a biblical worldview reveal themselves in a very realistic way: "He has told you, O man, what is good; and what does the LORD require of you but to do justice, and to love kindness, and to walk humbly with your God?" (ESV).

When we are given the command to embrace a biblical worldview, it means we show humility and kindness while we engage the world to find the goodness, beauty, and truth of God in a way that glorifies Him. In time, a biblical worldview means that we desire goodness because we desire Christ, ensuring we truly see and know what it means to be in His steps.

". . . a biblical worldview means that we desire goodness because we desire Christ, ensuring we truly see and know what it means to be in His steps."

Having a Christian, biblical worldview is more than just doing good deeds or saying you are a Christian. Professor Nathaniel Valle makes this point, while also explaining what a Christian worldview involves—discovering God's truth about everything in life through Scripture and a relationship with Jesus Christ. By growing in your knowledge and understanding of Scripture and by growing closer to Jesus, you will begin to see the world through His eyes and you *will* "be in His steps." With this perspective, you can encourage and share God's truth with others in our current culture without conforming " . . . to the pattern of this world, but be(ing) transformed by the renewing of your mind. Then you will be able to test and approve what God's will is—his good, pleasing and perfect will" (Romans 12:2, NIV).

Define the Concept of Worldview

Proverbs 23:7a,
"For as a man thinketh in his heart, so is he . . ." (KJV).

As you begin your coursework at Liberty University, it is important to identify and reflect on your **worldview**. Merriam-Webster.com defines the concept of worldview as "a particular philosophy of life or conception of the world" (2015). James Sire (1997), author of *The Universe Next Door: A Basic Worldview Catalog,* offers this explanation "A worldview is a set of presuppositions (assumptions which may be true, partially true, or entirely false) which we hold (consciously or subconsciously, consistently or inconsistently) about the basic make-up of our world" (p. 16). Even if you have never consciously considered your worldview, you *do* have one, and it guides every one of your actions and decisions. Because your worldview is all-encompassing, it affects your thinking on every aspect of life, from what you view as right and wrong to how you spend your money and your time to what you think politically; it even impacts how you treat others.

When you begin reflecting on your worldview and how you came to adopt it, you engage in "thinking about thinking," something also called "metacognition." Merriam-Webster.com defines **metacognition** as an "awareness or analysis of one's own learning or thinking processes" (2015). Most of the time, we don't think about our worldview, even though it permeates our lives (as we unconsciously try to make sense of our world by reflecting on our experiences). Many people have not asked the deep questions of life, nor have they considered how their answers might connect to each other. That doesn't mean, however, that they lack a worldview. Instead, they simply are not aware of what has shaped their thinking. However, identifying the factors that shape their thinking is an essential step because these factors influence and build their identity, as Proverbs 23:7a explains "For as *he thinks* in his heart, *so* is *he*" (AMP).

Photo by Ty Hester © Liberty University.

Everyone has a worldview. What is yours? Proverbs 23:7a, "For as *he thinks* in his heart, *so* is *he*" (AMP).

Examine the Way You View the World

KEY CONCEPT

I John 1:5–7,
"This is the message we have heard from him and proclaim to you, that God is light, and in him is no darkness at all. If we say we have fellowship with him while we walk in darkness, we lie and do not practice the truth. But if we walk in the light, as he is in the light, we have fellowship with one another, and the blood of Jesus his Son cleanses us from all sin" (English Standard Version).

Once you recognize that everyone has a worldview, it is critical to evaluate the origins of your own. What do you value in life? What is important to you? Your values impact the choices that you make in life and how you view the world around you. They contribute to your worldview.

In the pages that follow, take some time to respond to the questions regarding your beliefs and values. Be honest with yourself. Then, share your responses with a friend or family member. Invite them to share their answers, as well. Your thoughts and values will likely be different from others, but that doesn't make your ideals any less valuable or vice versa. However, knowing where you stand on an issue and your reasoning for it is necessary for character building and growing in your interpersonal relationships and in your relationship with Christ.

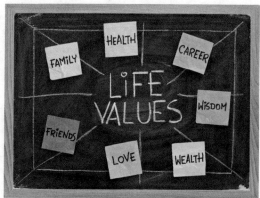

© 2015 by marekulisasz. Used under license of Shutterstock, Inc.

"What do you value in life? What is important to you? Your values impact the choices that you make in life and how you view the world around you." What do you value in life?

Personal Reflection

To evaluate your worldview, ask yourself the following questions and use the spaces provided to record your answers.

What are my core beliefs about the world and the people in it? Consider your beliefs about: God, Jesus, and the Holy Spirit; the origin of the world; the nature of man; mankind's role in the world; mankind's relationship with God, Jesus, and the Holy Spirit; man/woman's social responsibilities and personal interactions with others.

God is one w/ J + HS, He is the creator of all. We were created in His own image

How did I come to think about things the way I do?

upbringing, my faith

What has shaped my attitudes?

God's effect on my life

Does everyone else have an equally valid worldview? Are they all correct, in other words? If each of us has a right to our own beliefs, we have free will—after all, does that mean everyone has **correct** beliefs? Why or why not?

_____

_____

_____

_____

_____

How can I tell if my beliefs are correct?

_____ I can't, trust / faith _____

_____

_____

_____

_____

The author of the book _Elements of a Christian Worldview,_ Michael Palmer (1998), explains that worldview can help us answer the deep questions of life,

> Through our worldview, we determine priorities, explain our relationship to God and fellow human beings, assess the meaning of events, and justify our actions. Our worldview even speaks to the most ordinary practices in everyday life, including the types of things we read and view, the types of entertainment and leisure activities we seek, our approach to work, and much more. (p. 24)

With this in mind, evaluate your perspective even further . . .

Photo by David Duncan
© _Liberty University._

"Through our worldview, we explain our relationship to God and fellow human beings . . ." Michael Palmer.

What are my priorities in life?

_____ God _____

_____ Family _____

_____ myself - studies _____

_____

What kind of relationship do I have with God?

_____ Steady, maranthan _____

_____

_____

_____

How do I treat other people? Why?

_____ *tru w/ kindness + grace* _____

_____ *b/c God gave me to* _____

_____ *me 1st* _____

_____

Why do bad things happen to me/others? How do I respond when these things happen?

_____ *ser God* _____

_____ *broken* _____

_____ *world* _____

_____

Why do I do the things I do? (Consider basic decisions and actions, shortcomings and sins, acts of kindness, etc.)

_____

_____

_____

_____

Continue in this reflective process. In the space provided, ask yourself questions that address elements of your life: entertainment, recreation, work, family, education, exercise, and so on. To get you started, an example has been provided. Feel free to draw some of your questions out of Michael Palmer's (1998) explanation of a worldview.

Your Question	Your Answer
Example:	Example:
Why did I go see that movie?	*I wanted to see the movie, American Sniper, because I had heard the story of Chris Kyle on the news, and I wanted to know more about it.*
How did it impact me?	*The movie made me think about the sacrifices that men and women make to serve and protect others. It made me aware of the pain their families experience while they are away. It also painted a realistic picture of how difficult it can be to adjust to life at home after serving in a war-torn country, especially after losing brothers/sisters in arms.*

Why?	Even though my grandparents and uncles served faithfully in the armed forces, my knowledge of their sacrifices has always been second hand and carefully told. I have no personal experiences to draw from, apart from their stories, the news, and other narratives, from friends and other forms— movies, television shows, books, etc.

Photo by Kevin Manguiob
© Liberty University

Liberty University's mascot, Sparky, welcomes alumni and visitors home for homecoming weekend.

Identify the Main Tenets of a Christian Worldview

2 Timothy 3:14–17,
"But as for you, continue in what you have learned and have become convinced of, because you know those from whom you learned it, and how from infancy you have known the Holy Scriptures, which are able to make you wise for salvation through faith in Christ Jesus. All Scripture is God-breathed and is useful for teaching, rebuking, correcting and training in righteousness, so that the servant of God may be thoroughly equipped for every good work" (NIV).

While there are many worldviews that seek to answer life's basic questions, Liberty University was founded and focuses on a **Christian worldview**, which is an overall concept of the world and our part in it, grounded on God's authority, which He reveals to us through the Bible. Often, when we talk about a biblical worldview, we describe the Bible as the lens through which we view the world. The Bible reveals God's truth to us, and through it, we gain a correct perspective on all that we encounter in the world. We can discern what is right and wrong and what is truth or fiction, based on what we learn from studying God's Word and applying it to dilemmas we encounter. In the Bible, we can identify the main principles of a Christian worldview; these include the existence and identity of God—the Father, the Son, and the Holy Spirit, the creation of the world and mankind, the fall of mankind, mankind's redemption through God's Son, Jesus Christ, and the revelation of God's love and plans for mankind through Jesus, the Holy Spirit, and the Bible.

© 2015 by Phakawee. Used under license of Shutterstock, Inc.

"A Christian worldview is an overall concept of the world and our part in it, grounded on God's authority, which He reveals to us through the Bible."

Biblical Worldview Tenet	Support from Scripture
1. God exists in three persons: God, the Father; God, the Son (Jesus), and God, the Holy Spirit.	*"Then God said, "'Let us make mankind in our image, in our likeness, so that they may rule over the fish in the sea and the birds in the sky, over the livestock and all the wild animals, and over all the creatures that move along the ground'"* Genesis 1:26. *"For there are three that bear record in heaven, the Father, the Word, and the Holy Ghost: and these three are one"* I John 5:7, KJV. Read John 14 for an explanation in Jesus' own words.
2. God created the world.	*"In the beginning, God created the heavens and the earth"* Genesis 1:1.
3. God created mankind (us) in His image.	*"So God created mankind in his own image, in the image of God he created them; male and female he created them"* Genesis 1:27.
4. Mankind sinned against God and continues to do so.	*"For everyone has sinned; we all fall short of God's glorious standard"* Romans 3:23.
5. In order to redeem mankind, God sent His Son, Jesus, to live a perfect human life and give His life to pay our sin debt.	*"For God so loved the world that He gave His one and only Son, that whoever believes in him shall not perish but have eternal life"* John 3:16.
6. To receive Jesus' redemption, we must confess our sins and ask Jesus to forgive our sins and to change our lives forever through a relationship with Him.	*"Jesus answered, 'I am the way and the truth and the life. No one comes to the Father except through me'"* John 14:6. *"This is the message we have heard from him and declare to you: God is light; in him there is no darkness at all. If we claim to have fellowship with him and yet walk in the darkness, we lie and do not live out the truth. But if we walk in the light, as he is in the light, we have fellowship with one another, and the blood of Jesus, his Son, purifies us from all sin. If we claim to be without sin, we deceive ourselves and the truth is not in us. If we confess our sins, he is faithful and just and will forgive us our sins and purify us from all unrighteousness. If we claim we have not sinned, we make him out to be a liar and his word is not in us"* I John 1:5-10.

7. God reveals Himself to us through Jesus and the Holy Spirit.	*"In the past God spoke to our forefathers through the prophets at many times and in various ways, but in these last days he has spoken to us by His Son, whom He appointed heir of all things, and through whom He made the universe"* Hebrews 1:1-2. *"And I will ask the Father, and he will give you another advocate to help you and be with you forever—the Spirit of truth. The world cannot accept him, because it neither sees him nor knows him. But you know him, for he lives with you and will be in you"* John 14:16-17.
8. God reveals Himself to us through the Bible.	*"All Scripture is God-breathed and is useful for teaching, rebuking, correcting and training in righteousness so that the servant of God may be thoroughly equipped for every good work"* 2 Timothy 3:16-17.

As explained, each of these tenets establishes the foundation of a Christian worldview: 1. God's existence and identity: Father, Son, and Holy Spirit; 2. Creation of our world; 3. Creation of man; 4. The problem of sin; 5. Jesus came to help us overcome our problem of sin; 6. We must confess our sin and ask for reconciliation through Jesus; 7. God reveals Himself to us through Jesus and the Holy Spirit; 8. God gave us the Bible as our guide to life. Ultimately, a Christian worldview is propelled through a saving relationship with Jesus Christ (as indicated in tenet #6). To learn more about a relationship with Christ, read "The Ultimate Cornerstone: Our Altitude and Our Salvation" at the conclusion of this textbook.

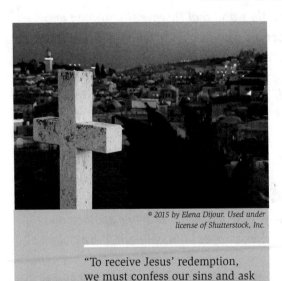

"To receive Jesus' redemption, we must confess our sins and ask Jesus to forgive our sins and to change our lives forever through a relationship with Him."

It's important to recognize that just as a Christian worldview grounds our thinking, it should also determine our actions. When we choose to follow a biblical worldview, our choice is borne out in how we live each moment. What we choose to read, do, and how we act, day by day, should reflect our choice to live biblically. The way to determine the correctness of any action is to compare it to the standard established in the Bible through careful and consistent Bible study.

Personal Reflection

Take a look at the following main tenets of a Christian worldview and dive into the Bible to find additional scriptural support for each of these beliefs. Record your findings in the space provided. In the third column provided, evaluate your own beliefs and compare them to each of these truths.

Biblical Worldview Tenet	Support from Scripture	Your Conclusions
1. God exists in three persons: God, the Father; God, the Son (Jesus), and God, the Holy Spirit.		
2. God created the world.		
3. God created mankind (us) in His image.		
4. Mankind sinned against God and continues to do so.		
5. In order to redeem mankind, God sent His Son, Jesus, to live a perfect human life and give His life to pay our sin debt.		
6. To receive Jesus' redemption, we must confess our sins and ask Jesus to forgive our sins and to change our lives forever through a relationship with Him.		
7. God reveals Himself to us through Jesus and the Holy Spirit.		
8. God reveals Himself to us through the Bible.		

Identify Liberty University's Core Values

I John 1–4,

"That which was from the beginning, which we have heard, which we have seen with our eyes, which we have looked at and our hands have touched—this we proclaim concerning the Word of life. The life appeared; we have seen it and testify to it, and we proclaim to you the eternal life, which was with the Father and has appeared to us. We proclaim to you what we have seen and heard, so that you also may have fellowship with us. And our fellowship is with the Father and with his Son, Jesus Christ. We write this to make our joy complete" (NIV).

© 2015 by Rawpixel. Used under license of Shutterstock, Inc.

"Without apology our mission is to educate Champions for Christ who are prepared to also utilize their education to become lifelong agents of cultural transformation and exponents of the Great Commission" Dr. Ronald S. Godwin.

As mentioned previously, a Christian worldview is "an overall concept of the world and our part in it, grounded on God's authority, which He reveals to us through the Bible." Liberty University was developed and operates today with this biblically based perspective. Former Provost and friend of the University, Dr. Ronald S. Godwin explains this further, "Without apology our mission is to educate Champions for Christ who are prepared to also utilize their education to become lifelong agents of cultural transformation and exponents of the Great Commission. To this end we are both grateful and proud that Liberty graduates are increasingly taking their place in positions of leadership in America and around the globe" (Falwell & Godwin, 2014). The Doctrinal Statement provides a comprehensive explanation of the Christian worldview upheld at Liberty University.

Personal Reflection

In your choice to attend Liberty University, evaluate how your values and the elements of your worldview align with Liberty's Doctrinal Statement. The instruction you receive here will shape you as you develop skills for your future profession and as you develop and strengthen your walk with Christ.

_____

_____

_____

_____

_____

_____

Doctrinal Statement

We affirm our belief in one God, infinite Spirit, creator, and sustainer of all things, who exists eternally in three persons, God the Father, God the Son, and God the Holy Spirit. These three are one in essence but distinct in person and function.

We affirm that the Father is the first person of the Trinity and the source of all that God is and does. From Him the Son is eternally generated and from Them the Spirit eternally proceeds. He is the designer of creation, the speaker of revelation, the author of redemption, and the sovereign of history.

We affirm that the Lord Jesus Christ is the second person of the Trinity, eternally begotten from the Father. He is God. He was conceived by the virgin Mary through a miracle of the Holy Spirit. He lives forever as perfect God and perfect man: two distinct natures inseparably united in one person.

We affirm that the Holy Spirit is the third person of the Trinity, proceeding from the Father and the Son and equal in deity. He is the giver of all life, active in the creating and ordering of the universe; He is the agent of inspiration and the new birth; He restrains sin and Satan; and He indwells and sanctifies all believers.

We affirm that all things were created by God. Angels were created as ministering agents, though some, under the leadership of Satan, fell from their sinless state to become agents of evil. The universe was created in six historical days and is continuously sustained by God; thus it both reflects His glory and reveals His truth. Human beings were directly created, not evolved, in the very image of God. As reasoning moral agents, they are responsible under God for understanding and governing themselves and the world.

(continues)

Ruth

Q: *What is your favorite Dr. Falwell quote?*

A: *"'Don't quit!' What a testimony that was for me during the 4–5 years I took online courses."*

President Jerry Falwell

"Many universities abandoned their original Christian mission when they achieved academic and athletic prominence. Often, the founding principle was compromised because of financial needs and pressure from donors who did not share the founding values of the institution. We believe that God has blessed Liberty University financially so this pattern is not repeated here" (Falwell, 2014).

Cheryl, 30-something, graduate

Q: *What brought you to Liberty University?*

A: "I was first interested in Liberty U because it was one of the first universities to work around my hectic schedule. I very simply would not have been able to further my education in a brick-and-mortar environment."

Dr. A. Pierre Guillermin, first president of LU

"Liberty has made a tremendous impact all over the world and it will continue to be a very strong Christian institution, so long as it is consistent and committed to its Christian faith . . . That really is what makes it distinctive. To my knowledge there is not another university in the world that has had such an impact because of its Christian orientation" (Menard, 2012).

Ruth

Q: *How does your worldview fit in with the message and purpose of LU?*

Q: "Training Champions for Christ at LU is part of our job in being a testimony to each and every one we come in contact with."

We affirm that the Bible, both Old and New Testaments, though written by men, was supernaturally inspired by God so that all its words are the written true revelation of God; it is therefore inerrant in the originals and authoritative in all matters. It is to be understood by all through the illumination of the Holy Spirit, its meaning determined by the historical, grammatical, and literary use of the author's language, comparing Scripture with Scripture.

We affirm that Adam, the first man, willfully disobeyed God, bringing sin and death into the world. As a result, all persons are sinners from conception, which is evidenced in their willful acts of sin; and they are therefore subject to eternal punishment, under the just condemnation of a holy God.

We affirm that Jesus Christ offered Himself as a sacrifice by the appointment of the Father. He fulfilled the demands of God by His obedient life, died on the cross in full substitution and payment for the sins of all, was buried, and on the third day He arose physically and bodily from the dead. He ascended into heaven where He now intercedes for all believers.

We affirm that each person can be saved only through the work of Jesus Christ, through repentance of sin and by faith alone in Him as Savior. The believer is declared righteous, born again by the Holy Spirit, turned from sin, and assured of heaven.

We affirm that the Holy Spirit indwells all who are born again, conforming them to the likeness of Jesus Christ. This is a process completed only in Heaven. Every believer is responsible to live in obedience to the Word of God in separation from sin.

We affirm that a church is a local assembly of baptized believers, under the discipline of the Word of God and the lordship of Christ, organized to carry out the commission to evangelize, to teach, and to administer the ordinances of believer's baptism and the Lord's table. Its offices are pastors and deacons, and it is self-governing. It functions through the ministry of gifts given by the Holy Spirit to each believer.

We affirm that the return of Christ for all believers is imminent. It will be followed by seven years of great tribulation, and then the coming of Christ to establish His earthly kingdom for a thousand years. The unsaved will then be raised and judged according to their works and separated forever from God in hell. The saved, having been raised, will live forever in heaven in fellowship with God.

Approved by the Liberty University Board of Trustees, November 12, 2010

Generate Ideas to Implement a Biblical Worldview

Philippians 4:7–9,
"And the peace of God, which passeth all understanding, shall keep your hearts and minds through Christ Jesus. Finally, brethren, whatsoever things are true, whatsoever things are honest, whatsoever things are just, whatsoever things are pure, whatsoever things are lovely, whatsoever things are of good report; if there be any virtue, and if there be any praise, think on these things. Those things, which ye have both learned, and received, and heard, and seen in me, do: and the God of peace shall be with you" (King James Version).

In his essay, "Is Theology Poetry" (1980), C. S. Lewis, former atheist turned Christian apologist, stated "I believe in Christianity in the same way as I believe that the sun has risen. Not because I see it, but that by *it*, I see *everything* else." This quote captures the essence of what it means to have a biblical worldview, approaching the world through the lens of God's camera, His Word. Having a biblical worldview encompasses what you take in to your heart and mind and what you pour out into the lives of others.

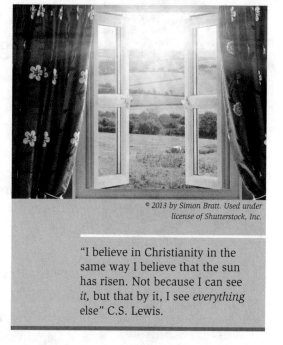

© 2013 by Simon Bratt. Used under license of Shutterstock, Inc.

"I believe in Christianity in the same way I believe that the sun has risen. Not because I can see *it*, but that by it, I see *everything* else" C.S. Lewis.

Taking It All in

When you were growing up, did you ever hear the phrase "garbage in—garbage out?" The concept is clear-cut: If a person watches a TV show or movie or reads a book with profanity, sooner or later that profanity could become a part of his vocabulary, a part of him. Proverbs 23:7a confirms this, "For as a man thinketh, so is he" (KJV).

Part of getting a quality liberal arts education involves studying a wide array of content, both Christian and secular. So, how do you approach the culture with a biblical worldview and avoid the culture influencing and defining you? The answer is also clear-cut: Take

Terry

Q: *What do you value in life?*

A: "I value relationships, those with my family and those of people God brings in to my life."

in the information, let it add to your learning, but filter everything through God's Word. Ask yourself these questions while studying:

1. What message is the author trying to communicate?

2. Do I agree/disagree with the author's message? Why?

3. What does the Bible say about the author's point of view?

4. What does the Bible say about my point of view?

5. How does all of this information impact me?

Thinking critically through your learning process will not only help you grow as a scholar, but it will also strengthen your faith. Finally, pray for discernment as you approach your studies, and the Holy Spirit will guide your heart and mind. Philippians 4:4–9 affirms this, "Rejoice in the Lord always. I will say it again: Rejoice! Let your gentleness be evident to all. The Lord is near. Do not be anxious about anything, but in every situation, by prayer and petition, with thanksgiving, present your requests to God. And the peace of God, which transcends all understanding, will guard your hearts and your minds in Christ Jesus. Finally, brothers and sisters, whatever is true, whatever is noble, whatever is right, whatever is pure, whatever is lovely, whatever is admirable—if anything is excellent or praiseworthy—think about such things. Whatever you have learned or received or heard from me, or seen in me—put it into practice. And the God of peace will be with you" (NIV).

Pouring into Others

Living a life that reflects a biblical worldview involves absorbing information through God's truth, and it also involves what you pour into the lives of others. Galatians 5:13–26 explains this concept beautifully:

> You, my brothers and sisters, were called to be free. But do not use your freedom to indulge the flesh; rather, serve one another humbly in love. For the entire law is fulfilled in keeping this one command: "Love your neighbor as yourself." If you bite and devour each other, watch out or you will be destroyed by each other.

> So I say, walk by the Spirit, and you will not gratify the desires of the flesh. For the flesh desires what is contrary to the Spirit, and the Spirit what is contrary to the flesh. They are in conflict with each other, so that you are not to do whatever you want. But if you are led by the Spirit, you are not under the law.

> The acts of the flesh are obvious: sexual immorality, impurity and debauchery; idolatry and witchcraft; hatred, discord, jealousy, fits of rage, selfish ambition, dissensions, factions and envy; drunkenness, orgies, and the like. I warn you, as I did before, that those who live like this will not inherit the kingdom of God.

© 2013 by R. Gino Santa Maria. Used under license of Shutterstock, Inc.

Jesus gave us the perfect example of what it means to show love and goodness to others when He washed His disciples' feet. (Read the story in John 13.)

But the fruit of the Spirit is love, joy, peace, forbearance, kindness, goodness, faithfulness, gentleness and self-control. Against such things there is no law. Those who belong to Christ Jesus have crucified the flesh with its passions and desires. Since we live by the Spirit, let us keep in step with the Spirit. Let us not become conceited, provoking and envying each other. (NIV)

What do you pour into the lives of others? When faced with a trying situation, do you respond in the flesh or do you respond with the fruit of the Spirit? You may be thinking, "It depends on what kind of situation it is." That's a very honest response because we all have our buttons, and when pushed, they bring us to a breaking point. It is human nature to respond in the flesh, especially when someone pushes those sensitive buttons, so it is critical that you cover yourself in prayer and fill yourself with the fruits of the Spirit: love, joy, peace, forbearance, kindness, goodness, faithfulness, gentleness, and self-control.

Cheryl

Q: *What do you value in life?*

A: "I value many things in life. However, the top five of my values all revolve around my faith base and my family."

Bearing Fruit

Love

The first fruit of the Spirit mentioned in Galatians 5 is love. The *Merriam-Webster Dictionary* (2013) defines **love** as a "strong affection for another arising out of kinship or personal ties" (*Merriam-Webster.com*). Love, however, is so much more than a strong affection. In I John 4:8, we learn that God is love; love is forgiveness, acceptance, and sacrifice.

Corrie ten Boom's (1971) story serves as a profound example of a believer pouring out love into the lives of others. In her book, *The Hiding Place,* Corrie tells of her family's bravery when they hid people in their home during the Jewish Holocaust to help them escape Nazi cruelty. When the Nazis discovered the ten Boom's kindness, they raided the home and dragged the family and those in hiding away to concentration camps. Ultimately, Corrie and her sister Betsie were sent to Ravensbruck Death Camp in Germany. Betsie died there, but Corrie lived to tell their story.

After World War II, Corrie went around Germany speaking to people about the love of Jesus and His forgiveness. After one of her talks, a man approached her and told her that he was a guard at Ravensbruck. He thanked her for her message, stretched out his hand to shake hers, and asked for her forgiveness. Corrie remembered

© 2015 by Jinga. Used under license of Shutterstock, Inc.

"'How grateful I am for your message, Fraulein,' he said. 'To think that, as you say, He has washed my sins away!' His hand was thrust out to shake mine," —Corrie ten Boom.

this man as one of the cruelest guards in the camp, and she wrestled with extending forgiveness to him. The outcome follows in her words:

> It was at a church service in Munich that I saw him, a former S.S. man who had stood guard at the shower room door in the processing center at Ravensbruck. He was the first of our actual jailers that I had seen since that time. And suddenly it was all there—the roomful of mocking men, the heaps of clothing, Betsie's pain-blanched face.
>
> He came up to me as the church was emptying, beaming and bowing. "How grateful I am for your message, Fraulein," he said. "To think that, as you say, He has washed my sins away!" His hand was thrust out to shake mine. And I, who had preached so often to the people in Bloemendaal the need to forgive, kept my hand at my side.
>
> Even as the angry, vengeful thoughts boiled through me, I saw the sin of them. Jesus Christ had died for this man; was I going to ask for more? Lord Jesus, I prayed, forgive me and help me to forgive him. I tried to smile; I struggled to raise my hand. I could not. I felt nothing, not the slightest spark of warmth or charity. And so again I breathed a silent prayer. Jesus, I prayed, I cannot forgive him. Give me Your forgiveness.
>
> As I took his hand the most incredible thing happened. From my shoulder along my arm and through my hand a current seemed to pass from me to him, while into my heart sprang a love for this stranger that almost overwhelmed me. And so I discovered that it is not on our forgiveness any more than on our goodness that the world's healing hinges, but on His. When He tells us to love our enemies, He gives, along with the command, the love itself. (ten Boom, 1971)

When put to the ultimate test, Corrie ten Boom chose to pour out love into the life of her former persecutor. Her relationship with Jesus Christ made this impossible action a possibility.

Joy

Merriam-Webster (2013) defines joy as "a feeling of great happiness" (*Merriam-Webster.com*). Legendary evangelist, Billy Graham elaborates further, "Joy cannot be pursued. It comes from within. It is a state of being. It does not depend on circumstances, but triumphs over circumstances. It produces a gentleness of spirit and a magnetic personality" (Goodreads, Inc., 2014a). A beautiful Christian lady, who triumphed over her own circumstances and lives a life of joy, is Joni Eareckson Tada.

When Joni was 18 years old, she injured herself in a swimming accident in Chesapeake Bay, resulting in quadriplegia. Confined to a wheelchair, Joni fought feelings of anger and depression, but her faith in Jesus Christ and God's promise to give her a "hope and a future" (Jeremiah 29:11) helped her overcome her circumstances and approach life with joy. Joni began painting with a brush between her teeth. Today, she's an accomplished artist, author, speaker, and wife. She also founded Joni and Friends, an outreach designed to "advance disability ministry and changing the church and communities around the world" (Joni and Friends: International Disability Center, 2009–2014a).

God has your future in the palm of His hand and has your best interests at heart. Regardless of your circumstances, He wants you to live in joy, just as Joni has, "Jesus went without comfort so that you might have it. He postponed joy so that you might share in it. He willingly chose isolation so that you might never be alone in your hurt and sorrow. He had no real fellowship so that fellowship might be yours, this moment. This alone is enough cause for great gratitude!" (Goodreads, Inc., 2014c).

Peace

Catholic friar, St. Francis of Assisi, lived a life of **peace**, which according to Merriam-Webster (2013) is "a state of tranquility or quiet: as a freedom from civil disturbance . . . freedom from disquieting or oppressive thoughts or emotions . . . harmony in personal relations" (*Merriam-Webster.com*). Born into a well-to-do family, Francis abandoned a life of financial security and embraced a life of poverty, longing to live the way Christ lived. Men and women alike responded to the gospel message and Francis' way of life, which led to the establishment of the Franciscan Orders: the Friars Minor, Order of St. Clare, and the Third Order. Francis even braved the conflict of the Crusades in an effort to share the message of peace and Christ's love with Muslims in Egypt. He even managed to deliver this message of peace to the Sultan of Egypt, al-Kamil and earned his respect, giving "him permission (it is said) to visit the sacred places in the Holy Land" (Brady, I. C., OFM., 2014). St. Francis lived a life that bore many fruits, and his prayer invokes God's peace in all areas of life:

© 2015 by Zvonimir Atletic.
Used under license of Shutterstock, Inc.

"Lord, make me an instrument of Thy peace"—St. Francis of Assisi.

> Lord, make me an instrument of Thy peace;
> where there is hatred, let me sow love;
> where there is injury, pardon;
> where there is doubt, faith;
> where there is despair, hope;
> where there is darkness, light;
> and where there is sadness, joy.

Ruth

Q: *What do you value in life?*

A: "My children and family come second to God, being a testimony to them and loving them as God loves me."

O Divine Master,
grant that I may not so much seek to be consoled as to console;
to be understood, as to understand;
to be loved, as to love;
for it is in giving that we receive,
it is in pardoning that we are pardoned,
and it is in dying that we are born to eternal life.

Amen.

(World Prayers Project, n. d.)

Forbearance

The fruit of the Spirit, **forbearance**, is "the quality of someone who is patient and able to deal with a difficult person or situation without becoming angry" according to Merriam-Webster (*Merriam-Webster.com*, 2013). Forbearance means the same as the words patience, tolerance, and endurance. Dr. Martin Luther King, Jr. is a prime example of a Christian who showed forbearance to others in the midst of dark circumstances, like the segregation in America before the Civil Rights Movement.

In the 1950s, King served as a Baptist minister. He spearheaded the Civil Rights Movement, which led to the Civil Rights Act of 1964 and the Voting Rights Act of 1965. He won the Nobel Peace Prize in 1964. In 1968, before King could see the full fruition of his dream of peace and equality, he was assassinated (The Biography Channel Website, 2014a).

King's "I Have a Dream" and "I've Been to the Mountaintop" speeches are iconic pieces of American history, inspiring and beautifully written and delivered, especially in the context of the cultural conflicts King faced. His words continue to inspire others today to endure through difficult times, "If you can't fly then run, if you can't run then walk, if you can't walk then crawl, but whatever you do you have to keep moving forward" (Goodreads, Inc., 2014d).

Shannon Bream

"Now is not the time to stand silently by as your most deeply held beliefs are being questioned in the public square. Speaking up is rarely easy when the world is actively waiting to discredit and misconstrue what you have to say—but we have Christ as our model" (Menard, 2013).

Kindness

The definition of **kindness** is compassion for others. Bono, lead singer of U2, walks in compassion in his walk with Christ. In his own words, he explains compassion and Christianity, "To me, a faith in Jesus Christ that is not aligned with the poor . . . it's nothing" (Hardaway & Epictrek.com, 2009). Bono aligns himself with the poor, hurting, and hungry as a humanitarian and activist raising awareness and funds for disease prevention and education through relief concerts and organizations, such as RED, ONE, and EDUN (TED Conferences LLC., 2014). His passion and compassion for others is seen in his actions and through his words, as he encourages others to extend compassion, "God is in the slums, in the cardboard boxes where the poor play house. God is in the silence of a mother who has infected her child with a virus that will end both their lives. God is in the cries heard under the rubble of war. God is in the debris of wasted opportunity and lives, and God is with us if we are with them" (Compassion International, Inc., 2014).

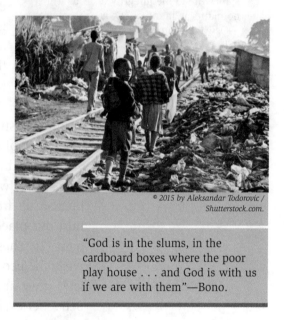

© 2015 by Aleksandar Todorovic / Shutterstock.com.

"To me, a faith in Jesus Christ that is not aligned with the poor . . . it's nothing"—Bono.

Goodness

Goodness is the fruit of ministry. Catholic nun and missionary, Mother Teresa, led a life full of ministry, as she reached out to the people in the slums of Calcutta (Kolkata), West Bengal, India. Originally a teacher and principal at St. Mary's School for Girls in Calcutta, Mother Teresa felt the Lord Jesus calling her to a life of ministry to the poorest of the poor. She founded the Missionaries of Charity Sisters to work toward this end, "Let us touch the dying, the poor, the lonely and the unwanted according to the graces we have received and let us not be ashamed or slow to do the humble work" (Brainy Quote, 2014). Mother Teresa established a school, "a leper colony, an orphanage, a nursing home, a family clinic and a string of mobile health clinics" to care for the "dying, the poor, the lonely, and the unwanted" (The Biography Channel Website, 2014b). She traveled across the globe extending care and developing ministries for those in dire need. In 1979, she received the Nobel Peace Prize for her humanitarian efforts, which she continued until her death in 1997.

© 2015 by Aleksandar Todorovic / Shutterstock.com.

"God is in the slums, in the cardboard boxes where the poor play house . . . and God is with us if we are with them"—Bono.

Faithfulness

Merriam-Webster (2013) explains that **faithfulness** is "having or showing true and constant support or loyalty; deserving trust; keeping your promises or doing what you are supposed to do" (*Merriam-Webster.com*). Known for his classic devotional work, *My Utmost for His Highest*, Oswald Chambers never knew fame during his lifetime, though he had published a few works. While studying the arts at the University of Edinburgh, he felt called to pursue ministry studies. During his lifetime, he served the Lord faithfully as a teacher, a speaker, and a chaplain during World War I. He died at the young age of 43, resulting from complications of an emergency appendectomy (McCasland, 2014). About faithfulness and integrity, Chambers said, "It is

© 2015 by CURAphotography.
Used under license of Shutterstock, Inc.

". . . the greatest to see of all is spiritual courage; oh, to see a person who will stand true to the integrity of Jesus Christ no matter what he or she goes through!" —Oswald Chambers.

a great thing to see physical courage, and greater still to see moral courage, but the greatest to see of all is spiritual courage; oh, to see a person who will stand true to the integrity of Jesus Christ no matter what he or she goes through!" (Joni and Friends: International Disability Center, 2009–2014b).

Self-Control

The final fruit of the Spirit is **self-control**. Self-control is "restraint exercised over one's own impulses, emotions, or desires" according to Merriam-Webster (*Merriam-Webster.com*, 2013). Francis A. Schaeffer was a noted author, philosopher, theologian, apologist, and missionary to Switzerland. While he and his wife, Edith, served as missionaries, they began a ministry called L'Abri, which means "The Shelter." Francis and Edith invited people to take shelter in their Swiss chalet. At L'Abri, the Schaeffers gathered together with their guests, offering them food and conversation, specifically to find answers to their questions about philosophy, theology, and other relevant topics of concern.

Opening up their home to strangers was an adventure that required restraint over their own reactions, especially when people took advantage of their hospitality. Schaeffer explained, "In about the first three years of L'Abri all our wedding presents were wiped out. Our sheets were torn. Holes were burned in our rugs. Indeed once a whole curtain almost burned up from somebody smoking in our living room . . . drugs came into our place. People vomited in our rooms" (Christianbook.com, 2014, para. 2). These challenges did not deter the Schaeffer's; they continued to welcome people into their home and ministry. As a result, the L'Abri ministry grew and exists internationally today. In his book *Art and the Bible*, Schaeffer explained what it means to have self-control through any circumstance, "When a man comes under the blood of Christ, his whole capacity as a man is refashioned. His soul is saved, yes, but so are his mind and his body. True spirituality means the lordship of Christ over the total man" (Goodreads, Inc., 2014b).

Personal Reflection

Consider what you have read regarding the Fruits of the Spirit and how others have poured out love, joy, peace, etc. into the lives of those around them. Now, consider the ways that the Fruits of the Spirit are at work in your own life. Reflect on those by providing answers to the questions in this chart.

Love	
How have you extended love to those around you?	
How can you extend love to those around you who may not deserve it?	
Joy	
What brings you joy in life?	
What circumstances do you find stunt your joy?	
How can you overcome those circumstances and embrace life with a joyful spirit?	
Peace	
Where do you find peace in times of conflict?	
How can you extend the peace of God to others?	
Forbearance	
Who in your life tests your patience?	
How can you inspire them with your forbearance and endurance?	
Kindness	
How have you shown compassion to those around you who are hurting?	
How can you extend kindness to others?	
Goodness	
What ministry work do you do?	

In what ministries would you like to get involved?	
How does/could your investment in ministries bless the lives of others?	
Faithfulness	
In what areas of your life have you been faithful?	
How might the people in your life benefit from your faithfulness in all circumstances?	
Self-Control	
In what way(s) have you exercised self-control in your life?	
What areas of your life require self-control?	
How can the people in your life (your family and friends) benefit from your ability to show restraint in your reactions to things that upset you?	

Biblical Worldview: Implementation

© 2015 by Antonio Gravante. Used under license of Shutterstock, Inc.

". . . find little ways that you can show love, joy, peace, forbearance, kindness, goodness, faithfulness, and self-control to others in your life, for in doing so, you will also be sharing those fruits with Jesus..."

Approaching the world through the lens of the Bible's truth can change your life and the lives of those around you remarkably. In order to generate this change, you must first know Jesus Christ as the Lord and Savior of your life (for more information about making this decision, see "Our Altitude and Our Salvation" in the Final Cornerstone of this textbook). You must also remember to use scripture to filter all that your mind takes in and remember to pray for discernment through the process. Additionally, find little ways that you can show love, joy, peace, forbearance, kindness, goodness, faithfulness, and self-control to others in your life, for in doing so, you will also be sharing those fruits with Jesus, just as the scripture states, "The King will reply, 'Truly I tell you, whatever you did for one of the least of these brothers and sisters of mine, you did for me'" (Matthew 25:40, NIV).

BUILDING BLOCKS

We learned a lot about the concept of worldview and what it means to embrace a biblical or Christian worldview in this chapter. We've defined what a worldview is, noting that the Bible tells us that "for as he thinks in his heart, so he is" (Proverbs 23:7a, AMP). Your worldview is the set of presuppositions you hold about the world and your place in it.

What is your worldview? Recall that everyone has a worldview, even if it is something you have never really thought much about. You may be influenced by family teachings, tradition, and the culture around you in adopting your worldview, despite what you may think. You've been invited to consider how your worldview answers the basic questions of life. What has influenced your thinking and helped develop your worldview?

For Christians, answers to the basic questions of life can be found in God's Word, the Bible.

Following are some questions you should be able to answer as you continue evaluating your worldview.

Question	Your Question
What answers have you found or adopted regarding the basic questions of life?	
On what authority do you base the surety of your answers?	
What is the foundation of your worldview?	
How does your worldview influence your thinking as a student?	
What does your worldview indicate about your character? (Think back to what you read about the Fruits of the Spirit.)	

When Dr. Jerry Falwell established Liberty University, he also identified the core values that were to guide the development of our university. These values and principles are faith tools. These develop in each of us as we grow in our understanding (what Christians sometimes refer to as our "walk with the Lord"). List the values and principles.	
Do you believe it is important to develop these "fruits" in your life, even as you are developing an understanding of your major course of study? Why or why not?	

At Liberty University, our faculty desire to help you develop and grow in your academic skills and your character qualities. We believe that learning topically while growing spiritually makes for a complete education.

TOOL BOX

Biblical Foundations

- **The Bible**—The first order of business in developing a Christian world-view is to spend time in the Bible on a consistent basis. Careful and continued study of God's Word will lay the groundwork for understanding what a biblical worldview is. Print Bibles are still around, and many believers still prefer them, but there is also a variety of electronic options available. These tools offer everything from simple reading sessions to advanced language studies, linking Scripture with the commentaries of biblical scholars who leverage their years of study to help add background, context, and insight to the passages you are reading.

- **Bible Classes**—As a student at Liberty, one of the classes you will be required to take is *A Survey of Biblical Literature*. This class offers a solid grounding in the totality of God's Word. For further study, you can take additional Bible classes, in a variety of topics, and plug them into the electives section of your degree. This will allow you to grow in your knowledge while simultaneously working toward your goal of a college degree.

- **Additional Bible Study**—In addition to reading your Bible and taking Bible classes, there are a number of other ways to improve your knowledge of God's Word. The most common approach is to attend church services on a regular basis, either locally or online. You might also consider subscribing to the podcast of a favorite pastor/teacher, using a devotional in print/app form, or listening to Liberty's live broadcasts of Convocation.

Theological Foundations

- **Theology Classes**—While studying the Bible will serve as the foundation of your biblical worldview, theological studies will act as the structure. Systematic theology groups the teachings of the Bible, so you can study all that the Bible teaches about the big questions in life. While at Liberty, you will take a theological survey course, which will cover the biblical perspectives on issues such as the nature of existence, the nature of knowledge, and the person of Jesus Christ. These courses will aid you in developing an understanding of how you view the world

Christian Action/Service

- **Actions Speak Louder Than Words**—This old saying could never be truer than when considered in light of a worldview. You can share your thoughts and beliefs (worldview) day and night; however, if your actions contradict that worldview, then that may not be the actual worldview you possess. Be careful to consider each task and issue you approach, through the lens of your biblical worldview. As an example, ask yourself, "How does my belief about the value of people inform the way I approach my giving or political views?" Do your actions match up with your beliefs? The answers to this question will allow you to work toward developing a consistent worldview, one where your beliefs, thoughts, and actions align.

Additional resources and links to specific sites, worksheets, and apps can be located by accessing the Breaking Ground website:

www.breakinggroundlu.com

References

The Biography Channel Website. (2014a). *Martin Luther King, Jr.* Retrieved from http://www.biography.com/people/martin-luther-king-jr-9365086

The Biography Channel Website. (2014b). *Mother Teresa.* Retrieved from http://www.biography.com/people/mother-teresa-9504160?page = 1

Brady, I. C. & OFM. (2014). *The Franciscan rule.* Retrieved from http://www.britannica.com/EBchecked/topic/216793/Saint-Francis-of-Assisi/2421/The-Franciscan-rule

Mother Teresa, Brainy Quotes (2014). Quotes.net. Retrieved from (URL) Brainy Quote. (2014). *Mother Teresa quotes.* Retrieved from http://www.brainyquote.com/quotes/authors/m/mother_teresa.html#fTYUl2gKCrXZStIe.99

Christianbook.com, LLC. (2014). *Meet Francis Schaeffer.* Retrieved from http://www.christianbook.com/html/authors/581.html

Compassion International, Inc. (2014). *Famous quotes about children.* Retrieved from http://www.compassion.com/child-advocacy/find-your-voice/famous-quotes/

Faithfulness. (n.d.). In *Merriam-Webster.com.* Retrieved from http://www.merriam-webster.com/dictionary/faithfulness

Falwell, J. & Godwin, R. (2014). *Message from the president and the provost.* Retrieved from http://www.liberty.edu/index.cfm?PID = 27045

Falwell, M. (2008). *Jerry Falwell: His life and legacy.* New York, NY: Howard Books.

Forbearance. (n.d.). In *Merriam-Webster.com.* Retrieved from http://www.merriam-webster.com/dictionary/forbearance

Fralik, M. (2011). *College and career success.* Dubuque, IA: Kendall Hunt Publishing Company.

Goodreads, Inc. (2014a). *Billy Graham: Quotes.* Retrieved from http://www.goodreads.com/author/quotes/40328.Billy_Graham?page = 2

Goodreads, Inc. (2014b). *Francis August Schaeffer: Quotes.* Retrieved from http://www.goodreads.com/author/quotes/601678.Francis_A_Schaeffer?page = 2

Goodreads, Inc. (2014c). *Joni Eareckson Tada: Quotes.* Retrieved from http://www.goodreads.com/author/quotes/3715.Joni_Eareckson_Tada

Goodreads, Inc. (2014d). *Martin Luther King, Jr.: Quotes.* Retrieved from http://www.goodreads.com/author/quotes/23924.Martin_Luther_King_Jr

Hardaway, J. E. & Epictrek.com. (2009). *Quotes: Bono.* Retrieved from http://epictrek.com/Epictrek/BonoQuotes.html

Joni and Friends: International Disability Center. (2009–2014a). About us. Retrieved from http://www.joniandfriends.org/about-us/

Joni and Friends: International Disability Center. (2009–2014b). Joni's favorite quotes. Retrieved from http://www.joniandfriends.org/jonis-corner/jonis-favorite-quotes/

Joy. (n.d.). In *Merriam-Webster.com.* Retrieved from http://www.merriam-webster.com/dictionary/joy

Lewis, C. S. (1980). Is Theology poetry? In C. S. Lewis (Ed.), *The Weight of Glory.* New York, NY: Harper Collins.

Love. (n.d.). In *Merriam-Webster.com.* Retrieved from http://www.merriam-webster.com/dictionary/love

McCasland, D. (Ed.). (2014). *Oswald Chambers' bio.* Retrieved from http://utmost.org/oswald-chambers-bio/

Menard, D. (2013). *40th Commencement: Celebrating historic accomplishments, continuous growth.* Retrieved from http://www.liberty.edu/aboutliberty/index.cfm?PID = 24995&MID = 91512

Metacognition. (n.d.). In *Merriam-Webster.com.* Retrieved January 25, 2015, from http://www.merriam-webster.com/dictionary/metacognition

Palmer, M. (1998). Elements of a Christian worldview, Ch. 1 In M. Palmer (Ed.), *Elements of a Christian worldview* (p. 24). Foreword by Russell P. Spittler. Springfield, MO: Logion Press.

Peace. (n.d.). In *Merriam-Webster.com.* Retrieved from http://www.merriam-webster.com/dictionary/peace

Self-Control. (n.d.). In *Merriam-Webster.com.* Retrieved from http://www.merriam-webster.com/dictionary/self-control

Sire, James. The Universe Next Door: A Basic Worldview Catalog, 3rd ed., (Downers Grove: InterVarsity Press, 1997), 16.

TED Conferences LLC. (2014). *Speakers Bono: Musician, activist.* Retrieved from http://www.ted.com/speakers/bono.html

World Prayers Project. (n.d.). *World Prayers.* Retrieved from http://www.worldprayers.org/archive/prayers/invocations/lord_make_me_an_instrument.html

Worldview. (n.d.). Retrieved December 12, 2014, from http://www.merriam-webster.com/dictionary/worldview

Chapter 5

Goals: Building Materials

In this chapter, you will:

- Define success.
- Establish educational goals.
- Determine the necessity of time management.
- Set priorities and plan good use of time.
- Determine valuable, goal-setting character traits.

THE BUILDING MATERIALS

After choosing the perfect structure, designing the floor plan, carefully outlining the blue prints, and determining the plan for the site, it is time to collect the materials needed to begin the building process. In order to do this, you must develop a shopping list of necessary materials required for different stages of the build. You need to know how much of each product you should purchase, so you do not have an insufficient supply or excessive amounts of materials to return. You need to choose high quality, lasting materials, so you may rest in the assurance that your building will not crumble in the elements. In education, making a list of academic goals and priorities will help you manage your time effectively and become more self-aware of your behaviors and the factors that motivate you toward lasting academic success.

© 2015 by 06photo. Used under license of Shutterstock, Inc.

Luke 6:47–48,
"As for everyone who comes to me and hears my words and puts them into practice, I will show you what they are like. They are like a man building a house, who dug down deep and laid the foundation on rock. When a flood came, the torrent struck that house but could not shake it, because it was well built" (NIV).

THE CORNERSTONE

Psalms 37:4, "Take delight in the Lord, and He will give you the desires of your heart" (NIV).

Dr. Falwell, founder of Liberty University, used to tell his students they needed to choose a Big Hairy Audacious Goal (BHAG) for their lives. My mom attended Liberty University in 1971 when it was called Lynchburg Bible College. She learned, very quickly, the merit in Dr. Falwell's BHAG message, and when she became a mother, she extended that message to her children as well.

When my brother, John, and I were children, we watched the Wonderful World of Disney on Sunday nights with Mom and Dad. We did not watch a lot of television, so this was a real treat. John and I would camp out on the floor in front of the TV and eat a small bowl of freshly popped popcorn and drink a cold glass of orange juice (weird combination, I know, but it worked). Mom and Dad would join us for the feature presentation. I remember being so excited as Tinker Bell would fly to the top of Cinderella's Castle and set off the fireworks in the opening credits. Mom would say, "One of these days, kids, we're going to get you to Disney World. You can see that castle and Tinker Bell for yourself." John and I would smile, sip our orange juice, and take in yet another story, this time brought to life through the TV screen. For Mom, the promise of taking us to Disney World was a BHAG; it involved many years of planning and saving.

Finally, when I was a teenager, she took us to Disney World's Magic Kingdom. We rode Dumbo, Snow White's Scary Adventures, Peter Pan, and Mr. Toad's Wild Ride. We went on the Jungle Cruise and climbed the Swiss Family Robinson Tree House. We rode the Pirates of the Caribbean and visited the Enchanted Tikki Room. We braved the mountains: Splash Mountain, Big Thunder Mountain, and Space Mountain. As the day drew to a close, we took in the wonder of Main Street USA and Cinderella's Castle, lit up brilliantly with twinkle lights. John and I anxiously awaited Tinker Bell's appearance in the distance, remembering Mom's promise that Tinker Bell would wave her wand and the fireworks would begin.

© 2013 by Ivan Cholakov. Used under license of Shutterstock, Inc.

Mom would say, "One of these days, kids, we're going to get you to Disney World. You can see that castle and Tinker Bell for yourself."

© 2013 by Gladskikh Tatiana. Used under license of Shutterstock, Inc.

What is your BHAG?

As we waited, however, Mom heard thunder in the distance. She panicked; all she could think about was getting us back to the car safely without risking our while lives dodging thunderbolts in the vast parking lot. She ushered us quickly out of the park, and we missed Tinker Bell. It was not until we got on the ferry departing the Magic Kingdom that Mom realized the thunder she heard was actually just the fireworks show at EPCOT. We missed witnessing Tinker Bell light up the sky, and for my part, I began to doubt that the fairy even existed.

After that experience, we teased Mom over the years about Tinker Bell's flight, telling her that she must have imagined it from our nights of watching it happen on the Wonderful World of Disney when we were younger. Despite our taunts, she insisted that Tinker Bell really flew to the Castle and set off fireworks; we just missed it.

Nine years after our Disney trip, I was engaged to be married. When my fiancé (now husband), Terry, told me and my parents that he was taking me to Disney World for our honeymoon, Mom's response was, "Great! Now you can see Tinker Bell!" Knowing the story, Terry laughed; we all did.

Cut to the honeymoon—as Terry and I made our way down Main Street USA after a fun-filled day in the park, we grabbed some ice cream. With our delicious treat in hand, we walked toward the exit to beat the crowds to our bus. All of the sudden, Jiminy Cricket's voice echoed through the loud speaker announcing the fireworks show. We turned around just in time to see Tinker Bell, gleaming brightly and flying toward the highest turret of the Castle. Terry and I looked at each other, our eyes wide with wonder and amazement and glistening with tears.

My Mom had told us the truth over the years, and her BHAG was realized in that precious moment shared between a new husband and wife. It was almost 20 years in the making, yet she did not give up, much like the Parable of the Persistent Widow in Luke 18:1–8,

"Then Jesus told his disciples a parable to show them that they should always pray and not give up. He said: 'In a certain town there was a judge who neither feared God nor cared what people thought. And there was a widow in that town who kept coming to him with the plea, 'Grant me justice against my adversary.' For some time he refused. But finally he said to himself, 'Even though I don't fear God or care what people think, yet because this widow keeps bothering me, I will see that she gets justice, so that she won't eventually come and attack me!' And the Lord said, 'Listen to what the unjust judge says. And will not God bring about justice for his chosen ones, who cry out to him day and night? Will he keep putting them off? I tell you, he will see that they get justice, and quickly. . . .'" (NIV)

Just as the widow kept after the judge, Mom persisted in her playful vision for her children. Through taunts and disbelief, she was unshaken.

Dr. Falwell used to say, "You do not determine a man's greatness by his talent or wealth, as the world does, but rather by what it takes to discourage him" (Falwell, 1997, p. 43). What is your BHAG? Whatever it may be, whether it is academic, professional, spiritual, or personal, do not be discouraged; do not give up! In Psalms 37:4, you are promised, "Take delight in the Lord, and He will give you the desires of your heart" (NIV). Your persistence will pay off, and when it does, rejoice in the wonder and amazement of that precious moment.

© Mooshny/Shutterstock.com.

Psalms 37:4,
"Take delight in the Lord, and He will give you the desires of your heart" (NIV).

Define Success

Micah 6:8,
"He has shown you, O mortal, what is good.
And what does the LORD require of you?
To act justly and to love mercy
and to walk humbly with your God" (NIV).

Dr. Jerry Falwell, Sr.

"God never called anyone to be a quitter. The word 'retreat' should not be in the Christian's vocabulary. The only way is upward and onward for the Lord" (Falwell, 1997, p. 150).

Defining success may sound easy enough, but it is truly a difficult task. Watkins (2014) explains this dilemma perfectly in the article "Defining Success," "Like beauty, success is in the eye of the beholder. As a result, success can have a thousand definitions" (p. 68). Success is a popular topic. If you doubt it, just perform a Google search for the word "success" and be amazed when about 1,110,000,000 results pop up in 0.34 seconds. Success is popular because it is something everyone wants to achieve, so knowing what success really means, by analyzing the practical, personal, and biblical definitions and what it takes to achieve success, is essential.

Merriam-Webster.com (2015) defines success as a "favorable or desired outcome; also: the attainment of wealth, favor, or eminence." This definition encapsulates most existing explanations when exploring the concept of success in dictionaries, online resources, articles, journals, and books; nearly all of the definitions showcase a need for achievement in different areas of life: financial, social, professional, physical, spiritual, and so on. As Watkins (2014) suggested, there are "a thousand definitions." However, we don't need thousands of definitions; we just need one that will serve us as relevant to any and every aspect of life. As a result, our practical definition of **success** is simply the achievement of an objective or goal.

With our practical definition in mind, we must determine what goals we want to achieve in life. This step is a personal one and requires a look inward. In the article, "Success is Overrated," author Tyler Ward (2013) explains that "We all have a deeply felt need to be successful. Call it whatever you want—being faithful, meeting expectations, winning—but feeling successful is a healthy part of being fully human. The problem is, when we inherit our ideas of success, we are driven by another person's definition and miss the unique existence only you or I can live" (para. 4). Ward (2013) encourages his

© 2013 by Greg Epperson. Used under license of Shutterstock, Inc.

". . .feeling successful is a healthy part of being fully human. The problem is, when we inherit our ideas of success, we are driven by another person's definition and miss the unique existence only you or I can live"
—Tyler Ward.

readers to set aside society's definitions of success and evaluate their own by considering: what success looks like in their own lives, their motives toward achieving success, and the sacrifices involved along the way. Take a moment to evaluate these considerations for yourself and determine what success means to you as an individual.

Personal Reflection

What does success look like to you?

Personal Goals	Reasons/Motives	Sacrifices Involved
What goals do you want to achieve in your lifetime?	What are your reasons/ motives for achieving these goals?	What sacrifices might you have to make in order to achieve these goals?
kids	answrs	self
school	self improvement	time

While our practical and personal definitions of success are essential, even more so is God's definition. As a result, we must consult our primary resource for seeking how God defines success, His Word, and we must consider how His definition should impact our own perceptions. Joshua 1:7 8 states:

> Be strong and very courageous. Be careful to obey all the law my servant Moses gave you; do not turn from it to the right or to the left, that you may be successful wherever you go. Keep this Book of the Law always on your lips; meditate on it day and night, so that you may be careful to do everything written in it. Then you will be prosperous and successful (NIV).

Look carefully at this portion of the scripture, "Be careful to obey all the law my servant Moses gave you; do not turn from it to the right or to the left, that you may be successful wherever you go." To be successful, according to God's Word, you must be obedient to His teachings and faithful in your relationship with Him; faithfulness is key here, not veering from

Dr. Jerry Falwell, Sr.

"It is my conviction that whatever is required to make a good Christian also makes a good citizen" (Falwell, 1997, p. 379).

the path. In his book, *What God Thinks When We Fail*, Steven Roy (2013) explains this further:

> ...all of us, as followers of Christ, can be faithful to God. Faithfulness does not require extraordinary gifts or a large stage or public notoriety. It's not dependent on having a certain amount of money or education. It's not dependent on good luck or fortuitous circumstances or knowing the right people. Every one of us can love God. Every one of us can be a loving servant to our neighbors. . . . If we humble ourselves to receive God's love, and if we trust him to change our hearts and empower us to live a life of humble, loving faithfulness, every one of us can be truly successful. (p. 52–53)

Therefore, God defines success as faithfulness, just as "The Parable of the Talents" in Matthew 25:21 affirms, "His lord said to him, 'Well done, good and faithful servant; you have been faithful over a few things, I will make you ruler over many things. Enter into the joy of your lord'" (NKJV).

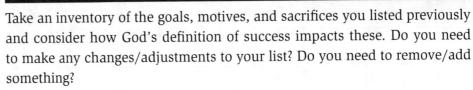

Personal Reflection

Take an inventory of the goals, motives, and sacrifices you listed previously and consider how God's definition of success impacts these. Do you need to make any changes/adjustments to your list? Do you need to remove/add something?

Roger

Q: How did you determine your goals for college study?

Did you begin with your goals set, or did they take shape as you made progress? How did you refine your goals?

A: "I began my time at Liberty University with a goal: graduate with an MAT degree in Secondary Education, History and to become a licensed and certified teacher in the Commonwealth of Virginia. This goal morphed and expanded to include a Special Education endorsement as I examined the shrinking educational workforce. Having a second endorsement would open up more opportunities for employment. I would only need to add a few additional classes to receive this degree. Furthermore, I felt that I could use the knowledge to help my adopted children with their academic issues."

Personal Goals	Reasons/Motives	Sacrifices Involved
What goals do you want to achieve in your lifetime?	What are your reasons/motives for achieving these goals?	What sacrifices might you have to make in order to achieve these goals?

Establish Educational Goals

Proverbs 9:9–11,
"Instruct the wise and they will be wiser still; teach the righteous and they will add to their learning. The fear of the LORD is the beginning of wisdom, and knowledge of the Holy One is understanding. For through wisdom your days will be many, and years will be added to your life" (NIV).

In the article "Goal Setting Strategies," Jordan (2006) found that "Professional achievers have a common characteristic and that is they are big at writing down their goals" (para. 8). As Jordan explained, in order to achieve success in life, it is important to establish goals. So, how do you determine which areas should draw your focus for success? In the book, *Today Matters*, author John Maxwell (2004) identifies 12 categories in life to consider when pursuing success; he calls this list the "Daily Dozen" (p. 24). He also establishes a goal/objective to provide direction toward achieving success in each area, as seen here:

© 2015 by wavebreakmedia. Used under license of Shutterstock, Inc.

In the article "Goal Setting Strategies," Jordan (2006) found that "Professional achievers have a common characteristic and that is they are big at writing down their goals" (para. 8).

Categories in Life	Daily Dozen
	Objective to Achieve Success
Attitude	Choose and display the right attitudes daily.
Priorities	Determine and act on important priorities daily.
Health	Know and follow healthy guidelines daily.
Family	Communicate with and care for family daily.
Thinking	Practice and develop good thinking daily.
Commitment	Make and keep proper commitments daily.
Finances	Make and properly manage dollars daily.
Faith	Deepen and live out faith daily.
Relationships	Initiate and invest in solid relationships.
Generosity	Plan for and model generosity daily.
Values	Embrace and practice good values daily.
Growth	Seek and experience improvements daily.

Cheryl

Q: *How did you determine your goals for college study?*

A: "My goals for college study revolved around my desire to understand people. However, I wanted my undergrad to be through a Christian filter."

Q: *What goals did you set up for yourself when entering college?*

A: "I had quite a gap between beginning college, and returning to complete my degree. My FIRST goal I set for myself upon returning to my undergrad, was to complete it. It was a HUGE goal for me, and I had to focus on one assignment, and one class . . . at a time."

One of the most important words in Maxwell's "Daily Dozen" is the word "daily." In order to achieve success, you must also establish objectives for success, and you must work toward accomplishing those goals daily. It is the constant, chipping away every day at the goal that brings it to completion. With this in mind, take a moment to write down your goals in each area of the "Daily Dozen." Your goal may be the same as the one determined by Maxwell, but this is an opportunity for you to be specific about the traits/goals that you wish to accomplish personally.

Dr. Elmer Towns

"You must go out and fulfill your dream. An idea is never yours until you write it down" (McKay, 2009).

Maddy

Q: *How did you determine your goals for college study? Did you begin with your goals set, or did they take shape as you made progress? How did you refine your goals?*

A: "When I graduated high school, I had goals set, but they've completely changed since that time. I've changed my major, and have even started pursuing hobbies that could develop into different careers. The refining of my goals has been a large amount of trial and error."

Terry

Q: *How did you determine your goals for college study?*

A: "I started out with a large goal, to earn an upper level position at work. From this I developed a series of goals, or a roadmap, to reach that goal."

Q: *Did you begin with your goals set, or did they take shape as you made progress?*

A: "Some took shape as I got into the program and learned what I could handle and what was difficult for me."

Personal Reflection

My Daily Dozen		
Categories in Life	**Objective to Achieve Success**	**Personal Objective**
Attitude	Choose and display the right attitudes daily.	
Priorities	Determine and act on important priorities daily.	
Health	Know and follow healthy guidelines daily.	
Family	Communicate with and care for family daily.	
Thinking	Practice and develop good thinking daily.	
Commitment	Make and keep proper commitments daily.	
Finances	Make and properly manage dollars daily.	
Faith	Deepen and live out faith daily.	
Relationships	Initiate and invest in solid relationships.	
Generosity	Plan for and model generosity daily.	
Values	Embrace and practice good values daily.	
Growth	Seek and experience improvements daily.	

Not only is the exercise of determining goals a characteristic of professional achievers as Jordan asserts (2006), but it is also a spiritual exercise. In Habakkuk 2:2–4, the Lord instructs us:

> And the Lord answered me, and said, 'Write the vision, and make it plain upon tables, that he may run that readeth it. For the vision is yet for an appointed time, but at the end it shall speak, and not lie: though it tarry, wait for it; because it will surely come, it will not tarry. Behold, his soul which is lifted up is not upright in him: but the just shall live by his faith' (KJV).

In this passage, the Lord gives specific instruction to his prophet Habakkuk, who is awaiting deliverance for the people of Judah out of the hands of the Chaldeans (Babylonians). Even though the Lord provided this instruction during a time of war, a careful analysis can reveal its relevance in most areas of everyday life. Take a look at this breakdown of Habakkuk 2:2–4 and observe how it relates perfectly to goal setting.

Habakkuk 2:2–4	Goal Setting Application
Write the vision.	Establish your goal.
Make it plain upon tables.	Make your goal specific and understandable.
That he may run that readeth it.	Share it with others, so that they can help keep you accountable.
For the vision is yet for an appointed time.	Stay focused; it will be achieved in the future.
But at the end it shall speak, and not lie.	The progress/lack of progress you make will be evident.
Though it tarry, wait for it.	Some goals take a long time to achieve, so be patient.
Because it will surely come, it will not tarry.	The goal will be accomplished by its determined time.
Behold, his soul which is lifted up is not upright in him: but the just shall live by faith.	Remain faithful to your goal.

Emily

Share a realistic goal.

"Start studying for a test at least three days prior to a test."

Share an unrealistic goal.

"Being able to finish all your work for all your classes in one or two days is unrealistic."

Alissa Keith

"Take charge/responsibility of your own education. No one cares more about your educational success than you; figure out now how you will complete your educational journey."

Roger

Q: Have you achieved the specific goals (educational, career, other) that you set in college?

What goals did you set up for yourself when entering college?

How did your goals change throughout your experience?

A: "I have enjoyed the foresight of two college experiences, first as a 19 year-old in New York, and second as an experienced middle-aged adult. In the first college experience, I had no clear vision of what I wanted to do with my life. I felt that I would figure it out as I went along. As a result, I wasted a lot of time, effort, and money. The administration was less than helpful in describing what I needed for my major in order to graduate. In my last semester, the registrar told me that I still needed 15 liberal arts credits in order to finish my courses. I had enough credit hours but I didn't realize that music courses did not qualify for liberal arts credits. That resulted in spending more time and money in order to receive a diploma. But here at Liberty University, I kept closely in touch with my academic advisors. Every course taken was purposeful and was in accordance to the degree plan. Every course was available every semester, so I didn't have to do any course juggling."

Just like in everyday life, if you want to be successful in college, you must establish goals to target and to measure your achievement. To confirm this point, consider this study conducted by Morisano, Hirsh, Peterson, Pihl, and Shore (2010). In a four-month time period, these professionals evaluated whether or not a goal-setting program would have a positive impact on students and their academic progress and performance. Morisano and team observed that "students who completed the goal-setting intervention displayed significant improvements in academic performance compared with the control group" and concluded that the goal-setting program proved "to be a quick, effective, and inexpensive intervention for struggling undergraduate students" (2010). With these findings in mind, consider setting your own educational goals using the strategy outlined in Habakkuk 2:2–4.

Personal Reflection

Using the strategy outlined in Habakkuk 2:2–4 set your own academic goals.

Strategy	Application
List academic goals. **Example:** *I want to earn an A in my English Composition course.*	

Make sure your goals are specific and understandable.

Example: *The bolded elements of the academic goal make it specific and understandable: I want to earn an **A** in my **English Composition** course.*

Who will keep you accountable?

Example: *I'll ask my husband, my best friend, and my parents to be my accountability partners.*

What strategies will help keep you focused?

Example: *I'll create a chart, call on friends, establish personal incentives, and read and study my Bible to stay positive.*

Terry

Share a realistic goal.

"I believe a realistic goal is moving up in my company."

Share an unrealistic goal.

"Owning that company, but I could certainly own my own company."

Alexandra Barnett

"Explain to your family your educational goals, expectations for study time, and how your education will benefit them. Let them know that you obtaining your degree is a team effort and you are counting on them to support you. Develop a plan that allows your family to celebrate your accomplishments with you."

Cheryl

Q: *How did your goals change throughout your experience?*

A: "As I met goals, I would reevaluate myself, and create NEW goals, to constantly keep moving forward. That has been so VERY important to me throughout my educational path . . . to keep moving forward. I have often had large gaps of time when I struggled to keep moving forward, and not GIVE UP, because of circumstances. Instead, God taught me the amazing concept of His timing. Adaptation is also integral to my philosophy of moving forward. For example: looking at an obstacle, and not being able to go over it . . . so going around it, under it, or THROUGH it, instead."

Cheryl

Q: *What is a favorite Bible verse that has kept you focused on your goals?*

A: "Romans 8:28, 'And we know that in all things God works for the good of those who love him, who[a] have been called according to his purpose' (NIV). I have claimed this verse and the promises within, just about every single day. I often CLING to it . . . especially when things get REALLY rough in my life. This verse gives me hope for how things will work out."

Terry

Q: *Have you achieved the specific goals (educational, career, other) that you set in college?*

A: "Most of them, not all of them can happen at this point. I've completed my degree and while completing my degree was able to apply some of the information I learned directly to my job. This has helped me progress towards my other goal of achieving an upper level position."

Alexandra Barnett

"Continue to remind yourself that the next four years will pass either way. At the end of those four years you can either have the same level of education you have today, or you can have earned your Bachelor's degree!"

In what ways, will you keep track of your progress? **Example:** *Like with weight loss, if my goal is to lose ten pounds in one month, at the end of the month, the scale will show the results. Tracking progress by using a chart or a daily journal are great strategies for showing where you've been compared to where you are at the end of the determined time. In academics, keeping track of my grade via my course records is a great way to track progress in my English course.*	
Be patient. Identify which goals are short and long-term goals. **Example:** *There are two types of goals: short-term and long-term. I need to identify which are short-term goals (like good grades on the assignments or 2–3 pounds of loss) and which are long-term goals (the A in your English Composition course or the 10-pound weight loss). I need to celebrate the short-term goals that add up as I await the results of my long-term goals. This will help me stay focused and patient in the process.*	
Establish the determined completion date of your goals. **Example:** *My English Composition course is an 8-week course, so at the end of the 8 weeks, I will complete my goal of earning an A in that course.*	

Identify scripture that will encourage you and help keep you faithful to your goal. **Example:** *Hebrews 10:23–25, "Let us hold unswervingly to the hope we profess, for he who promised is faithful. And let us consider how we may spur one another on toward love and good deeds, not giving up meeting together, as some are in the habit of doing, but encouraging one another—and all the more as you see the Day approaching" (NIV).*	

Another strategy is the SMART goal-setting strategy. SMART is an acronym that stands for setting Specific, Meaningful and Measurable, Actionable, Realistic, and Timed goals. The chart below, found in Cuseo, Thompson, Campagna, and Fecas's (2013) text, *Thriving in College and Beyond*, provides details for using this strategy to determine and modify your goals.

Whatever strategy you use to determine your academic goals will prove beneficial, as observed in the study conducted by Morisano, et al. (2010). As long as you are identifying, working toward, and praying for your personal academic vision, you will be many steps closer to bringing your vision into fruition.

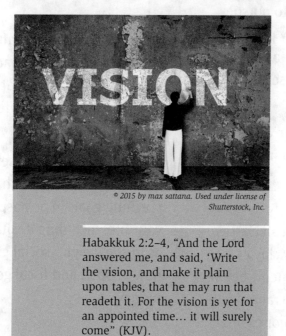

© 2015 by max sattana. Used under license of Shutterstock, Inc.

Habakkuk 2:2–4, "And the Lord answered me, and said, 'Write the vision, and make it plain upon tables, that he may run that readeth it. For the vision is yet for an appointed time… it will surely come" (KJV).

Cheryl

Q: *Did you begin with your goals set, or did they take shape as you made progress?*

A: "They definitely became clearer, as I progressed."

Q: *Have you achieved the specific goals (educational, career, and other) that you set in college?*

A: "Yes, and no. I have met some, then made new ones. Others, I have not quite completed as yet, and I continue to work towards them."

Tim

Q: *How did you determine your goals for college study? Did you begin with your goals set, or did they take shape as you made progress? How did you refine your goals? Have you achieved the specific goals (educational, career, other) that you set in college? What goals did you set up for yourself when entering college? How did your goals change throughout your experience?*

A: "My personal goals for college study did not really take shape until I had actually participated in a few classes. My study habits are not necessarily the best, simply because my schedule fluctuates so much. Therefore, I study whenever I get a chance and typically on a lot of weekends. My specific goal was to graduate quickly; however, because of work it has taken much longer than I expected. Therefore, my goal went from graduating quickly to simply completing one class each sub term or term. This has helped me to be able to complete my goal and I am now on track to graduate sooner than I expected."

A SMART Method of Goal Setting

A popular mnemonic device for remembering the key components of a well-designed goal is the acronym "SMART" (Doran, 1981; Meyer, 2003).

A **SMART** goal is one that is:

Specific: States exactly what the goal is and what will be done to achieve it.

Example: I'll achieve at least a "B" average this term by spending 25 hours per week on my course work outside of class and by using the effective learning strategies described in this book. (As opposed to the non-specific goal, "I'm really going to work hard.")

Meaningful (and **M**easurable): A goal that really matters to the individual, for which progress can be steadily measured or tracked.

Example: I will achieve at least a "B" average this term because it will enable to me to get into a field that I really want to pursue as a career, and I will measure my progress toward this goal by keeping track of the grades I'm earning in all my courses through-out the term.

Actionable: Identifies the concrete actions or behaviors that will be engaged in to reach the goal.

Example: I will achieve at least a "B" average this term by (1) attending all classes, (2) taking detailed notes in all my classes, (3) completing all reading assignments before their due dates, and (4) avoiding cramming by studying in advance of all my major exams.

Realistic: A goal capable of being achieved or attained.

Example: Achieving a "B" average this term will be a realistic goal for me because my course load is manageable and I will not be working at my part-time job for more than 15 hours per week.

Timed: A goal that is broken down into a timeline that includes short-range, mid-range, and long-range steps.

Example: To achieve at least a "B" average this term, first I'll acquire the information I need to learn by taking complete notes in class and on my assigned readings (short-range step). Second, I'll study the information I've acquired from my notes and readings in short study sessions held in advance of major exams (mid-range step). Third, I'll hold a final review session for all information previously studied on the day before my exams, and after exams I'll review my test results as feedback to determine what I did well and what I need to do better in order to maintain at least a "B" average (long-range step).

Note: The strategy for setting SMART goals is a transferable process that can be applied to reaching goals in any aspect or dimension of your life, including health-related goals such as losing weight, social goals such as meeting new people, and fiscal goals such as saving money.

Cari Smith: "Setting goals is important in all aspects of life. As you set your educational goals, think about the following questions: Why are you in school? What do you want to accomplish once you obtain your degree?

When do you plan to graduate? Write the goal down, share it with family and friends, and post it somewhere prominent as a reminder of your purpose.

Example: I am going to school to earn a business degree. This will afford me the opportunity to obtain a job in a major corporation. Having a good job will allow me to provide for my family's needs and even some of their wants. I plan to graduate in May 2017.

Example: I am returning to school to obtain my degree in nursing. This will give me the opportunity to have a career, once my children begin school fulltime. I think it will help me be a better role model to my children. I plan to graduate in December 2018.

Now that you have a target date, look at the courses you have yet to complete. How many classes will you need to take each term to graduate in May 2017? Is this still a feasible goal? If not, adjust your target graduation date. It is important to ensure that the goal you are setting is attainable. You want to set yourself up for success, not failure."

Mark Heideman

"When setting out to complete each task, think 'baby steps.' Thinking about completing a task can often be overwhelming; however, once you begin a task it often becomes less overwhelming as it's put into perspective. Therefore, break each task into smaller, doable tasks and schedule several small windows of time to complete each task. The goal is to simply get started rather than trying to complete the entire task at once."

Terry

Q: *What is a favorite Bible verse that has kept you focused on your goals?*

A: *Psalm 91, the entire chapter is really powerful, but here are some highlights:*

Whoever dwells in the shelter of the Most High will rest in the shadow of the Almighty.

² I will say of the LORD, "He is my refuge and my fortress, my God, in whom I trust." ...

³ If you say, "The LORD is my refuge," and you make the Most High your dwelling,

⁴ no harm will overtake you, no disaster will come near your tent.

⁵ For he will command his angels concerning you to guard you in all your ways;

⁶ they will lift you up in their hands, so that you will not strike your foot against a stone.

⁷ You will tread on the lion and the cobra; you will trample the great lion and the serpent.

⁸ "Because he loves me," says the LORD, "I will rescue him; I will protect him, for he acknowledges my name.

⁹ He will call on me, and I will answer him; I will be with him in trouble, I will deliver him and honor him.

¹⁰ With long life I will satisfy him and show him my salvation" (NIV).

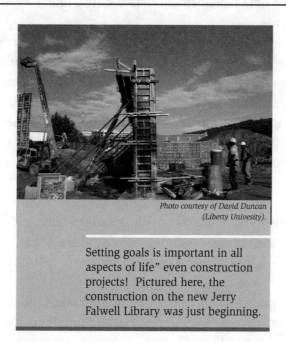

Photo courtesy of David Duncan (Liberty Univesity).

Setting goals is important in all aspects of life" even construction projects! Pictured here, the construction on the new Jerry Falwell Library was just beginning.

Determine the Necessity of Time Management

Ecc. 8:6,
"For there is a proper time and procedure for every matter" (NIV).

Alissa Keith

"Everyone has time for the things that are important to them."

Cari Smith

"Each person has 24 hours in a day. It is what you do with your time that determines your success."

Dr. Jerry Falwell, Sr.

"God is always right on time. There are no panic buttons near the throne. The Holy Trinity has never gone into emergency session. Everything is under control and going according to plan" (*Falwell: An Autobiography*, p. 408).

Why is Time Management Important?

As you consider how your plans become goals and goals become accomplishments, it is vital to consider the importance of **time management**. When you take on college study, you are probably adding this new commitment to an already-busy life. Many new online learners have full-time jobs, families, and a full life *before* registering to take college courses. The responsibilities of church, family, and work all require a commitment of time for success, and the same is true of college study. Some new college students impulsively respond to a desire for a college education, without first considering how college coursework will fit into a busy life. We take up the subject of time management here because this is a critical ingredient for college success.

Online students work with near-total independence, outside the weekly course deadlines. Students, who opt to take courses online, may erroneously believe that their time spent on their coursework is much less than if they were residential students. However, trading in the time spent getting to and attending classes for freedom to set your own schedule is not the only consideration. Online learners are responsible to independently read and study textbooks and must complete assignments on a regular schedule provided in the course. Those who believe they can simply complete the week's reading, viewing, and assignments after every other commitment is fulfilled are likely to fall behind in reading and studying and are likely to fail to meet course assignment deadlines, as well. It is critical to take a realistic view of the time required to create success, and to plan a schedule which recognizes this as a priority.

Research demonstrates that the ability to manage time well is a critical driver of student success (Erickson, Peters, & Strommer, 2006). Further, the

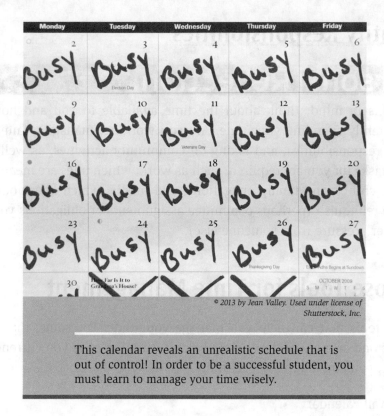

This calendar reveals an unrealistic schedule that is out of control! In order to be a successful student, you must learn to manage your time wisely.

© 2013 by Jean Valley. Used under license of Shutterstock, Inc.

Terry

Q: *Are you a good manager of time?*

A: "Sometimes I'm better at it than others, but overall, I would say yes."

Q: *Do you believe that time management is a natural gift, or do you have to work at it?*

A: "I certainly believe you can learn time management, but just like everything else, it requires focus and discipline."

Q: *How do you balance competing demands in your life?*

A: "It's a matter of having a plan and working the plan. I allot certain time for each activity that needs my attention and try to shed those that aren't important for me at this time. It's important to remember that there is a limit to the amount of time you have."

Q: *What prompted you to consider time management a necessary skill (if you do)?*

A: "Anytime you have a family, time management is a necessary skill . . . just for survival."

Q: *What is non-negotiable in your schedule?*

A: "Family, they are the most important investment in my life . . . they are my support structure, without them, I wouldn't have been able to accomplish this."

Q: *What did you have to give up for college success?*

A: "I was lucky and didn't have to give up anything, but I did have to use whatever free time I had to help complete my work."

ability to set goals, make wise choices, and manage competing priorities for how to use the precious resource of time can be a strategy for success not only in your college work, but also in life. Those who report being successful managers of their time also report themselves as happier, too (Myers, 2000). Good time management is beneficial in every area of your life, not just your college work.

Strategies for Managing Your Time

Time management begins by evaluating the options for how you might spend your time. It is important to look at what you are currently committed to, as well as what opportunities you wish to take advantage of in the future. You will need to determine how much time you need for each commitment or event. Your time is valuable, so you must also prioritize and decide which tasks are worthy of that time. Consider this: the most effective and busy person and the one who accomplishes the least each have the same amount of time to work with. God gives each of us 168 hours per week—24 hours each day—to manage. How we prioritize and carry out our plans can make a difference in whether we are successful or not. That said, successful managers of time are able to identify responsibilities that are important to them and are able to make and keep a schedule to accomplish their goals.

Alexandra Barnett

"Are you a morning person or a night owl? Complete your schoolwork during the time of day when you are at your best. You can often complete as much work in 30 minutes during your "prime time," as you can in two hours when you are tired or unable to concentrate well."

Identify Responsibilities

Personal Reflection

With this in mind, think about the time available to you and how you are currently spending your time. Are you working, managing family and church responsibilities, and taking on community activities, as well? Note which tasks for you are required, such as work; which ones are meaningful, such as church and family obligations; and finally, which ones you might need to relinquish (perhaps committee assignments or obligations you took on under pressure from someone else).

Choose Tools for Time Management

Gather tools that can help you manage your time. For some, that would include one or more of the choices below. Mark the ones you currently use or think you could apply successfully.

_____Wall calendar

_____Desk calendar

_____Family calendar (on the refrigerator, perhaps)

_____Pocket-size annual or biannual calendar

_____Smartphone calendar application

_____Personal computer calendar application

Emily

Q: *What prompted you to consider time management a necessary skill (if you do)?*

A: "When I wasn't doing very well in classes and I just felt like I didn't have a good balance of anything."

Tim

Q: *What is non-negotiable in your schedule? Why? What did you have to give up for college success?*

A: "Something that is non-negotiable in my schedule is my work schedule and field duty. I personally have had to give up sleep, set meal times, and many fun events so that I could complete my course work."

Photo courtesy of Kevin Manguiob.

Liberty students are served by several pedestrian tunnels. Time management can provide the light at the end of the tunnel when you are a busy student!

There are advantages and disadvantages for each type of tool. Only you can know what works best for you. Consider whether the tools you use are ones that you can synchronize and which others (such as family members) can see and edit, as well. You may have to experiment to find the best options for your situation.

© 2015 by val lawless. Used under license of Shutterstock, Inc.

"Consider this: the most effective and busy person and the one who accomplishes the least each have the same amount of time to work with. God gives each of us 168 hours per week—24 hours each day—to manage."

Roger

Q: *Are you a good manager of time?*

A: "Time management is a learned skill. A person is not born managing time. I have never seen a baby wear a watch. One must continually work at managing time wisely. I can spend hours working on a paper while watching television or I can spend half that time completing my paper at the library desk. It's important to get away from distractions to complete work in a timely fashion. In the end, I will have more time to do what I want to do. I also like to reward myself for productive behavior. If I work diligently for one hour, I will give myself a ten-minute break doing something fun and relaxing."

Ruth

Q: *How did you determine your goals for college study?*

A: "Since it was later in life when I began to work on my college degree, it was for my personal satisfaction to earn the degree. Because of my past years as a Sunday school teacher, for my cognates, I chose Religion and Business because of my position at LU."

KEY CONCEPT

Establish Your Priorities and Plan Your Use of Time

1 Samuel 12:23,
"I will teach you the way that is good and right" (NIV).

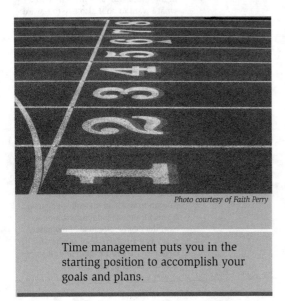

Photo courtesy of Faith Perry

Time management puts you in the starting position to accomplish your goals and plans.

After you consider the time you have available, and you have gathered the tools you will need to manage your time, you will need to set priorities for how you spend your time. There may well be more opportunities than you are able to take advantage of. Some things, such as work, demand priority placement in your schedule. Other things, such as a favorite television show or leisure reading, may not be as important. You will want to rank these considerations, in order of importance to you. Things of highest priority should go into your plans first, and you can work your way down in priority order, until you have to decide between lower-ranking options. To prioritize effectively you must create a personal time management plan that will help you defeat procrastination and avoid distractions.

Create a Personal Time Management Plan

Mark Heideman

"Plan your time by writing down everything you want to do or accomplish."

Effective use of your time begins with having a well-considered time management plan. While taking time to create a plan for how you use your time may seem like a waste of valuable time, it is actually a way to become more efficient. Once you have evaluated what is important to you and determined which tasks contribute to your overall goals, it is time to establish your routines for time management.

Good time management should be done on three different levels: long-range planning, weekly planning, and daily planning. Consider these different planning time frames when evaluating how to manage your time effectively.

1.   Long-range, or term (or semester) planning

Long-range planning allows you to see all of the upcoming responsibilities and commitments that you have. Consider using a monthly calendar, and put in all of your work and family time commitments. This would include things like travel for work, extra time spent outside of work on job-related tasks, family events such as weddings, birthdays, or weekend travels, and so on. This calendar should include all of the unique (non-repeating) responsibilities you have. Once you have included all of the work and family commitments, gather your course charts, and put in all the course assignments by due date. You may begin to see some weeks or weekends that are very busy. For example, suppose you are taking part in a family wedding that begins with out of town travel on Thursday and ends with a brunch on Sunday morning after the wedding. If this coincides with the same week(end) a term paper is due on the following Monday, you will need to plan ahead to accomplish the work. Failing to gather this information onto a single calendar can result in discovering at the last minute that you have far too much to do and far too little time to accomplish it.

© 2015 by tadamichi. Used under license of Shutterstock, Inc.

"Consider using a monthly calendar, and put in all of your work and family time commitments. This would include things like travel for work, extra time spent outside of work on job-related tasks, family events such as weddings, birthdays, or weekend travels, and so on."

2. Weekly or routine planning

This shorter-term plan allows you to acknowledge the routine of your life. For example, if your regular work schedule is from 9:00 a.m. to 5:00 p.m. on weekdays, note that in your calendar. That time will be reserved only for work and can, therefore, never be available for school assignments. Think through your week and add in all the commitments you are currently responsible to complete. This can include your softball team, your Girl Scout troupe, Sunday school teaching and preparation, commuting to and from your child's music lessons or sports team events, and so on. Put in regular times for exercise if you do that routinely. Only you can determine what needs to go into this version of the calendar. What times will you plan for course reading, study, and assignment-completion? If you are taking two, three-credit courses, you should plan on at least twelve hours each week, at minimum, to complete your reading, presentations, and course assignments. Remember, this has to be a routine part of your life if you hope to achieve academic success.

As you place your responsibilities in the calendar, consider whether there are any routine events that you can relinquish to others. Maybe it is time to step down from a volunteer role for a time? Perhaps your bowling league can get along without you, at least while you are in school? You need not consider these as permanent changes but ones that you might consider which can free up valuable time that you will need for reading, study, and mastery of course material. As you consider tasks that are important to you, keep in mind that you should avoid letting others dictate your priorities.

Mark Heideman

"If you need to eliminate any item, begin with the lowest priority."

Cheryl

Q: *Are you a good manager of time?*

A: "When I need to be . . . yes."

Q: *Do you believe that time management is a natural gift, or do you have to work at it?*

A: "Not for me. I definitely have to work at it. Taking the (optional) Study Skills class at Liberty U was so incredibly helpful. I remember telling my Professor at the time how I wish it had been my FIRST class at LU, as the class taught me HOW to study. I learned tools in that class that I utilize, whenever I do ANY kind of work at my desk. My favorite tools for studying are my to-do-list, and my BRIGHT highlighters, BRIGHT post-its, and BRIGHT colored index cards. They work for my individual learning style."

© 2015 by Aleshyn Andrei. Used under license of Shutterstock, Inc.

"While we are creatures of habit, it is important to give yourself some 'down' or unplanned time."

Kristy Motte

"Don't forget to schedule in personal time each week of the term. Even just an hour or two each week gives you something to look forward to, motivation to get other tasks completed on time, and the ability to refresh/refocus in the midst of a busy week."

Sherry Dickerson

"Use the calendar tool in your Outlook school email to schedule due dates for all of your assignments at the beginning of the term. Avoid missing deadlines by setting up reminders and checking them off as you complete your assignments."

Consider giving up responsibilities which are a drain on your time and which do not bring you satisfaction.

3. Daily planning

This is the sort of planning that many of us already do as a daily "to-do" list. Think of this plan as a check-off listing of the tasks you want to accomplish. It is best to plan this list at the end of one day for the next or first thing each morning. Prioritize the things that must get done, such as an appointment with the dentist. In addition, you can list some things you would like to accomplish if time allows. This sort of inclusion might be for things like pleasure shopping, washing the car, or picking up dry-cleaning. These tasks may be accomplished most any day that you have time available.

Many people take great pleasure in checking off the tasks on their daily "to-do" list. Seeing your plans come to fruition can be fulfilling, particularly if you have planned well and can achieve most of what is on your list each day. The items which do not get completed can be moved to the next day's list until each is accomplished.

As you are planning your monthly, weekly, and daily schedules, avoid the urge to fill up every moment with planned activities. While we are creatures of habit, it is important to give yourself some "down" or unplanned time. Additionally, a realistic plan is one that acknowledges that life can be very unpredictable; you never know when the unexpected event outside your control will happen. Giving yourself additional time that is unplanned and uncommitted is being realistic, avoiding the stress you will face if something interferes and challenges your all-too-full schedule.

Defeating Procrastination

Procrastination can be a terrible drain on your time management, as well as your productivity. It is important to think about it, so you are able to avoid it when you are tempted. The word **procrastination** is defined by the Merriam-Webster dictionary as "to put off intentionally and habitually" (*Merriam-Webster.com*, 2015). However, another entry is even more discouraging, defining procrastination as "to put off doing something, especially out of *habitual carelessness or laziness* (emphasis added)" (*TheFreeDictionary.com*, 2015). Looking at that definition can be rather convicting, can't it? With either definition, it is important to recognize that procrastination merely prolongs the time required to perform a needed task. Sometimes, we procrastinate until the last possible moment that something can be done or even later. In that case, the work is completed poorly, if at all, and does not represent a sincere best effort. Sadly, research shows that most college students procrastinate (Steele, 2007).

Some students believe (incorrectly) that they perform their best work "under pressure" of time to get assignments completed. Others allow too much time to pass before beginning work on important assignments, falsely allowing themselves the handicap of too little time to finish well. In this circumstance, students rationalize that a poor performance is due to too little time to finish well, rather than facing the fact that it was poor use of time that was actually to blame (Chu & Cho, 2005; Rhodewalt & Vohs, 2005). Do not allow yourself to fall prey to faulty thinking which promotes the tendency to procrastinate your important school tasks. Instead, adopt strategies that can help you avoid procrastination. These strategies include:

- Set a time or deadline that you will begin an assignment.
- Plan a budget of time for large assignments, breaking it up into smaller tasks.
- Begin with a small portion of the work, so you can begin to make progress.
- On the other hand, tackle a large piece of the work. This enables you to feel mastery over the larger task, since you are well underway with it.
- Avoid commiserating about the task with others.

Dealing with Distractions

Often, students struggle to complete their work not because they are not interested, but because there are just too many good options for how to spend time. Are you familiar with the story related in Luke 10:38–42?

> "As Jesus and his disciples were on their way, he came to a village where a woman named Martha opened her home to him. She had a sister called Mary, who sat at the Lord's feet listening to what he said. But Martha was distracted by all the preparations that had to be made. She came to him and asked, "Lord, don't you care that my sister has left me to do the work by myself? Tell her to help me!"
>
> "Martha, Martha," the Lord answered, "you are worried and upset about many things, but few things are needed—or indeed only one. Mary has chosen what is better, and it will not be taken away from her." (NIV)

In this Bible story, Martha was not uninterested in what her Lord was teaching, but she was distracted by other tasks. She had not correctly

Hanna Bruce

"Begin studying and completing assignments early in the week. It seems that those unexpected life events always seem to "pop up" near the end of the week. If you have spaced out your work, starting on the first day of the module, when something goes awry on Saturday, you won't feel behind in your studies."

Debra Magnuson

"You can always work ahead in each week. That way if an emergency arises the day of the deadline, you won't be stressed out about turning in an assignment late."

Sherrie Welfel

"Get a weekly/monthly planner when opened to a page, a full week is visible. Utilize erasable colored pencils to color code your individual course assignments and personal events!"

© 2015 by Blend Images. Used under license of Shutterstock, Inc.

"Think of ways to spend meaningful time with family, while still maintaining your commitment to your course work. Consider things like working together to make simple meals…"

Mark Heideman

"Assign amounts of time to each item by projecting the amount of time you 'think' each will take. It's always a good idea to add 10% or 20% to the time as we often underestimate our time."

Alexandra Barnett

"Plan out your week by determining what you need to study when and what assignments you will complete when to avoid last minute, less than stellar assignment submissions."

prioritized what she should be doing and had chosen poorly. Too often, students do the same thing. There are a dizzying number of options for how to spend time, and many of them are good choices. Good time management requires making the **best** use of time and avoiding anything that will distract from that choice. Sometimes, it is necessary to limit the number of activities you agree to or the number of organizations to which you promise your time. Take a careful look at the commitments you give your time now. Are there any responsibilities that you can share with others, cease temporarily, or even abandon for the long term?

Do not feel that you must give up family responsibilities and time together, but consider how you might give time to your family in a different way. Does your family spend several hours in front of the television each night as "family time?" That may not fit your schedule as an online learner, as you may need to spend time reading or viewing course presentations online. Think of ways to spend meaningful time with family, while still maintaining your commitment to your course work. Consider things like working together to make simple meals, spending time around the table at mealtime (not in front of the television), coming up with review games together, reading stories or devotionals together, taking family walks, and other meaningful and fun ways to give time to your family.

Though distractions may come in the form of activities, they can also be a bit more insidious. While you are working, are you often distracted? Distractions might crop up as a ringing phone (or text message arriving), the lure of Facebook, or internet or phone games. What can you do to limit the intrusion of these sort of distractors? Consider adopting the following practices when you are doing your course work in order to be prepared for success:

- Turn off your phone or leave it in another room. There is nothing so urgent that it cannot wait until you have completed your planned study time.
- Use restraint in opening additional tabs on your computer. Do not be available to your email, or Facebook, or . . . anything that might distract you.
- Set a timer for your work. Once you have worked for the planned period of time, take a break. You may allow yourself some time with one of the distractors mentioned above (phone, Facebook, etc.), but

again, set yourself a time limit, and use the timer to let you know when the time is up.

- Let family and friends know your work plans and ask that they help you stick to your plan. For family, set some clear signals, such as a closed door or a note on the door to remind others to respect your study time.
- Use headphones. This can help you avoid hearing any auditory distractors and also be a visual clue for family that you are "in the zone" for classwork.
- Avoid family distractions by arising early in the morning to do your course work. This can help you finish the tasks you want to accomplish before the day officially begins.
- Do not attempt marathon study sessions, "massed practice," or cramming. What we refer to as "spaced practice" (studying in small increments of time spread out over time) is much more effective for your learning and is less likely to cause you to fall to distractions.
- Do not begin a work/study session when you are hungry or thirsty. Take care of those needs first so you will not be distracted by thinking about foods/beverages.

Mark Heideman

"Allow for reward time. Everyone needs to relax, so reward time is beneficial."

Emily

Q: *Do you believe that time management is a natural gift, or do you have to work at it?*

A: "I think it varies. Some people are naturally better at it but I think everyone has to work at it."

Personal Reflection

Setting Priorities Exercise

The life of the online learner is certainly a *full* life: each day presents challenges to even the plans for completing your college work in a timely, thoughtful way. The following exercise will help you think about how you manage your time with a focus on prioritizing your time to achieve the tasks that are important to you.

Imagine that the list below is your own personal to-do list. Given the many tasks, responsibilities, and activities that are demanding your time, how will you spend the time from now until bedtime? Using the tasks below, prioritized them from 1 (do this first) through 12 (do this last). You need not include every choice, but you may not leave out, for example, the children's activities (even if you do not have children) to make the time work out before bedtime (midnight).

(HINT: You may want to do this with a pencil so you can make changes as you evaluate the options.)

Tim

Q: *What prompted you to consider time management a necessary skill (if you do)?*

A: "Time management is something that everyone must work at. Time management is not a natural gift that everyone receives; it is something that requires discipline. The best way to balance your personal life, school, and work is with what I call a 'tasker.' First, you need to get a dry-erase board and dry-erase markers. Next, you need to get your course syllabus and schedule along with your work schedule. Mark out your course schedule into sectors and then add your work schedule to that schedule. With each input, you will draw a box beside it. Finally, hang the dry erase board beside, above, under, or in front of your television. As your course work moves along, you can add in personal task or events. Yes, this is the same thing as a day planner. However, with a dry erase board beside your television nagging you to do your course work- it is much more effective. Once you complete a specific task, put a check in the box. This will help to keep you motivated as you complete your course work and will be a constant reminder to do your course work."

Ruth

Q: *Are you a good manager of time?*

A: "Yes."

Q: *Do you believe that time management is a natural gift, or do you have to work at it?*

A: "You have to work at it."

Q: *How do you balance competing demands in your life?*

A: "Family is always first, then plan ahead for all things necessary, even the smallest things."

Q: *What prompted you to consider time management a necessary skill (if you do)?*

A: "Raising three children as a single Mom."

Q: *What is non-negotiable in your schedule?*

A: "Putting family first in case of emergency. It's my responsibility."

It's Thursday, 4:30 p.m. Here are the many tasks that lie ahead for you:

_____Pick up the children from daycare.

_____Prepare dinner, serve it, and clean up.

_____Work on your history paper, which requires a number of drafts over a few weeks.

_____Your Discussion Board thread is due tonight.

_____There are two presentations for this week's work that you have not viewed.

_____An assignment is due on Monday for your other course. You first will need to read the two chapters of the textbook for that course.

_____The children have homework.

_____Bath time/bedtime for the children should be completed by 9 p.m. Don't forget to read a bedtime story and pray with them!

_____Your favorite show is on television tonight at 10:00 p.m.

_____You teach a weekly Sunday school class, but haven't yet read this week's lesson.

_____You did your morning Bible study this morning, but slept in a bit, so you didn't have time to exercise yet today.

_____Two weeks ago, you had agreed to meet with friends for coffee to celebrate a birthday. You don't see these friends very often and have been looking forward to this time.

Setting Priorities Exercise, a Second Look

Did you have difficulty fitting everything from the Setting Priorities Exercise into the time available? If so, what does that indicate to you? You may be surprised to learn that you were not expected to be able to find a way to fit everything shown there into the evening hours allowed. Those tasks were simply too time-consuming to be able to do them all and certainly not to do them well! Many students find themselves in a similar situation with more to do than will fit into the time allowed. If this situation is uncomfortably close to home, it is time to rethink priorities.

During your time as an online college student, you may have to relinquish some responsibilities. This may involve handing off some duties you do not enjoy, but it also may mean deferring, for a time, tasks you find fulfilling. Perhaps it is time for someone else to step up to teach the Sunday school class, or take your spot on the bowling league, or some other task you are enjoying now. As mentioned previously, these changes do not have to be permanent, but making these changes for a season can provide room in your schedule to allow academic work.

Think carefully about how you can arrange your time and commitments so that you can be successful in the long run. You will want to put your priorities in order: God, family, work/school. Notice that even though school is critical in this time of your life, it is not the primary task of your life. Nevertheless, ensure that you plan sufficient time to complete your work well. This is a balancing act and may require a few revisions before you get it just right for yourself and your commitments. Take heart, as the Bible assures us that "the wise in heart will know the proper time and procedure" Ecclesiastes 8:5 (NIV). Pray that God will grant you wisdom to plan your time well.

Personal Reflection

Time Management: Lists

Time is a wonderful gift from God. While we do not know how many years we will be granted here on Earth, we do know that everyone has the same 24 hours each day, with 168 hours each week. The busiest person utilizes the same amount of time each day as the least accomplished person who only manages to spend the day on the couch, watching TV or playing computer games! What does your current use of time indicate about you? This activity will help you see how much time you truly have left to "manage" once you determine what time you currently have committed to your daily activities and tasks. Complete the chart provided below to see where you stand now. Simply write in the hours spent on each activity and total up each column.

	Mon.	Tues.	Wed.	Thurs.	Fri.	Sat.	Sun.	Weekly Total
Commuting	2	3	2	3	2	2	1	15
Work	2	2	2	2	2	0	0	10
Eating	1.5	1.5	2	1.5	1.5	2	2	12
Exercise	1	0	1	0	1	0	0	3
Home chores	1	2	1	2	1	1	0	8
Family time	2	1	2	1	2	6	4	18
Social time	0	1	0	1	0	1	1	4
Volunteering	1	1	1	1	1	0	0	5
Worship	0	0	0	0	0	0	2	2
Prayer/Bible study	.5	.5	.5	.5	.5	.5	1	4

								total
Personal grooming/ hygiene	1	1	1	1	1	1	2	8
Entertainment (TV, movies, games, etc.)	1	0	1	0	1	2	1	6
Shopping	1	0	1	0	1	0	1	4
Sleeping	7	7	7	7	7	8	8	51
Other	1	1	1	1	1	1	1	7
Daily Total								
Time Left (24-daily total) (168-weekly total)								

Maddy

Q: *Are you a good manager of time? Do you believe that time management is a natural gift, or do you have to work at it? How do you balance competing demands in your life?*

A: "I am a good manager of time when I have a specific motivation to do so. The general idea of 'free time' never seems like a good enough reason, but having a particular event to go to does motivate me to get work done. I believe that there is some natural ability in time management, but like all gifts and abilities, it must be nurtured and developed or it will go to waste. As someone who isn't very good at managing my time, I sometimes stay up late to make sure I get things done, simply because I didn't do what I needed to in the normal daytime hours."

Michael Marrano

"Use an 'organizer' such as the MS Outlook features in your LU Webmail account. Set up task and calendar reminders to help keep yourself organized and on schedule."

Once you complete the chart, answer the following questions thoroughly.

1. How much time do you have available on a daily basis? Take the total hours committed for each day and subtract from 24.

  M___ T___ W___ R___ F___ S___ S___

2. How much time do you have available on a weekly basis? Take your weekly total and subtract it from 168. _____

3. Do you think there is enough time "left" to accomplish what you need to do each week when you are doing online college work? Explain.

4. Are there areas that you think you may need to make some changes in the weeks ahead? If so, how will you implement those changes? If you do not see the need for changes, explain why.

The Bible says, in Psalm 90:12, "So teach us to number our days, that we may apply our hearts unto wisdom." If we ask God to help us manage our time wisely, He will!

Determine Valuable, Goal-Setting Character Traits

Proverbs 1:5,
"Let the wise listen and add to their learning,
and let the discerning get guidance" (NIV).

A successful life and education involves more than mastering objectives, achieving goals, managing time, and setting priorities. While all of these elements are critical to success, they would be nothing if not deeply rooted in godly character traits. In order to be truly successful, you must adopt valuable, goal-setting behaviors. These character traits can be found in 2 Timothy 4:7 when Paul writes to Timothy, reflecting on his life and ministry, "I have fought the good fight, I have finished the race, I have kept the faith" (NIV). This verse draws attention to the following godly qualities: wisdom, honesty, determination, diligence, respect, and faithfulness.

"I have fought the good fight..."

Fighting the good fight involves the character traits of wisdom and honesty:

Wisdom

Merriam-Webster.com defines wisdom as "knowledge of what is proper or reasonable: good sense of judgment" (2015). Discerning what fights are worth fighting and what goals are worth pursuing is an essential part of possessing wisdom. When the Apostle Paul wrote this letter to Timothy, he was imprisoned in Rome, and he was martyred shortly afterwards. Recognizing that his time on earth may be limited (v.6, "the time of my departure is near"), Paul notes that he has "fought the *good fight*." In other words, Paul explains that he chose wisely when he abandoned persecuting Christians and committed his life to Christ and spreading the gospel message, even if it meant losing his own life.

In one of his sermons, Dr. Jerry Falwell, Sr. told a story that explains this concept more. Students often approached Dr. Jerry wondering if God was calling them to be pastors. His standard response was "If you can keep from preaching—don't preach. If you can keep from going to the mission field—stay home. If God has put His hand upon you, He will make you a flop in everything else you try to do." Dr. Jerry Falwell, Sr. goes on to

Cheryl

Q: *How do you balance competing demands in your life?*

A: "Prioritization and my to-do-list (with check marks, so I can see progress, and visually diagram what is left to do, each day)."

Q: *What is non-negotiable in your schedule? Why?*

A: "My family's medical situations.

It is amazing the stress that a single parent has, to get everything 'done.' I know scheduling and time-management is challenging for all adult learners. However, I have to give extra props to single parents, as there are huge sacrifices made, in order to take care of the needs of children and school. I cannot even estimate the number of days that I had (and still do) familial medical and emergency situations. This has been the second biggest challenge with my education (first being finances).

Assignment deadlines are a nightmare when the medical needs of the family and educational 'deadlines' have a conflict. Time management is the ONLY tool I used, that helped me to be successful with my incredibly hectic schedule. I very simply could NOT have done well, if I left all of my assignments until the last minute."

Q: *What did you have to give up for college success?*

A: "Free time . . . and reading for pleasure."

Roger

Q: *Do you believe that time management is a natural gift, or do you have to work at it? How do you balance competing demands in your life?*

A: "One strategy I have developed is to prioritize my responsibilities into categories: urgent, important, can wait. I also have maintained a list of those things which I need to do on a regular basis and devote a portion of time for that. For example, I teach Sunday school so I have devoted a time slot in my week for that. And if there is any reading involved, I will reserve a few minutes at the start and end of the day for reading."

explain that "The call of God is without repentance" (Falwell, 1973, p.165). As you choose goals in life, choose wisely and follow God's call and leading in your life.

Honesty

Honesty is "fairness and straightforwardness of character" according to *Merriam-Webster.com* (2015). Part of being successful on your road toward completing your goals is fighting a fair fight, choosing honesty and trustworthiness instead of backhanded behaviors and cowardice, speaking the truth in love and having integrity in every interaction. In the same sermon, Dr. Falwell explained the importance of this trait, as well, "There is an old Chinese proverb, 'You can't carve rotten wood.' We need strength of character, toughness of fiber. Then God can carve upon us and make us into instruments He can use" (p. 169). The Apostle Paul was certainly an instrument used by the Lord. In his reflection, he chooses his words carefully and observes that he "fought the good fight." He doesn't say that he fought it perfectly, but he recognizes that he chose his battle correctly and does not express regret. Paul is honest in his reflection, as he was honest in living. Paul did not veer from the truth of Christ's message throughout his ministry and imprisonment, even when staring death in the face.

As you work toward achieving your goals, you must be honest with yourself. Have you chosen good goals, as Paul chose a "good fight?" In the article, "Ayn Rand's Objectivist Virtues as the Foundation for Morality and Success in Business," the author, Younkins (2012) explains that "Honesty means being in accord with reality. Honesty is basic to the structure of human relationships in virtually all contexts. Dishonesty is self-defeating because it involves being in conflict with reality." Reflecting honestly on your choices and motives is a necessary step toward working in harmony with others, as you make each goal and strive for successful completion of it. Have you been honest with others as you have worked toward your goal? Have you been honest with yourself? If the answer is "no" to either of these questions, determine what you can do to be honest and fair in all of your actions and interactions.

Photo courtesy of Thomas Road Baptist Church.

"Nothing of eternal importance is ever accomplished apart from prayer."—Dr. Jerry Falwell, Sr.

"I have finished the race..."

Finishing the race involves the qualities of determination and diligence, two closely related—but not identical—characteristics:

Determination and Diligence

Merriam-Webster.com (2015) defines determination as "a quality that makes you continue trying to do or achieve something that is difficult," and it defines diligence as the "steady, earnest, and energetic (painstaking) effort" involved in achievement. Paul compares his Christian ministry to a race in this portion of verse 7. Paul recognizes that his ministry is at its end as he shares that he has "finished the race." Paul's ministry reflected earnest effort toward sharing the gospel with people who were not receptive, even cruel; it took determination and diligence to finish his race.

If you plan to run a race successfully, you must train to do so. You must work hard to ensure that you finish the race and finish well. In order to do this, you must determine to train daily and work with diligence toward that end. Training is not easy; it involves discipline in regards to daily exercises, practicing, and dieting. Former Heavyweight Champion, Muhammad Ali explained this perfectly, "I hated every minute of training, but I said, 'Don't quit. Suffer now and live the rest of your life as a champion'" (Velasquez, 2015). You must determine that crossing the finish line is worth the work that it will take to get there.

In the movie, *Rocky Balboa*, Sylvester Stallone's character, Rocky, shares some practical advice about determination with his son:

> Let me tell you something you already know. The world ain't all sunshine and rainbows. It's a very mean and nasty place and I don't care how tough you are it will beat you to your knees and keep you there permanently if you let it. You, me, or nobody is gonna hit as hard as life. But it ain't about how hard ya hit. It's about how hard you can get hit and keep moving forward. How much you can take and keep moving forward. That's how winning is done! (2006)

If you are at all familiar with the Rocky films, you know that Rocky starts out as an underdog boxer, who is given shot to fight in the ring with Apollo Creed, the narrative's World Heavyweight Champion. Rocky establishes a personal goal to train so that he can "go the distance" with Creed, an accomplishment that no one else has achieved,

> Cause all I wanna do is go the distance. Nobody's ever gone the distance with Creed, and if I can go that distance, you see, and that bell rings and I'm still standin', I'm gonna know for the first time in my life, see, that I weren't just another bum from the neighborhood. (1976)

"Go the distance" is exactly what Rocky does because of his determination and his diligence.

Joe Super

"If all you're getting out of the class is academic knowledge, you're missing out. As you go through the course, and as your education becomes a part of your life for a time, I hope you grow spirituality by learning more about perseverance."

Cari Smith

"Obtaining a degree includes sacrifice. You have to make a conscious decision to put aside some of your extra-curricular activity and you have to be willing to say 'no.'"

Dr. Jerry Falwell, Sr.

"It always costs you something to do a work for the Lord. If it does not cost you anything, it is not worth doing" (*Falwell: An Autobiography*, p. 206).

© 2015 by Petrenko Andriy. Used under license of Shutterstock, Inc.

"But it ain't about how hard ya hit. It's about how hard you can get hit and keep moving forward. How much you can take and keep moving forward. That's how winning is done!"—Rocky Balboa, 2006.

Dr. Jerry Falwell, Sr.

"Faith is believing what God says in spite of the circumstances. Faith is simply taking God at His Word," (*Falwell: An Autobiography*, p. 126).

President Jerry Falwell

"The key is perseverance. Your ultimate success will be determined not by what it takes to knock you down, but by what it takes to keep you down" (Falwell, 2014).

"I have kept the faith."

Keeping the faith involves accountability through respect and faithfulness.

Respect and Faithfulness

One of the ways that Merriam-Webster.com defines respect is as "a feeling or understanding that someone or something is important, serious, etc., and should be treated in an appropriate way" is one of the ways that Merriam-Webster.com defines respect. When you are faithful, you show "true and constant support or loyalty; deserving trust: keeping your promises or doing what you are supposed to do" (*Merriam-Webster.com*, 2015). In order to respect his faith, Paul had to defend it, guard it, and keep it safe; he had to be loyal to it. Paul kept the gospel message alive through three missionary journeys and two Roman imprisonments; this spanned 20 years of his life. As God inspired, Paul wrote about his faith in Jesus Christ and Christ's redemption for mankind; he wrote guidelines for how we can/should walk in faith through a relationship with Jesus. He preserved his faith through this documentation that is now housed in 14 books of the New Testament. What a legacy of faithfulness and respect for God's truth Paul left behind!

Another example of "keeping the faith," is Carnegie Mellon University Professor, Randy Pausch, who lost his battle with pancreatic cancer in 2008. A year prior to that, Carnegie Mellon asked him to present a lecture in a series entitled "Journeys." Pausch really wanted to give this lecture, even though his wife, Jai, knowing his tendency to pour himself into his work, resisted the idea because she "wanted all" of him, and she didn't want anything to interfere with the precious time he had left to spend with her and their three young children. While he empathized with his wife's concerns, Pausch also felt that this recorded lecture could give his children a piece of him after his death. He explained,

> One thing I've learned is that when parents tell children things, it doesn't hurt to get some external validation. If I can get an audience to laugh and clap at the right time, maybe that would add gravitas to what I'm telling my kids. (Pausch, 2008, p. 9)

Ultimately, Jai yielded and supported Randy as he began working on his "last lecture." Recognizing that this lecture might be the last time loved ones would see him alive, Randy wanted to choose the best legacy and advice to leave his children, and he realized that his audience "might expect the talk to be about dying. But it had to be about living." He chose the title "Really Achieving Your Childhood Dreams."

True to his promise to Jai, Pausch's "Last Lecture" was recorded and can now be viewed on YouTube. Pausch also documented his advice to his children and others about "Really Achieving Your Childhood Dreams" in his book entitled, *The Last Lecture*. Pausch committed to delivering this message, knowing what it would mean for his children:

> Under the ruse of giving an academic lecture, I was trying to put myself in a bottle that would one day wash up on the beach for my children. If I were a painter, I would have painted for them. If I were a musician, I would have composed music. But I am a lecturer. So I lectured. (p. x)

Because he "kept the faith" by delivering a message about really living, while dying, Pausch's bottle did indeed wash up on the beach for his children, and this legacy continues to encourage others to this day.

© 2015 by R. Gino Santa Maria. Used under license of Shutterstock, Inc.

"I was trying to put myself in a bottle that would one day wash up on the beach for my children" —Randy Pausch, 2008.

Reflection Time

In II Timothy 4:7, Paul shares the secret ingredients to the success of his ministry, the godly qualities of wisdom, honesty, determination, diligence, respect, and faithfulness. One overarching quality found throughout the verse is Paul's willingness to reflect honestly on his own actions. **Self-reflection**, the "careful thought about your own behaviors and beliefs," is one of the most critical components toward achieving success. Dr. Jerry explained self-reflection this way,

> You must learn the success of failure. Some of you will go home and fail at a task. You will have an evangelistic campaign or a youth banquet and the meeting will flop. You'll end up with egg on your face. How you react to failure will determine whether you will attain greatness. Failure is inevitable in life. All men fail at least once; many of us fail several times. What one does with failure determines his character. (Falwell, 1973, p. 165)

Carefully evaluating the success of your achievement or the failure of your flop will help you determine how to move forward successfully in the future.

While evaluating, you must be honest with yourself and avoid something social psychologists refer to as "the **fundamental attribution error**," which is explained practically in Sherman's article, "Why We Don't Give Each Other a Break" (2014), "When we see someone doing something, we tend to think it relates to their personality rather than the situation the person might be in." For instance, if your boss doesn't call you back, you might think she is being dismissive or rude, when in fact she may have had a medical emergency or situation that kept her from calling you back. What

Roger

Q: What did you have to give up for college success? What is non-negotiable in your schedule?

A: "Managing a family, work, church, and school is tricky, like learning to juggle. It doesn't pay to be successful at school or work while being a failure at home. I must devote some time for family things. When I'm not in school I will take my wife and kids out shopping or bowling. If I have an errand to perform, I will bring one of the children with me. If I have to go to the library to study, I might take a child with the promise that after an hour, I will do something he likes to do for fun. I will reserve time to date my wife. That's a bit trickier these days since we our built in babysitter moved out (our adult daughter).

There is no excuse for failing to work hard. Since I paid for my education (and am still paying for LU with student loans) I refused to waste my time by not putting in the effort. It costs too much to redo a class. So I completed my work on time and studied hard for exams. In the end, I was rewarded with a 4.0 GPA and a good job."

Dr. Jerry Falwell, Sr.

"What would you do for God, if you were sure you couldn't fail?" (Miller, 2007).

Dr. Jerry Falwell, Sr.

"If God's people will see nothing but the goal line, will accept nothing but victory, will pay any price, will suffer any hurt and hardship, will refuse to be discouraged or disheartened, we cannot help but win; because we are charged with the power of God's Holy Spirit" (Falwell, 1997, p. 236).

Dr. Jerry Falwell, Sr.

"God has a vision for you. Don't settle for second best. Don't ever retire. Don't ever quit. Let your vision become an obsessive reality" (Falwell, 1997, p. 479).

Sherman goes on to explain is that "we make the fundamental attribution error…about other people but rarely ourselves. When we do things, we always have a good reason. It's other people we see as defective" (2014). Remember Rocky Balboa's speech to his son that you read about earlier? Rocky warns his son about the fundamental attribution error too:

> Now, if you know what you're worth, then go out and get what you're worth. But you gotta be willing to take the hits, and not pointing fingers saying you ain't where you wanna be because of him, or her, or anybody. Cowards do that and that ain't you. You're better than that! I'm always gonna love you, no matter what. No matter what happens. You're my son and you're my blood. You're the best thing in my life. But until you start believing in yourself, you ain't gonna have a life. (2006)

As Rocky suggests, in pursuing your personal goals, you have to avoid pointing fingers at others. Blame accomplishes nothing. However, if you take responsibility for your failures and learn from them instead, you will have a chance at success. Learn from process of honest self-reflection, so you can say with the Apostle Paul,

> I have fought the good fight, I have finished the race, I have kept the faith. Now there is in store for me the crown of righteousness, which the Lord, the righteous Judge, will award to me on that day—and not only to me, but also to all who have longed for his appearing. (II Timothy 4:7-8, NIV)

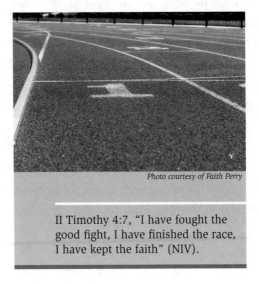

Photo courtesy of Faith Perry

II Timothy 4:7, "I have fought the good fight, I have finished the race, I have kept the faith" (NIV).

BUILDING BLOCKS

This chapter has hopefully helped focus your attention on two areas critical to your success: goal setting and time management. Goals are the foundation of your success, and good time management practices can help bring your goals to completion. When you go from having unrealistic dreams, wishing for certain things to happen, to an achieving goal-setter, you set concrete plans to move forward in your accomplishments. Managing your time well helps you take advantage of the time you have been given to see your plans fulfilled.

Personal Reflection

Recall that goal-setting can be divided into short-term and long-term goals. Consider creating some SMART goals, which are **S**pecific, **M**easured, **A**chievable, **R**ealistic, and **T**imed.

Goal #1:_____

S _____

M _____

A _____

R _____

T _____

Goal #2:_____

S _____

M _____

A _____

R _____

T _____

Goal #3:_____

S _____

M _____

A _____

R _____

T _____

You can set SMART goals for any area of your life: work, family, spiritual/prayer concerns. Carefully evaluate the goals you have made in the past, thinking about how SMART goals may have differed from what you planned. Does achieving a goal in one area of your life make you likely to achieve goals in other areas? Why or why not? How might you plan to coordinate goal-setting for best effect?

Personal Reflection

What biblical guidance do you have for setting your goals? In the book of Genesis, we read the account of God's creation of the Earth and all that live in it. The first chapter begins, "In the beginning, God created the heavens and the earth" (Genesis 1:1). On each of the six days of creation, God adds to what He has created, extending and developing the Earth from its initial formlessness and void. On closer examination, we can see that God goes about the process of creation in a very orderly way. Orderliness is one of God's characteristics. In the Bible, we learn to model ourselves on God's character. What do you see in yourself that can mirror God's orderliness? How can you apply that characteristic to your work as you attempt to begin well in online education?

_____

_____

_____

_____

_____

_____

_____

_____

Personal Reflection

Mastering the skill of time management is critical for success in college and beyond. Time is one of our most powerful personal resources; the better we manage it, the more likely we are to achieve our goals and gain control of our lives.

> Ponder Galatians 6:7 and 6:9: "Do not be deceived: God cannot be mocked. A man reaps what he sows" (NIV). "Let us not become weary in doing good, for at the proper time, we will reap a harvest if we do not give up." (NIV)

Do you see the relationship between these two verses as they relate to your use of time? Consider the implications of procrastination versus timeliness in light of these verses. What do they have to say about your stewardship of the time God has given you? Think about what your responsibilities are in regard to your use of time. Do you need to make any changes? Make some notes here about what you think needs to change:

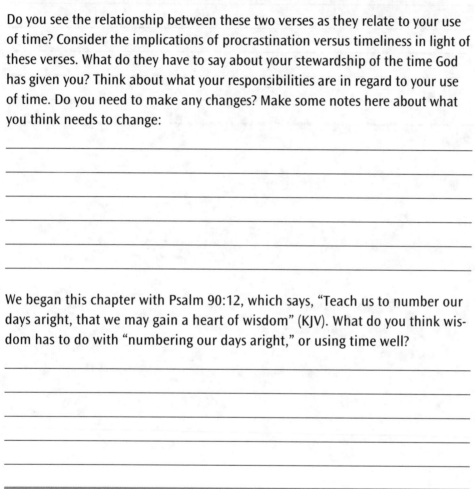

_____

_____

_____

_____

_____

_____

We began this chapter with Psalm 90:12, which says, "Teach us to number our days aright, that we may gain a heart of wisdom" (KJV). What do you think wisdom has to do with "numbering our days aright," or using time well?

_____

_____

_____

_____

_____

Personal Reflection

In Luke 2:53, it says that "Jesus grew in wisdom and stature and favor with God and men" (NIV). What does that verse indicate to you about the balance we should try to achieve in our lives? How does this balance look when you evaluate your use of time?

_____

_____

_____

_____

_____

_____

_____

TOOL BOX

Attaining Self-Awareness

Focus 2—The Liberty University Career Center has adopted the Focus 2 software to assist you in the process of assessing your interests, options, talents, and values. Liberty University students may register and use the tool for free. Once registered, you will work your way through a series of self-assessments, each designed to explore and expose different aspects of your interests, talents, and values. Upon completing the assessments, you will be able to explore a large database of degree and career options, each cross-referenced against your results in order to show you which are most compatible with your goals.

Establishing Goals

Programs at Liberty—Having explored which degrees may be best suited for your interests and talents, you can jump on the Liberty University website to review the different degree options available to you. With over 250 programs, you are sure to find something that piques your interest.
  www.liberty.edu/admissions

Degree Completion Plan Audit—Once you have chosen a specific degree program, Liberty's Degree Completion Plan (DCP) Audit can help keep you on track. Your personal degree audit is located within your Liberty University account. Here you will be able to see where your transfer credits fit into your existing program, the courses you are currently enrolled in, as well as a listing of the courses you need to take in order to complete your program.

Course Guides—After you use the DCP Audit to determine which classes you need to take, you can use the Liberty University Course Guides to help you narrow down your exact choices for the next term. Each course guide offers you a look at the course syllabus, as well as the schedule of readings and assignments. This information is extremely valuable when you are trying to determine what your workload will be for the next term.
  www.liberty.edu/online/course-guides

Course Sequencing—Each degree completion plan lists a suggested course sequence. Following this suggested order of classes will ensure that you are fully prepared for the next level of courses in your program.

Academic Advising—While Liberty University does everything possible to provide a comprehensive list of tools for the completely independent learner, there are always those who would prefer to speak with a live person when planning their next courses or making decisions that will affect their degree program. If you are that type of person, Liberty has a dedicated team of Academic Advisors to assist you. Advising is available by email, online chat, and by phone.

www.liberty.edu/online/academic-advisors

Staying Motivated

Aside from the plethora of tools that Liberty University has made available to help you set your goals, there are an even larger number of tools to help you stay motivated and achieve your goals.

Degree Completion Plan (DCP) Audit—Mentioned earlier, this tool will plug each course you take into your own custom degree plan. Watching your plan fill up as you near completion acts as a huge motivational tool.

Calendars—As calendars are available in both paper and electronic formats, these are a wonderful tool that any student can use to plot out short-term, mid-range, and long-term goals. Most electronic calendars will even sync across your devices, enabling you to keep close tabs on your progress.

Applications and Sites—Beyond the basic calendar, there are a vast array of goal-setting and motivational tools. Some of these are easily accessible checklists enabling you to map out the short-term steps toward a larger goal. As you check off the smaller items on your list, you see a nice visual representation of your progress. More aggressive applications will allow you to sign up for an account, set a series of goals, and then have your bank account charged a small fee if you happen to wander off course. You can review the Breaking Ground website for a listing of various applications and sites, along with brief descriptions.

Additional resources, and links to specific sites, worksheets, and apps can be located by accessing the Breaking Ground website:

(www.breakinggroundlu.com)

References

Chartoff, R., Tempeton, K. K., Winkler, C., Winkler, D. (Producer), & Stallone, S. (Director). (2006). *Rocky Balboa* [Motion picture]. United States: Metro-Goldwyn-Mayer.

Chartoff, R., Winkler, I. (Producer) & Avildsen, J. G. (Director). (1976). *Rocky* [Motion Picture]. United States: United Artists.

Chu, A. H. C., & Cho, J. N. (2005). Rethinking procrastination: Positive effects of "active" procrastination behavior on attitudes and performance. *The Journal of Social Psychology, 145*(3), 245–264.

Determination. (n.d.). In *Merriam-Webster.com*. Retrieved from http://www.merriam-webster.com/dictionary/determination

Diligent. (n.d.). In *Merriam-Webster.com*. Retrieved from http://www.merriam-webster.com/dictionary/diligent

Doran, G. T. (1981). There's a S.M.A.R.T. way to write management's goals and objectives. *Management Review, 70*(11), 35–36.

Erickson, B. L., Peters, C. B., & Strommer, D. W. (2006). *Teaching first-year college students.* San Francisco, CA: Jossey-Bass.

Faithfulness. (n.d.). In *Merriam-Webster.com*. Retrieved from http://www.merriam-webster.com/dictionary/faithful

Falwell, J. (1973). *Capturing a town for Christ.* Old Tappan, NJ: Fleming H. Revell.

Falwell, J. (1997). *Falwell: An autobiography.* Lynchburg, VA: Liberty House Publishers.

Falwell, J. (2014). *Press quotes.* Retrieved from http://www.liberty.edu/aboutliberty/index.cfm?PID = 26726

Falwell, M. (2008). *Jerry Falwell: His life and legacy.* New York, NY: Howard Books.

Honesty. (n.d.). In *Merriam-Webster.com*. Retrieved from http://www.merriam-webster .com/dictionary/honesty

Jordan, M. (2006). Goal setting strategies. *Charter, 77*(1), 36–37. Retrieved from http://search.proquest.com/docview/195553684?accountid = 12085

Maxwell, J. C. (2004). *Today matters: 12 daily practices to guarantee tomorrow's success.* New York: Warner Faith.

McKay, D. (2009). *Dr. Elmer Towns speaks at convocation.* Retrieved from http://www.liberty.edu/news/index.cfm?PID = 18495&MID = 5840

Meyer, P. J. (2003). *Attitude is everything: If you want to succeed above and beyond.* Waco, TX: Meyer Resource Group.

Miller, R. L. (2007). Farewell to my boss and friend, Dr. Jerry Falwell. *The Biblical Evangelist, 38*(4). Retrieved from http://www.biblicalevangelist.org/index.php?id = 539&issue = Volume + 38 % 2C + Number + 4

Morisano, D., Hirsh, J. B., Peterson, J. B., Pihl, R. O., & Shore, B. M. (2010). Setting, elaborating, and reflecting on personal goals improves academic performance. *Journal of Applied Psychology, 95*(2), 255–264. DOI:10.1037/a0018478

Myers, D. G. (2000). The funds, friends, and faith of happy people. *American Psychologist, 55*, 56–67.

Organization. (n.d.). In *Merriam-Webster.com*. Retrieved from http://www.merriam-webster.com/dictionary/organization

Procrastination. (2015). In *TheFreeDictionary.com*. Retrieved February 24, 2015 from http://www.thefreedictionary.com/dictionary/procrastination

Procrastination. (2015). In *Merriam-Webster.com*. Retrieved February 24, 2015, from http://www.merriam-webster.com/dictionary/procrastination

Rhodewalt, F., & Vohs, K. D. (2005). Defensive strategies, motivation, and the self. In A. Elliot & C. Dweck (Eds.), *Handbook of competence and motivation* (pp. 548–565). New York, NY: Guilford Press.

Roy, S. (2013, February 1). Seeing success through God's eyes: God sees. *Christianity Today; Men of Integrity*. Retrieved from http://www.christianitytoday.com/moi/2013/001/february/god-sees.html

Self-reflection. (n.d.). In *Merriam-Webster.com*. Retrieved from http://www.merriam-webster.com/dictionary/self-reflection

Sherman, M. (2014, June 20). Why we don't give each other a break: Annoyed? Peeved? The fundamental attribution error explains it all. *Psychology Today*. Retrieved from https://www.psychologytoday.com/blog/real-men-dont-write-blogs/201406/why-we-dont-give-each-other-break

Steel, P. (2007). The nature of procrastination: A meta-analytic and theoretical-review of quintessential self-regulatory failure. *Psychological Bulletin, 133*(1), 65–94. DOI: 10.1037/0033-2909.133.1.65

Success. (n.d.). In *Merriam-Webster.com*. Retrieved from http://www.merriam-webster.com/dictionary/success

Velazquez, E. (2015). How Ali Became the Greatest. *Muscle and Performance*. Retrieved March 4, 2015 from http://www.muscleandperformancemag.com/training/2012/2/how-ali-became-the-greatest

Ward, T. (2013, September 24). Success is overrated. *Relevant Magazine*. Retrieved from http://www.relevantmagazine.com/life/career-money/success-overrated#wHuJbFUVmxlXZYDA.99

Watkins, R. (2004). Defining success. *Distance Learning, 1*(2), 33–34. Retrieved from http://search.proquest.com/docview/230683851?accountid=12085

Wisdom. (n.d.). In *Merriam-Webster.com*. Retrieved from http://www.merriam-webster.com/dictionary/wisdom

Younkins, E. W. (2012). Ayn Rand's Objectivist virtues as the foundation for morality and success in business. *Journal of Ayn Rand Studies, 12*(2), 237–262. Retrieved from http://www.quebecoislibre.org/jars12_2eyounkins-2.pdf

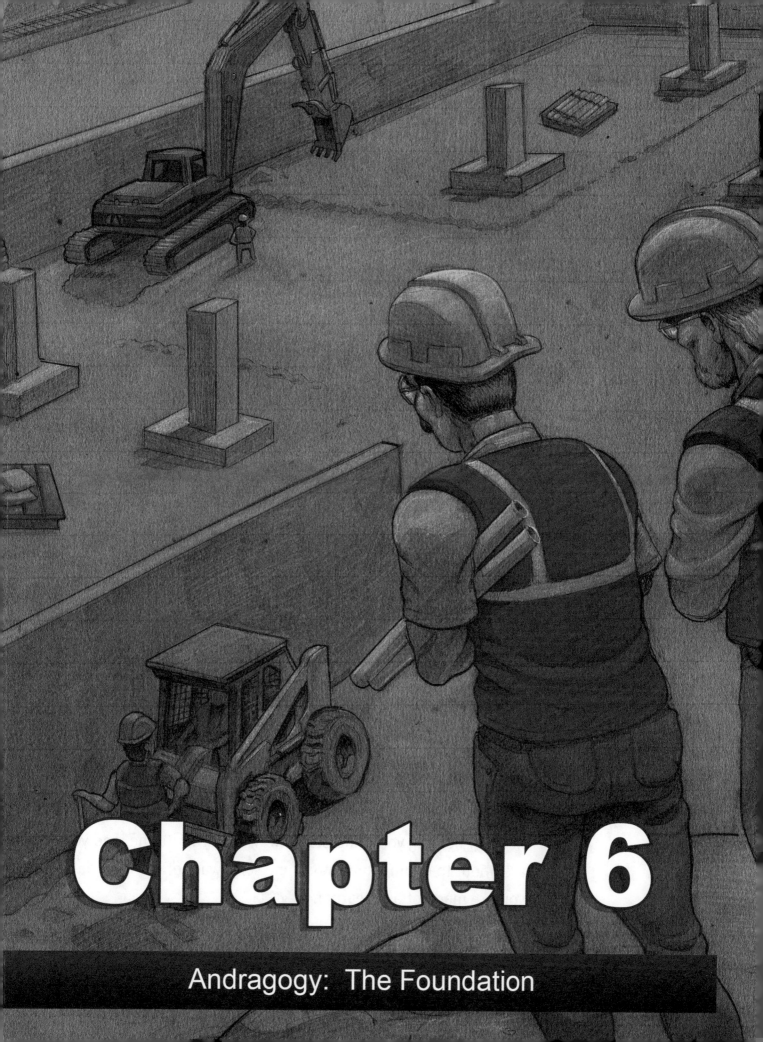

Chapter 6

Andragogy: The Foundation

In this chapter, you will:

- Define pedagogy and andragogy.
- Explore what makes you an adult learner.
- Examine the six assumptions of andragogy.

THE FOUNDATION

The task of establishing a firm foundation is pivotal to the success of any building project. If the appropriate calculations are not done, your foundation may not support the load that will eventually bear down on it. If the wrong material is chosen, then the foundation may develop cracks, leaks, or even cave in from the pressure of the surrounding dirt. Establishing a foundation for your educational journey is every bit as important and every bit as technical. There are considerations you must make in order to ensure that you will hold up under the pressure, and you need to know what material you are working with in order to avoid cracks and leaks. Coming to understand who you are as an adult learner will help you to establish the firm foundation you need by helping you understand how to distribute the load you are about to endure and to become self-aware of the material you are made of as a learner.

© 2013 by iQoncept. Used under license of Shutterstock, Inc.

I Cor. 3:11,
"For no one can lay any foundation other than what is being laid, which is Jesus Christ" (NET).

THE CORNERSTONE

John 14:1–2, "Let not your heart be troubled: ye believe in God, believe also in me. In my Father's house are many mansions: if it were not so, I would have told you. I go to prepare a place for you" (KJV).

"Imagine yourself as a living house. God comes in to rebuild that house. At first, perhaps, you can understand what He is doing. He is getting the drains right and stopping the leaks in the roof and so on; you knew that those jobs needed doing and so you are not surprised. But presently He starts knocking the house about in a way that hurts abominably and does not seem to make any sense. What on earth is He up to? The explanation is that He is building quite a different house from the one you thought of—throwing out a new wing here, putting on an extra floor there, running up towers, making courtyards. You thought you were being made into a decent little cottage: but He is building a palace. He intends to come and live in it Himself" (Lewis, 1996, p. 176).

Photo courtesy of David Duncan (Liberty University).

Build a strong foundation by understanding how you learn.

I put off completing my master's degree for many years and for a variety of reasons, but the three primary ones were insecurity, time investment, and convenience. Through it all, the Lord was at work, and I wondered "What on earth is He up to?"

When I originally considered pursuing my master's degree, I was terribly insecure. I honestly didn't think I was smart enough to earn a master's degree; all of the people I knew with a graduate degree were intellectual and interesting. When I compared myself to them, I just didn't think that I measured up. Additionally, the degree I wanted required that I take the Graduate Record Exam (GRE) in order to complete the application process. Realizing this, test anxiety immediately set in, fueling my insecurity, so I decided to wait until I thought I was smarter or until I had the time to study to prepare for it.

Additionally, I did not feel that I had the time to invest in the degree because I taught English to high school students; my day was long and filled with preparing lessons, helping students, and grading papers. When I got home, the last thing I wanted to do was study for a class of my own. I simply had no time if I wanted to have a life outside of the classroom.

Finally, I dreaded the inconvenience of attending a physical campus. I was older now, and the fun of attending courses with younger students just didn't inspire like it did when I was working on my undergraduate degree. Also, when I explored my degree options, I would have to travel to campus to attend courses. Though campus was only 30 minutes away, this would be an hour of my day that would be erased as a result of travel time. This simply would not do!

My fears, however, began to subside a little when I discovered that Liberty University was offering my degree in the online format. Finally, a school had established a program meant for the busy adult with responsibilities and a fast-paced life! I would be able to work from home for all of my coursework, and even though I still had to take the dreaded GRE, I recognized that this new opportunity was worth setting aside some fun time to prepare for the test. My husband, Terry, decided to take the GRE, too, so he and I spent quality time together at restaurants and coffee shops with flashcards of Latin roots and a GRE study book. Finally, Terry and I passed the test, applied for our programs, and began working toward degree completion.

Many years later, I recognized that God was at work in my life, as C. S. Lewis' quote suggests. He was breaking down the walls that I had built up with my fears of being inconvenienced, my reluctance to surrender valuable relaxing time, and my feelings of insecurity; He wanted to build me up with the truth of His Word that "I can do all things through Christ who strengthens me" (Philippians 4:13, NKJV). He wanted to make me palatial, and I was almost willing to settle on the cottage.

As you learn what it means to be an adult learner, with all of your responsibilities and people in your care, remember Philippians 4:6–7, "Be anxious for nothing, but in everything by prayer and supplication, with thanksgiving, let your requests be made known to God; and the peace of God, which surpasses all understanding, will guard your hearts and minds through Christ Jesus" (NKJV). Don't let your fears get in the way of God's big, palatial plans for you! Let Jesus' words reassure you that though the growing pains may "hurt abominably and don't seem to make any sense" (Lewis, 1996, p. 176), He has big plans for you; "Let not your heart be troubled: ye believe in God, believe also in me. In my Father's house are many mansions: if it were not so, I would have told you. I go to prepare a place for you" (John 14:1–2, KJV).

The Lord "wanted to make me palatial, and I was almost willing to settle on the cottage."

Define Pedagogy and Andragogy

> Hebrews 5:13-14,
> "For everyone who lives on milk is inexperienced in the message of righteousness, because he is an infant. But solid food is for the mature, whose perceptions are trained by practice to discern both good and evil" (NET).

Hebrews 5:13–14 acts as an excellent illustration of the differences between pedagogy (ped-uh-goh-jee) and andragogy (an-druh-goh-jee), which are educational theories that seek to describe the different ways that children and adults learn. Like those who "live on milk," young learners typically require direction and guidance and often rely on a mature teacher to them. On the other hand, the adult learner has years of practice and experience, which they can refer to when attempting to solve a problem. Pedagogy and andragogy are commonly seen as competing perspectives on learning, separated by a distinct line-in-the-sand, with children on one side and adults on the other (Knowles, Holton & Swanson, 2011). However, the distinction between the two is not always so clear. As you dig into the concepts that define child and adult learners, you will see that the two theories are very well defined, but in real life there is often a significant amount of overlap.

Pedagogy

The term **pedagogy** comes from the Greek words, *paid*, meaning "child" and *agogus*, meaning "leader of." Put the two together, and it is easy to see how the term pedagogy has come to be defined as "the art and science of teaching children" (Knowles et al., 2011, loc. 1160). The concept of teaching children has existed since Cain and Abel but was developed into a more formal structure during the seventh century in Europe. Over time, the concept evolved from a framework for educating children into a much broader theory of educating in general, coming to be defined as "the art and science of teaching" (Wurm, 2005, p. 159). However, the original concept of pedagogy as a theory for educating children seems to be making a comeback as theories of adult learning emerge.

2013 by hxdbzxy. Used under license of Shutterstock, Inc.

With pedagogy, the learner is conditioned to be dependent upon the instructor. Adults tend to be far more independent, and self-directed (Knowles et al., 2011, loc. 2135).

Pedagogy is *broadly* defined by the following assumptions of the learner:

- **Need to know**—It is not essential that the learner understand "why" he or she needs to learn.

- **Self-concept**—The learner is conditioned to be dependent upon the instructor for direction.

- **Experience**—The learner has a limited amount of experience with the subject matter and must rely upon the teacher's experience and knowledge.

- **Readiness to learn**—The learner has no say in determining when learning will take place. This is the responsibility of the instructor.

- **Orientation to learning**—Learning is centered on the content being taught and is intended for future application.

- **Motivation to learn**—The learner is motivated, primarily, by external factors.

(Knowles et al., 2011)

Andragogy

The term **andragogy** comes from the Greek words *aner*, meaning "man," and *agogus*, meaning "leader of." So, andragogy is defined as "the art and science of helping adults learn." (Knowles et al., 2011, loc. 5019). The concept of andragogy, or adult learning, has existed as a formal inquiry since the early 1800s, when Alexander Kapp first published a study regarding the matter. Between 1833 and the mid-1900s, bits and pieces were added to the idea of how adults learn, but no formal, cohesive theory had been established. Through the early 1900s, the concept of andragogy began to take shape, and in the 1960s, Malcolm Knowles popularized the concept as a single, cohesive way of understanding how adults learn (Chan, 2010).

Andragogy is *broadly* defined by the following assumptions of the learner:

- **Need to know**—The learner typically needs to understand "why" something is important before he or she will be open to a new learning experience.

- **Self-concept**—The learner is independent and self-directed.

- **Experience**—The learner possesses a vast set of experiences, which act as a foundation for learning new information.

- **Readiness to learn**—Learning should be relevant and is best conducted when the learner is in a transitional stage regarding his or her social role.

Terry Conner

"In childhood you are establishing the foundation for your education, and in adulthood, you are adding on or enhancing the building by applying theories to your education and your career."

Cheryl

"Going to school as an adult learner is dramatically different than as a younger 'college' student."

- **Orientation to learning**—The learner is a problem solver who learns best in the context of real-world situations that are immediately applicable.

- **Motivation to learn**—The learner is motivated by primarily internal factors.

(Knowles et al., 2011; Taylor & Kroth, 2009; Wurm, 2005)

While pedagogy and andragogy tend to be viewed as competing theories—one describing the way that children learn and the other describing how adults learn—this does not have to be the case. People develop varying levels of self-directedness and independence as they gain experience in life. Some people will become more independent very early on, while others may remain more dependent until later in life. This means that there is plenty of room for these two theories to overlap with one another. (Knowles et al., 2011; Wurm, 2005).

Considering this brief introduction to the concepts of pedagogy and andragogy, it is easy to see how we can observe the principles of each at play in our key verse, Hebrews 5:13–14. The principles of pedagogy can be seen in those who have gone back to needing milk. These believers need more guidance and direction in their spiritual journey, much like a child who relies upon a teacher for direction and experience. Meanwhile, more mature believers subsist on solid food. As adult learners, they need less direction and guidance in their walk, and their experience in the faith enables them to make sound, godly, decisions.

Tim

"There is definitely a major difference between when I was learning at a younger age and how I learn now. I have found 'shortcuts' that have helped me more than I ever imagined. Some of these shortcuts have allowed me to learn at a faster pace and help me complete my course work on time."

Personal Reflection

Take a moment to fill in the following chart with the primary assumptions of pedagogy and andragogy. Be sure to rephrase each assumption in your own words, as this will help you to internalize the concepts.

Pedagogy		Andragogy
	Need to know	
	Self-concept	
	Experience	
	Readiness to learn	

Pedagogy		Andragogy
	Orientation to learn	
	Motivation to learn	

Cheryl

"As a young college student (living on campus), the only things I had to focus on were my education and my social life. As an adult learner, I am responsible for more than just me. My 'time' no longer belongs to 'me.' I must insert here, that I would have it no other way."

Think about the aforementioned definitions, then make a list of learning experiences in your life that have fallen into each of these two categories. Try to list at least five in each column. This exercise allows you to relate each concept with experiences you are already familiar with. Each connection you make will make it easier for you to remember what these concepts mean.

Pedagogy
For example:
High school class, U.S. History

Andragogy

Learning new software on YouTube

Explore What Makes You an Adult Learner

I Cor. 13:11,
"When I was a child, I talked like a child, I thought like a child, I reasoned like a child. But when I became an adult, I set aside childish ways" (NET).

Where do you fall in the scheme of things? If you have a little bit of age on you, then you may be pretty quick to jump on the adult learning band wagon, but what about those of you who are just coming out of high school? Where do you fit? Many of you might not consider yourselves to be "adults" yet. At the same time, some of you who have been an adult for quite some time now. The question you need to ask yourself is, when should you consider yourself an adult?

Here are some possible ways we could determine if a person is an adult:

- **Biologically**—Based on the ability of the individual to reproduce

- **Legally**—As the laws of a given jurisdiction dictate that an individual has the rights of an adult

- **Socially**—As an individual takes on roles that would typically be associated with being an adult

- **Psychologically**—Once an individual comes to see him- or herself as independent

(Knowles et al., 2011; Taylor & Kroth, 2009)

Which of these definitions should we use? Well, it would be hard to argue that you suddenly became an adult in an instant, at least as it relates to your willingness or ability to learn. So, it would be safe to say that the biological or legal definitions may not be the best definitions to help us in understanding where you fall in the spectrum of learning. On the other hand, we can see that both the social and psychological definitions describe the kinds of thought processes we would expect to be associated with an adult learner. For our purposes, it might be best to consider the implications of combining these two definitions as we explore the assumptions of how adults learn (Knowles et al., 2011).

Roger

"As an adult returning to the classroom after many years, I lacked confidence. I wondered if I could really do the work and complete with other, brighter, younger students. After the first class, I realized that I had the tools of perseverance, a strong internal drive to achieve, proven time management experience, greater organizational skills, and maturity. I didn't have these things as a young college student."

© 2013 by Gelpi JM. Used under license of Shutterstock, Inc.

"When should you consider yourself an adult?"

Examine the Six Assumptions of Andragogy

Matthew 16:5–12,

"When the disciples went to the other side, they forgot to take bread. 'Watch out,' Jesus said to them, 'Beware of the yeast of the Pharisees and Sadducees.' So they began to discuss this among themselves, saying, 'It is because we brought no bread.' When Jesus learned of this, he said, 'You who have such little faith! Why are you arguing among yourselves about having no bread? Do you still not understand? Don't you remember the five loaves for the five thousand, and how many baskets you took up? Or the seven loaves for the four thousand and how many baskets you took up? How could you not understand that I was not speaking to you about bread? But beware of the yeast of the Pharisees and Sadducees!' Then they understood that he had not told them to be on guard against the yeast in bread, but against the teaching of the Pharisees and Sadducees" (NET).

1. Need to Know

Ruth

Q: *Were you surprised in the difference in your learning as an adult, compared to what you remember when you were in school as a child?*

A: *"No, I wasn't surprised. I knew I would appreciate it more and wanted to learn."*

The disciples didn't really get it; they figured that Jesus' warning had to mean something important, but what was it? They were struggling to grasp what Jesus was saying to them about the yeast. This was an important warning, but they lacked the appropriate understanding to appreciate it. They didn't know *why* it was important. So, Jesus addressed them again; this time He was very clear about why this statement was so important. Only then did the disciples come to understand what Jesus was trying to tell them. They came to understand *why* Jesus' statement was so profound, and suddenly, His words were no longer lost on them.

The concept of "need to know" describes the adult learners' need to understand *why* a particular topic is valuable to them before they invest the time and effort into learning about it (Knowles et al., 2011; Merriam & Bierema, 2013; Taylor & Kroth, 2009). Adult learners are considered to be very practical and focused on real-world issues that exist in their lives (Wurm, 2005); before valuable time can be set aside to learn something new, they want to be sure that the return is worth the investment. They are not likely to set aside an excessive amount of time to learn about something that is not going to impact their lives (Knowles et al., 2011; Taylor & Kroth, 2009; Wurm, 2005).

What this means for you, as an online adult learner, is that you will want to spend some time before each term, class, week, or assignment, assessing the impact that the information you are about to learn will have on your life. Some classes or assignments in your major could be easy to assess as they directly relate to your goals, but what about classes or assignments that are difficult to connect with? Do they lack value for you? The most likely answer is no, but this doesn't mean that you won't need to dig a little to make a connection. A good place to start your inquiry is in the syllabus, as it typically contains a detailed description and rationale for the course. If you are still struggling to find the relevance, email your instructors; they care deeply about their disciplines and would be more than willing to help.

In the passage below, Dr. Emily W. Heady, Ph. D., Liberty University's Vice Provost for Undergraduate Education, the Dean of the College of General Studies, and English Professor explains the importance of a liberal arts education and how it relates to our "need to know" as adult learners. She emphasizes the connection between these elements and how a balanced learning experience can strengthen our ability to impact our culture for Christ.

Mary Dixon

"Adult learners can be wonderful leaders. Life experience has given them perspectives and opportunities that translate well into independent and creative thinking. Use those skills that you have developed and apply them to study and learning in the same way that you applied them to employment or negotiating life experience. Perseverance is a big asset and a great model for others to follow! You can show the less experienced learner a thing or two."

"Why" a Liberal Arts Education?

Emily W. Heady, Ph.D.

What Is a Liberal Arts University?

When I was a high school student beginning my college search, I received a number of recruiting letters and flyers from universities offering "liberal arts degrees." At the time, I didn't know what that meant—though, to be fair, I wasn't able to find a clear understanding of the liberal arts in many of the recruiting materials I reviewed either. I had a vague association that liberal arts universities had well-groomed campuses, small classes, and a vibrant arts scene, and generally, they did have all those things. What they also had—and what I didn't appreciate at the time—was a curriculum organized around the principles that have made American higher education the best in the world.

On a most basic level, a liberal arts university—and Liberty University counts itself among them—has a curriculum designed to give students a broad introduction to a variety of academic disciplines, such as math, science, literature, history, social science, and the arts. At most schools, this broad approach is reflected in general education core, that group of courses that all students must complete regardless of their majors. Liberty's accreditor SACS-COC, in fact, requires that the general education core cover a variety of disciplines, an approach that is common nationwide. For SACS-COC, the presence of a rich general education component differentiates a university from a trade school, which focuses more narrowly on the specific knowledge and skills used in a particular line of work. A trade school graduate will likely be a fine electrician or dental assistant, but she will not necessarily be able to adapt quickly or easily to a new career field. By contrast, because their training has focused less on particular job skills and procedures and more on broad competencies such as communication, critical thinking, and mathematical or scientific reasoning, graduates of a university are prepared not just to succeed in whatever job they attain after graduation, but also to adjust flexibly to the demands that nearly any workplace might present in the future. Their well-roundedness makes them broadly capable.

Universities that align themselves with the liberal arts tradition generally do an excellent job preparing well-rounded graduates, but unfortunately, many of them have lost the Christian ideals and beliefs underlying their pedagogical approach. In *On Christian Doctrine*, Augustine says he wants "every good and true Christian to understand that wherever truth may be found, it belongs to his Master" (II.18.28). A more pop-culture version of this statement, "All truth is God's truth," is so commonly quoted it seems cliché. Of course, knowing truth is not enough to assure a full and rich relationship with Christ, but the liberal arts university recognizes knowledge as an important part of truth-seeking, and it is set up to help students to find truth more readily. A liberal arts university that embraces the Christian underpinnings of its curriculum acknowledges that God can and should be visible in a variety of places in a variety of ways—through completing math problems and seeing the principles that organize the universe, through encountering literature and seeing the ways God uses language to speak to us, and through tracing the hand of providence in history. In so doing, it assures that its students have many opportunities to know God through the world He made.

On a daily basis, you may spend some time wondering why you have to take all the classes that are on your DCP. If you're training to be a pastor, why would you need to take MATH 115? Would it be better to take another homiletics class? Besides the obvious answer—that everyone needs to do math at some point in his life—a liberal arts university would answer that you need to take MATH 115 because mathematical reasoning skills are important for you to be well-rounded and adaptable. Beyond this, math has spiritual value, in that it is a powerful way of observing the logical principles by which creation functions. At Liberty, we try to make these connections between Christianity and the academic content of the courses obvious, not to foist a biblical application where it does not belong, but rather to reveal connections that we might have otherwise missed.

From a practical point of view, too, a liberal arts approach to education makes sense: it just works better. In his landmark book *The Idea of a University*, John Henry Newman argues that different types of knowledge represent different levels of learning, from shallow to extremely deep. The most basic sort of knowledge, which Newman calls *notional assent*, is something like book knowledge—an answer you have memorized in response to a question. This sort of knowledge, though basic, is important. In some areas that have little clear application to your life or career, you may not progress much beyond notional assent, but in other areas, book knowledge serves as a gateway to other more powerful types of learning. When you start making connections between book knowledge and the world you live in, you end up with a more powerful form of knowledge that Newman calls *real assent*. *Real assent* is knowledge that you know to be true because you have tested it out enough to know you believe it; it is something you know for yourself, not just because an authority told you so. The highest form of knowledge for Newman, the *illative sense*, is knowledge that runs so deep in a person that it becomes a way of understanding the world—something that becomes a means of organizing new information as it comes. It is knowledge that becomes part of the very way we think.

At a liberal arts university, as you tour through various disciplines and see truth from a variety of perspectives, you'll begin to see connections: the ways, for instance, that biblical hermeneutics and literary scholarship intertwine; the applications of statistics to organizational behavior; the ways that history can help us to understand current events—even the ways that math can enrich your pastoral ministry. These connections drive knowledge more deeply into you, past the part of your brain that memorizes answers and into the part of the self that helps you to make wise decisions. Connections turn notional assents into real assents, and real assents, if practiced for long enough, start to become part of the self. Recent research on brain-based pedagogy has arrived at similar conclusions: the more connections we make when we learn, the better and more permanent that learning is.

Because of the wide variety of subjects you will encounter at Liberty, and because you'll be asked to complete coursework in areas that may sound unappetizing—or downright awful—to you, you may have days where you wish you were a student at a trade school, or that you could do nothing but take classes in your major. When those moments come, though, you can know with confidence that the challenges you are facing will prepare you both to be a better follower of Christ now and to be a better practitioner of your chosen career in the future. Your hard work—even in fields that you don't want to plow—will be rewarded with a different way of seeing God's work in the world. Your disciplined efforts to see things from more than one perspective will require your brain to do unfamiliar and difficult things, but it will also make you much more able to understand the perspectives of people who are not like you, who do not think like you, and who cannot meet you in the middle. Your training, in short, will enable you to live your own life with excellence and to generously reach out to others in ways you couldn't do before—and in ways that others most likely will not be able to do for you.

Personal Reflection

How might this explanation of a liberal arts education help to satisfy your "need to know" when you are faced with taking a course in your degree program that you are not excited about? How might that impact your learning experience in that class?

_____

_____

_____

How might your learning experience be different if you had not learned about the intent of a liberal arts education, and your "need to know" had not been satisfied?

_____

_____

_____

_____

2. Self-Concept

1 Peter 2:16, "Live as free people, not using your freedom as a pretext for evil, but as God's slaves" (NET).

According to I Peter 2:16, you are to live as a free person beholden only to God. You have a free mind and a free spirit, which lead you down paths of interest and discovery. You are naturally inclined to be self-directing and independent. Your natural state is to gravitate away from the direction of your parents and teachers and to head off into the world to live and learn.

The assumption of "self-concept" informs us that adult learners are independent and self-directed individuals (Knowles et al., 2011; Taylor & Kroth, 2009; Wurm, 2005). They are used to taking responsibility for themselves and making their own decisions, so they tend to struggle with situations where they feel that the ability to decide for themselves has been taken away. Adult learners desire to be viewed as independent and capable of making decisions on their own and may shut down when placed in a learning situation where their independence appears to be overlooked (Knowles et al., 2011; Merriam & Bierema, 2013; Taylor & Kroth, 2009). Adult learners are most invested when they are actively engaged in the learning process, meaning they are able to make choices and decisions regarding their learning (Wurm, 2005).

As an online college student and an adult learner, you have a significant amount of choice in deciding when, where, and how you will go about completing your work, but there are still some limits, which are to be expected. You have the benefit of being able to decide which program you would like to pursue and even the order in which you will take many of your classes. At the same time, there are a number of required courses that you may need to take in order to complete your degree. This can be a big sticking point for students. It is not unusual to hear the question, "I'm studying to be a pastor. Why do I need to take a math class?" The resistance to the math class is based, partially, on the student feeling that his or her decision-making ability has been taken away. In this scenario, it would be best to think back to the concept of "need to know" and try to find the value in the course that is being required. Understanding this need will help you address these issues when you encounter them.

Maddy

Q: *Were you surprised in the difference in your learning as an adult, compared to what you remember when you were in school as a child? What differences were there?*

A: "The main difference I've noticed is that now I actually have to study. It wasn't really a surprise, because I had been told that college would be harder than any other schooling I had faced. It was more of a disappointment that adults were right."

Terry

Q: *Were you surprised in the difference in your learning as an adult, compared to what you remember when you were in school as a child?*

A: "Not so much the difference between how I learned, but my investment in that learning. As a child, it was more passive, now as an adult I'm actively engaged in the material and applying it to my life as I go through the program, which is pretty cool."

Personal Reflection

Can you recall a situation that you have faced as an adult, where you resisted a learning opportunity due to feeling that your decision-making ability was taken away?

Yes / No

Since awareness is the key to avoiding problems, jot down some of the issues related to self-concept you might face as you work to complete your degree. Then, take a minute to brainstorm a couple of strategies to keep these issues from becoming obstacles.

Issues	Strategies

Roger

"When I first entered college at age 19, I was immature, inexperienced, trying to figure out what I wanted to do. I procrastinated and waited till the last minute to study or get my homework completed. I occasionally skipped classes and did not have the same passion and drive to achieve. By the time I graduated, I had developed better skills but it was not there at the beginning. I was satisfied with C's."

3. Prior Experience

Hebrews 5:14, "But solid food is for the mature, whose perceptions are trained by practice to discern both good and evil" (NET).

As an adult believer, you are able to analyze new spiritual teachings by testing them against what you already know about God based on biblical truth. You have the experience to know that each new teaching must be filtered through Scripture. If it holds up with what you know to be true in the Bible, you may incorporate this concept into your knowledge base. At the same time, you can reject any new spiritual teaching that does not stand up to the test of Scripture.

The concept of "prior experience" brings several different issues to the table. It reminds us that adult learners bring a vast amount of life experience with them when they enter the classroom and that their store of experience will continue to grow over time (Knowles et al., 2011; Taylor & Kroth, 2009). These experiences are the learners' best resource for learning and act as a foundation upon which to build new understandings and through which they can test the validity of new information (Merriam & Bierema, 2013; Taylor & Kroth, 2009; Wurm, 2005). Adult learners are deeply connected to their experiences and see them as part of who they are as a person. Keep in mind that this experience also has the potential to hinder the learning experience. With a wealth of life experience comes an established way of thinking. Those deeply routed thoughts and views can make it difficult for adult learners to open themselves to new learning experiences. (Knowles et al., 2011; Merriam & Bierema, 2013).

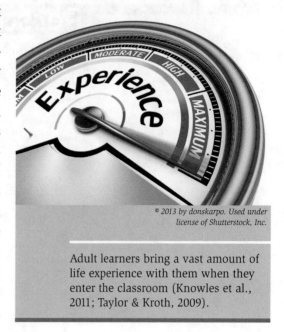

© 2013 by donskarpo. Used under license of Shutterstock, Inc.

Adult learners bring a vast amount of life experience with them when they enter the classroom (Knowles et al., 2011; Taylor & Kroth, 2009).

Learning from a distance can be difficult, but you have the opportunity to make it an extremely personal endeavor. You have a storehouse of past experiences that you can use to help you connect with the information in your online classes. Taking a basic math course can be connected to your experiences paying the household bills or managing a small business. Studying a passage of Scripture on forgiveness can be connected to several past experiences where you struggled to forgive someone, and a lesson on how adults learn can be related back to previous learning experiences you have had at work or in other educational environments. The key is to use these experiences to connect with and remember the information you are learning. They will help you to internalize the concepts, which will increase the likelihood that you will store the information in your long-term memory.

Katie Robinson

"Adult learners bring something to learning that other students cannot: experience. Because of this advantage, adult learners have the unique opportunity to enrich their learning with past experience opposed to attempting to apply learning to future experience, which can be further disconnected."

Additionally, adult learners use their past experience to help them determine the validity of new information. As you listen to information in your classes, you are much more prone to accept or dismiss things based on your past experiences with similar situations or information. Information that does not pass the sniff test can be addressed with peers or the instructor. You might find that this new information needs to be considered in the light of experience you do not yet possess or that the specific concept is simply not as clear-cut as you thought. Either way, you have the potential to gain a deeper understanding by using your experiences as you consider what you are learning.

Personal Reflection

Take a moment to describe a situation where considering your past experience has helped you to understand new information.

_____

_____

_____

_____

_____

List a couple of experiences from your life that you use to filter new information.

_____

_____

_____

_____

_____

4. Readiness to Learn

Acts 3:19, "Therefore repent and turn back so that your sins may be wiped out" (NET).

One moment you are set in your life, and the next you experience a transition like no other: you have made a decision to become a follower of Christ, but you have so much to learn. Can you think of a time when you wanted to read or know more? You are voracious in your consumption of information regarding your newfound faith. You are completely open and ready to learn.

Adult learners' "readiness to learn" is heavily related to their social role, but they are most receptive to learning when they are transitioning into a new social role (Knowles et al., 2011; Merriam & Bierema, 2013; Taylor & Kroth, 2009). This period of transition creates what is referred to as a "teachable moment" where the learner is open to new information (Merriam & Bierema, 2013). Results of large-scale polling show that the vast majority of adults who were involved in some type of formal education cited their jobs as the reason (Merriam, Caffarella, & Baumgartner as cited in Merriam & Bierema, 2013).

Office personnel will maintain their job readiness but are not typically open to learning about management tasks unless the possibility of moving into a management position exists. A mother of 20 years loves her children, but she most likely will not read through a stack of parenting books, while

Emily

"In college you actually want to learn more and retain it all. In high school, you learn it and as long as you pass your test you don't really care if you remember it in the long run."

an expectant mother tends to read anything she can get her hands on that relates to parenting.

If you are among the vast majority of adults, you have returned to school for some transitional reason related to work. Some of you have been promoted or are seeking a promotion, some of you are transitioning to a new career field, and others of you are trying to transition from high school into your first career. You are in the middle of your "teachable moment" and eager to absorb the knowledge before you.

Personal Reflection

In the first column, make a list of the major transitional stages or life-tasks in which you were most open to learning new information. In the second column, describe what you were most open to learn about.

Transition/life-task   **What did you want to learn?**

_____   _____

_____   _____

_____   _____

_____   _____

5. Orientation to Learn

> 2 Timothy 3:16–17, "Every scripture is inspired by God and useful for teaching, for reproof, for correction, and for training in righteousness, that the person dedicated to God may be capable and equipped for every good work" (NET).

As believers, we turn to the Scriptures on a daily basis for spiritual sustenance, but we also find ourselves searching the Bible or praying for answers when we encounter problems in life.

If a close friend does something to harm you, you might seek guidance and find an answer in Matt 18:15–17:

> "If your brother sins, go and show him his fault when the two of you are alone. If he listens to you, you have regained your brother. But if he does not listen, take one or two others with you, so that at the testimony of two or three witnesses every matter may be established. If he refuses to listen to them, tell it to the church. If he refuses to listen to the church, treat him like a Gentile or a tax collector" (NET).

If you are struggling with anger, you might seek advice in Ephesians 4:26:

> "Be angry and do not sin; do not let the sun go down on the cause of your anger" (NET).

Emily

"You have to really spend time studying and apply [what you are learning] to life to retain it."

Adult learners want to be able to utilize the new information they are learning immediately in order to solve real-world problems (Merriam & Bierema, 2013; Taylor & Kroth, 2009).

Nathaniel Valle

"The best way to apply information from this course is by thinking not only about what you're learning, but how you interact with your professor to master whatever you're studying. Interacting with your instructor through andragogical instruction will help you realize that nearly every career utilizes some type of it. Whether in your college courses or your personal life, allow yourself to accept constructive criticism and never be afraid to ask any questions!"

If you were beginning a new marriage, you might spend time studying 1 Corinthians 13:4–7:

"Love is patient, love is kind, it is not envious. Love does not brag, it is not puffed up. It is not rude, it is not self-serving, it is not easily angered or resentful. It is not glad about injustice, but rejoices in the truth. It bears all things, believes all things, hopes all things, endures all things" (NET).

The assumption of "orientation to learn" refers to the tendency of adult learners to be oriented toward learning when they feel it will assist them in solving a problem or performing a specific task (Knowles et al., 2011; Merriam & Bierema, 2013; Taylor & Kroth, 2009). Adult learners want to be able to utilize the new information they are learning immediately in order to solve real-world problems (Merriam & Bierema, 2013; Taylor & Kroth, 2009), so they desire learning situations that are practical in nature (Knowles et al., 2011; Wurm, 2005).

You have probably run into many situations where you needed to find the answer to a problem or needed to perform a task that you were unsure of, and you turned to the Internet. You may have searched for "how to tie a tie" or "How do I do _____ in Microsoft Excel?" or even something more serious such as "What are the treatment options for _____ type of cancer?" A friend of mine taught himself leatherworking because he could not find a wallet to suit his needs. The point is that adult learners are problem solvers; they seek information that they can immediately apply to their real-life situations. Some of the topics that adults research are not topics that they would even be interested in if the topic were not presenting them with some kind of problem to solve.

As you enter the realm of online education, your problem might be bigger than "how to tie a tie." You are looking for knowledge and a degree so that you can change careers, obtain a promotion, or find employment that will allow you to support your family. You believe that learning about a particular field and earning a degree in that field will help you to solve your problem. This is a long-term goal though, so it will be easy to lose sight of the finish line. Use the assumption of "orientation" to your advantage and think about how your individual classes and lessons can help you to solve everyday problems in your life. This will keep things relevant and help you to stay motivated as you work toward your degree.

Personal Reflection

Use this exercise to explore the application of this principle in your own life. In the space provided, describe a real-world problem that you needed to solve, then provide an explanation as to how you went about learning the information necessary to solve the problem.

For Example:

Problem: Needed to learn how to combine two cells into one in Excel 2010 for a project.

Solution: I searched the Internet for "Combine words from two cells into a single cell in Excel 2010." The results returned a YouTube video that I was able to watch. I learned how to use the "concat" formula to accomplish my goal.

Problem: _____

Solution: _____

_____

_____

_____

Problem: _____

Solution: _____

_____

_____

_____

6. Motivation to Learn

Matt 6:21, "For where your treasure is, there your heart will be also" (NET).

Money itself is not a horrible thing, but the love of money is warned against explicitly. Money is just an item, something that is external to your being. You might want it, or need it, so that you can pay bills or buy groceries, but the internal motivation might actually be that you need to support your family. When you love money, then money becomes the object or goal; you chase the money in the hopes that it will bring you satisfaction. In either situation, it is the internal motivations that drive you toward your goal.

The assumption of "motivation to learn" informs us that adult learners are internally motivated to learn (Knowles et al., 2011; Merriam & Bierema, 2013; Taylor & Kroth, 2009) in order to achieve their goals and gain personal fulfillment (Merriam & Bierema, 2013; Taylor & Kroth, 2009). The driving

T. Marcus Christian

"One of the best things to remember about Andragogy is that it describes the motivation for adult learning. This can be your motivation to be the first in your family to complete college or it can be the motivation to get a new job. Whatever motivates you to work hard is going to be the thing that gets you your degree."

forces behind adult learners' motivations are their "values, beliefs, and opinions" (Wurm, 2005, p. 160). When a learning situation is presented that is not initiated by an internal motivation, it is important that a connection be made to adult learners' interests or needs (Merriam & Bierema, 2013).

As you begin your journey into online adult education, it will be crucial for you to understand the internal motivations that are driving you. As mentioned a little earlier in the chapter, earning a degree is a long-term goal, and losing your motivation is a real possibility. It is important to assess what brought you here and what is going to keep you working when you are ready to quit. Purposefully seeking to connect the information you are learning with your needs is an invaluable way to stay motivated. You might also try writing down a list of your motivators and keeping it near your computer, in your wallet, or as a note on your smartphone.

Personal Reflection

Think about the influences and motivational factors in your life right now. Categorize them based on whether they are internal or external factors.

External	Internal
_____	_____
_____	_____
_____	_____
_____	_____
_____	_____

Alissa Keith

"Professors can lead students to knowledge, but they can't make them learn. As an adult learner, you must choose to learn that knowledge to reach your own personal goals."

Now, take another look at your list. Circle those influencers that are most significant and ask yourself why these are so important to you. You will often find that what seems like an external influence can often be tied to an internal motivation. Do you find this to be the case here? Explain your answer in the space provided.

_____

_____

_____

_____

_____

_____

_____

_____

BUILDING BLOCKS

Summary and Conclusion

This chapter compares the differences in learning orientation and focus of those who are pedagogical versus andragogical learners. You have had the opportunity to examine the features of each type of learner and the instruction that is geared to the needs of each. As you evaluate yourself, do you see yourself more as a pedagogical learner or one who can benefit from the features of instruction for learners who are more self-directed, those we describe as andragogical learners?

Consider how each of the assumptions of learners (need to know; self-concept; experience; readiness to learn; orientation; motivation to learn) fits either those learning through the process of pedagogy or those who are ready for adult learning, also referred to as andragogy.

As you consider this, I'll use myself as an example for a particular topic, **learning physics**.

- For **need to know**, I would take this course because it is required for a program of study that I want, but I am not particularly interested in physics, per se. Based on this context, I am a pedagogical learner for physics.

- My **self-concept** and **experience** are both quite dependent on the teacher's instruction, as this is a course that I am not very familiar with and actually somewhat fearful of taking! I am planning to be led almost entirely by the instructor, rather than my own initiative.

- My **readiness to learn** is based on my need to learn this information to move forward with the program of study, but I am unable to move forward, I believe, without the instructor.

- While I am always motivated to do well, my **orientation** for this course is to master it so I can move on to other topics in the program.

- As a result, my **motivation** is based on the need to master this before moving on.

Can you see from this example that I am primarily a pedagogical learner with this topic?

In other instances, I may be an andragogical learner. Let's look at how this would play out if I decide to learn German for an upcoming family trip to our ancestral homeland, Germany.

- My drive to master the language is based on my desire to speak the language with distant family members. I understand the "why" (**need to know**).

- I am quite independent in learning the language, as it can benefit my trip, and is something I am choosing for myself, so it satisfies the **self-concept** component of andragogical learning.

- My background with travel assures me that my experiences will be heightened if I am able to speak the language of the country I am visiting, so I am eager to begin (**experience**).

- The relevance to my trip is obvious, so I am anxious to begin studying German as soon as possible (**readiness to learn**).

- Both my **orientation to learning** and **motivation to learn** are heightened by the prospect of being able to master a new skill that will be readily applicable on my family trip. I want to learn this new language to enrich my experience of another country and to enable me to speak with distant family members in their language.

Do you see that you might be an andragogical learner in one situation and yet a pedagogical one in another? In some instances, you may discover that you have a mixed collection of descriptors that fits your learning readiness and preferences.

Personal Reflection

Using the chart on the following page, choose a couple of examples from your own life, and keep in mind that you may not find yourself to be purely pedagogical or purely andragogical: Your responses may be a mix.

Assumptions	Example 1	Example 2	You 1	You 2
	Physics	Learning German		
Need to know	Pedagogy Required course; but low interest	Andragogy I want this skill to aid me in an upcoming trip		
Self-concept	Pedagogy Dependent on teacher to calm my fears and lead me	Andragogy I see myself as a learner who is gaining a skill that will be beneficial to me		
Experience	Pedagogy No experience in my background; dependent on instructor	Andragogy My travel background helps me understand that speaking the language of the country is of benefit to me		
Readiness to learn	Pedagogy Based on my need in my program, but dependent on my instructor	Andragogy Eager to begin, because I have plans to use this soon		
Orientation to learn	Pedagogy Determined to master this so I can move forward in my program	Andragogy Excitement for new skill development		
Motivation to learn	Pedagogy I need to master this before moving on to the next subject in my program of study	Andragogy My upcoming trip keeps me excited to learn more and speak with my distant family		

Psalm 25:4, "Show me your ways, Lord, teach me your paths" (NIV).

Luke 2:52, "And Jesus grew in wisdom and stature, and in favor with God and man" (NIV).

Think about the aforementioned two verses. In the first one, the Psalmist is apparently eager to learn the lessons that God has to teach him. Do you suppose this is a godly student who is learning with andragogy? On the other hand, the verse from Luke describes Jesus' growth from a young boy to a young man. We could presume that as a young boy He learned as all young students do: with pedagogy. As He grew in stature and *wisdom*, this would change to a more mature learning or andragogy. It is difficult for some people to think of the human Jesus, who came to earth as a baby, taking on human form, even as He remained fully God. As a human child, He learned and grew, as this verse tells us.

Personal Reflection

What parallels do you see in Jesus' growth and your own as a learner?

_____

_____

_____

_____

_____

_____

TOOL BOX

Career Center—If you are in that transitional period between careers, positions, or organizations, consider using the Liberty Career Center to explore your skills, marketability, and career options.

www.liberty.edu/careercenter

Course Guides—Since you won't be able to access the official syllabus until shortly before your classes begin, consider reviewing the Course Guides on the Liberty University Online website. These are samples of the syllabi for various courses. You will still be able to review the course description and rationale, but the official syllabus may contain slight differences.

www.liberty.edu/online/course-guides

Credit by exam—Aside from work experience, you may possess enough knowledge or experience in a subject area to take a special exam and receive credit for courses without having to sit through them. While you have most likely heard of the CLEP exam, there are several other ways to earn credit by exam. Many Dantes Subject Standardized tests (DSSTs), Excelsior exams, and NOCTI Business assessments can help you earn credit for information you are already familiar with. Liberty University also offers an Institutional Challenge Exam (ICE), which can be used to earn credit for certain classes that might not be available on the other exams.

Equivalency credit—Liberty acknowledges the experience you have by awarding credit for many different job experiences, professional licenses, and military service. Much of this credit can be earned by submitting the appropriate documentation to the Transfer Evaluation Office.

On-demand learning—While you are working your way through your degree, you may find yourself needing to acquire new skills that you don't necessarily want to take an additional class to learn. What are you going to do when you need to know how to use spreadsheet software for a business class, how to understand basic statistical information for a research class, or how to format a paper in APA for your psychology class? Consider using some of the on-demand resources that Liberty has made available to you, like Atomic Learning, Tutor.com, and the Online Writing Center.

Portfolio credit—If you possess life experience that is not accepted by automatic transfer, you might consider utilizing the portfolio process in order to earn credit for your experience. In order to earn portfolio credit, you will need to take GEED 205; in this course, you will be taught how to put together a portfolio and submit it for review. From there, you will be able to submit additional portfolios on your own. Submitted portfolios are reviewed by the appropriate academic departments in order to determine if credit will be awarded or not.

Syllabi—The syllabus for each class contains a course description, rationale, and a set of measurable learning outcomes. These will assist you in establishing the "why" behind each course. The official syllabus will be available to you as soon as you gain access to your courses; typically, access is granted the week before classes begin.

Additional resources and links to specific sites, worksheets, and apps can be located by accessing the Breaking Ground website:

www.breakinggroundlu.com

References

Chan, S. (2010). Applications of andragogy in multi-disciplined teaching and learning. *Journal of Adult Education, 39*(2), 25–35. Retrieved from http://search.proquest.com/docview/871911642

Knowles, M.S., Holton, E. F., & Swanson, R. A. (2011). *The adult learner: The definitive classic in adult education and human resource development* (7th ed.). [Kindle Edition]. Retrieved from Amazon.com

Lewis, C. S. (1996). *Mere Christianity*. New York, NY: Simon and Schuster.

Merriam, S. B., & Bierema, L. L. (2013). *Adult learning: linking theory and practice*. [Kindle Edition]. Retrieved from Amazon.com

Taylor, B., & Kroth, M. (2009). Andragogy's transition into the future: Meta-analysis of andragogy and its search for a measurable instrument. *Journal of Adult Education, 38*(1), 1–11. Retrieved from http://search.proquest.com/docview/204494009

Wurm, K. B. (2005). Andragogy in survey education. *Surveying and Land Information Science, 65*(3), 159–162. Retrieved from http://search.proquest.com/docview/202972619

Chapter 7

Learning Theories: The Structure

In this chapter you will:

- Identify the elements of learning style preferences and your personal learning gifts.

- Determine learning strategies that align with your learning preferences for maximum effectiveness and learning efficiency.

STRUCTURE AND FRAMING

When constructing a building, the structure's framing provides a network of interconnected materials that serve a critical function. Though the framing is internal and not prominently visible when the building is completed, it determines the size, height, and overall design of the building by providing the form and dimensions of the completed structure. Just as in a construction project, the structure and framing of an individual's learning strength is his or her learning style. It is the frame, if you will, of the way each of us interacts with the world around us to best gain information. God has given each of us individual learning style gifts, and if we use these gifts to their best effect, the finished results can be strong and beautiful! This chapter will help you understand the concept of learning style and will guide you in maximizing the use of the learning gifts God has given you.

© 2013 by VLADGRIN. Used under license of Shutterstock, Inc.

Psalm 139:14,
"I praise you because I am **fearfully and wonderfully made**; your works are wonderful, I know that full well" (NLT).

THE CORNERSTONE

I Corinthians 12:5–6, "There are different kinds of gifts, but the same Spirit distributes them. There are different kinds of service, but the same Lord. There are different kinds of working, but in all of them and in everyone it is the same God at work" (NIV).

Renowned gospel singer Doug Oldham came to Thomas Road Baptist Church in the 1970s to help Dr. Jerry Falwell, Sr. promote and raise funds for the college (Liberty University) he planned to establish. When describing Doug, Dr. Falwell wrote, "He has sung for presidents and royalty. Doug Oldham is as fine a singer as there is and he is a master communicator. But the important thing to me is that he has remained true to his Lord and his calling" (Cox, 2010). In his lifetime, he recorded 66 albums, won two Dove Awards, sang many of the songs written by gospel songwriters Bill and Gloria Gaither, and performed for six U.S. Presidents and the Queen of England. While others knew him as a "master communicator," I knew him as "Grandpa."

My grandpa, Doug, was the only son of Dale and Polly Oldham. Dale served as the preacher of Park Place Church of God and hosted the Christian Brotherhood Hour radio show in Anderson, Indiana. Polly played the organ during church services. Dale and Polly raised Doug in the knowledge of Christ and encouraged his natural singing abilities, which later led to his profession as minister of music at various churches and ultimately, his own ministry of music that lasted until his death in 2010.

Being the only son of a preacher, Doug learned how to lead two lives . . . one for church and one for his own pleasure. When he married my grandmother, Laura Lee Makings, a simple yet beautiful girl from the Nebraska prairie, that double life continued. Together, they had three children: Paula, Karen, and Rebekah. Grandpa behaved badly in those early years of marriage and was unfaithful to my grandmother many times. Each time, he would apologize for his bad behavior and would find another minister of music position at a different church and repeat the pattern. It was not until my grandma left with the three little girls that my grandpa experienced a true conversion experience, committing his life to Christ. He then spent the next months winning back my grandma's heart and her trust and spent the rest of his life telling others the story of God's mercy and grace in his life.

After my grandpa passed away in 2010, a good friend and colleague of mine, Vangie Alban, came up to me at the family visitation and gave me a

Photo courtesy of Paula Johnson

Married 58 years, Doug and Laura Lee Oldham dedicated their lives to sharing Christ's love with others through testimony and song.

Photo courtesy of Thomas Road Baptist Church.

In this picture, Dr. Falwell and Doug Oldham worship on the platform of Thomas Road Baptist Church together.

comforting hug. She then told me about a time when she was facing a terribly difficult, personal trial, and my grandpa comforted her with these words, "Ministries are born out of adversity." These words reflected the way he lived his life, and without that adversity in his own life, he would not have been able to touch so many other lives. While the enemy "intended to harm" him, "God intended it for good to accomplish what is now being done, the saving of many lives" (Genesis 50:20, NIV).

My great-grandpa, Dale, and grandpa, Doug, both impacted the lives of others for Christ; however, they arrived at their ministries in different ways. PaPa Dale was faithful from the start, while PaPa Doug learned the hard way. Though they learned differently, both were effective ministers of God's message of grace, love, and forgiveness, because both were willing. As you realize your own style of learning, consider ways that you can use your abilities, not only as you learn in your courses, but also as you live for the Lord, "There are different kinds of gifts, but the same Spirit distributes them. There are different kinds of service, but the same Lord. There are different kinds of working, but in all of them and in everyone it is the same God at work" (I Corinthians 12:5–6, NIV).

Identify the Elements of Learning Style Preferences and Your Personal Learning Style Gifts

Genesis 1:26, 31,
"Then God said, 'Let us make mankind in our image, in our likeness' God saw all that he had made, and it was very good" (NIV).

The Bible reassures us that while we have different gifts from God, we are all precious in His sight and perfect as He created us. In other words, no matter what our strengths and individual differences, we are all created by God to be like Him. The Bible confirms God's approval just a few verses later: All that God made was pleasing to Him! What a wonderful comfort to know that how we learn best is designed and approved by God!

Identifying your learning preferences can help you to choose effective strategies for learning in school and on the job. Recognizing your preferred learning environment can help you increase effectiveness as you learn.

Silvia Graham

"Reduced to essentials, learning styles refer to the way we better channel information. For instance, some people take in information best through visual stimuli, some through auditory, and others through tactile processes. Knowing how we best cognitively approach the world might help us succeed academically."

What Are Learning Preferences?

Just as each individual has a unique personality, each individual has a unique learning style. It is important to remember that there are no good or bad learning styles. Your learning style is simply your preferred way of learning. By understanding your learning style, you can maximize your potential by choosing the learning techniques that work best for you. Each individual also has a preferred learning environment. Knowing about your preferred learning environment and learning style helps you to be more productive, to increase achievement, to be more creative, to improve problem solving, to make good decisions, and to learn effectively. Knowing about how you learn best helps to reduce frustration and increase your confidence in learning.

Photo courtesy of David Duncan (Liberty University).

Students are on their way to convocation. Liberty University hosts speakers in convocation from across the country and around the world!

(continues)

Barbara Sherman

". . . learning styles are the ways we concentrate on, process, and internalize and remember new and difficult information or skills. These styles often vary with age, achievement level, culture . . . and gender."

Gary Price has developed the Productivity Environmental Preference Survey (PEPS), which identifies 20 different elements of learning style and environment, including the immediate environment, emotional factors, sociological needs, and physical needs. As you read the description of each of these elements, think about your preferences.

1. **Sound.** Some students need a quiet environment for study, whereas others find it distracting if it is too quiet.

   - If you prefer quiet, use the library or find another quiet place. If you cannot find a quiet place, sound-blocking earphones or earplugs may be helpful. Remember that not all people need a quiet environment for study.

   - If you study better with sound, play soft music or study in open areas. Use headphones for your music if you are studying with those who prefer quiet.

2. **Light.** Some students prefer bright light to see what they are studying, whereas others find bright light uncomfortable or irritating.

   - If you prefer bright light, study near a window with light shining over your shoulder or invest in a good study lamp.

   - If you prefer dim lights, sit away from direct sunlight or use a shaded light.

Katie Robinson

"We are all hard-wired oh so differently with various strengths and weaknesses, and this extends to how our minds work and how we learn. Research has shown that when a student is self-aware and understands how he or she learns, that student can use meta-cognition when approaching new material. Discovering one's learning style can greatly help when refining study skills. In this way, we can 'learn to learn.'"

3. **Temperature.** Some students perform better in cool temperatures and others prefer warmer temperatures.

   - If you prefer a warm environment, remember to bring your sweater or jacket. Sit near a window or other source of heat.

   - If you prefer a cooler environment, study in a well-ventilated environment or even outside in the shade.

4. **Design.** Some students study best in a more formal environment or less formal environment.

   - If you prefer a formal environment, sit in a straight chair and use a desk.

   - If you prefer an informal environment, sit on the sofa or a soft chair or on some pillows on the floor.

5. **Motivation.** Some students are self-motivated to learn, and others lack motivation.

   - If you are self-motivated, you usually like school and enjoy learning on your own.

- If you lack motivation, think about your reasons for attending college and review the material in the motivation chapter of this book.

6. **Persistence.** Some students finish what they start, whereas others have many things going on at once and may not finish what they have started.

    - If you are persistent, you generally finish what you start.

    - If you lack persistence, you may get bored or distracted easily. You may find it easier to break tasks into small steps and work steadily toward completing assignments on time. Think about your college and career goals to increase motivation and persistence.

7. **Responsibility (conforming).** This element has a unique meaning in the area of learning style.

    - Some students like to please others by doing what is asked of them. They complete assignments to please the professor.

    - Other students are less likely to conform. They prefer to complete assignments because they want to, rather than because someone else wants the assignment done. These students may need to look for something interesting and personally meaningful in school assignments.

8. **Structure.** Students prefer more or less structure.

    - Students who prefer structure want the teacher to give details about how to complete the assignment. They need clear directions before completing an assignment.

    - Students who prefer less structure want the teacher to give assignments in which the students can choose the topic and organize the material on their own.

9. **Alone/peer.** Some students prefer to study alone, and others prefer to study with others.

    - You may find other people distracting and prefer to study alone. You need to study in a private area.

    - You may enjoy working in a group, because talking with others helps you to learn.

10. **Authority figures present.** Some students are more or less independent learners.

Photo courtesy of Joel Coleman (Liberty University).

This chandelier hangs in the Grand Lobby of the DeMoss Learning Center. Notice the brass eagle detailed here, an homage to the Liberty mascot.

Shaun D. Curran

"All too often students journey through our education with the belief that 'one size fits all' when it comes to studying and understanding the information they need to learn. This belief does little more than limit students and put their abilities in a box. Instead of the 'one size fits all' attitude towards learning, you should approach your education with the 'my size fits me' approach. This approach means understanding your learning style as much as you can, and using appropriate strategies that help make learning easier."

(continues)

- Some students prefer to have the professor available to guide learning. In the college environment, students may prefer traditional face-to-face classes.

- Others prefer to work on their own. In the college environment, students may prefer online classes or independent study.

11. **Several ways.** Some students learn in several ways, and others have definite preferences.

   - Some students like variety and can learn either on their own or with others.

   - Some students definitely prefer learning on their own or prefer learning with others.

12. **Auditory.** Some students prefer to learn through listening and talking.

   - Those who prefer auditory learning find it easier to learn through lectures, audio materials, discussion, and oral directions.

   - Those who do not prefer auditory learning may find their minds wandering during lectures and become confused by oral directions. They do not learn through others talking about the topic. These students should read the material before the lecture and take notes during the lecture. Review the notes periodically to remember the material.

13. **Visual.** Some students prefer to learn through reading or seeing things.

   - Those who prefer visual learning benefit from pictures and reading.

   - Those who are not visual learners may dislike reading. If auditory learning is preferred, view the presentation first to hear the lecturer talk about the subject and then do the reading. It is important to do the reading because not all the material is covered in the presentation.

14. **Tactile.** Some students prefer to touch the material as they learn.

   - Students who prefer tactile learning prefer manipulative and three-dimensional materials. They learn from working with models and writing. Taking notes is one of the best tactile learning strategies.

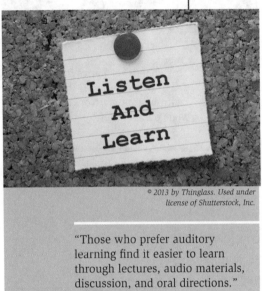

© 2013 by Thinglass. Used under license of Shutterstock, Inc.

"Those who prefer auditory learning find it easier to learn through lectures, audio materials, discussion, and oral directions."

© 2013 by Andrey Shadrin. Used under license of Shutterstock, Inc.

"Visual learners benefit from pictures and reading."

- Students who are not tactile learners can focus on visual or auditory strategies for learning.

15. **Kinesthetic.** Kinesthetic learning is related to tactile learning. Students prefer to learn by acting out material to be learned or moving around while learning.

   - Students who prefer kinesthetic learning enjoy field trips, drama, and becoming physically involved with learning. For example, they can learn fractions by slicing an apple into parts or manipulating blocks. It is important to be actively involved in learning.

   - Students who are not kinesthetic learners will use another preferred method of learning such as auditory or visual.

16. **Intake.** Some students need to chew or drink something while learning.

   - If you prefer intake while learning, drink water and have nutritious snacks such as fruits and vegetables.

   - Some students do not need intake to study and find food items distracting.

17. **Evening/morning.** Some students are more awake in the morning and prefer to go to bed early at night. If this is your preference, schedule your most challenging studying in the morning and do your routine tasks later.

18. **Late morning.** Some students are more awake from 10:00 a.m. until noon. If this is your preference, use this time for studying. Use other times for more routine tasks.

19. **Afternoon.** Some students are more productive in the afternoon. If this is your preference, schedule your study time in the afternoon. Do your routine tasks at other times.

20. **Mobility.** Some students like to move around while studying.

   - If you prefer mobility, you may find it difficult to sit still for a long time. Take a break every 15 or 20 minutes to move around. When choosing an occupation, consider one that requires you to move around.

   - If you don't need to move around while studying, a stationary desk and chair are sufficient to help you concentrate on learning.

© 2013 by suphakit73. Used under license of Shutterstock, Inc.

Kinesthetic learners enjoy learning through movement and hands-on projects.

Shaun D. Curran

"The purpose of learning styles is not to generate frustration, but to show you that what strategies work for one student may not work for you, and that simply staring at a computer screen in hopes that somehow you 'get' what is being taught may not be the most effective way to learn. Auditory learners may benefit from reading texts aloud and recording themselves, while kinesthetic learners may benefit from using flashcards to best master the material. Visual learners may be at a benefit in online classrooms, but this does not mean people with other types of learning styles cannot enjoy the rewarding freedom of an online education."

Jenny Walter

"Finding out the style that best suits you can help you throughout college. Have some fun learning more about yourself."

T. Marcus Christian

"You learn differently than any other student. There are special ways you can focus your attention depending on your learning style. Once you find the learning style that works best for you, the world of learning will open wide."

Mary Dixon

"God has made us unique and gifted us in a variety of ways. The way we process information and learn is one of those. Get to know yourself; get acquainted with God's gifts in you. Experiment until you know what works best for you because God has a plan that he will bring to completion as you cooperate with him. You are God's work of art, so show it in all that you do."

We know that individuals are different. I love the expression, "You're unique . . . just like everyone else!" Break that down, and here is what it means: God created each of us in His image, but we are all special and precious to Him. Even if you are an identical twin, you and your sibling are different. Your appearance may make it very difficult for others to tell you apart, but you may yet be very different when it comes to your learning style preferences. You are unique, so celebrate what God has given you as learning style gifts.

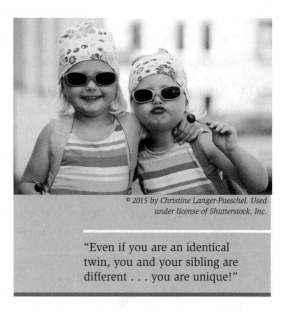

© 2015 by Christine Langer-Pueschel. Used under license of Shutterstock, Inc.

"Even if you are an identical twin, you and your sibling are different . . . you are unique!"

WORKSHEET

Go to the textbook companion website, Breaking Ground LU, at "www.breakinggroundlu.com". Click on the **My Power Learning** link to take a learning styles inventory and learn about strategies that may be particularly helpful for your learning preference. Then, return here to resume reading.

After completing the My Power Learning inventory

Roger

"As an online learner, I knew about different learning styles and was aware of how I learn best. I am not strongly kinesthetic or experiential. Nor am I strongly visual or acoustic. I am a wonderful blend of learning styles and can easily move from one mode of learning to another. I guess you can say, I love to learn about new things. I appreciate teachers who can present learning in a variety of styles, because they all appeal to me. So when I teach, I like to change my style and present information in several different ways by utilizing the senses, because people learn differently. They do not all process information the way I do. I have to show my wife how to perform certain computer applications. If I simply tell her how to do it, she will become confused and flustered, because that is not her learning style."

Were you surprised by what you found out about yourself, or were you easily able to predict your learning styles preference? Some students are very aware of their learning preferences, while others may be taken by surprise, having always just listened to lectures and taken notes, along with reading the textbook. Did your responses overwhelmingly fall into a single category, or did your answers range across the style choices? While some students are very heavily one type of learner, others may find strengths in a couple of categories. Still others discover that they score fairly evenly across the categories, with no clear preference. No matter what results you found from this exercise, you can be confident that you are perfectly set for learning just the way God made you!

Personal Reflection

1. What learning style preference(s) did you discover for yourself?

_____

_____

_____

2. Were you able to predict the results you discovered in the assessment?

_____

_____

_____

3. Are you solidly a single style, or do you have a mix of learning style preferences?

_____

_____

_____

Visual 7.3
Auditory 3.2
Kinesthetic 5.4

Let's turn next to examine learning strategies that best match each of the three learning styles we have identified: visual, auditory, and kinesthetic learners. For those who find strengths in a pair of categories, you can be confident utilizing strategies from both of your learning styles. Experiment to find what suits you best. Did you find that you are a total mix of learning styles? Rejoice! This means that God has given you a host of learning strategies to work with: You can be successful with nearly every strategy outlined here. Praise Him for His generosity to you!

Determine Learning Strategies that Align with Your Learning Preferences for Maximum Effectiveness and Learning Efficiency

I Cor. 12:6,
"There are different kinds of working, but in all of them and in everyone it is the same God at work" (NIV).

Barbara Sherman

"Confucius stated: 'I hear and I forget; I see and I remember; I do and I understand.' Therefore, in studying, it is wise to first lean on your own preferences but, then, to also attempt to comprehend/process information in as many ways as you can."

It's a comfort to recall that no matter what learning techniques work for each of us, we are designed by God, and designed to be like Him. While some students find that there are many, many strategies that can help them learn easily, others have a more limited range of options to use. In any case, it is wise to try different strategies, rather than simply relying on what you have always done in the past. Your traditional strategies may be replaced when you discover new ones that are even more effective for you. Very few learners are all one way when it comes to learning style preference, so you may find that you are most efficient and effective when you apply a mix of strategies. Some learning tasks require a change of strategy, too. What works for you when you are learning a new concept may be different from what you do when you are trying to master a list of facts that must be memorized. No matter what you discover in terms of the strategies that work for you, know that you are unique, just as God designed you!

Visual Learning Strategies

Use as many visual resources as you can.

- When choosing a learning environment, position yourself with as few visual distractors as possible. Never work in front of the television!

- Read textbooks to gain information when possible.

© 2015 by Dan Kosmayer. Used under license of Shutterstock, Inc.

Use colorful highlighters to mark main ideas, themes, and so on in your notes.

- Preview chapters, looking for main ideas, examining pictures, charts, graphics.

- In a presentation that is auditory (lecture or online course presentation), take notes to convert auditory stimuli to visual ones.

- Use colorful highlighters to mark main ideas, themes, and so on in your notes.

- Make flashcards of your noted information. Keep them with you and practice with them when you have a few moments to study: waiting in line, sitting in traffic, and so forth.

- When studying, review your notes or flashcards. Then put them away and see if you can rewrite them from memory. Rewriting is a powerful tool to build your memory of the visual stimulus.

- When selecting how to do course assignments, choose written work when possible, such as papers, PowerPoints, and so on.

- Students who prefer visual learning experiences usually work best without auditory distractions, so no music, for example, in the background, except perhaps quiet classical music without vocals.

- Create a concept map of what you are trying to learn.

Dr. Jerry Falwell, Sr.

"Life is filled with glorious opportunities brilliantly disguised as unsolvable problems" (Falwell, 1996, p. 97).

Alissa Keith

"Learn however you learn best, even if it means standing on your head to memorize math facts."

Personal Reflection

1. What visual learning strategies have you used previously?

_____

_____

_____

2. Which strategies for visual learning would you like to incorporate in your reading and study practices?

_____

_____

_____

Auditory Learning Strategies

Use as many auditory resources as possible. Create them if necessary!

- When reading course materials or PowerPoint presentations, read aloud.

- If you must read silently, try to "hear" the words as you are reading.

© 2015 by gpointstudio. Used under license of Shutterstock, Inc.

Study with a friend, so you can talk over what you are learning.

Nathaniel Valle

"Knowing how you learn makes you a more equipped student as well as a holistic learner. If you struggle to understand a concept or information, think about how you're attempting to understand it; are you maximizing your natural style? Find ways to make your learning work for you."

- Preview a textbook chapter by looking over the material in the chapter. Talk about what you see, so that you get an auditory stimulus of what you will be reading about. Talk your way through charts, pictograms, graphs, and so forth.

- Study with a buddy, so you can talk over what you are learning.

- Rehearse aloud what you are trying to learn. Add rhythm if possible.

- Join a study group to enable you to hear what others are saying about what you are studying. You can do this online with video conferencing software.

- Create flashcards for the material you want to learn. Practice with them repeatedly, aloud.

- Make a recording of the material on your flashcards and play it while you do other things (driving, etc.).

- Choose to make oral presentations for course assignments when possible. Record a video, make an audio clip, or something that employs your auditory learning strengths.

- Master what you are trying to learn by teaching it to someone else.

- If music is helpful to you, then use it while you are studying. Choose instrumental music to avoid being distracted by the lyrics of familiar music. (Use vocal music as your break-time entertainment.)

- Write a song or jingle filled with facts you want to remember, and sing it to a familiar tune.

- Turn your textbook into an auditory resource by reading it aloud. Record it so you can review it later.

- Use your computer's read-aloud function to have the e-textbook read to you.

Personal Reflection

1. What auditory learning strategies have you used previously?

_____

_____

_____

2. Which strategies for auditory learning would you like to incorporate in your reading and study practices?

_____

_____

_____

_____

Kinesthetic Learning Strategies

Use as much physical interaction with what you are learning as possible.

- For online work, have your computer where you can move your chair, wiggle, and so on. Be as comfortable as possible, but resist the urge to use your bed as a work area.

- You may consider abandoning the chair altogether and stretch out on the floor to do your work.

- Try to work in briefer time frames, perhaps 20–25 minutes at a time. Take frequent breaks to stretch, move around, and refresh yourself. Quickly get back to your work, however.

- As you read from a textbook, follow along with your finger. Subvocalize (move your lips while reading silently) to make reading a kinesthetic activity.

- Make notes on what you are reading. Color-code them with highlighters.

- Make models to represent what you are learning.

- Create a card game so you can manipulate the information on each card as you are trying to master it.

- Create flashcards to use for study time. When you are using them, pace, rock, or otherwise be active as you work.

- Music is a good background for you, but use only music with no vocals. Keep it as a quiet background.

- Think ACTIVE learning. Use your body as much as possible to engage what you are trying to learn.

- If possible, choose hands-on activities for coursework presentations. Be creative with video, PowerPoint, or other presentation methods that take advantage of your kinesthetic learning style.

- Outdoor study may work well for you.

© 2015 by Lucky Business. Used under license of Shutterstock, Inc.

Outdoor study may work well for you if you benefit from kinesthetic learning strategies.

Terry Conner

"The key to learning is not just understanding your learning style, but knowing how to apply it in the online environment. If you're a kinesthetic learner, find ways to bring the information out from the book and into your living room."

Michael Shenkle

"The topic of individual learning styles is one of my favorites, because it has such wide-ranging implications. Not only has it helped me understand my successes and failures in education, but it also has helped me better communicate with my family members by understanding how they receive and process information. By looking for ways to tailor my educational and relational interactions to a specific learning style, I have found greater success in both areas."

Personal Reflection

1. What kinesthetic learning strategies have you used previously?

_____

_____

_____

2. Which strategies for kinesthetic learning would you like to incorporate in your reading and study practices?

_____

_____

_____

There are some strategies that are helpful for all learning styles. Flash cards can be useful for every learner, particularly if adapted to an individual's learning style. Auditory learners benefit from reading/quizzing the cards aloud, or by creating flash cards on a tablet, like the iPad. Record the information and quiz yourself. Visual learners benefit by seeing the information on the card, enhanced with colored ink or highlighting. Kinesthetic learners benefit most from the act of making the cards: writing the words and definitions/dates and so on helps in mastery. Reviewing the cards while moving (walking, pacing, or acting out) adds to the kinesthetic experience.

What other strategies do you think can be adapted for use by every learner? While it is important to understand and develop the particular strengths of your learning style, you should not ignore the strategies that can help other learners. Often, students have more than a single strong inclination for learning style, so you will want to practice strategies that will touch both/all of your learning strengths.

Photo courtesy of Dave Moquin.

Liberty Mountain boasts beautiful sunset views.

Tim

"Before starting my online courses, I did know a lot about my learning style. However, I did not know what strategies worked best with my learning style. The course offered by Liberty did help me learn more about my learning style and what I would need to do to complete my courses in a timely manner with high grades."

Multiple Intelligences

In 1904, the French psychologist Alfred Binet developed the IQ test, which provided a single score to measure intelligence. This once widely used and accepted test came into question because it measured the intelligence of individuals in schools in a particular culture. In different cultures and different situations, the test was less valid. As an alternative to traditional IQ tests, Harvard professor Howard Gardner developed the theory of multiple intelligences. He looked at intelligence in a broader and more inclusive way than people had done in the past.

Howard Gardner observed famous musicians, artists, athletes, scientists, inventors, naturalists, and others who were recognized contributors to society to formulate a more meaningful definition of intelligence. He defined **intelligence** as the human ability to solve problems or design or compose something valued in at least one culture. His definition broadens the scope of human potential. He identified eight different intelligences: musical, interpersonal, logical–mathematical, spatial, bodily-kinesthetic, linguistic, intrapersonal, and naturalist. He selected these intelligences because they are all represented by an area in the brain and are valued in different cultures. Howard Gardner has proposed adding existential intelligence to the list. He defines existential intelligence as the capacity to ask profound questions about the meaning of life and death. This intelligence is the cornerstone of art, religion, and philosophy. His theory can help us to understand and use many different kinds of talents.

Within the theory of multiple intelligences, learning style is defined as intelligences put to work. These intelligences are measured by looking at performance in activities associated with each intelligence. A key idea in this theory is that most people can develop all of their intelligences and become relatively competent in each area. Another key idea is that these intelligences work together in complex ways to make us unique. For example, an athlete uses bodily-kinesthetic intelligence to run, kick, or jump. They use spatial intelligence to keep their eye on the ball and hit it. They also need linguistic and interpersonal skills to be good members of a team.

Developing intelligences is a product of three factors:

1. Biological endowment based on heredity and genetics

2. Personal life history

3. Cultural and historical background

Terry

Q: *When you began as an online learner, did you know anything about your learning style?*

A: "Yes"

Q: *What is your learning style?*

A: "I'm more of an auditory learner, but I'm equally versed in all three styles."

Q: *How did you learn about it?*

A: "A teacher in high school"

Q: *Were you able to take advantage of what you learned (or knew) about yourself?*

A: "Yes, it has helped me tremendously by informing me how best to study."

Q: *Why does choosing the correct strategies for learning matter, anyway?*

A: "If we choose a style that is outside of ours, we run the risk of becoming frustrated since the learning won't come easily."

For example, Wolfgang Amadeus Mozart was born with musical talent (biological endowment). Members of his family were musicians who encouraged Mozart in music (personal life history). Mozart lived in Europe during a time when music flourished and wealthy patrons were willing to pay composers (cultural and historical background).

Each individual's life history contains crystallizers that promote the development of the intelligences and paralyzers that inhibit the development of the intelligences. These crystallizers and paralyzers often take place in early childhood. For example, Einstein was given a magnetic compass when he was four years old. He became so interested in the compass that he started on his journey of exploring the universe. An example of a paralyzer is being embarrassed or feeling humiliated about your math skills in elementary school so that you begin to lose confidence in your ability to do math. Paralyzers involve shame, guilt, fear, and anger and prevent intelligence from being developed.

From *College and Career Success*, 5/e by Marsha Fralick. Copyright © 2011 by Kendall Hunt Publishing Company. Reprinted by permission.

WORKSHEET

Go to the textbook companion website, Breaking Ground LU, at "www.breakinggroundlu.com" to learn more about Multiple Intelligences and evaluate your Multiple Intelligences strengths. Then, return here to reflect on what you have identified as your strengths and areas that you may want to develop more.

Personal Reflection

According to Gardner's theory, what are your most developed intelligences? Are there any you need to improve?

_____

_____

_____

_____

_____

_____

_____

_____

_____

_____

_____

_____

_____

_____

_____

_____

_____

_____

_____

_____

_____

Developing Your E-Learning Strategies

Students who are independent learners or introverts who enjoy individual learning in a quiet place may prefer online learning. Students who prefer having a professor to guide learning with immediate feedback and extraverts who are energized by social interaction may prefer traditional classroom education. However, because of work, family, and time constraints, online learning might be a convenient way to access education. No matter what your learning style, you are able to take advantage of online learning.

Here are some suggestions for successful e-learning experiences.

- The most important factor in online learning is to **log in regularly** and complete the work in a systematic way. Set goals for what you need to accomplish each week and do the work a step at a time. Get in the habit of regularly doing your online study, just as you would attend a traditional course each week.

- It is important to **carefully read the instructions** for the assignments and **ask for help** if you need it. Your online professor will not know when you need help unless you ask.

- **Have a backup plan** if your computer crashes or your Internet connection is interrupted. Public libraries offer computers with Internet, free for their patrons' use, where you can do your work if you have technical problems at home. Do you have a library card? If not, be sure to sign up for one before you need it!

- Remember to **participate** in the online discussion boards. This is part of your grade and a good way to learn from other students and apply what you have learned. The advantage of online communication is that you have time to think about your responses.

- **Check your grades** online to make sure you are completing all the requirements. Make sure to look for comments from your professor to guide you in future similar assignments.

Celebrate your success as you complete your online studies. Online learning becomes easier with experience.

From *College and Career Success*, 5/e by Marsha Fralick. Copyright © 2011 by Kendall Hunt Publishing Company. Reprinted by permission.

Keys to Success

We are responsible for what happens in our lives. We make decisions and choices that create the future. Our behavior leads to success or failure. Too often, we believe that we are victims of circumstance. When looking at our lives, we often look for others to blame for how our lives are going:

- My grandparents did it to me. I inherited these genes.

- My parents did it to me. My childhood experiences shaped who I am.

- My teacher did it to me. He gave me a poor grade.

- My boss did it to me. She gave me a poor evaluation.

- The government did it to me. All my money goes to taxes.

- Society did it to me. I have no opportunity.

These factors are powerful influences in our lives, but we are still left with choices. Concentration camp survivor Viktor Frankl wrote a book, *Man's Search for Meaning,* in which he describes his experiences and how he survived his ordeal. His parents, brother, and wife died in the camps. He suffered starvation and torture. Through all of his sufferings and imprisonment, he still maintained that he was a free man because he could make choices.

> We who lived in concentration camps can remember the men who walked through the huts comforting others, giving away their last piece of bread. They may have been few in number, but they offer sufficient proof that everything can be taken from a man but one thing: the last of the human freedoms—to choose one's attitude in any given set of circumstances, to choose one's own way. . .
>
> Fundamentally, therefore, any man can, even under such circumstances, decide what shall become of him—mentally and spiritually. He may retain his human dignity even in a concentration camp.*

*Viktor Frankl, *Man's Search for Meaning* (New York: Pocket Books, 1963), 104–5.

Viktor Frankl could not choose his circumstances at that time, but he did choose his attitude. He decided how he would respond to the situation. He realized that he still had the freedom to make choices. He used his memory and imagination to exercise his freedom. When times were the most difficult, he would imagine that he was in the classroom lecturing to his students about psychology.

(continues)

Photo by Ty Hester © Liberty University.

Celebrate your success as you complete your online studies. Online learning becomes easier with experience.

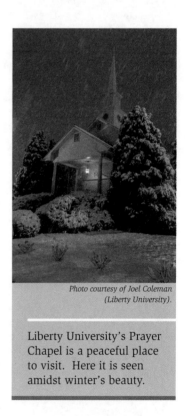

Photo courtesy of Joel Coleman (Liberty University).

Liberty University's Prayer Chapel is a peaceful place to visit. Here it is seen amidst winter's beauty.

© 2015 by Featureflash / Shutterstock.com

Christopher Reeve's wife embraces him with a congratulatory kiss as Reeve's Star on the Hollywood Walk of Fame is unveiled

He eventually did get out of the concentration camp and became a famous psychiatrist.

Christopher Reeve is another example of a person who maintained his freedom to make choices in difficult circumstances. Reeve, who once played the character Superman, was paralyzed from the neck down as the result of an accident he suffered when he was thrown from his horse. When he first awoke after the accident, he saw little reason for living. With the help of his family, he made the decision to keep fighting and do as much as he could to promote research on spinal cord injuries.

He succeeded in raising awareness and money for this cause. As a result, there have been many advancements in the study and treatment of spinal cord injuries. Reeve believed that he and others in similar circumstances would walk again some day. Sadly, Reeve passed away in 2004. However, his advocacy for the cause of finding a cure for spinal injuries has led to research that will help others in the future.

Hopefully, none of you will ever have to experience the circumstances faced by Viktor Frankl or Christopher Reeve, but we all face challenging situations. It is empowering to think that our behavior is more a function of our decisions than of our circumstances. It is not productive to look around and find someone to blame for your problems. Psychologist Abraham Maslow says that instead of blaming, we should see how we can make the best of the situation.

One can spend a lifetime assigning blame, finding a cause, "out there" for all the troubles that exist. Contrast this with the responsible attitude of confronting the situation, bad or good, and instead of asking, "What caused the trouble? Who was to blame?" asking, "How can I handle the present situation to make the best of it?"

Author Stephen Covey suggests that we look at the word responsibility as "response-ability." It is the ability to choose responses and make decisions about the future. When you are dealing with a problem, it is useful to ask yourself what decisions *you* made that led to the problem. How did *you* create the situation? If you created the problem, *you* can create a solution.

At times, you may ask, "How did I create this?" and find that the answer is that you did not create the situation. We certainly do not create earthquakes or hurricanes, for example. But we do create or at least contribute to many of the things that happen to us. Even if you did not create your circumstances, you can create your reaction to the situation. In the case of an earthquake, you can decide to panic or find the best course of action at the moment.

(continues)

Stephen Covey believes that we can use our resourcefulness and initiative in dealing with most problems. When his children were growing up and they asked him how to solve a certain problem, he would say, "Use your R and I!" He meant resourcefulness and initiative. He notes that adults can use this R and I to get good jobs.

But the people who end up with the good jobs are the proactive ones who are solutions to problems, not problems themselves, who seize the initiative to do whatever is necessary, consistent with correct principles, to get the job done.

Use your resourcefulness and initiative to create the future that you want.

From *College and Career Success*, 5/e by Marsha Fralick. Copyright © 2011 by Kendall Hunt Publishing Company. Reprinted by permission.

Photo courtesy of Joel Coleman (Liberty University).

Light-covered trees line the sidewalks in preparation for Christmas.

BUILDING BLOCKS

In the Bible, we read about the Israelites, God's chosen people, who left Egypt and wandered in the desert for 40 years, finally coming to the land that God had promised to give them. As their leader Moses was about to send the Israelites across the Jordan River into their new land, he spoke to them, giving farewell instructions that would carry them forward to success. Here is a bit of what he told them:

Deuteronomy 6:1–12

[1] These are the commands, decrees and laws the LORD your **God directed me to teach you** to observe in the land that you are crossing the Jordan to possess,[2] so that you, your children and their children after them may fear the LORD your God as long as you live by keeping all his decrees and commands that I give you, and so that you may enjoy long life.

[4] Hear, O Israel: The LORD our God, the LORD is one. Love the LORD your God with all your heart and with all your soul and with all your strength.[6] These commandments that I give you today are to be on your hearts.[7] Impress them on your children. **Talk about them when you sit** at home and **when you walk** along the road, **when you lie down and when you get up**.[8] Tie them as **symbols on your hands** and bind them **on your foreheads**.[9] **Write them** on the **doorframes of your houses** and **on your gates** . . .[12] be careful that you do not forget the LORD, who brought you out of Egypt, out of the land of slavery (NIV).

Notice the highlighted words in the passage. Do you see that God was using a variety of methods to help His chosen people remember what He was having Moses teach them? He encouraged them to use auditory methods (by talking about the commands, decrees, and laws). He gave them kinesthetic ways to remember, too (referring to walking, lying down, and getting up). He used visual methods as well, when he told them to put the symbols where they would see it: on their hands, foreheads, doorframes, and gates. God wanted to be sure that His people could learn in any of their preferred methods. Just as the Israelites could learn best by using the methods that they individually preferred, you can, too! Choose strategies that play to your strengths and use them frequently as you try to learn and do so efficiently. Do not simply rely on whatever methods you have used in the past, such as note-taking, but also, try to develop your learning skills by selecting new strategies within your preferred learning style. This can help you learn more in less time, which is an important consideration for a busy online learner.

Be careful to choose a learning environment that suits you best. While some students seek absolute quiet in a room far from friends or family, others will be able to thrive in a more active, busy environment. You may determine that you are best served in a cool room, spread out on the floor to learn, or you may prefer the structure of a desk in the library. Whatever your learning style preferences, choose strategies that match them, in order to gain maximum benefit from your time committed to study.

TOOL BOX

Visual

- **In Your Online Classroom**—Lessons in the online classroom are delivered through varying media in order to address the different ways that students prefer to consume information. Students who prefer visual learning experiences should look for charts, diagrams, and video presentations.

- **Mind Mapping**—Some students tend to do better when they can see a visual representation of a concept, so the use of mind mapping as a study tool can be very helpful. You can use presentation software like PowerPoint or you can utilize mind mapping websites/software to help you develop your visual aids.

- **Note-Taking**—Take your own notes, using a text or word processing program, while you watch videos or listen to lectures. For lessons that are already written out, you might consider using the highlighting or underlining feature in your word processing program.

Auditory

- **In Your Online Classroom**—Lessons in the online classroom are delivered through varying media in order to address the different ways that students prefer to consume information. Students who prefer auditory learning experiences may want to pay particular attention to narrated slide presentations, basic audio lectures, or even consider downloading audio lectures from iTunes U, if available.

- **Podcasts**—These are online audio broadcasts that typically offer the ability to subscribe to regular content. There are several programs and apps that you can use to help you locate and subscribe to podcasts on a range of topics. One of the big benefits of podcasts is the ability to have them automatically downloaded to your mobile device and then listen to them as you commute to and from work.

- **Discussions**—While much of the discussion in online classrooms is done through email or the Discussion Board forum, you can speak with others about what you are learning. Consider discussing relevant course topics with friends or family. This will afford you the opportunity to review the information verbally.

- **Text-to-Speech Software**—Students who prefer auditory learning experiences often find themselves struggling when they are in a course that requires an extensive amount of reading. In these circumstances, you could consider using a text-to-speech program that will read the text to you. This creates a sort of audio book and enhances the auditory learner's ability to absorb the material.

Kinesthetic

- **In Your Online Classroom**—Lessons in the online classroom are delivered through various media in order to address the different ways that students prefer to consume information. As a student who prefers kinesthetic learning experiences, you will want to be on the lookout for interactive tutorials and assignments that ask you to create or develop things on your own.

- **Demonstrations/Labs**—Many courses, especially in the math and science areas, will offer online labs. These labs offer you the opportunity to interact with materials in the same way you might in a residential classroom. A classic example is the online dissection labs in biology that allow you to virtually dissect a frog.

- **Building or Designing on Your Own**—While taking basic tests and quizzes may not be a favorite for students who prefer kinesthetic learning experiences, creating them can be a huge help. Consider writing your own tests/quizzes in a word processing program or use an online quiz-making site.

Additional resources and links to specific sites, worksheets, and apps can be located by accessing the Breaking Ground website:

www.breakinggroundlu.com

References

Cox, R. (2010). *Doug and Laura Lee*. Retrieved from http://www.dougoldham.com/

Falwell, J. (1997). *Falwell: An autobiography*. Lynchburg, VA: Liberty House Publishers.

Fralick, M. (2011). *College and career success*. Dubuque, IA: Kendall Hunt Publishing Company.

Price, G. E. "Productivity Environmental Preference Survey." Price Systems, Inc., Box 1818, Lawrence, KS 66044-8818.

Chapter 8

Information Literacy: The Plumbing

In this chapter, you will:

- Explore the definition and importance of information literacy.
- Develop a strategy for research.
- Identify and avoid plagiarism.

THE PLUMBING

When tasked to plumb a new building, the inexperienced or unskilled plumber might accidentally use the wrong type of pipe or incorrectly fuse the pieces together, leading to contaminants in the water or a breach in the integrity of the system. This is not unlike an inexperienced or unskilled student choosing to use the wrong resources or inadvertently plagiarizing while patching together the first research paper. On the other hand, a master plumber would analyze and plan the job so as to protect the purity of the water and the integrity of the system. In the same way, a student who is information literate will be more than capable of selecting appropriate resources and skillfully citing his or her work.

© 2013 by Paul Fleet. Used under license of Shutterstock, Inc.

Acts 17:11,
"These Jews were more open-minded than those in Thessalonica, for they eagerly received the message, examining the scriptures carefully every day to see if these things were so" (NET).

THE CORNERSTONE

Philippians 1:9–10, "And this is my prayer: that your love may abound more and more in knowledge and depth of insight, so that you may be able to discern what is best and may be pure and blameless for the day of Christ" (NIV).

After visiting "A Bug's Life: It's Tough to Be a Bug," a 4-D experience found in the Tree of Life at Disney's Animal Kingdom, my daughter, Laura Grace, peppered me with questions, specifically about one character in the show, the Termitator. In the program, the Termitator is a termite that spews acid (water) at its predators (the audience). The Termitator fascinated Laura Grace, so she begged to know more about termites on our way to our home-away-from-home that evening. She asked me, hoping that I would be the authority on the topic, since I know everything else (or at least that's what she thinks).

My basic knowledge of termites was limited to two facts: termites live in mounds, and they like to eat wood. That simply did not satisfy my curious six-year-old's brain. She wanted to know if the acid was poisonous. I explained that the acid in the show was just water, but she still wanted to know if the real acid was poisonous. In a moment of information desperation, I grabbed my smart phone and did a quick search for termites. I quickly scrolled past Wikipedia and landed on an entomology site for children. My, oh, my! Information overload! This led to many more questions and answers about termite behaviors, habitats, diet, and more.

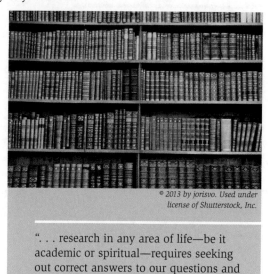

© 2013 by jorisvo. Used under license of Shutterstock, Inc.

"... research in any area of life—be it academic or spiritual—requires seeking out correct answers to our questions and relying on the best authoritative sources available to us."

Laura and I had a great time engaging each other in conversation and learning about termites, of all things. I felt like I became the informed hero to her inquisitive brain, until she said the words that humbled me instantly, "Mommy, would you please ask the phone . . . ?" I don't even remember the rest of her question. With those words, Laura put me in my place. I didn't know everything. I had to go to another source to track down information, and she knew it. However, her meaning was not judgmental; she just recognized the source of information (not her mommy, sadly) and longed to know more.

Much like my termite conversation with Laura Grace, research in any area of life—be it academic or spiritual—requires seeking out correct answers to

© 2015 by wavebreakmedia.
Used under license of Shutterstock, Inc.

You don't have to know it all, as long as you know where to look for reliable and accurate information!

our questions and relying on the best authoritative sources available to us. Research requires checking and double-checking the facts to be sure that they are correct, choosing the best resource rather than the most convenient. In our spiritual walk, our authoritative resource is God's Word; in academics, we also must be selective, actively searching out the information and not relying only on what we already know. I was not the authority on the subject of termites; I knew it, and because of that, I sought out assistance. The beautiful thing is, I didn't have to know it all because I knew where to go to find the reliable information. In your academic pursuits, remember that you do not have to know the answers to everything; just select the best resource(s) and remember Paul's words in Philippians 1:9–10, "And this is my prayer: that your love may abound more and more in knowledge and depth of insight, so that you may be able to discern what is best and may be pure and blameless for the day of Christ" (NIV).

Explore the Definition and Importance of Information Literacy

Ecc, 1:13,
"I applied my mind to study and to explore by wisdom all that is done under the heavens. What a heavy burden God has laid on mankind!" (KJV).

We're now living in an era commonly referred to as the "information and communication" age, because more information is being produced and communicated in today's world than at any other time in history (Breivik, 1998; Cairncross, 2001; Thornburg, 1994). Since information is being generated and disseminated at such a rapid rate, **"information literacy"**—the ability to search for, locate, and evaluate information for relevance and accuracy—is now an essential 21st-century skill for managing and making sense of the overload of information that's currently available to us. If you dedicate yourself to improving your information literacy skills, you'll improve not only your academic performance in college, but also your career performance beyond college. This chapter is designed to strengthen your skills in this key area.

In addition to assignments relating to material covered in course readings and class lectures, you are likely to be assigned research projects that involve writing in response to information you locate and evaluate on your own. One of the key outcomes of a college education is for students to become self-reliant, lifelong learners. One key characteristic of a self-reliant, lifelong learner is information literacy. When you're information literate, you become a critical consumer of information: you know where and how to find credible information whenever you need it (National Forum on Information Literacy, 2005).

Terry

"I learned research skills initially in my high school courses, but more thoroughly in my English classes in college."

© 2013 by Gts. Used under license of Shutterstock, Inc.

"One key characteristic of a self-reliant, lifelong learner is information literacy. When you're information literate, you become a critical consumer of information: you know where and how to find credible information whenever you need it" (National Forum on Information Literacy, 2005).

Develop a Strategy for Research

Hebrews 4:12,

"For the word of God is quick, and powerful, and sharper than any two-edged sword, piercing even to the dividing asunder of soul and spirit, and of the joints and marrow, and is a discerner of the thoughts and intents of the heart" (KJV).

The following is a six-step process for locating, evaluating, and using information to write research papers and reports in college (and beyond). This process can also be used to research information for oral presentations and group projects.

Terry

Q: *What is information literacy?*

A: "Information Literacy is the ability to know how to get information and determining the validity of that information."

1. Define a Research Topic/Question

Be sure that your research topic is relevant to the assignment and that its scope is neither too narrow, leaving you with too little available information on the topic, nor too broad, leaving you with too much information to cover within the maximum number of pages allowed for your paper or report.

If you have any doubts about your topic's relevance or scope, before going any further, seek feedback from your instructor or from a professional in your college library.

2. Locate Potential Sources of Information

You have two major types of resources you can use to search for and locate information:

- **Print resources**—for example, card catalogs, published indexes, and guidebooks; and

- **Online resources**—for example, online card catalogs, Internet search engines, and electronic databases.

As an online student, the bulk of your research will be done using online resources. As an active student at Liberty University, you can search through thousands of full-text scholarly articles by accessing the online library. If you can't locate what you are looking for there, the library also offers interlibrary loan services and will mail material to your home or scan copies of some articles that are not currently available online.

© 2013 by koya979. Used under license of Shutterstock, Inc.

"As an online student, the bulk of your research will be done using online resources."

However, the first question to ask yourself about potential sources is whether they are acceptable to the instructor who assigned your research paper. Before you begin the information-search process, be sure to read the assignment instructions carefully so that you know what sources your instructor requires or prefers. Since different information-search tools are likely to generate different types of information, it's best not to rely exclusively on just one research tool. The following is a list of key information search tools and terms.

Roger

"[Information Literacy] is a skill that continues to change over time. I picked up some of these skills while asking questions at the library. As technology continues to advance, there are more and more tools available to research topics. The best thing that helped me was when I had to take a class that taught me how to perform searches to find the best sources. With online tools at the student's disposal, researching topics should not be as time consuming."

Key Information Search Tools and Terms

Abstract—A concise summary of the source's content, usually appearing at the beginning of an article, which can help you to decide quickly whether the source is relevant to your research topic.

Catalog—A library database containing information about what information sources the library owns and where they are located. Libraries may still have some or all parts of their catalogs available on cards (i.e., in a card catalog); however, most catalogs are now in electronic form and can be searched by typing in a topic heading, author, topic, or keyword.

Citation—A reference to an information source (e.g., book, article, web page) that provides enough information to allow the reader to retrieve the source. Citations used in a college research paper must be given in a standard format, such as APA or MLA format.

Database—A collection of data (information) that has been organized to make the information easily accessible and retrievable. A database may include:

1. Reference citations—for example, author, date, and publication source,
2. Abstracts—summaries of the contents of scholarly articles,
3. Full-length documents, or
4. A combination of 1, 2, and 3.

(continues)

Descriptor (a.k.a. subject heading)—A keyword or key phrase in the index of a database (card or catalog) that describes the subjects or content areas found within it, enabling you to quickly locate sources relevant to your research topic. For example, emotional disorders may be a descriptor for a psychology database to help researchers find information related to anxiety and depression. (Some descriptors or subject headings will be accompanied by suggestions for different words or phrases that you can use in your search.)

Index—An alphabetical listing of topics contained in a database.

Keyword—A word used to search multiple databases by matching the search word to items found in different databases. Keywords are very specific, so if the exact word is not found in the database, any information related to the topic you're researching that doesn't exactly match the keyword will be missed. For example, if the keyword is college, it will not pick up relevant sources that may have university instead of college in their titles.

Search engine—A computer-run program that allows you to search for information across the entire Internet or at a particular website. For regularly updated summaries of different electronic search engines, how they work, and the types of information they generate, check the websites searchenginewatch.com/reports and researchbuzz.com.

Search thesaurus—A list of words or phrases with similar meaning, allowing you to identify which of these words or phrases could be used as keywords, descriptors, or subject headings in the database. This feature enables you to choose the best search terms before beginning the search process.

Subscription database—A database that can only be accessed through a paid subscription. You may be able to access through

Roger

"Not all research evidence is the same. For example, using Wikipedia is not a valid academic source because the imbedded information is not based upon scholarly research. One must examine the abstract, author, supporting documents, the data gathered to determine if it is appropriate academic material for citation in a paper."

(continues)

your college or university library because most electronic data-bases available in libraries are paid for through subscriptions.

URL (uniform resource locator)—An Internet address consisting of a series of letters and/or numbers that pinpoints the exact location of an information resource (e.g., www.breakinggroundlu.com)

Joe Super

"The library—go early, go often."

Wildcard—A symbol, such as an asterisk (*), question mark (?), or exclamation point (!), that may be used to substitute different letters into a search word or phrase, so that an electronic search will be performed on all variations of the word represented by the symbol. For example, an asterisk at the end of the keyword econom* may be used to search for all information sources containing the words economy, economical, or economist.

Source: Hacker and Fister (2010)

When you locate a source, your first step is to evaluate its relevance to your paper's topic. One strategy for efficiently determining the relevance of a source is to ask if it will help you answer one or more of the following questions about your topic: Who? What? When? Where? Why? How?

Personal Reflection

Look back at the list of key information search tools and terms and make note of any terms or definitions that were unfamiliar to you.

_____

_____

_____

_____

_____

_____

_____

_____

_____

3. Evaluate the Credibility and Quality of Your Sources

The primary purpose of your sources is to provide documentation—references that support or confirm your conclusions. Since sources of information can vary widely in terms of their accuracy and quality, you'll need to think critically and make sound judgments about what are solid sources to select and use as documentation. The Internet has made this selection process more challenging, because most of its posted information is self-published and not subjected to the same quality control measures as information published in journals and books—which go to press only after they are reviewed for acceptance by a neutral panel of experts and are carefully edited by a professional editor. Listed below are some criteria to help you critically evaluate the quality of the sources you locate:

Terry

"In today's information age, anyone who wants to can put information out for public consumption. Just as I would verify that my mechanic can work on cars, I need to evaluate whether the author behind a source is knowledgeable in the area they claim they are."

Credible—Is the source written by an authority or expert in the field, such as someone with an advanced educational degree or professional experience relating to the topic? For example, if your topic relates to an international issue, a highly credible source would be an author who has an advanced degree in international relations or professional experience in international affairs.

Scholarly—Is the source a scholarly publication that has been reviewed by a panel or board of impartial experts in the field before being published? If the source is written in formal style and includes references to other published sources, this is a good indication that it's a scholarly reference. Journal articles that have been "peer-reviewed" or "peer-refereed" have been reviewed, evaluated, and approved for publication by other experts in the field. This is a good indication that the source is a scholarly publication. Professional journals (e.g., the *New England Journal of Medicine*) are peer-reviewed, but popular magazines (e.g., *Newsweek*) and popular websites (e.g., Wikipedia) are not. Liberty University offers current students free access to several subscription databases, which are more likely to contain scholarly, peer-reviewed sources that are more closely monitored for quality than free databases available to you on the Internet.

Current—Is it a recent or current source of information? In certain fields of study, such as the natural and social sciences, recent references may be strongly preferred because new data is generated rapidly in these fields and information can become quickly outdated. In other fields, such as history and philosophy, older references may be viewed as classics, and citing them is perfectly acceptable. If you're not sure whether current references are strongly preferred, check the specific assignment instructions and then email your instructor if you are still unsure.

Objective—Is the author likely to be impartial or unbiased toward the subject? One way to answer this question is to consider how the professional positions or personal backgrounds of the authors may influence their ideas or their interpretation of evidence. Scholars should be impartial pursuers of truth who attempt to maximize their objectivity and minimize their level of emotional and political involvement with the topic. They should also not be in a position to gain personally or financially from favoring a certain conclusion about the topic. To assess the objectivity of a website, always ask yourself why the site was created, what its objective or purpose is, and who sponsors it.

Mary Dixon

"Education is a process in which we must develop ideas and execute them. It is not harvesting information."

Research articles you locate may also demonstrate a lack of objectivity. Suppose your topic relates to a controversial political issue such as global warming and you find an article written by a researcher who works for or consults with an industry that would incur significant costs to switch to more ecologically efficient sources of energy. It would be reasonable to suspect that this researcher has a conflict of interest and may be biased toward reaching a conclusion that financially benefits his employer (and himself). In this case, the objectivity of the article may be questionable, and you may not want to use it as a source in your paper. If scholars are not neutral, it increases the risk that they will find what they want to find. In scientific research, this risk is referred to as experimenter bias, and it stems from the natural tendency for people to see what they expect to see or what they hope to see (King, 2010; Rosenthal, 1966). When evaluating an article, ask yourself the following questions to check for bias:

1. Is the author a member of a special-interest group or political or religious organization that could affect the article's objectivity?

2. Does the author consider alternative and opposing viewpoints and deal with those viewpoints fairly?

3. Does the author use words that convey a sense of rationality and objectivity, or are they characterized by emotionality and an inflammatory tone?

If you think an article may lack complete objectivity, but still find that it's well written and contains good information and arguments, you can cite it in your paper; however, be sure you demonstrate critical thinking by noting that its conclusions may have been biased by the author's background or position.

Personal Reflection

The question of credibility can be applied to more than just research. Think about the last news story you heard or read; then evaluate that story using the three questions of credibility.

Subject of the story: _____

Special interests: _____

Alternative views: _____

Subjective wording: _____

Based on your evaluation, was this a credible story, or was there a bias that skewed the reporting?

_____

_____

_____

_____

4. Evaluate the Quantity and Variety of Your Sources

Your research will be judged not only in terms of the quality of your individual sources, but also in terms of the overall set or total collection of references you used throughout your paper. Your total set of references is likely to be judged in terms of the following two criteria:

Quantity of References—Have you cited a sufficient number of references? As a general rule, it is better to use a larger rather than smaller number of references because it will provide your paper with a stronger research foundation and a greater number of perspectives. In addition, using multiple sources allows more opportunity to demonstrate the higher-level thinking skill of synthesis because you can demonstrate your ability to integrate information from different sources. Keep in mind that this is a general rule and that some assignments may require you to use a specific number of references. Be sure you know what is required for each assignment before you begin.

Variety of References—Have you used different types of sources? For some research papers and some professors, the variety of references you use matters as much as (or more than) the sheer quantity. You can intentionally vary your sources by drawing on different types of references, such as:

- Books,

- Scholarly journal articles written by professionals and research scholars in the field,

Mary Dixon

"We can access so much information that it is tempting to circumvent our own thought process by borrowing the thought processes of others. This does not help us to learn, nor does it help us to develop characteristics that will honor God."

- Magazine or newspaper articles written by journalists,

- Course readings or class notes, and

- Personal interviews or personal experiences.

You can also vary your references in terms of using **primary sources**—firsthand information or original documents (e.g., research experiments or novels)—and **secondary sources**—publications that rely on or respond to primary sources (e.g., a textbook or a newspaper article that critically reviews a novel or movie). Lastly, varying your references by including a balanced blend of older, classic sources and newer, cutting-edge references may also be desirable. This combination will enable you to demonstrate how certain ideas have changed or evolved over time or how certain ideas have withstood the test of time and continue to remain important.

In the end, the individual assignment instructions and the purpose of your writing should be the major factor in the variety of references you use.

5. Use Your Sources as Stepping Stones to Your Own Ideas and Conclusions

Your paper should represent something more than an accumulation of ideas gathered from other people. Simply collecting and compiling the ideas of others will result in a final product that reads more like a high school book report than a college research paper. It's your name that appears on the front cover of the paper. Your sources just provide the raw material for your paper; it's your job to shape that raw material into a finished product that's uniquely your own. Do not just report or describe information you've drawn from your sources; instead, react to them, draw conclusions from them, and use them as evidence to support your reactions and conclusions.

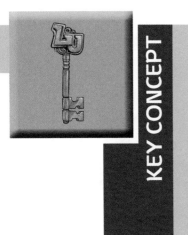

Identify and Avoid Plagiarism

I Timothy 2:1-3,
"I exhort therefore, that, first of all, supplications, prayers, intercessions, and giving of thanks, be made for all men; For kings, and for all that are in authority; that we may lead a quiet and peaceable life in all godliness and honesty. For this is good and acceptable in the sight of God our Saviour" (KJV).

Before you can move on to the sixth step in the research process, properly citing your sources, you need to become familiar with the concepts of academic integrity and plagiarism.

Jenny Walter

"Plagiarism is defined as using anyone's words or ideas as your own. Whether you include the exact words from another, summarize or paraphrase another's thoughts, always give that person the credit."

What Is Academic Integrity?

Academic integrity involves avoiding the unethical practice of stealing the ideas of others, whether they are the ideas of peers (e.g., cheating on exams) or the words and ideas of authorities that have been used in a written paper (plagiarism). When writing papers and reports, students with academic integrity give credit where credit is due: they carefully cite and reference their sources.

What Exactly Is Plagiarism?

Plagiarism is a violation of academic integrity that involves the intentional or unintentional use of someone else's work without acknowledging it, giving the reader the impression that it's the writer's original work.

Common Forms of Plagiarism

1. Paying someone, or paying a service, for a paper and turning it in as your own work

2. Submitting an entire paper, or portion thereof, that was written by someone else

© 2013 by Sielan. Used under license of Shutterstock, Inc.

Copying and pasting is a form of plagiarism when you don't give credit to the original source.

3. Copying sections of someone else's work and inserting it into your own work

4. Cutting paragraphs from separate sources and pasting them into the body of your own paper

5. Paraphrasing (rewording) someone else's words or ideas without citing that person as a source

6. Not placing quotation marks around someone else's exact words that appear in the body of your paper

7. Failing to cite the source of factual information in your paper that's not common knowledge

8. Submitting all or part of a paper that you have previously submitted, as new work, is considered self-plagiarism.

(Academic Integrity at Princeton, 2011; Purdue Online Writing Lab, 2012).

From *Thriving in College and Beyond*, 3/e by Joseph B. Cuseo, Aaron Thompson, Michele Campagna and Viki S. Fecas. Copyright © 2013 by Kendall Hunt Publishing Company. Reprinted by permission.

T. Marcus Christian

"One of the easiest ways to plagiarize is to wait until the last minute to complete an assignment. When you do that, it is easier to borrow from other sources. Save yourself from failure and plan to complete assignments long before they are due."

A Christian Worldview: Avoiding Plagiarism

While there are general rules that all academics follow regarding the avoidance of plagiarism, the Christian academic must also look at this issue using their biblical worldview. Dr. Emily Heady, Vice Provost for Undergraduate Education and Dean for the College of General Studies at Liberty University, shares how to apply a biblical worldview to this topic.

Almost anyone who has taught for any length of time has a story about a student who plagiarized in an unusually brazen (and sometimes laughable) way—the one, for instance, about the student who forgot to remove the hyperlinks when he cut and pasted a Wikipedia article, or the one about the student who plagiarized an article written by his professor, or the one about the student who denied that he could have plagiarized his paper because "[his] roommate wrote the essay for [him]." While students like these (thankfully) come along only rarely, they make a lasting impression—and not a good one. On the one hand, their instructors remember them because they made an extraordinarily poor decision that, more often than not, resulted in their failing the course they were taking. More than this, though, they are memorable for what their poor decision to plagiarize says about them as a person. Instead of using their God-given intellect, talents, and time to complete the requirements for the classes they were taking, these students chose to co-opt others' thoughts and labor, claiming them as their own without acknowledging it. In short, they chose to steal rather than to work.

(continues)

Alissa Keith

"If it doesn't come from your own brain, then cite it. It's better to over-cite than under-cite."

Mary Dixon

"Be true to yourself, and in turn, be true to others. Give credit where credit is due."

As Christians striving to integrate faith and learning, we have an opportunity to develop further our Christian worldview every time we complete an assignment for a class or write something another will read. In part, this means that we avoid the behaviors of the sorts of students mentioned earlier—we can choose to work rather than to steal, and thus maintain high standards of academic honesty. At the same time, we can think about the way that practicing Christian virtues such as gratitude, generosity, humility, honesty, integrity, and industriousness gives us an opportunity to develop ourselves in ways that will allow us to bring God glory through all we do, whether in the classroom or anywhere else we may go.

The first two virtues that we can develop by maintaining a high standard of academic integrity—which both conveniently begin with the letter "g"—go hand-in-hand: *gratitude* and *generosity*. Grateful people are also generous people; when we recognize that what we have has been given to us as a gift rather than as an entitlement, we are more likely to share what we have with others.

© 2013 by Sielan. Used under license of Shutterstock, Inc.

"Practicing Christian virtues such as gratitude, generosity, humility, honesty, integrity, and industriousness gives us an opportunity to develop ourselves in ways that will allow us to bring God glory through all we do."

When we write papers or complete academic assignments of any sort, we depend on the hard work of those who came before. In a broad sense, we operate within the confines of the discipline we study; if we are majoring in psychology, for instance, we are indebted to Erickson, Freud, and many others who helped to shape the way we understand the rules and principles that govern the human mind. More specifically, if we are writing a paper or a discussion board post, we are building on the work of others who came before, including our instructors, the authors of our textbooks, and anyone whose work we consulted while we were formulating our own thoughts and ideas. The best way to express our gratitude to those whose work preceded us is to thank them with a correct citation that follows the formatting conventions of our fields of study.

In turn, our grateful acknowledgment of our debt to others' work helps us to give a generous gift to our own readers as well—the ability to enter into a productive scholarly conversation. If a student of mine is working on a project such as a thesis or a seminar paper, one of the first pieces of research advice I give is to find a great article, then read everything listed in that article's bibliography or works cited page. The reason is not that I want my students to take a shortcut; rather, it is that I want them to benefit from the generosity of others who have invited them to share their scholarly conversation. What could be better than having Christians in the conversations that drive change in academic disciplines and workplaces across the world?

(continues)

In addition to gratitude and generosity, writing a paper with a high degree of academic integrity requires another two related virtues, *humility* and *honesty*. While humility requires us to put others ahead of ourselves, it does NOT require us to think less of ourselves than is warranted; rather, it involves having a right view of ourselves and our own abilities, one which acknowledges that everything good in us comes from God. When we value ourselves rightly, we also find it easier to appreciate the giftedness and contributions of others, for we see their skills as evidence of God's goodness. Thus, the humble student feels no shame in giving credit where credit is due, via a proper citation or a cogent summary of another's work, because the student holds his or her own skills and talents loosely.

It follows, then, that humble students are also honest. They know what work they have done by themselves, and they are open and truthful about what they have gleaned from others. Sometimes, though, it takes hard, detailed work to be honest. During the research process, careful and correct note-taking allows you later on to give credit where credit is due—remember that it will be hard to cite a quotation properly if you can't remember where you found it!

Finally, students completing academic assignments have the opportunity to develop two virtues that begin with the letter "i": *integrity* and *industriousness*. Of all the virtues discussed here, these are perhaps the most obviously applicable to an academic context. Integrity means that we are the same people in private as we are in public; it means we have nothing to hide. Imagine that your course instructor watched you through all phases of your writing process—research, reading, note-taking, drafting, and editing. Would your instructor find that you were operating with integrity as you note others' ideas and then develop your own, or would your instructor discover that you are taking shortcuts to make your work look more impressive than it really was?

The best way to operate with integrity is to make sure that you have worked hard. Of course, we all spend a little bit of time fighting distraction when we are working (I know that my house is never cleaner than on days when I have a major project to complete!), and we all struggle to keep our eyes open when we are reading a pile of articles on a less-than-interesting topic. Yet working industriously is a choice we make. If we research diligently—not reading everything we could, but reading enough to have a thorough understanding of our topic—take careful notes, draft conscientiously, and edit in such a way as to produce a finished project of which we can be proud, then we have put ourselves in a position to demonstrate all these virtues to their fullest. We will find it easy to be humbly grateful for the work others have

Mary Dixon

"Honor God's work in yourself and his work in others by citing information and ideas that you use to become truly educated."

Mark Heideman

"Do not minimize the importance of adhering to Academic Writing Standards such as APA, Turabian, etc. Students often say 'I won't use this after college,' which is sometimes true but writing standards hone in on other writing skills such as spelling/grammar, formatting, professional looking documents, etc."

(continues)

done because we will have a thorough knowledge of what everyone has contributed, and in turn, we will be able to operate with honesty and integrity because we will have nothing to hide. This will have the final benefit of giving us an opportunity to contribute generously to our field of study.

Of course, schools across the country have strict policies against plagiarism and other types of academic misconduct (cheating, falsification, etc.). Liberty University (like its secular peers) values academic integrity and holds its students to high standards. We have set rules about what is allowed and not allowed, and we publish them in obvious places such as the academic catalog and even some course syllabi. Should students violate these rules, there are consequences, ranging from minor grade deductions to failure in a class to expulsion from the university. Liberty is unlike its secular peers, though, in the reason it has these rules: the intimate connection between Christian worldview and academic ethics. We publish and enforce policies about academic ethics not only to protect the academic reputation of Liberty University, but also because the best way to learn about the Christian worldview is to put it into practice. Like driving a car, being an effective Christian requires not just knowing but doing—studying the driver's manual and getting out on the road.

As you journey to your degree, we hope and pray that you'll not only stay out of trouble by maintaining the highest academic standards, but also that you'll think of your assignments as opportunities to put your worldview into practice.

Katie Robinson

"Information literacy and avoiding plagiarism isn't just about avoiding the trespass of taking credit for someone else's work. Instead, writing a body of work that includes thorough research and support from other sources (documented correctly, of course) serves to demonstrate that the writer has done his or her job well in presenting good, solid information that is backed up by other researchers."

Cite Your Sources with Integrity—The Sixth Step in the Research Process

Now that you are familiar with the concepts of academic integrity and plagiarism, it's time to discuss the primary technique you can employ to practice academic integrity and avoid plagiarism. By citing and referencing your sources, you demonstrate intellectual honesty by giving credit where credit is due. You credit others whose ideas you've borrowed and you credit yourself for the careful research you've done.

When should sources be cited? You should cite the source of anything you include in your paper that does not represent your own work or thoughts. This includes other people's words, ideas, statistics, research findings, and visual work (e.g., diagrams, pictures, or drawings). There is only one exception to this rule: You don't need to cite sources for

"By citing and referencing your sources, you demonstrate intellectual honesty by giving credit where credit is due."

information that's common knowledge—that is, information that most people already know. For example, common knowledge includes well-known facts (e.g., the Earth is the third planet from the Sun) and familiar dates (e.g., the Declaration of Independence was signed in 1776).

The Quote, the Paraphrase, and the Summary

Presenting the Research of Published Professionals Appropriately

When using research and support within academic writing, you may want to share the ideas of experienced professionals, who have conducted research regarding your writing topic, with your audience. In order to use the documented research of these published professionals as evidence for support within your own writing, you must give credit to them by sharing and citing their ideas appropriately; this can be achieved in one of three ways: the quote, the paraphrase, and the summary:

Quote: When you quote a source, you use the exact words of the original author. You typically use quotes when you want to provide evidence or a powerful argument from the original author, and you believe that using your own words would lessen the impact of that information. In most cases, you will enclose a quote with quotation marks.

Paraphrase: When you paraphrase a passage, you provide a detailed accounting of the original author's ideas and argument, but you use your own words. Paraphrases simplify an idea or argument for your reader. A paraphrase can be as long as the original passage, but with additional context from you, it could be longer than the original.

Summary: A summary is a *brief* representation of the original author's ideas or argument; just like in the paraphrase, you use your own words when you summarize. To keep a summary brief, you only want to give your readers a big-picture overview of the most important points that the original author made.

The Quote, the Paraphrase, and the Summary—In Action

Read the following paragraph from Chapter 6:

> *Learning from a distance can be difficult, but you have the opportunity to make it an extremely personal endeavor. You have a storehouse of experiences that you can use to help you connect*

(continues)

---

with the information in your online classes. Taking a basic math course can be connected to your experiences paying the household bills or managing a small business. Studying a passage of scripture on forgiveness can be connected to several past experiences where you struggled to forgive someone, and a lesson on how adults learn can be related back to previous learning experiences you have had at work or in other educational environments. The key is to use these experiences to connect with and remember the information you are learning. They will help you to internalize the concepts, which will increase the likelihood that you will store the information in your long-term memory (Hassenpflug, Traphagen, & Conner, 2014, p. 164).

Using the aforementioned excerpt as the source text, an example of a quote, a paraphrase, and a summary in action is provided:

Quote: "The key is to use these experiences to connect with and remember the information you are learning" (Hassenpflug, Traphagen, & Conner, 2014, p. 164).

Paraphrase: You can personalize your learning by seeking and identifying the connections between what you are learning and your past experiences. Use what you know from experience to help you remember what you are learning now. Making these connections can help you consolidate information in your memory and build your success (Hassenpflug, Traphagen, & Conner, 2014, p. 164).

Summary: According to Hassenpflug, Traphagen, & Conner (2014), adult learners can improve their chances of learning new material by linking new information to things they already know.

Ramona Myers

"Rules to help avoid plagiarism (I call this the 'sandwich method'):

(1) Introduce the source with a signal phrase before providing the source information. Often, this signal phrase will include the name of the author (and in APA, the year in parenthesis). This is the 'top bun' of the sandwich.

(2) Source material may be written as a Direct Quote, a Summary, or a Paraphrase. This is the 'meat' and the 'condiments' of the sandwich.

(3) The 'bottom bun' of source material involves finalizing the source with an ending citation."

The Internet has allowed us to gain easy access to an extraordinary amount of information and has made research much easier—that's the good news. The bad news is that it has also made proper citation more challenging. Determining the true "owner" or original author of information posted online isn't as clear-cut as it is for published books and articles. If you have any doubt, print it out and check it out with your instructor or a professional librarian. If you don't have the time or opportunity to consult with either one of them, then play it safe and cite the source in your paper. If you cannot find the name of an author, at least cite the website, the date of the posted information (if available), and the date you accessed or downloaded it.

Remember: As a general rule, whenever you're unsure about the need to cite a source, it's better to cite it and risk being corrected for over-citing than it is to run the risk of being accused of plagiarism—a serious violation of academic integrity that can have grave consequences (e.g., probation, suspension, or expulsion).

Where and how should sources be cited? Sources should be cited in two places: (1) the body of your paper (in-text citations) and (2) the reference section at the end of your paper (also known as a "bibliography" or "works cited" section).

How you should cite your sources depends on the referencing style of the particular academic field or discipline in which you are writing your paper, so be sure that you know the citation style your instructor prefers. It's likely that you will be expected to use one of three referencing styles during your time at Liberty:

1. **MLA Style**—standing for the Modern Language Association—the citation style commonly used in the humanities and fine arts (e.g., English and theatre arts); or

2. **APA Style**—standing for the American Psychological Association—the citation style most commonly used in the social and natural sciences (e.g., sociology and anthropology).

3. **Turabian Style**—named for the original author, Kate L. Turabian, and very similar to Chicago Style—the citation style commonly used in religion courses here at Liberty.

Be aware of the referencing style that is expected or preferred by your instructor before you begin to write your paper.

The key elements when citing another author's work in the body of your paper are the last name of the author, the date of publication, and, in situations where you are quoting, the page number from which the information was retrieved. When citing the same works in your references section, you will need to include additional information. Refer to the specific writing manual for details, as the exact information and formatting required will vary by style.

Examples (in APA):

- When quoting—include the author's last name, publication date, and page number

- When paraphrasing—include the author's last name and publication date (a page number is encouraged, but is not required)

- When summarizing—include the author's last name and publication date

If you paraphrase or summarize several ideas from the same source within the same paragraph, and if you are not mixing in the ideas of other authors, you do not need to cite the author after every single sentence; cite the source only once at the end of the paragraph. However, you do need to include a citation immediately following each quotation.

Personal Reflection

Take a look back at the definition and forms of plagiarism described in the early part of this chapter. List those forms of plagiarism that you were not aware of or weren't sure actually represented plagiarism.

_____

_____

_____

_____

_____

BUILDING BLOCKS

Summary and Conclusion

The key skill discussed in this chapter—research (information literacy)—is a powerful, transferable skill that can be applied across different academic subjects that you encounter in college and across different work situations you encounter beyond college.

Research, writing, and speaking are interrelated and complementary sets of success tools. Research skills are needed to acquire high-quality ideas from others, and both writing and speaking skills are needed to actively stimulate your own thinking about the ideas you acquire and as vehicles for communicating your ideas to others. Said in another way, research skills enable you to locate, evaluate, and integrate information, while writing and speaking skills enable you to comprehend, communicate, and demonstrate your mastery of that information to others.

These three key skills have always been relevant to the educational and professional success of college students and college alumni, but they are even more critical for success in today's information and communication age. Furthermore, as discussed earlier, they are valued highly by employers.

Crime and Punishment: Plagiarism and Its Consequences

Because of the ease with which internet sources can be copied and pasted, it is now common for college students to submit assignments using text that has been lifted off the Web. In response to this trend many universities now subscribe to websites that match the content of students' papers with content from books and online sources. To monitor plagiarism in their classes, faculty members require students to submit their papers through these websites. At Liberty University, we use a tool called SafeAssign. The SafeAssign tool compares students' work to find matches with previously published work. The match may be to a work by a well-known source or to another student's work. The SafeAssign service can be described as a dumb tool, as it does not make judgments, it only finds matching words. It is the responsibility of faculty and students to carefully evaluate the matches to determine if matching words are common knowledge, properly cited paraphrases or quoted material, or at worst, plagiarism. If students are caught plagiarizing, for a first offense, they typically receive an F for the assignment or the course. A second offense can result in dismissal or expulsion from college.

Source: http://www.plagiarism.org/index.html

Personal Reflection

1. Why do you think students plagiarize? What do you suspect are the primary motives, reasons, or causes? (*Hint:* Remember what Dr. Heady had to say about this.)

2. What do you think is a fair or just penalty for those found guilty of a first plagiarism violation? What is fair for those who commit a second violation?

3. How do you think plagiarism could be most effectively reduced or prevented from happening in the first place?

4. Do Christian students have any additional responsibilities when it comes to ethical behavior when producing written work? Why or why not?

TOOL BOX

Become Information Literate

Search for Quality Sources

Research Guides—Research guides are yet another invaluable resource provided to Liberty University students by the school's librarians. Research guides are informational pages that explain the details of various resources and processes. You can locate information and tutorials on how to use the various, subject-specific databases, as well as gain direct access to thousands of media and web resources. Research guides can be located on the library website.

The Jerry Falwell Library—The Jerry Falwell Library is the primary means by which you will search for and locate scholarly journal articles, media, and web resources as you work to complete academic projects for your classes. Not only does the library house thousands of full-text online resources, but the staff will also mail out physical media to online students.

www.liberty.edu/library

Cite Your Work

Citation Software—For help in citing your sources and building a reference page, Liberty University offers free Citation Software to active LUO students. The software can be used on both Mac and PC and allows you to fill out a brief survey of information regarding each of your sources; then, it formats your information based on the citation style you indicate. Be sure to check the results, as you are ultimately responsible for ensuring the accuracy of your work. You can locate a link to this resource on the Breaking Ground website.

Writing Aids from the LUO Writing Center—If you are looking for a checklist of a writing style's basic elements, this site is the place to go. You can quickly review all of the writing basics, as well as verify that you have met the required elements for standard citations types and even review samples of entire papers written in the various formats.

www.liberty.edu/onlinewritingcenter

Additional resources and links to specific sites, worksheets, and apps can be located by accessing the Breaking Ground website:

www.breakinggroundlu.com/

References

Academic Integrity at Princeton. (2011). *Examples of plagiarism*. Retrieved from http://www.princeton.edu/pr/pub/integrity

Breivik, P. S. (1998). *Student learning in the information age*. Phoenix, AZ: The Oryx Press.

Cairncross, F. C. (2001). *The death of distance: How the communication revolution is changing our lives*. Cambridge, MA: Harvard Business School Press.

Hacker, D. & Fister, B. (2010). *Research and documentation in the electronic age* (5th ed.). Boston, MA: Bedford/St. Martin's.

Hassenpflug, A. S., Traphagen, A. D., & Conner, J. J. (2014). *Breaking ground: Keys for successful online learning*. Dubuque, IA: Kendall/Hunt Pub. Co.

King, G. (2010, April). A hard unsolved problem? Post-treatment bias in big social science questions. Presentation made at the Hard Problems in Social Science Symposium, Institute for Quantitative Social Science, Harvard University, Cambridge, MA.

National Forum on Information Literacy. (2005). *Forum overview*. Retrieved from http://www.infolit.org

Purdue University Online Writing Lab. (2012). *Writing a research paper*. Retrieved from http://owl.english.purdue.edu

Rosenthal, R. (1966). *Experimenter effects in behavioral research*. New York, NY: Appleton-Century-Crofts.

Thornburg, D. D. (1994). *Education in the communication age*. San Carlos, CA: Starsong.

Chapter 9

Academic Writing: The Lighting

In this chapter, you will:

- Determine the importance of writing.
- Select different writing strategies for active learning.
- Identify and use the essential stages of academic writing.

ELECTRICITY

In a construction project, every room requires electricity, just as in education, every class requires some sort of writing assignment. In a building, each room has different electrical needs, from wiring the lighting fixtures and the appliances to providing power to the air conditioning system. The builder must refer to the blueprints to determine where the wiring should go. The same is true for academic writing; each class will have different objectives that must be accomplished through writing. The author must refer to his or her writing blueprints (resources such as instructions, rubric, prewriting, etc.) to determine what to address when working on the assignment.

© 2013 by ??. Used under license of Shutterstock, Inc.

I Corinthians 14:40,
"Let all things be done decently and in order" (KJV).

THE CORNERSTONE

James 1:2–5, "Consider it pure joy, my brothers and sisters, whenever you face trials of many kinds, because you know that the testing of your faith produces perseverance. Let perseverance finish its work so that you may be mature and complete, not lacking anything. If any of you lacks wisdom, you should ask God, who gives generously to all without finding fault, and it will be given to you" (NIV).

Fruitful Endeavors

Writing is hard work! The process itself takes diligence, patience, and perseverance. Like most worthwhile endeavors in life, the investment in these virtues yields a fruitful harvest. To illustrate, my little family learned the joys of diligence, patience, and perseverance in an outing that inspired a delicious blackberry cobbler.

One beautiful, sunny, Virginia morning in the early fall, our six-year-old daughter, Laura Grace, told us that she wanted to pick blackberries. My husband, Terry, looked online for a local orchard that offered the picking experience and found Morris' Orchard in Monroe, VA. Surrounded by luscious, green hills and Virginia's Blue Ridge Mountains, Morris' Orchard not only offers blackberry picking, but depending on the season, it also offers pink lemonade slushies, peaches, apples, apple donuts, pumpkins, and Christmas trees. We love any excuse to visit.

© 2013 by Rock and Wasp. Used under license of Shutterstock, Inc.

"Writing is hard work! The process itself takes diligence, patience, and perseverance. Like most worthwhile endeavors in life, the investment in these virtues yields a fruitful harvest."

Terry and I loaded Laura Grace and her one-year-old sister, Marianna, into our blueberry blue 4 × 4 and headed to the orchard. Once we arrived at the orchard, friendly bunnies and goats greeted us, and our daughters giggled with excitement. Terry and I ushered the girls into the big, red barn that features jams, jellies, salsas, and various peanut treats; we picked up our yellow bucket and headed toward the rows of blackberry bushes.

Terry selected a row that was a little off the beaten path; those rows tend to be less frequented by orchard visitors and yield more fruitful opportunities. Terry told Laura Grace that she should look for clusters of berries that had turned black and juicy. Laura Grace determined that she wanted to find the biggest and juiciest blackberry of the day and began her search. Marianna was more interested in the pretty pink and red berries that were not quite ripe. She picked one after another and handed them all to me, so proud of herself.

As we lifted up vines, picked clusters of berries, plopped them in our plastic yellow bucket, and moved toward the next bush, I noticed that our hands were all stained with a deep red, berry juice. Marianna also had some convicting stains on her face and around her mouth—somebody had been sneaking a berry or two. We all worked so hard in the fall sunshine that our clothes stuck to our skin, sweat rolled down our faces, and our stomachs growled for lunch. We headed back to the big, red barn to pay for our bucket, brimming full of ripe blackberries. Terry treated us to pink lemonade slushies . . . yum! Then, we headed home for lunch, showers, and naps.

Having rinsed off the blackberries and pondering what to make, Terry decided to bake his Nanny's famous cobbler. We took the blackberry cobbler to Sunday lunch with our family. It was a hit! The combination of tart berry with the sweetness of the cobbler made our mouths long for more. People kept sneaking back into the kitchen and heaping another spoonful into their bowls. It was heavenly! Laura Grace told our family that the secret ingredient in the cobbler was the biggest, juiciest berry that she found. Marianna just smiled, said "Mmmm," and begged for more.

© RoJo Images

"Just like our blackberry adventure, writing is chore, and it is worth completing . . . knowing that the Lord has delicious things in store for you."

All of our perspiration and diligence paid off in that delicious, please-give-me-another-spoonful dessert and in the memory we shared with our two precious, hardworking daughters. The end product was truly amazing, but the journey itself helped us grow together as a family, toiling in the blackberry row with a united purpose.

Just like our blackberry adventure, writing is a chore, and it is worth completing. When you commit to the process, invest yourself in the hard work, and see the final product, the trial itself will make you a better, stronger writer. Not only that, but just as it says in James 1:2–5, the efforts will produce perseverance and maturity in your character. So, approach opportunities to write with giggles and excitement, knowing that the Lord has delicious things in store for you.

Determine the Importance of Writing

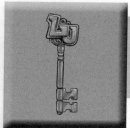

Jeremiah 30:1–3 says,
"The word that came to Jeremiah from the Lord, saying,[2] Thus speaketh the Lord God of Israel, saying, Write thee all the words that I have spoken unto thee in a book.[3] For, lo, the days come, saith the Lord, that I will bring again the captivity of my people Israel and Judah, saith the Lord: and I will cause them to return to the land that I gave to their fathers, and they shall possess it" (NIV).

How do you feel about writing? Do you love it? Do you hate it? Is it something you approach with joy or with dread, or are you indifferent? Regardless of how you approach writing, our Heavenly Father also has His own perspective. Writing is important to God. In Jeremiah 30:1–3, He tells Jeremiah to write a book to document the wondrous miracles that He would perform.

The Bible is God's love story for us. If we did not have the Bible, how else would we know that He sent His only Son, Jesus, as a Holy Sacrifice for our sins, so that we could be redeemed? It is no coincidence that God inspired men to write these words, so that we would know His redemption and love. Without these writings, without these willing hearts who wrote what the Lord asked of them, we would be lost.

Today, writing is important for a myriad of reasons. We communicate via letters, emails, social media, and texting. We develop resumes, portfolios, and cover letters for job hunting. We write essays and reports in academic settings. Writing should be important to us for practical reasons and also because writing is important to God. The Bible is an expression of His love for us through writing, through living words! He molded us in His image as creative beings, so embrace that creativity and start writing!

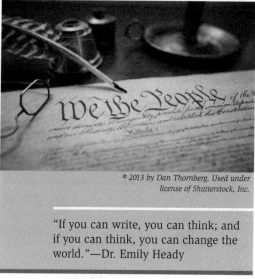

© 2013 by Dan Thornberg. Used under license of Shutterstock, Inc.

"If you can write, you can think; and if you can think, you can change the world."—Dr. Emily Heady

Katie Robinson

"While some students struggle with their writing process at first, developing the skills of communicating through written word presents a student with a source of empowerment. It is through writing that we can communicate with permanence."

Select Different Writing Strategies for Active Learning

Proverbs 9:9,
"Instruct the wise and they will be wiser still; teach the righteous and they will add to their learning" (NIV).

Photo courtesy of Aaron Traphagen

"Using different writing strategies as you approach your academics will help you gain wisdom with each new learning experience."

Several different writing strategies exist that can enrich your learning experiences. Joseph Cuseo (2013), a psychology professor specializing in the first year experience for college students, discusses these strategies in his text, *Thriving in College and Beyond*; the strategies include: writing to learn, writing to listen, writing to read, writing to remember, writing to organize, writing to study, writing to understand, writing to create, writing to discuss, and writing to solve problems. Using these different writing strategies as you approach your academics will help you gain wisdom with each new learning experience. Determine which of these approaches will benefit you as you study the academic content of your online classes.

T. Marcus Christian

"One of the best ways to ensure you stay on the right path is to write well. Writing, along with any other skill, takes time and practice. When you write well, you will find your pathways opening."

WRITING STRATEGIES FOR ACTIVE LEARNING		
Writing to . . .	**What does it Mean?**	**How do I do it?**
Learn	Write for your benefit, rather than for a specific, graded assignment.	▪ Gather notes from a document to support a new concept.
Listen	Write while listening to a lecture, recording, etc. to capture the gist of what you have heard.	▪ Write a brief summary of what you have heard in a lecture. ▪ Jot down questions and ideas throughout the lesson to deepen understanding of new concepts.
Read	Writing while reading keeps you focused on the content and aids in comprehension.	▪ Take notes by outlining main points.

WRITING STRATEGIES FOR ACTIVE LEARNING		
Writing to . . .	*What does it Mean?*	*How do I do it?*
Remember	The physical act and visual representation involved in transferring important concepts to paper solidifies the content in your mind, and as a result, you will be able to remember the information later.	▪ Create a list of key terms, definitions, and concepts.
Organize	Breaking down the main points of a topic into categories/concepts can promote orderly thinking and assists in the process of completing more advanced projects and writing assignments.	▪ Label index cards with the appropriate category and write a summary of the relevant information; if using a resource, be sure to write the source information on the back of the card to keep track of where you retrieved the information. ▪ Outline your main points in the order in which you wish to remember/use them.
Study	Writing to study helps you prepare for assessments of all kinds.	▪ Create your own study guide by looking over the information that will be covered on the test and write down questions that you would ask your students on the test if you were the professor.
Understand	Writing down what you have read or heard in your own words is a good way to assess whether or not you understood the concepts presented in the lesson. This practice helps you reflect and analyze where your learning is lacking and what needs further clarification.	▪ Summaries ▪ K-W-L activities, list what you know, want to know, what you learned

Emily

Q: *Are you a good writer?*

A: "I'm a decent writer, and I became one by developing a wide vocabulary and learning how to use it properly. Plus, I use my imagination."

Terry Conner

"Communication, in any form, but specifically in the written form, is imperative for your post-collegiate success. In a recent study of what employers look for in new employees, employers listed communication (both verbal and written) and problem solving skills as the most desirable qualities for new hires."

Mary Dixon

"Richard Reeves said, 'Writing energy is like anything else. The more you put in, the more you get out.' Treat writing like the work it is. Make a plan, focus on the task, start, and keep at it until the job is done."

Maddy

Q: *Are you a good writer? How did/do you become one? Describe your process of learning about good academic research/writing.*

A: "I believe I am a good writer, and I am entirely certain it is due to the excellent English teachers I have had. Three in particular come to mind: one who taught me how to outline and write a good paper, one who taught me how to research, and one who taught me to love doing those things."

WRITING STRATEGIES FOR ACTIVE LEARNING		
Writing to . . .	*What does it Mean?*	*How do I do it?*
Create	When it is time to complete a project or an assignment, a great place to start is to write down ideas as they come to you. The act of writing allows ideas to take a place on paper before they are forgotten. Once on paper, the good ideas can be developed further, and the bad ideas can be material for a good laugh later on. If you don't write the creative ideas down, you will likely forget them later.	■ Freewriting, brainstorming
Discuss	Before discussing a topic, preparing for the discussion by writing down key points can help the conversation go smoothly. It can also help keep you focused on the topic and result in a productive and meaningful meeting.	■ Listing ideas/questions, creating an agenda for focused and productive discussion
Problem Solving	Writing can assist with problem solving by helping you keep track of your thought process. Why did you make that choice? Why not make this choice? This kind of record can help you/others make better future decisions.	■ Documenting the process by writing it down and organizing it based on topic, order of importance, or order of required steps. Include the "why" behind the selected process

Personal Reflection

Proverbs 9:9 says, "Instruct the wise and they will be wiser still; teach the righteous and they will add to their learning." Based on what you have learned about how to use writing to enhance your learning experience, how can you *add* to your learning? As you work on assignments in your class, jot down how you can/do use each of these strategies in the column provided below.

USE WRITING STRATEGIES FOR ACTIVE LEARNING		
Writing to . . .	*What does it mean?*	*How can/do I use this strategy?*
Learn	Write for your benefit, rather than for a specific, graded assignment.	
Listen	Write while listening to a lecture, recording, etc. to capture the gist of what you have heard.	
Read	Writing while reading keeps you focused on the content and aids in comprehension.	
Remember	The physical act and visual representation involved in transferring important concepts to paper solidifies the content in your mind, and as a result, you will be able to remember the information later.	
Organize	Breaking down the main points of a topic into categories/concepts can promote orderly thinking and assists in the process of completing more advanced projects and writing assignments.	
Study	Writing to study helps you prepare for assessments of all kinds.	

Terry

Q: *Why is learning about writing important?*

A: "It is how we communicate; oftentimes, it's the first impression someone has of you in a work environment. Being able to communicate clearly is an essential skill."

Michael Shenkle

"Fair or not, we are judged by the quality of our writing. Even the strongest of ideas can be lost in poor composition or less-than-ideal grammar. Regardless of your current level of expertise, I strongly encourage you to commit to improving this aspect of your academic and professional skill set. In the words of Dr. Emily Heady, 'If you can write, you can think; and if you can think, you can change the world.'"

USE WRITING STRATEGIES FOR ACTIVE LEARNING		
Writing to . . .	**What does it mean?**	**How can/do I use this strategy?**
Understand	Writing down what you have read or heard in your own words is a good way to assess whether or not you understood the concepts presented in the lesson. This practice helps you reflect and analyze where your learning is lacking and what needs further clarification.	
Create	When it is time to complete a project or an assignment, a great place to start is to write down ideas as they come to you. The act of writing allows ideas to take a place on paper before they are forgotten. Once on paper, the good ideas can be developed further, and the bad ideas can be material for a good laugh later on. If you don't write the creative ideas down, you will likely forget them later.	
Discuss	Before discussing a topic, preparing for the discussion by writing down key points can help the conversation go smoothly. It can also help keep you focused on the topic and result in a productive and meaningful meeting.	
Problem Solving	Writing can assist with problem solving by helping you keep track of your thought process. Why did you make that choice? Why not make this choice? This kind of record can help you/others make better future decisions.	

Identify and Use the Essential Stages of Academic Writing

I Corinthians 14:40,
"Let all things be done decently and in order" (KJV).

Even in academic writing, it is essential that you do things "decently and in order" as I Corinthians 14:40 suggests. In order to create an organized and polished piece of writing, it is important to identify and use the essential stages of academic writing. A way to remember these ten basic steps easily is through the mnemonic device: SOW AND REAP.

Study the instructions and grading expectations.
Obtain a main topic.
Write down a list of subtopics that complement the main topic.

Acquire resources and quotes to add support for your subtopics.
Number subtopics in logical order.
Draft the writing assignment.

Revise to improve content, organization, style, etc.
Edit by focusing on spelling, punctuation, and grammar mistakes.
Ask someone you trust to read and review your writing.
Prepare the final draft by implementing recommended changes.

These organized steps are designed to help you achieve maximum success on any writing assignment you tackle. As you begin writing papers and reports for your college courses, be sure to follow each step carefully and completely.

Stephanie A. Hobson

"Writing well is hard work—even for your professors! But it is possible if you think of writing as a process. A good paper doesn't just happen by putting your fingers on the keyboard and hoping for inspiration. In fact, most of the work comes before you even start to draft your paper. Brainstorming, grouping together ideas, outlining, researching, drafting, revising, and proofreading are all important steps to producing a great paper. If you plan ahead so that you can work through all of these steps, you will see great improvement in your writing and grades!"

Study the Instructions and Grading Expectations

At the beginning of your course, you will receive a course syllabus. In the syllabus, assignment overviews and grading procedures are generally provided. Check the syllabus for your course and see if there are any instructions provided within it regarding the assignment. Detailed assignment instructions can often be found in a document or web page that corresponds

Betsey Caballero

"Follow directions carefully and ALWAYS proofread your assignments!"

Terry

Q: *Describe a great professor.*

A: "A great professor is one who is attentive and responds quickly with feedback on assignments and or responses to questions. They will also hold you accountable for the information they are supposed to teach. After all, they are the stewards of that discipline."

directly with the assignment. Take a look at the instructions and break them down into their simplest forms, like a checklist, and use this as a reference when you begin working on the assignment.

For example, in a culinary arts course, you may have an assignment that looks something like this:

Favorite Recipe Essay: Assignment Instructions
Write a five-paragraph essay (500 words minimum) that explains important steps someone else might need to follow if they wanted to create your favorite recipe. Use APA formatting style to format your paper and to cite any sources that you use within the essay.

Breaking down the instructions in their simplest form would look like this:

- ☐ Five-paragraph essay
- ☐ 500 words minimum
- ☐ Steps to make favorite recipe
- ☐ APA formatting
- ☐ Cite sources used

Additionally, be sure to review the assignment's **rubric**. This is the tool that your professor will use to grade your writing assignment. Look at the expectations detailed within it and use it to make sure that you address all of the requirements.

For the Favorite Recipe Essay, the rubric would look like the one provided here. Notice the different categories that will be evaluated: content, organization, grammar and mechanics, and formatting. Also, notice that there are three different areas for scoring: excellent/good; fair/decent; poor/deficient. Use the expectations described in the "Excellent/Good" category as a checklist when writing to ensure that you will earn the best score on your essay.

Grading Rubric: Essay Sample

	Excellent/Good- 3	Fair/Decent- 2	Poor/Deficient- 1
Content	Essay content *meets* the expectations and includes the following elements: ■ Thesis statement establishes the main topic(s) and point/direction of the essay.	Essay content *mostly meets* the expectations and includes the following elements: ■ Thesis statement establishes the main topic(s) and point/direction of the essay.	Essay content *does not meet* expectations: ■ Thesis statement may be missing or does not establish the topics/point of the essay.
	■ Thoroughly addresses the main topic(s) of the assignment and remains focused throughout the piece. ■ Explains the topic(s), providing essential details and support that strengthens the content.	■ Addresses the main topic(s) of the assignment and mostly remains focused on the topic(s) throughout the piece. ■ Explains the topic(s) and provides details and support; more substantial support may be necessary.	■ The main topic(s) may be unclear or vague; focus is limited. ■ No support is provided, or support, if provided, does not pertain to the assigned topic.
Organization	Essay organization *meets* the expectations and includes the following elements: ■ Strong introduction paragraph with attention getter, explanatory transition sentences, and a comprehensive thesis statement. ■ Three body paragraphs that follow the sequence outlined in the thesis, each beginning with a topic sentence and concluding with a sentence that wraps up the main points of the paragraph and transitions into the next paragraph. ■ A conclusion paragraph reviews the main points addressed within the essay and provides a final, convincing application.	Essay organization *mostly meets* the expectations and includes the following elements: ■ Introduction paragraph with attention getter and a thesis statement. ■ Three body paragraphs that follow the sequence outlined in the thesis statement; transitions may exist but may be weak. ■ A conclusion paragraph includes a statement that reviews the main points addressed within the essay and provides a final application. The application may not be convincing or effective.	Essay organization *does not meet* expectations: ■ Lacks structure and organization altogether. ■ Key elements are missing: introduction paragraph, three body paragraphs, transition sentences, concluding paragraph, etc. ■ The direction of the piece is unclear and points appear to be scattered and disconnected. ■ No application is provided; the essay just ends.
Grammar and Mechanics	Essay is *free* from grammatical, spelling, and punctuation *errors*.	Essay is *mostly free* from grammatical, spelling, and punctuation *errors* (more than *3-5 mistakes*).	Essay *contains numerous* grammatical, spelling, and punctuation *errors* (more than *5 mistakes*).
Formatting	Essay *meets* the following criteria: ■ Follows the parameters of the assignment instructions. ■ Formatting of essay/citations follows APA guidelines. ■ Meets the minimum word count. ■ Honor statement is signed.	Essay *mostly meets* the following criteria; it is *missing no more than 1* of the required pieces: ■ Follows the parameters of the assignment instructions. ■ Formatting of essay/citations follows APA guidelines. ■ Meets the minimum word count. ■ Honor statement is signed.	Essay *does not* meet the following criteria; it is *missing 2 or more* of the required pieces: ■ Follows the parameters of the assignment instructions. ■ Formatting of essay/citations follows APA guidelines. ■ Meets the minimum word count. ■ Honor statement is signed.
Total: /12			

Photos courtesy of Dave Moquin

Every sunset casts brilliant, vivid colors across the sky as it descends into the night; while it sets, the sun's positions and hues vary, revealing majestic stages of a beautiful process. Just as the stages of the sunset, everything in life requires a process of some kind, even the skill of writing; in order to write well, to achieve your purpose, and to write beautifully, you must complete strategic stages in a purposeful and beautiful process.

Obtain a Main Topic

What is going to be the main topic for your assignment? Look at the instructions for your assignment. Pick out the key words from the instructions and identify the main topic that you will need to address within the assignment.

For example, remember when we broke down the instructions into their simplest form for the culinary arts course? This was the list we generated:

- Five-paragraph essay
- 500 words minimum
- Steps to make favorite recipé
- APA formatting
- Cite sources used

Of the key words listed above, which one relates to the main topic?

- Steps to make favorite recipe

As you write this essay, you want to make sure that your content centers on explaining the steps to making your favorite recipe. For the purpose of our example, let's choose "Building a Delicious Pizza" as our main topic.

Sometimes, the assignment instructions will allow you to choose your own topic. In cases like this, look at the instructions for the type/mode of writing that you need to use when addressing the topic you selected. Some forms of writing used in academics include analysis, argument, classification, comparison/contrast, definition, description, illustration, or narration. Be sure that you include the elements required of that writing mode to ensure that you are meeting the requirements of the assignment.

Write Down a List of Subtopics that Complement the Main Topic

This is an opportunity to brainstorm and write down any ideas that you may have about your main topic. The prewriting steps, beginning with this one, are critical elements of the writing process; Lindemann (as cited by Kolb, Longest, & Jensen, 2001) explains that "scholars of composition are in agreement that this activity helps students generate, organize, and explore new ideas" (2013). No idea is necessarily wrong in this phase; you can always eliminate irrelevant pieces after you have done your research and acquired the resources you plan to use.

To assist in the brainstorming process, Susan Winebrenner (2012), founder of Education Consulting Service and author of multiple learning resources for educators, developed a graphic organizer to assist with the part of the prewriting process. Below is a template that can be used to brainstorm about possible suptopics for an essay's main topic.

Graphic Organizer: Essay Sample

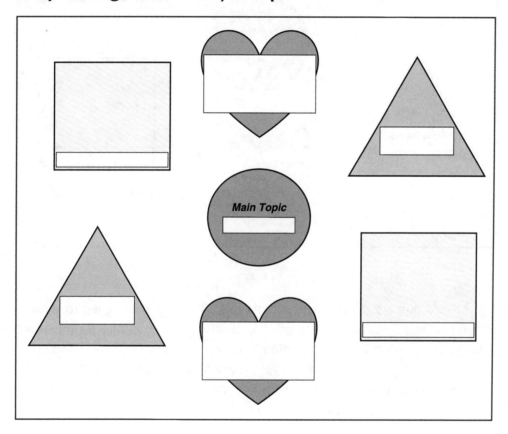

For the culinary arts essay, the subtopics for "Building a Delicious Pizza" may include:

1. Baking Tools
2. Oven Style
3. Toppings
4. Sauce
5. Crust
6. Restaurants.

We have listed these subtopic ideas in the following graphic organizer.

Subtopic Ideas: Essay Sample

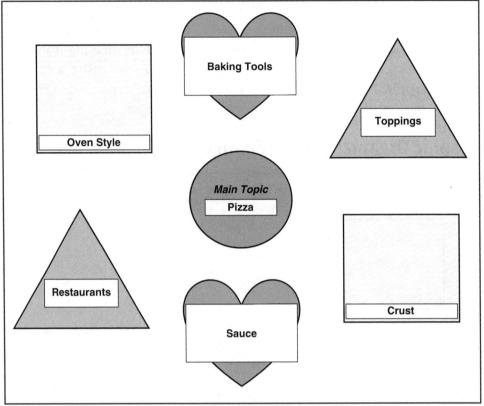

Since our assignment instructions indicated that we needed to write a five-paragraph essay, we only need to choose three subtopics for our three body paragraphs. Our introduction and conclusion will provide the other two required paragraphs. As a result, we will need to eliminate three of the six subtopics. These subtopics can be eliminated after the next step in our SOW AND REAP process.

Acquire Resources and Quotes to Add Support for Your Subtopics

During this step in the SOW AND REAP writing process, you will need to do your research about your main topic and your subtopics. For academic writing, it is important to select authoritative resources on the topic; to be clear, there is a lot of information on the Internet that is just plain garbage. In order to avoid using inaccurate information in your essay, be sure that professionals, who know their subject matter through training and experience, have written the resources you plan to use; searching through an academic database that will identify journal articles on your topic is a great place to start to find reliable resources.

After researching the different subtopics for "Building a Delicious Pizza," the following quotes/resources might prove valuable for our example.

Source Information: Essay Sample

1. Baking Tools

Source Information

After researching this subtopic, there was nothing relevant to the topic.

2. Oven Style

Source Information

After researching this subtopic, there was nothing relevant to the main idea of this essay.

3. Toppings

Source Information

Tranell, K. (2014). Which is healthier? *Health*, 28(4), 142. Retrieved from http://search.ebscohost.com.ezproxy.liberty.edu:2048/login. aspx?direct=true&db=s3h&AN=95394162&site=ehost-live&scope=site

Quote

"…pizza sauce is often simply crushed tomatoes, since mozzarella is the star ingredient (which explains pizza's relatively high saturated-fat content)."

4. Sauce

Source Information

Singh, P. & Goyal, G. K. (2011). Functionality of pizza ingredients. *British Food Journal, 113*(11), 1322 –1338. Retrieved from http://www.emeraldinsight.com.ezproxy.liberty.edu:2048/doi/full/10.1108/00070701111179960

Quote

"Nutrition experts believe that the functional components of food that may reduce the risk of cancer include traditional nutrients such as lycopene in tomatoes, have antioxidant properties, which protect cells against damage from oxidation. The key: tomato sauce, super-rich in the antioxidant lycopene, which may help save you from heart disease, prostate cancer, and Alzheimer's disease, according to many studies."

(continues)

5. Crust

Source Information

Hillebrand, M. (2005). How to formulate pizza crusts. *Baking Management, 9*(2), 38–39. Retrieved from http://search.proquest.com/docview/220856330?accountid=12085

Quote

"A crispy crust is dense, hard, and, as its name implies, crispy. It typically is found in the supermarket's frozen aisle. Thin crusts range between 1/8- and 1/4-in. thick."

"Thick crusts, on the other hand, range between 1/2- and 1-in. thick. They can have raised or flat edges and are made either flat or pan-style. A flat, or hearth-style, crust has a chewy consistency."

6. Restaurant

Source Information

Nothing stuck out as relevant to the topic of making a pizza when searching restaurants and pizza together.

7. Additional Information

Source Information

Lehmann, T. A. (2004). Pizza trends in the United States. *Cereal Foods World, 49*(2), 60–61. Retrieved from http://search.proquest.com/docview/230372339?accountid=12085

Quote

"In the last 45 years, pizza has evolved from a relative nobody to what is now possibly the single most popular food item consumed in the United States today."

After researching the subtopics, we have a better idea of which subtopics need to be eliminated. For the purpose of our culinary arts example, we will eliminate the subtopics: baking tools, oven style, and restaurants and focus on the different ingredient categories throughout our essay.

Number Subtopics in Logical Order

In this stage of the SOW AND REAP process, you will organize your ideas into a logical order. See the graphic organizer provided below with the main topic and subtopics for the essay "Building a Delicious Pizza."

Determining Subtopics: Essay Sample

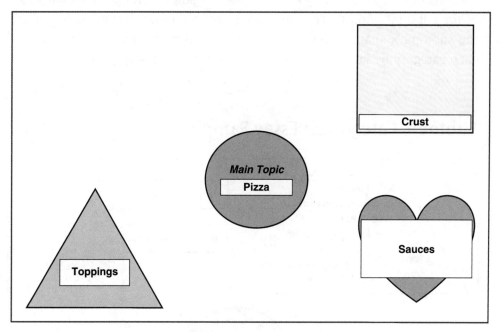

Now that you have determined your subtopics, you need to establish the order in which you wish to discuss them within your assignment. We will use Roman numerals to determine the order of the topics.

Ordering Subtopics: Essay Sample

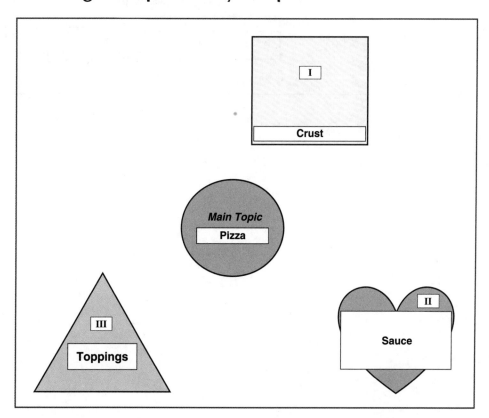

Based on the research you have conducted, your subtopics will need their own list of categories that you will want to address within the explanation of the subtopic. Add these categories to the subtopics by branching off of the subtopic's shape. Then, determine the order that you wish to discuss each category by labeling it with a capital letter, beginning with A.

Subtopic Categories: Essay Sample

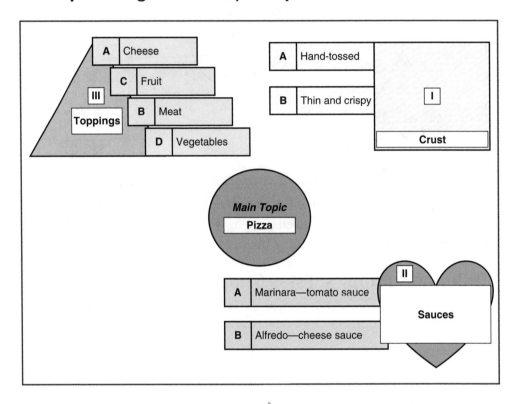

If you'd like to go into more detail about each category, you can add subcategories and assign numbers to each subcategory to organize them, as well. See the example below.

Subcategory Details: Essay Sample

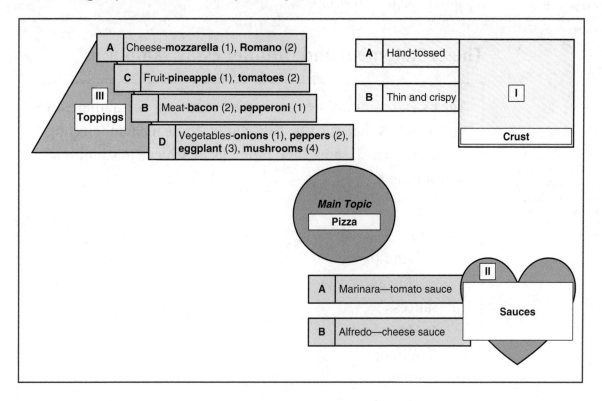

Hanna Bruce

"A concise, yet informative thesis statement can make all the difference in a paper. Try to write one sentence that includes all the majors points of your paper. This will be your roadmap for writing and will help the reader know exactly what you plan to discuss."

Josh Gerstner

"Avoid being a narrator in your writing. In other words, do not write, 'This paper is about . . .' or 'I have chosen Topic X as my subject, and the following . . .' Let your thesis statement do the work."

Based on the order you assign the different categories, you can then design your assignment's outline, your **thesis statement** (One sentence that establishes the main topic(s) and point/direction of a piece of writing), and ultimately, the order of the different paragraphs within your paper. Notice the outline and the thesis statement below; these correspond with the graphic organizer you have developed.

Thesis Statement and Outline: Essay Sample

Thesis Statement: When craving a hot, cheesy pizza, there are many factors that must be considered; these include selecting the perfect crust, sauce, and toppings to achieve maximum deliciousness.

Outline

I. Crust
   A. Hand-tossed
   B. Thin and crispy
II. Sauces
   A. Marinara
   B. Alfredo
III. Toppings
   A. Cheese
      1. Mozzarella
      2. Romano
   B. Meat
      1. Pepperoni
      2. Bacon
   C. Fruit
      1. Pineapple
      2. Tomatoes
   D. Vegetables
      1. Onions
      2. Peppers
      3. Eggplant
      4. Mushrooms

After you complete your prewriting and outlining stage, you are ready to begin work on your rough draft.

Draft the Writing Assignment

In this step of the SOW AND REAP process, you will write the rough draft of your essay. For the rough draft, it is important not to worry about writing everything perfectly, but you do want to be sure that you include the main elements required of you in the assignment instructions. For our culinary arts example, it is time to refer to the list we broke down from the assignment instructions:

- Five-paragraph essay

- 500 words minimum

- Steps to make favorite recipe

- APA formatting

- Cite sources used

In your essay, you will need to be sure that you include all of these elements as best you can and in the order you established in your outline; then, in later stages, you can correct errors relating to grammar, spelling, and punctuation, wordiness, organization, formatting, and so on.

Kirsten Hoegh

"Give yourself plenty of time to work on your writing assignments. No first draft is perfect, and it is important to make sure that you double check your work for spelling, grammar, professional tone, formatting (APA, MLA, or Turabian), and of course to make sure that your ideas flow well. If you are new to the idea of formatting your essays in a specific style (APA, MLA, or Turabian), now is a good time to begin getting familiar with the style you will use for your major. Take advantage of the information available on Liberty's Online Writing Center webpage, and always feel free to ask your instructor for help with this. It is not as complicated as it may seem, but it is an important element in college writing."

Rough Draft: Essay Sample

Running Head: BUILDING THE PERFECT HOMEMADE PIZZA 1

Building the Perfect Homemade Pizza

T. Marcus Christian

Liberty University

PIZZA!!! Who doesn't like pizza? I know I like it. Sometimes it is good on a cool spring night while you are working on final exams. There are a lot of options too. Dominoes is probably the faster to deliver, but Papa John's is the best. You can make it yourself too. When craving a hot, cheesy pizza, there are many factors that must be considered; these include selecting the perfect crust, sauce, and toppings to achieve maximum deliciousness.

The first thing to consider when making or ordering the best pizza around. Crust. It's the thing that can make the pizza the tastiest of all. There are two kinds of crust. Hand tossed and thin and crispy. Hand-tossed is when pizza makers throw it in the air to toss it nice and round. Thin and crispty is when they roll it out really really thin and then cook it that way.

Now that you have the crust all figured out, you need to decide which kind of sauce you want. There are usually two options for sauce, although sometimes there are more. Red tomatoe sauce, sometimes called marina sauce and then there's white sauce called Alfredo sauce. There are other sauce options but these two are the two that are usually served at most places like Pizza Hut etc.

Toppings are important. They can make or brake the pizza. You can put anything on a pizza that you want but the most popular is cheese, meat, fruits and then there are vegetables. Some of the cheeses that are good on a pizza are mozzarella cheese and romano Cheese. Sometimes I put parmesean cheese on my pizza too. After the cheese is selected, there next choice is the succulent meats. There are so many meats to choose from but the most popular are bacon and pepperoni.

After Cheese and meats are chosen, next is fruits and vegteables. Some people put pine apple on there pizza but they usally have ham on it too. "Tomato's are a fruit." Then, vegtables. You can choose from almost any kind of vegtables you want to add to your pizza. There is onions, peppers, eggplants, and mushrooms that can go on the pizza.

So, now that you know what to put on the pizza, you shouldn't have any strife ordering one or making one from scratch if that's what you wanted too do but ordering is probably a lot easier. Hot and cheesy pizza is the best with the perfect crust, sauce and topings.

This will help you achieve maximum deliciousness.

David Hart

"Meet or exceed your target length. The assignment instructions give a minimum required length for written answers. If the required length is one paragraph, you should write at least three to five sentences. Therefore, you should not submit two sentences and expect to earn full credit for an answer. Also, remember that they should be substantive sentences. Rather than just assume your answer is sufficient, merely because you wrote three sentences, ask yourself if they sufficiently answer the question. An excellent answer is similar to an excellent sculpture or an excellent photograph: The strength of the finished work we see is determined by what is intentionally removed."

Revise to Improve Content, Organization, Style, Etc.

Revision is defined, according to Sommers (as cited in Witte, 1980) as "a sequence of changes in a composition, in which ideas, words, and phrases are added, deleted, moved, or changed throughout the writing of the work" (2013). In the revision stage, take a look at the rubric for your assignment; look specifically at the categories of the rubric that relate to content, organization, writing style, etc. Then, look at the column with the most possible points connected to it; change each description in this column to a question to ask about your essay. For example, below you will find the rubric for the "Favorite Recipe" assignment. Look at the Excellent/Good column:

Rubric Elements: Essay Sample

	Excellent/Good- 3
Content	Essay content *meets* the expectations and includes the following elements: ■ Thesis statement establishes the main topic(s) and point/direction of the essay. ■ Thoroughly addresses the main topic(s) of the assignment and remains focused throughout the piece. ■ Explains the topic(s), providing essential details and support that strengthens the content.
Organization	Essay organization *meets* the expectations and includes the following elements: ■ Strong introduction paragraph with attention getter, explanatory transition sentences, and a comprehensive thesis statement. ■ Three body paragraphs that follow the sequence outlined in the thesis, each beginning with a topic sentence and concluding with a sentence that wraps up the main points of the paragraph and transitions into the next paragraph. ■ A conclusion paragraph reviews the main points addressed within the essay and provides a final, convincing application.

Let's change the content and organization descriptions to questions to evaluate our essay:

☐ Is there a thesis statement that establishes the main topic(s) and point/direction of the essay?

☐ Does the essay thoroughly address the main topic(s) of the assignment and remain focused throughout the piece?

☐ Does the essay explain the topic(s), providing essential details and support that strengthens the content?

☐ Is there a strong introduction paragraph with attention getter, explanatory transition sentences, and a comprehensive thesis statement?

☐ Are there three body paragraphs that follow the sequence outlined in the thesis, each beginning with a topic sentence and concluding with a sentence that wraps up the main points of the paragraph and transitions into the next paragraph?

☐ Is there a conclusion paragraph that reviews the main points addressed within the essay and provides a final, convincing application?

If the answer is "no" to any of these questions, go back and add the missing pieces in the revision process.

Revised Draft: Essay Sample

Lisa Eppard

"Once your paper is written, read each individual sentence aloud to check for clarity/fluency. Sometimes, it's easier to "hear" our mistakes, especially when we read each sentence one at a time. If a sentence doesn't sound "natural," it probably needs revising. This is a great way to catch spelling errors, as well."

Building the Perfect Homemade Pizza

T. Marcus Christian

Liberty University

In his article tracking "Pizza Trends in the United States," Tom Lehmann explains that "In the last 45 years, pizza has evolved from a relative nobody to what is now possibly the single most popular food item consumed in the United States today" (2004). PIZZA!!! Who doesn't like pizza? Pizza's melted cheesy goodness appeals to food lovers of all ages. Any time during the year, pizza is the favorite answer to the question: "What's for dinner?" ~~I know I like it. Sometimes it!~~ It is especially good to chow down on a slice on a cool spring night while you are working on final exams. ~~There~~ For convenience, there are a lot of order-in or carry-out options at Dominoes, Pizza Hut, and PaPa Johns. ~~too. Dominoes is probably the faster to deliver, but Papa John's is the best~~. Sometimes, however, pizza is best when ~~You~~ you ~~can~~ make it yourself ~~too~~. When craving a hot, cheesy homemade pizza, there are many ~~factors~~ steps that must be considered; these include selecting the perfect crust, sauce, and toppings to achieve maximum deliciousness.

Dustin Williams

"After you finish writing a paragraph, reread that paragraph to make sure all of your sentences flow. Sometimes, it is beneficial to start with the last sentence in the paragraph and work backwards."

    The first thing to consider when making or ordering the best pizza around. Crust. It's the thing that can make the pizza the tastiest of all. ~~There are two kinds of crust. Hand tossed and thin and crispy.~~ The two most popular types of crust are hand-tossed and thin and crispy. Hand-tossed is when the ~~they~~ pizza maker ~~throw it~~ throws the dough up in the air ~~to~~ and toss~~es~~ it ~~nice~~ round and round. Thin and crispty is when pizza makers roll it out really really thin and then cook it that way. According to Melissa Hillebrand in her article "How to Formulate Pizza Crusts," "A crispy crust is dense, hard, and as its name implies, crispy" while thicker crusts have "a chewy consistency" aand "a lighter texture" (2005). Now that you have the crust all figured out, you need to decide which kind of sauce you want. ~~Now that you have the crust all figured out, you need to decide which kind of sauce you want.~~ In the second step of sauce selection, ~~There~~there are usually two options: marinara and Alfredo sauce. ~~for sauce, although sometimes there are more.~~ Red tomatoe sauce, sometimes called marina sauce and then there's white sauce called Alfredo sauce.

There are other sauce options but these two are the two that are usually served at most places, like Pizza Hut ~~etc..~~ The type of sauce you select can make a huge difference in the flavor of the pizza. Evidently, choosing a tomato-based sauce can even be a healthy decision according to Singh and Goyal in their article in the British Food Journal entitled, "Function-ality of Pizza Ingredients," "Nutrition experts believe that the functional components of food that may reduce the risk of cancer include traditional nutrients such as lycopene in tomatoes, have antioxidant properties, which protect cells against damage from oxidation" (2011).

The final step, topping selection, ~~Toppings are~~is very important. ~~They~~ Toppings can make or brake the pizza. You can put anything on a pizza that you want but the most popular is cheese, meat, fruits and then there are vegetables. ~~Some of the cheeses that are good on a pizza are m~~Mozzarella ~~cheese and~~ romano Cheese are the best cheeses to achieve that melted cheesy goodness pizza lovers crave. In the *Health* article "Which is Healthier?," the author asserts that "mozzarella is the star ingredient" of pizza (Tranell, 2014). ~~Sometimes I put parmesean~~ While mozzarella is the star ingredient parme-san cheese is a great accent cheese for ~~on my~~ pizza too. After the cheese is selected, the~~re~~ next choice is the succulent meats. There are so many meats to choose from but the most popular are bacon and pepperoni.

After choosing the Cheese and meats ~~are chosen~~, the last decision is to determine which ~~next is~~ fruits and vegteables to top the pizza. Some people put pine apple on there pizza but they usally have ham on it too. "Tomato's are also a popular fruit topping." ~~Then, vegtables. You can choose from almost~~There are all ~~any~~ kinds of vegtables ~~you want~~ to add to your pizza, such as: . ~~There is~~ onions, peppers, eggplants, and mushrooms~~, that can go on the pizza.~~

~~So, now that you know what to put on the pizza, you shouldn't have any strife ordering one or making one from scratch if that's what you want-ed too do but ordering is probably a lot easier.~~

Having determined the types of pizza toppings, cheese, and crust, making a pizza from scratch should be fun and easy. People of all ages love homemade pizza because it is an easy, fun, and delicious dinner, but each person may have a different idea of what makes a perfect pizza. Regardless of how those ideas differ, ~~Hot~~ hot and cheesy pizza is ~~the~~ best ~~with~~ after selecting the perfect type of crust, sauce and topings.~~.~~ ~~This~~ With all of these ingredients in place, ~~will help~~ your pizza will achieve maximum deliciousness.

References

Tranell, K. (2014). WHICH IS HEALTHIER?. *Health*, 28(4), 142.

Preeti Singh, G.K. Goyal, (2011) "Functionality of pizza ingredients", British Food Journal, Vol. 113 Iss: 11, pp.1322 - 1338

Hillebrand, M. (2005). How to formulate pizza crusts. *Baking Management, 9*(2), 38-39. Retrieved from http://search.proquest.com/docview/220856330?accountid=12085

Lehmann, T. A. (2004). Pizza trends in the united states. *Cereal Foods World, 49*(2), 60-61. Retrieved from http://search.proquest.com/docview/230372339?accountid=12085

Edit by Focusing on Spelling, Punctuation, Grammar, and Formatting Mistakes

Roger

Q: Are you a good writer? How did/ do you become one? Why is learning about writing important? Describe your process of learning about good academic research/writing.

A: "I was not born a good writer. I had to develop my writing skills. Years ago my college history teacher tried to tell me that my writing skills needed help. But I didn't know where to go to get the help. I learned to write over time and with experience. As computer spellchecking programs improved over time, so did the quality of my work. Today I grade the papers of students who do not proofread their work. They fail to properly reference and cite their sources. They rush through the assignments without really thinking about organizing their thoughts. They failed to answer all of the questions asked of them in the assignment and they have forgotten to examine the rubrics to determine how the paper will be graded. Quality writing takes time, energy, forethought and hard work. That is what is required of every college student."

While editing your revised paper, review the expectations in the rubric and be sure to check the areas that relate to editing: grammar and mechanics and formatting. Follow the same process you used when you revised your essay: look at the descriptions in the Excellent/Good column and change these to questions to evaluate your work.

Rubric Elements: Essay Sample

	Excellent/Good- 3
Grammar and Mechanics	Essay is *free* from grammatical, spelling, and punctuation *errors*.
Formatting	Essay *meets* the following criteria: ■ Follows the parameters of the assignment instructions. ■ Formatting of essay/citations follows APA guidelines. ■ Meets the minimum word count. ■ Honor statement is signed.

☐ Is the essay free from grammatical, spelling, and punctuation errors? Use the list below as a reference list of items to check in this part of the process.

- Spelling
- Run-Ons
- Fragments
- Comma usage
- Semi-colon usage
- Conjunction usage
- End punctuation
- Avoid second person point of view
  - ☐ (First person point of view may also be forbidden)
- Wordiness
- Awkward wording

Josh Gerstner

"A complete sentence has both a subject and a verb; a sentence fragment lacks one of the two. Note the difference, an write using only complete sentences."

Terri Washer

"Make sure that you proofread closely before submitting assignments. One great way to identify errors is to read your papers aloud. It's amazing how many errors you hear, but don't see."

- Sentence variety

- Contractions

- Passive voice

- Pronoun usage

☐ Does the essay follow the parameters of the assignment instructions?

- Remember those parameters were:

  ▫ Five-paragraph essay

  ▫ 500 words minimum

  ▫ Important steps to make favorite recipe

  ▫ APA formatting

  ▫ Cite sources used

☐ Does the essay follow APA guidelines for formatting essays/citations?

- Formatting style for essay: header, page numbers, title page, margins, and so on

- In-text citations

- Reference page

☐ Does the essay meet the minimum word count?

☐ Did I sign the honor statement?

- Honor statements may be attached to the assignment instructions, the assignment template, or within the course at the submission point. Wherever your signature is required, be sure to provide it.

If the answer is "no" to any of these questions, go back and correct the errors to avoid losing points. If you are unsure about correcting grammar errors, there are many Online resources available to you via Liberty University's Online Writing Center (OWC). The OWC is also staffed with writing specialists, who can give you feedback towards improving your writing; however, you need to plan ahead if you wish to use this service. As the final part of the editing process, use the spelling and grammar check feature provided by your computer program. Keep in mind that the spelling and grammar check is not going to catch every error within your assignment; it may even list something that is not an error at all. However, the spelling and grammar check may catch something you missed that can be quickly fixed, and as a result, you will be closer to a polished final product.

Edited Draft: Essay Sample

Running Head: BUILDING THE PERFECT HOMEMADE PIZZA 1

Building the Perfect Homemade Pizza

T. Marcus Christian

Liberty University

Building the Perfect Homemade Pizza

~~PIZZA!!! Who doesn't like pizza?~~ In his article tracking "Pizza Trends in the United States," Tom Lehmann (2004) explains that "In the last 45 years, pizza has evolved from a relative nobody to what is now possibly the single most popular food item consumed in the United States today. "~~(2004).~~ Pizza's melted cheesy goodness appeals to food lovers of all ages. Any time during the year, pizza is the favorite answer to the question: "What's for dinner?" It is especially good to chow down on a slice on a cool spring night while ~~you are~~ working on final exams. ~~There~~ For convenience, there are a lot of order-in or carry-out options ~~too, like~~at Dominoes, Pizza Hut, and ~~PaPa~~Papa Johns. Sometimes, however, pizza is best when ~~you make it yourself~~it is homemade. When craving a hot, cheesy homemade pizza, there are many steps that must be considered; these include selecting the perfect crust, sauce, and toppings to achieve maximum deliciousness.

The first thing to consider when making ~~or ordering~~ the best pizza ~~around. Crust~~is the crust. ~~It's~~ It is the thing that can make the pizza the tastiest of all. The two, most popular types of crust are hand-tossed and thin and crispy. Hand-tossed is when the pizza maker throws the dough up in the air and tosses it round and round. Thin and ~~crispty~~crispy is when pizza makers roll it out really~~really~~ thin and then cook it that way. According to Melissa Hillebrand (2005) in her article "How to Formulate Pizza Crusts," "A crispy crust is dense, hard, and as its name implies, crispy" while thicker crusts have "a chewy consistency" a~~a~~nd "a lighter texture." ~~(2005).~~ ~~Now that you have~~ Once the type of crust ~~all figured out,~~ is determined, ~~you need~~ it is time to decide which kind of sauce ~~you want~~to use.

In the second step of sauce selection, there are usually two options: marinara and Alfredo sauce. The familiar ~~Red~~ red ~~tomatoe~~tomato sauce, is sometimes called ~~marina~~marinara sauce, and then ~~there's~~ there is a white sauce called Alfredo sauce. ~~There are other sauce options but these two are the two that are usually served at most places, like Pizza Hut..~~The type of sauce ~~you select~~ can make a huge difference in the flavor of the pizza. ~~Evidently,~~ While both the red and the white sauce are delicious, choosing a tomato-based sauce can even be a healthy decision according to Singh and Goyal (2011) in their article in the British Food Journal entitled, "Functionality of Pizza Ingredients," "Nutrition experts believe that the functional components of food that may reduce the risk of cancer include traditional nutrients such as lycopene in tomatoes, have antioxidant properties, which protect cells against damage from oxidation." ~~(2011)~~.

The final step, topping selection, is very important. Toppings can make or ~~brake~~ break the pizza. ~~You~~ Pizza makers can put pretty much anything on a pizza ~~that you want~~ but the most popular ~~is~~ choices include: cheese, meat, fruits, and ~~then there are~~ vegetables. Mozzarella and ~~romano~~ Romano cheeses~~Cheese~~ are the best cheeses to achieve that melted cheesy goodness pizza lovers crave. In the *Health* article "Which is Healthier?," the author asserts that "mozzarella is the star ingredient" of pizza (Tranell, 2014). While mozzarella is the star ingredient, parmesan cheese is a great accent cheese for pizza too. After the cheese is selected, the next choice is the succulent meats. There are so many meats to choose from, but the most popular are bacon and pepperoni. After choosing the ~~Cheese~~ cheese and meats, the last decision is to determine which fruits and ~~vegteables~~ vegteables ~~to~~ should top the pizza. Some people put ~~pine apple~~pineapple on ~~there~~their pizza~~but they usally~~have ham on it too. "~~Tomato's~~Tomatoes are also a popular fruit topping." There are all kinds of ~~vegtables~~vegetables to add to ~~your~~ pizza, such as: onions, peppers, eggplants, and mushrooms.

Having determined the types of pizza toppings, cheese, and crust, making a pizza from scratch should be fun and easy. ~~People~~ It is no wonder that people of all ages love homemade pizza because it ~~is an easy, fun, and~~ can be a delicious dinner, but each person may have a different idea of what makes a perfect pizza. Regardless of how those ideas differ, hot and cheesy pizza is best after selecting the perfect type of crust, sauce, and ~~toping~~stoppings. With all of these ingredients in place, ~~your~~ a pizza maker's pie ~~pizza~~ will achieve maximum deliciousness.

References

Hillebrand, M. (2005). How to formulate pizza crusts. *Baking Management, 9*(2), 38-39. Retrieved from http://search.proquest.com/docview/220856330?accountid=12085

Lehmann, T. A. (2004). Pizza trends in the United States. *Cereal Foods World, 49*(2), 60-61. Retrieved from http://search.proquest.com/docview/230372339?accountid=12085

~~Preeti~~ Singh, P. & ~~G.K.~~ Goyal, G. K. (2011). "Functionality of pizza ingredients",. *British Food Journal,* ~~Vol.~~ *113*(~~Iss:~~ 11), ~~pp.~~1322 -- 1338. Retrieved from http://www.emeraldinsight.com.ezproxy.liberty.edu:2048/doi/full/10.1108/00070 01111179960

Tranell, K. (2014). ~~WHICH IS HEALTHIER~~Which is healthier? . *Health, 28*(4), 142. Retrieved from http://search.ebscohost.com.ezproxy.liberty.edu:2048/login.aspx?direct=true&db=s3h&AN=95394162&site=ehost-live&scope=site

~~Preeti Singh, G.K. Goyal, (2011) "Functionality of pizza ingredients", British Food Journal, Vol. 113 Iss: 11, pp.1322 - 1338~~

~~Hillebrand, M. (2005). How to formulate pizza crusts. *Baking Management, 9*(2), 38-39. Retrieved from http://search.proquest.com/docview/220856330?accountid=12085~~

~~Lehmann, T. A. (2004). Pizza trends in the united states. *Cereal Foods World, 49*(2), 60-61. Retrieved from http://search.proquest.com/docview/230372339?accountid=12085~~

Lisa Eppard

"If time permits, put your paper away overnight once it is written. Come back in a day or two and read it again with a fresh pair of eyes. It's amazing how easy it is to find errors when a little time has passed."

Josh Gerstner

"Consider your audience. The way you write for an undergraduate class should be different from how you write to a friend. Take note that writing for a class assignment should include a higher level of formality, which means proper attention should be given to capitalization, punctuation, and grammar."

Ask Someone You Trust to Review Your Writing

Consider reading your essay out loud to a family member or friend. This is not always an easy step, but it is a necessary one to take as explained in Kreuter's (2014) article "Writing Environments,"

> While a natural tendency, isolating our in-process writing from the eyes of others is frequently not a successful strategy for producing writing, nor for producing effective, convincing writing. On the whole, most successful writers share their in-process work with others—a trusted colleague or two or even an organized writing group—and at later stages with editors and colleagues with whom they have less familiar relationships. (p. 34)

When you take the chance and read your writing to someone else out loud, you will be surprised how many errors you missed when reading the assignment silently. When you identify those errors, make the changes as you note them.

You may also want to use a tutoring service to help you in the revision process. Liberty University's Online Writing Center is a wonderful resource for improving writing at any academic level. Tutor.com also provides review services for writing assignments. If you decide to use this type of service, it is important to submit your essay to them in advance of the assignment's due date, as they have a specified timeline appropriate to reviewing your writing. Check out the websites and processes involved to use these services.

Prepare the Final Draft by Implementing Recommended Changes

Make all of the necessary changes that you identified in the revising and editing stages; implement recommended changes by your friend or loved one, as well. Do a final read-through to ensure you caught everything that needed to be changed. As you do this final read-through, refer to your assignment instructions and rubric one last time.

Rubric: Essay Sample

	Excellent/Good- 3
Content	Essay content *meets* the expectations and includes the following elements: ▪ Thesis statement establishes the main topic(s) and point/direction of the essay. ▪ Thoroughly addresses the main topic(s) of the assignment and remains focused throughout the piece. ▪ Explains the topic(s), providing essential details and support that strengthens the content.
Organization	Essay organization *meets* the expectations and includes the following elements: ▪ Strong introduction paragraph with attention getter, explanatory transition sentences, and a comprehensive thesis statement.
	▪ Three body paragraphs that follow the sequence outlined in the thesis, each beginning with a topic sentence and concluding with a sentence that wraps up the main points of the paragraph and transitions into the next paragraph. ▪ A conclusion paragraph reviews the main points addressed within the essay and provides a final, convincing application.
Grammar and Mechanics	Essay is *free* from grammatical, spelling, and punctuation *errors*.
Formatting	Essay *meets* the following criteria: ▪ Follows the parameters of the assignment instructions. ▪ Formatting of essay/citations follows APA guidelines. ▪ Meets the minimum word count. ▪ Honor statement is signed.

Ask yourself these questions:

- ☐ Does my essay meet the following requirements?
  - ☐ Five-paragraph essay
  - ☐ 500 words minimum
  - ☐ Important steps to make favorite recipe
  - ☐ APA formatting
  - ☐ Cite sources used
- ☐ Does my essay meet the expectations listed in the Excellent/Good column of the rubric?

If the answer is "no" to either of these questions, go back and add the missing elements. Otherwise, you will lose points for the missing pieces.

Once you have completed this final evaluation, save your essay and submit your assignment.

Final Draft: Essay Sample

Building the Perfect Homemade Pizza

T. Marcus Christian

Liberty University

David Hart

"Finish well. Make sure that you follow the instructions for submitting the assignment. Sometimes students paste the text into Blackboard for something that should be attached as a Word document. Conversely, sometimes students attach a Word document for something that should be typed directly into Blackboard (such as a Discussion Board)."

Building the Perfect Homemade Pizza

In his article tracking "Pizza Trends in the United States," Tom Lehmann explains that "In the last 45 years, pizza has evolved from a relative nobody to what is now possibly the single most popular food item consumed in the United States today" (2004). Pizza's melted cheesy goodness appeals to food lovers of all ages. Any time during the year, pizza is the favorite answer to the question: "What's for dinner?" It is especially good to chow down on a slice on a cool, spring night while working on final exams. For convenience, there are a lot of order-in or carry-out options at Dominoes, Pizza Hut, and Papa Johns. Sometimes, however, pizza is best when it is homemade. When craving a hot, cheesy homemade pizza, there are many steps that must be considered; these include selecting the perfect crust, sauce, and toppings to achieve maximum deliciousness.

The first thing to consider when making the best pizza is the crust. It is the thing that can make the pizza the tastiest of all. The two, most popular types of crust are hand-tossed and thin and crispy. Hand-tossed is when the pizza maker throws the dough up in the air and tosses it round and round. Thin and crispy is when pizza makers roll it out really thin and then cook it that way. According to Melissa Hillebrand in her article "How to Formulate Pizza Crusts," "A crispy crust is dense, hard, and as its name implies, crispy" while thicker crusts have "a chewy consistency" and "a lighter texture" (2005). Once the type of crust is determined, it is time to decide which kind of sauce to use.

In the second step of sauce selection, there are usually two options: marinara and Alfredo sauce. The familiar red tomato sauce is sometimes called marinara sauce, and then there is a white sauce called Alfredo sauce. The type of sauce can make a huge difference in the flavor of the pizza. While both the red and the white sauce are delicious, choosing a tomato-based sauce can even be a healthy decision according to Singh and Goyal in their article in the British Food Journal entitled, "Function-ality of Pizza Ingredients," "Nutrition experts believe that the functional components of food that may reduce the risk of cancer include traditional nutrients such as lycopene in tomatoes, have antioxidant properties, which protect cells against damage from oxidation" (2011).

The final step, topping selection, is very important. Toppings can make or break the pizza. Pizza makers can put pretty much anything on a pizza but the most popular choices include: cheese, meat, fruits, and veg-etables. Mozzarella and Romano cheeses are the best cheeses to achieve that melted cheesy goodness pizza lovers crave. In the article "Which is Healthier?," the author asserts that "mozzarella is the star ingredient" of pizza (Tranell, 2014). While mozzarella is the star ingredient, parmesan cheese is a great accent cheese for pizza too. After the cheese is selected, the next choice is the succulent meats. There are so many meats to choose from, but the most popular are bacon and pepperoni. After choosing the cheese and meats, the last decision is to determine which fruits and vegetables should top the pizza. Some people put pineapple on their pizza. Tomatoes are also a popular fruit topping. There are all kinds of vegetables to add to pizza, such as: onions, peppers, eggplant, and mushrooms.

Having determined the types of pizza toppings, cheese, and crust, making a pizza from scratch should be fun and easy. It is no wonder that people of all ages love homemade pizza because it can be a delicious dinner, but each person may have a different idea of what makes a per-fect pizza. Regardless of how those ideas differ, hot and cheesy pizza is best after selecting the perfect type of crust, sauce, and toppings. With all of these ingredients in place, a pizza maker's pie will achieve maximum deliciousness.

References

Hillebrand, M. (2005). How to formulate pizza crusts. *Baking Management, 9*(2), 38-39. Retrieved from http://search.proquest.com/docview/220856330?accountid=12085

Lehmann, T. A. (2004). Pizza trends in the United States. *Cereal Foods World, 49*(2), 60-61. Retrieved from http://search.proquest.com/docview/230372339?accountid=12085

Preeti Singh, G.K. Goyal, (2011). Functionality of pizza ingredients. *British Food Journal, 113*(11), 1322 – 1338. Retrieved from http://www.emeraldinsight.com.ezproxy.liberty.edu:2048/doi/full/10.1108/00070701111179960

Tranell, K. (2014). Which is healthier? *Health, 28*(4), 142. Retrieved from http://search.ebscohost.com.ezproxy.liberty.edu:2048/login.aspx?direct=true&db=s3h&AN=95394162&site=ehost-live&scope=site

If you follow the SOW AND REAP writing steps carefully and completely, you will develop beautifully composed, organized, supported, and formatted pieces of writing. By taking the time to review the instructions and rubric for each writing assignment you encounter, you will have a clear idea of how your professor will assess your writing. From this point, you will be prepared to brainstorm, organize, and research your topic and subtopics. After completing these elements, writing the rough draft is a very natural process, followed by assessing your own draft through revision and editing. Finally, as you share your writing with your professor, classmates, friends, and loved ones, they will be impressed with your professional piece of writing—a most delicious harvest.

Personal Reflection

Use the brainstorming template below to organize key ideas, subtopics, subtopic categories, and subcategories for future writing assignments.

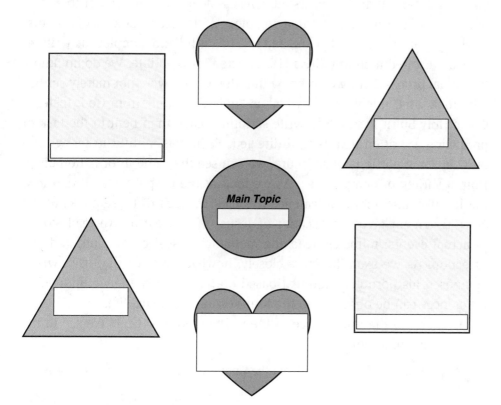

Main Topic

BUILDING BLOCKS

How Does a Christian Student Look at the Task of Writing?

As always, we use the lens of scripture to inform our thinking. For writing, there are two ways to do this. First, we look at how the Holy Scriptures came to be. Did you know that the Bible is not written by a single author (other than God's Holy Spirit, of course)? There are literally *dozens* of writers of the Bible. These writers lived over *hundreds* of years. While none understood that he was working on a huge collaborative effort, that was essentially the result. The Bible, as we know it, was not completely compiled until more than 300 years after Jesus' death. As we look at the unity of the Bible message, it is an amazing piece of literature: dozens of authors, working over hundreds of years, and it is beautiful and complete as written.

God inspired men to write as He directed for the Bible. We do not know the actual process, but we do know that the writers were not merely scribes who took what might be described as "holy dictation" from God. Instead, God's Holy Spirit led men to write scripture. Each man bent to the task of producing a written text as God directed. Each was faithful to his writing task. In some portions of scripture, we can see the same information given from a variety of perspectives. As we look at the gospel texts of Matthew, Mark, Luke, and John, we can see this clearly. Each of these books of the New Testament gives an account of Jesus' life on earth. We read stories of actual events: miracles, teaching moments, Jesus' crucifixion, and resurrection. As we examine more closely, however, we see that each writer composed his portion of the text based on his own experience. Individual differences can be observed in the four versions of Jesus' life.

We can see the importance of the written word to God. We see in the New Testament's John 1:1,

> "In the beginning was the Word and the Word was with God, and the Word was God" (NIV).

Wow! In this verse, we see Jesus named as the Word. Many times, we have seen the Bible described variously as "God's love letter to us" or "God's guidebook for life" or even the acronym BIBLE: basic instructions before leaving earth. None of these adequately express the beauty and majesty of God's Word, given to us in love.

As you consider your academic writing task, it may seem overwhelming. In Isaiah 40:8 we read, "The grass withers, the flower fades, but the Word of our God will stand forever" (ESV). What you are writing for school will not need to be that long-lasting, but it is important to do your best. Take the writing process in step-by-step tasks, and you can produce a written piece that speaks well for you while meeting the demands of the assignment. Pray this verse as a prayer as you begin:

> Psalm 19:14, "Let the words of my mouth, and the meditation of my heart, be acceptable in thy sight, O Lord, my strength, and my redeemer" (KJV).

Each time you have a writing assignment:

- Look carefully at your writing assignment. Determine the purpose and audience.

- Set a schedule for completing your work.

- Decide the steps that you should take in the writing process. Will you need to do research first?

- Determine sources to help you.

- Gather information, taking careful notes and determining citation information.

- Next, you must begin to organize your thoughts on how to present your ideas.

- Write a paragraph that conveys each idea you want to explore.

- Take a break when you have made a rough draft. When you come back, you will be refreshed.

- Revise your work to ensure that it is a succinct message that makes your points.

- Edit to eliminate grammar, spelling, punctuation, and capitalization mistakes that distract from what you are writing.

- Carefully check to ensure that you have properly cited each instance of "borrowing" the work, words, or ideas of others.

What Do You Do If You Are "Stuck?"

Sometimes, students find that once they have gathered information and made many notes, they have trouble continuing to the actual writing of the piece. You may face a period of difficulty with beginning the actual writing process, sometimes called "writer's block," just jump in and get going. Put pen to paper (or fingers to keyboard, as the case may be) and write what comes to mind. Do not judge what you are writing, just try to get your writing flowing. There will be opportunity to evaluate and revise later. At first, just try to capture your thoughts. As you proceed, you will organize your ideas into paragraphs, using one for each main idea you wish to convey. Make sure to keep careful notes as you work so you can properly cite any source material you are using. It is critical to avoid plagiarism, and keeping your notes organized by author or source will help you maintain your integrity as you "borrow" from the ideas of others.

Writing is a process, and by practicing, you will become better at it. Some students love to express their ideas in tweets, blogs, or texts but have difficulty writing for academic purposes. If that is your situation, take heart. Following the steps outlined in this chapter can help you create an organized, cogent, and meaningful written piece. The Bible tells us that "For the Spirit God gave us does not make us timid, but gives us power, love and self-discipline" (II Tim. 1:7, NIV). Take that message to heart, and let's get writing!

> Romans 5:1–5, "Therefore, since we have been justified through faith, we have peace with God through our Lord Jesus Christ, through whom we have gained access by faith into this grace in which we now stand. And we boast in the hope of the glory of God. Not only so, but we also glory in our sufferings, because we know that suffering produces perseverance; perseverance, character; and character, hope. And hope does not put us to shame, because God's love has been poured out into our hearts through the Holy Spirit, who has been given to us" (NIV).

TOOL BOX

Writing Tools

General Writing—For general paper writing, the most basic tool you will need is word processing software. Word processing software will allow you to write and edit anything from a paragraph to a novel and typically comes packaged with advanced editing and reference building tools. The most common programs for word processing are Microsoft Word (PC or Mac) and Pages (Mac). These programs can be expensive, but Liberty University works with different software companies to provide affordable options for current students. See the Breaking Ground website for a detailed list of the most current offerings.

Outlining and Note-Taking—For many writing strategies, you do not need word processing software. For these tasks, you might enjoy using one of the many note-taking programs or applications available. These programs are designed specifically for note-taking and are great for organizing your less formal thoughts. As an added bonus, most of these programs have applications that will work on multiple devices. This allows you to take notes on one device and have them instantly synchronized with your other devices. Other advanced features include the ability to add screenshots, voice memos, videos, and searchable text to your notes. See the Breaking Ground website for an updated list of programs and features.

Mind Mapping—Mind mapping tools allow you to create visual representations of information that might otherwise be found in an outline. These tools work wonders for those of you who are visual learners. There are too many examples to mention here, but check the website for some great options.

Writing Helps and Tutoring

SafeAssign—This tool, provided by Liberty, allows professors and students to check text-based assignments for potential plagiarism. Students will only access this tool if it has been made available for a particular assignments in their course, but professors are able to submit papers directly to SafeAssign at any point. The tool works by checking documents against an existing database of writing, as well as against various web sources.

Liberty University Online Writing Center—The Online Writing Center is another wonderful resource available to you as a Liberty student. Using this tool, you may submit your work for review by trained graders and receive high quality feedback to improve your writing. Live sessions may also be scheduled using a request form on the Writing Center website.
www.liberty.edu/onlinewritingcenter

Additional Tools—While Liberty has spent an enormous amount of time and money developing in-house tools, they have also developed strategic partnerships with outside entities. These partnerships are designed to offer you, the student, the best tools available as you work toward your degree. To find out what tools are available to assist you with your writing, please visit the Breaking Ground website.

Websites—Aside from the multitude of tools available to you through Liberty University, there are an even greater number of websites that promise to do just about everything possible to assist you in improving your writing. While many sites make claims that they will check your spelling, grammar, and sources, the best sites are those that educate you in the writing process. Spend some time at places like Purdue's Owl and dailygrammar.com to get quick tips and build your long-term writing skills.

Additional resources and links to specific sites, worksheets, and apps can be located by accessing the Breaking Ground website:

www.breakinggroundlu.com

References

Cuseo, J. B., Thompson, A., Campagna, M., & Fecas, V. S. (2013). *Thriving in college and beyond*. Dubuque, IA: Kendall Hunt Publishing Company.

Hillebrand, M. (2005). How to formulate pizza crusts. *Baking Management*, 9(2), 38–39. Retrieved from http://search.proquest.com/docview/220856330?accountid = 12085

Kolb, K. H., Longest, K. C., & Jensen, M. J. (2013). Assessing the writing process: Do writing-intensive first-year seminars change how students write? *Teaching Sociology, 41*(1), 20–31. Retrieved from http://search.proquest.com/docview/1282294461?accountid = 12085

Kreuter, N. (2014). Writing environments. *The Education Digest, 80*(2), 32–35. Retrieved from http://search.proquest.com/docview/1586076713?accountid = 12085

Lehmann, T. A. (2004). Pizza trends in the United States. *Cereal Foods World, 49*(2), 60–61. Retrieved from http://search.proquest.com/docview/230372339?accountid = 12085

Singh, P. & Goyal, G. K. (2011). Functionality of pizza ingredients. *British Food Journal, 113*(11), 1322–1338. Retrieved from http://www.emeraldinsight.com.ezproxy.liberty.edu:2048/doi/full/10.1108/00070701111179960

Tranell, K. (2014). Which is healthier? *Health, 28*(4), 142. Retrieved from http://search.ebscohost.com.ezproxy.liberty.edu:2048/login.aspx?direct = true&db = s3h&AN = 95394162&site = ehost-live&scope = site

Winebrenner, S. (2012). *Education Consulting Service, Inc.* Retrieved from http://susanwinebrenner.com/index.html.

Witte, S. (2013). Preaching what we practice: a study of revision. *Journal Of Curriculum & Instruction, 6*(2), 33–59. doi:10.3776/joci.2013.

Chapter 10

Career Planning: The Finishings

In this chapter, you will:

- Examine strategies for career exploration, planning, and development.
- Review action steps to take for your future career growth.
- Create documents to use in your future job search.

FINISHING

When constructing a building, whether a home, an office building, or a college library, an important step in the process is to complete the structure with finishing details. The finishings and furnishing are planned from the beginning as the final step in making the building ready for occupancy and use. Just as a building must be finished with wall treatments, window trims, baseboards, and painting, a careful plan of finishing must be completed in an academic program. This finishing would consist of careful exploration, evaluation, and preparation for a career, which is the capstone of the educational endeavor.

© 2013 by irin-k. Used under license of Shutterstock, Inc.

Galatians 6:4,
"Make a careful exploration of who you are and the work you have been given, and then sink yourself into that" (The Message).

THE CORNERSTONE

Philippians 1:6, "Being confident of this very thing, that he which hath begun a good work in you will perform it until the day of Jesus Christ" (KJV).

On May 15, 2007, Dr. Jerry Falwell went to be with the Lord. During his lifetime, he established Thomas Road Baptist Church and two schools, Liberty Christian Academy and Liberty University. He founded ministries, such as the Elim Home and the Liberty Godparent Home. He went on missions trips and encouraged his congregation and students to do the same. He generated political change and impacted his culture by using his pulpit and TV ministry as a platform to speak against sin and to share about salvation through Jesus Christ. Because of these ministries, he led multitudes to the Lord.

© 2015 by Artens. Used under license of Shutterstock, Inc.

"What role do you feel called to? What career plan is in store for you? Now's the time to think this through and to pray for God's guidance and discernment as you select courses and begin making decisions that will impact your career path."

As a college student, Jerry originally chose to study journalism and engineering at Lynchburg College, but after his conversion, he felt called to the ministry and transferred to Bible Baptist College in Springfield, Missouri. This decision was not an easy one. Many family members and friends worried that Jerry's decision to attend the Baptist Bible College was not the best plan for a young man with so many talents and options for a career. However, Jerry felt that God was calling him to serve Him, and he followed the call. Imagine what would have happened if he hadn't been sensitive to God's guidance in his life?

We are not all meant to be pastors, but if you are a child of God, you do have a call to serve Him. In Ephesians 4:11–16, the Apostle Paul talks about the many different roles that God's children serve in ministry:

"So Christ himself gave the apostles, the prophets, the evangelists, the pastors and teachers, to equip his people for works of service, so that the body of Christ may be built up until we all reach unity in the faith and in the knowledge of the Son of God and become mature, attaining to the whole measure of the fullness of Christ. Then we will no longer be infants, tossed back and forth by the waves, and blown here and there by every wind of teaching and by the cunning and craftiness of people in their deceitful scheming. Instead, speaking the truth in love, we will grow to become in every respect the mature body of him who is the head, that is, Christ. From him the whole body, joined and held together by every supporting ligament, grows and builds itself up in love, as each part does its work" (NIV).

What role do you feel called to? What career plan is in store for you? Now's the time to think this through and to pray for God's guidance and discernment, as you select courses and begin making decisions that will impact your career path.

Dr. Falwell's life verse was Philippians 1:6, "Being confident of this very thing, that he which hath begun a good work in you will perform it until the day of Jesus Christ" (KJV). Even though Dr. Falwell is in heaven with Jesus, his work continues now "until the day of Jesus Christ" in me and in you through the ministry of Liberty University. Today, I am thankful that Dr. Jerry was sensitive to God's calling in his life, and I pray that you will be sensitive to His calling in your life, knowing that God will use the "good work" He has begun in you to impact the lives of others for generations to come.

President Jerry Falwell

"Our Christian faculty and staff are so committed to the student body; they see their role here as a calling, not a job" (Falwell, 2014).

Dr. Elmer Towns, co-founder

"God has a plan for your life. I want to challenge you this year: Find that plan, and do it" (Liberty University News Service, 2014).

Dr. Elmer Towns

"What could God use you to do? What's your dream of doing something for God?" (McKay, 2009).

Alissa Keith

"In planning your career, follow your dream as long as that dream includes paying all your bills, living a contented life, and serving the Lord."

Photo courtesy of Cali Lowdermilk (Liberty University).

From 1990 until his passing in 2007, Dr. Jerry Falwell's office was in the Montview Mansion on the campus of Liberty University. An historic home, the Mansion is now used as a guest house and museum. Dr. Falwell's office has been preserved just as it was the day he died. The lights in his office are never turned off, representing the fact that his work continues through the lives of those hundreds of thousands of students he helped train to become "Young Champions for Christ."

Examine Strategies for Career Exploration, Planning, and Development

Jeremiah 29:11,

"For I know the plans I have for you," declares the Lord, "plans to prosper you and not to harm you, plans to give you hope and a future" (NIV).

This verse is a continuing theme throughout this textbook and with good reason: God promises that He has a plan for each of us. We know that God is good and generous and that He loves us. He tells us in Romans 8:28, "And we know that in all things God works for the good of those who love him, who have been called according to his purpose" (NIV). This is not a blanket promise that we will have just what we desire in all situations, but rather that God works things out for our *ultimate* benefit. As you look ahead to career growth and development, plan steps that lead you to the calling that God has for your life. This will be your path to blessing and fulfillment.

Even though this may be your first online college course, it is not too soon to consider what effects your degree will have on your future career. **Career planning** can be described as the ongoing process of looking at your interests and values, skills, experience, and aspirations, combined with academic development and growth, and ultimately, matching all of these elements to applicable work opportunities. You can begin this process now, but you will likely continue planning and adjusting throughout your life. Patterns of employment and career development have been changing, and most employees will have several "careers" over their working life (Clarke, 2009). Now is the time to look to the intersection of all of the career planning factors, including your interests, skills, and education, and examine how they relate to your personal career path.

As you are planning your career future, it is vital to look at the interests that you bring to the table. Often, a strong interest can be the beginning of a career path or a transition to a new one. Are there hobbies that you believe might develop into

Mary Dixon

"As Colossians 3:23–24 says, 'Whatever you do, work at it with all your heart, as working for the Lord, not for human masters, since you know that you will receive an inheritance from the Lord as a reward. It is the Lord Christ you are serving' (NIV). God has called you to a work that will bring about His kingdom. Seek His kingdom and then do all that He has given you to do. This is the service and the reward!"

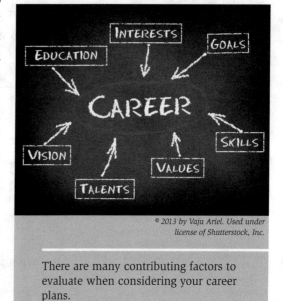

© 2013 by Vaju Ariel. Used under license of Shutterstock, Inc.

There are many contributing factors to evaluate when considering your career plans.

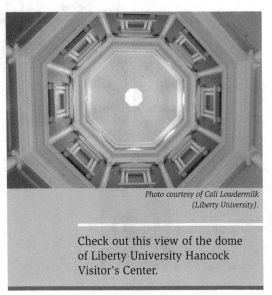

*Photo courtesy of Cali Lowdermilk
(Liberty University).*

Check out this view of the dome of Liberty University Hancock Visitor's Center.

a career opportunity? What values might influence the work you can or will engage? Think back to your consideration of personal goals and values in earlier chapters. How might what you identified there influence your choice of career?

The skills you have developed to date may serve you well in both your current work setting (if you work) and the career you will undertake in future. Begin by identifying skills or skill groups that you can continue or develop further for your employment.

Your education can certainly contribute to your employability. It is a safe guess that many students who are undertaking college courses online are already in the work force and hope to leverage additional education into a career or a promotion in current work. Education can also be the key to unlock a previously-unavailable career sector.

Personal Reflection

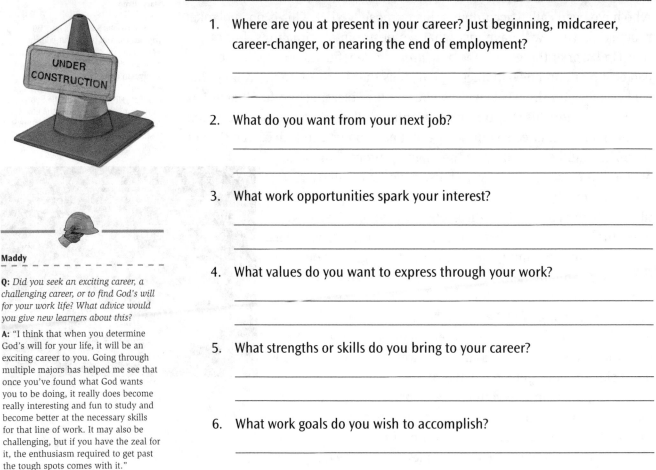

Maddy

Q: *Did you seek an exciting career, a challenging career, or to find God's will for your work life? What advice would you give new learners about this?*

A: "I think that when you determine God's will for your life, it will be an exciting career to you. Going through multiple majors has helped me see that once you've found what God wants you to be doing, it really does become really interesting and fun to study and become better at the necessary skills for that line of work. It may also be challenging, but if you have the zeal for it, the enthusiasm required to get past the tough spots comes with it."

1. Where are you at present in your career? Just beginning, midcareer, career-changer, or nearing the end of employment?

   _____

   _____

2. What do you want from your next job?

   _____

   _____

3. What work opportunities spark your interest?

   _____

   _____

4. What values do you want to express through your work?

   _____

   _____

5. What strengths or skills do you bring to your career?

   _____

   _____

6. What work goals do you wish to accomplish?

   _____

   _____

BREAKING GROUND

7. Thinking about work settings, do you prefer to work alone or as part of a group?

_____

_____

8. Do you prefer to work independently (for yourself), for a small company, or for a large corporation?

_____

_____

9. What sort of compromises are you willing to make for work? (Think about relocation, hours/days of work, and obligations to family and other demands.)

_____

_____

These are questions that you will continue to ask yourself across the breadth of your career, as the answers will continue to change. Employees who continue to grow and develop during their careers are of interest to employers. In today's economy, no single job is a final choice in your career path, unless you are approaching retirement.

Katie Robinson

"A college degree is more than a piece of paper or a lofty goal. Instead, students have the chance to learn more about themselves and use these lessons to help expand career opportunities. Perhaps, even, those lessons will help students discover areas of interest in careers that they hadn't previously thought to explore."

Dr. Jerry Falwell, Sr.

"I have an obligation to my children and to their children, to see to it that when I am gone I have left behind a legacy called freedom, liberty, morality and decency" (Falwell, 1997, p. 70).

Dr. Jerry Falwell, Sr.

"God never promised to keep you out of trouble; but He does promise to be with you through all your troubles" (Falwell, 1997, p. 98).

Terry

"Seek the Lord's will in your life; oftentimes, you'll find that it is both challenging and fulfilling in a way you've never known before."

Next, look at your interest across various work opportunities. Are there areas you would like to explore getting into? Perhaps your current college work is designed to help you move into an area that has piqued your interest. Take some time to explore the work available in the jobs or careers that interest you. A good place to start is the information provided by the Bureau of Labor Statistics, or BLS. The *Occupational Outlook Handbook* (*OOH*) has information about hundreds of jobs. It describes information in detail on compensation, education required, job duties, as well as growth or stagnation in the field (Sommers, 2012). *OOH* is published every two years. Occupations are broken into eleven large groups, with details about the kind of work involved, the conditions under which the work is done, and earning potential. Also included are details about education required to obtain the job, as well as the outlook for this job in future. Examining the *OOH* can also provide you with a clear picture of which occupations are growing, which are stagnating, and which are declining. This is important information for young workers who are considering making career choices that will have long-lasting effects. Consider these facts about the labor force projections:

Photo courtesy of Kevin Manguiob (Liberty University).

Students enjoy time at Snowlex, Liberty University's year-round ski facility.

Jennifer Griffin

Prov 3:6, "In all your ways acknowledge him, and he will make straight your paths" (ESV).

"Career planning is an important part of being a student. Whether you're starting your college journey at 18 years old or 68 years young, it's important to consider how you will use your education in the future. The Lord has placed in you a desire and passion for particular interests. You may have a natural inclination toward numbers and math, working with children and adults, or maybe the Lord has blessed you with an inquisitive mind with an aptitude for the sciences. No matter what your interests, you can be used by the Lord in any career! It is likely you will have many different jobs throughout your lifetime and your career will be formed as you move from one learning experience to another. No matter your profession, you can be certain the Lord has a special role for you in His plan. How he uses you will take many shapes and sizes. It delights the Lord when we follow His plan for our lives, and develop the passions He gives us!"

By 2020, there will be an additional 10 million workers (either working or looking for work).

As Baby Boomers age, the number of older workers will skyrocket, as that group's representation in the labor force grows nearly four times the rate of the total labor force.

Job growth in the 2010–2020 period will focus largely in the service industries.

The health-care sector will gain the most jobs and grow by 34% over the decade (Occupational Outlook Quarterly, 2012).

Other career information can be gleaned from the following resources:

The Department of Labor's **Occupation Exploration** site gives you an opportunity to learn about hundreds of different occupations in the United States. There are tools to help you, no matter where you are in the process of considering jobs and seeking employment.

The Bureau of Labor Statistics **Career Outlook** website narrows information to regional employment information.

U.S. Department of Labor's **O*NET OnLine** provides descriptions of more than 1000 careers, and is designed for use by job seekers, students, researchers.

The *Encyclopedia of Careers and Vocational Guidance, 16th ed.* is a multivolume compendium of data on a wide variety of careers. It provides qualifications, salary information, and advancement opportunities, as well.

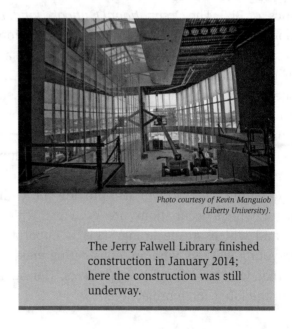

*Photo courtesy of Kevin Manguiob
(Liberty University).*

The Jerry Falwell Library finished construction in January 2014; here the construction was still underway.

Review Action Steps to Take for Your Future Career Growth

II Chronicles 15:7,
"But as for you, be strong and do not give up, for your work will be rewarded" (NIV).

The steps workers take to seek and secure employment has changed. Now, career-seekers use a variety of methods to find information on jobs and to promote themselves as candidates. Consider **networking** to build your circle of work colleagues. This can be a continual process of meeting others, determining how they may help you meet your career goals, and keeping in touch with them. Networking is defined by Merriam Webster's Dictionary as "the exchange of information or services among individuals, groups, or institutions; *specifically*: the cultivation of productive relationships for employment or business" (Merriam-webster.com, 2015).

"Career entrepreneurs use various ways of gaining success in their working lives, including contacts that can help them identify the right opportunities... They also recognize that they have something to offer to the people they are interested in, and they make attempts at establishing relationships that may require going an extra mile"(Korotov, Khapova, & Arthur, 2011, pp. 131). Networking is a way to build relationships that can help you meet

Photo courtesy of Joel Coleman (Liberty University).

This bench in the rooftop garden of DeMoss Hall features beautiful details in the iron, while supplying a place for students to relax.

T. Marcus Christian

"Career planning begins in your first semester of college. This is a time to explore the paths you hope to take with courses that may interest you. When you find that one set of classes that spikes your interest, you will finish school with a clear path and a smile."

Nathaniel Valle

"A professor once told me to 'think about your next step long before you have to walk.' As you think about that next step in your collegiate career, utilize the tools and knowledge you have gained in this course to plan beyond it. If you are already working in a professional career, consider how you can use INFT 101 to enhance your work environment and relationships."

Jenny Walter

"Now that you are actually in college, you want to choose the path of study you will walk down. Interests or advancement in your job can be a motivating factor in the course you will follow. If you are still unsure, looking at all of the different paths you can take with the various majors offered, can help you decide which course of study to follow."

your career goals. This can be as much about exchanging information with others as it is about seeking out mentors and those who can put a word in for you at just the right moment. Networking can seem just like casual socializing, but if it is done well, it is work!

Consider utilizing professional networking sites such as LinkedIn to advance your career opportunities.

A **personal mission statement** can be a tool for career development as well. It can help to "to crystallize what you want to express in your life, as it describes your values and how you wish to use them to effect change in your world" (Vozza, 2014). Your mission statement reveals what your values are and how you wish to use your life to express them. Your personal mission statement can be a guiding document as you think about your achievements and values, what you want to accomplish based on your skills, and the results you seek. Here is an example of a mission statement, written by Denise Morrison, CEO of Campbell Soup Company: "To serve as a leader, live a balanced life, and apply ethical principles to make a significant difference" (Quast, 2013). While the mission statement is personal and individual to you, it is not a once-and-done statement. You should review your personal mission statement from time to time and make adjustments as warranted.

Hanna Bruce

"Get to know someone who works in the field of your prospective profession. Ask this person about the pros and cons of his or her line of work, specific requirements that may be needed for the position and if he or she has any advice to pass along. This may help you determine whether or not this career is right for you."

Personal Reflection

Take a few moments to consider what your personal mission statement should say. What might be included in each category below?

VALUES	GOALS/ACTIONS	OUTCOMES

Your personal mission statement: _____

_____

Terry Conner

"It's never too late or too early to start thinking about your future employment. Seek out and research companies/industries that you think you'd be interested in joining. This serves a dual purpose; it can reinforce your desire to join that company and it can help you narrow the list of companies. Once you have this information you can then use the time to work on the skills that will make you more desirable to the company."

Job shadowing can be a way to glean valuable information during a typical workday. This allows you to see the everyday work an employee might encounter in a specific job or setting. Usually, job shadowing is a single-day experience, but longer experiences of shadowing, known as **Externship**

Experiences, can be beneficial, as well. This type of experience can be a good addition to your résumé if you are not working, nor have any experience in the field you are seeking to enter.

Volunteer work can give you opportunities to gain both experience and insights into different work settings and opportunities, while contributing your time and effort in service. This can be an excellent way to determine your interest in a long-term work commitment, while also helping you determine which settings you might enjoy the most. Volunteering your time can provide you opportunities to meet and work with professionals who may be able to advance your career with a recommendation in the future, based on the work (and work ethic) they observe during experiences with you.

Internships can pave the way to future career opportunities. Unlike shadowing, in which you are observing someone else's work, in an internship position, you are working alongside others in the profession you are considering. A major benefit of some internship programs is that you may earn either academic credit or financial compensation while working as an intern. Some internships are full-time positions, while others are temporary or part-time in nature. Seek internships with companies you consider excellent stepping stone to your work success. There are published guides that can help you in your search for information. *Petersons Internships* is one such guide which offers information for both undergraduate and graduate internships, including profiles for internships in more than a dozen employment categories. The Career Center and your local Chamber of Commerce or business group may also be of assistance in finding a suitable internship for you.

Finally, consider part-time work as a valuable résumé-building opportunity. If you have most of your time committed as a student, finding a part-time job that is relevant to your work goals can help you practice the skills you will need, while earning a small income as well.

Roger

"I was hired to teach a self-contained special education classroom at a public middle school. The amazing thing is that I was asked to come in for an interview three days before the start of the fall classes. My first day in the classroom was literally the first day of school! Since that day I received the educator of the year award for the entire school. I have had opportunities to take continuing education workshops and be certified as a highly qualified educator. I have had a positive impact on the lives of students with disabilities and have developed opportunities to bless fellow colleagues.

"But my greater joy is teaching as an online instructor for Liberty University School of Religion. I am truly blessed to interact with students from all across the country as well as students who are engaged with the military."

Tim

"The career path that I have chosen and been called to is in religion. I am not quite sure what it will entail; however, I do know that it is something that I use almost every day. Each day, I answer questions about different religions, God, and the Bible that Marines are curious about. I absolutely love talking about these matters with the Marines that I work with and I would love it if God opened the door for me to be a chaplain in any military service."

Tracey Good

"Have an end goal in mind. What type of job are you wanting to pursue? It's never too early to begin research within your field. We have a job database that is specific to Liberty University. It's our version of a monster.com and has jobs and internships from employers who are seeking Liberty talent. We have national and global positions listed. You can go to www.liberty.edu/lunetwork to join for FREE. You need to be aware of the job description of interest and know what skills you need to be achieving while taking your classes. This needs to be a part of your research process."

Create Documents to Use in Your Future Job Search

Matthew 7:7,
"**Ask** and it will be given to you; **seek** and you will find; **knock** and the door will be opened to you" (NIV).

Tracey Good

"As a Career Counselor, we meet with all majors and so would first encourage our students to take the Focus 2 Assessment. This will either help to confirm your major or will give them ideas on what types of jobs you could pursue within your area of strength. You will be tested on their interests (both work and leisure), personality, skills, and values."

Tracey Good

"The Career Center also helps with resumes, interviews, graduate school preparation, and more. Our students can visit www.liberty.edu/careers to help with their specific career planning needs."

Jess Cromley

"One strategy that I always found helpful in my undergraduate program was to request 'informational interviews' with the people who worked in a job I found exciting or interesting. Being able to ask questions like 'What is a typical day' or 'What is the hardest part of your job' allowed me to consider the answers as a way to determine if I could handle that in my own career."

As you begin to consider the path ahead in your career development plan, it may seem that the career opportunities you are pursuing are still a long way off, and you may become discouraged. Do not let the steps in the process deter your progress: Keep moving forward! This verse can help you think of the steps you will take: Ask, seek, knock. **Ask:** Verbalize what you are pursuing. **Seek:** This is an action verb that indicates that you will actively pursue opportunities to build your skills and hone your strengths. **Knock:** Look around you for those who can help you secure the job you want. Ask for their help with references, a job internship opportunity, or networking for your success.

Create Documents That Will Speak Well for You as You Build Your Career

1. **Transcript(s)**—You should keep updated copies of your transcript(s) from each school you have attended. This document is a concise display of the courses you have taken and the grades you earned. Often, employers give primary attention to the types of courses that you took, degrees you have completed, and the grade point average (GPA) you achieved. Contact the Registrar at each school you have attended to request copies of your transcript, usually for a nominal fee. Naturally, good grades reflect well on you and enhance your outlook for employment.

2. **Résumé**—Your résumé summarizes the experiences you have had. It is best done as a single page, but no more than two pages. The résumé highlights your achievements, not merely the work experiences you can claim. Notice the basic features of the following résumé template: Header, Objective, Body, References.

    The **Header** of your résumé gives your name and contact information. The information shared here should be your home address, personal phone number (home and/or cell), and personal email address. Avoid using your work address, phone number, or email. Ensure that your email address is professional in nature, avoiding overly personal nomenclature (e.g., aes27@gmail.com rather than foxymoma@gmail.com).

The **Objective** simply states what position you are seeking. It should be complete in only a sentence or two. An alternative here would be to describe the skills you will bring to a position. Include relevant work skills, which will be valuable in the job you are seeking.

The **Body** of your résumé is the meat of what you are sharing. You may have to work hard to encapsulate years of experience in a variety of jobs, or, if you are new to the working world, you may not have much to post here. In either case, begin with your most recent (or current) work or meaningful volunteer position. You should include your job title, the full name of the company your work(ed) for, its location, and your dates of employment. Briefly describe your responsibilities and accomplishments in the position you held. Include information that will set you apart from other candidates, such as promotions, additional responsibilities, awards and recognition, and so on. Be sure to use strong action verbs and a measure for the achievements you list in your résumé. Do not inflate any of your accomplishments but do not omit anything important that speaks of your skills and abilities.

The **References** section of your résumé should include names and full contact information of individuals who can speak of your skills, abilities, and results in work or volunteer settings. Never include a reference listing without first gaining permission from the individual whose name you wish to include. You may wish to simply include the phrase "Available upon request."

Sample Résumé Template

Contact information: centered (your full name, home address, phone numbers, and email address(es).

Job objective: Write a statement of your career goal, specific to the job you are applying for (or, for a general résumé, make this a broad statement).

Education: List college work, beginning with Liberty University and work backwards. Give dates of attendance and degree(s) or certificates earned, if any.

Awards and honors (optional, if there is room): This should include academic awards, but can also include awards from community groups (think Rotary Club, etc.) if they speak to your character traits that would make you a good employee.

(continues)

Nicole Lowes

"1) Before deciding on a career path I would recommend that students do some 'Job Shadowing.' Spend a day or two with a professional in your field of interest. Students typically have a preconceived idea of what a career looks like (possibly because they heard about it from a friend, or see it on television) when in actuality it is something very different. Students who take the time to job shadow sometimes realize that the career they thought they wanted is definitely not what they expected. This prevents them from changing majors multiple times throughout their college journey (i.e., if someone wants to become a nurse to help people and then realizes they can't handle blood).

2) Once a student has decided on a career path, it is important for them to research what it will take to actually work in that field. Many students believe that an undergraduate degree will get them the job of their dreams, which as we all know, is rarely the case. I think it is important to understand that most careers will take additional schooling beyond their initial BS degree. For instance, students think they can become a counselor with a degree in Psychology not realizing that it is going to take another 3 years for a masters and then 4000 hours of supervision. Or they think they can become a Physical Therapist with a degree in Health Science without understanding that Physical Therapy School is an additional 3-year program. So having the student understand what the full journey looks like to get them to the end goal is important.

3) Once a student has decided on their career path, it is important for them to figure out what skills are necessary in that career so they can begin developing them in their college years. Does the chosen career take excellent writing skills, strong attention to detail, and so on? How can they begin developing those skills while in college to prove they are a worthy candidate for a position in the field of their choice once they have successfully graduated?

4) Once a career path is chosen it is important to understand what is required in the transition between undergraduate programs and graduate programs. Many graduate programs require students to take specific courses before they are eligible for enrollment. So if a student chooses to go on to graduate school it is important to research that information during the junior/senior year to make sure he or she is meeting the requirements. That is, each Physical Therapy school requires different science courses as pre-reqs. It is important for student to know which courses they must take in order to be eligible for the school they desire to go to."

Community or college activities (again, optional, given space consider-ations): Name club leadership roles, team memberships, and so on, if they foster your career goal.

Memberships in professional organizations (optional): This might include honor societies, as well as groups that have a career focus. Leadership roles in these organizations could promote your employability.

Work experiences: Begin with your current employment, if you are working. This should be in reverse chronological order and may include not only paid employment, but also work as an intern, apprentice, or volunteer. Give the title of the job, the company you work(ed) for, your employment dates, and the major responsibilities you held. This can also be a place to highlight accomplishments within a job, such as a promotion.

Skills (not addressed previously): If you have a skill, which has not been addressed previously, include it here. Things to include are computer skills, languages you speak/write well, or any skill or experience, which your poten-tial employer may use.

References: You may simply put "Available upon request," or you can give details of your reference contact information. Three or four references should be sufficient. Include not only references who know your work hab-its, but also a personal reference who can speak to your character outside of work.

3. **Cover letter**—Your cover letter, like the resume' it will accompany, speaks for you. It is important to think carefully when crafting your cover letter. Your cover letter is best presented (like your resume) on high-quality, bright white paper. Do not try to impress a potential employer with fancy script, ink colors, or the like. That is not the way you want to stand out!

This is the time to be all-business. Your cover letter's job is to con-vince the reader that your résumé is worth a look. It should briefly introduce you, then give clues to why you would make an excellent candidate for a job, such as your skills, knowledge, and experiences. Finally, the cover letter should conclude by reiterating your interest in the position and noting that you are available for an interview. Close by thanking the reader for considering your application.

Your cover letter should be an evolving document, customized to each position for which you wish to apply. Read the job posting care-fully, noting the key words, and respond to them in your cover letter.

Since your cover letter speaks for you, ensure that you are succinct, complete, and have used correct grammar, capitalization, spelling, and punctuation. Do not let your prospects be ruined by a carelessly presented cover letter. Your cover letter gives the reader a first impression of you, so make sure it is a good one!

Here is a sample cover letter for you to consider: (Remember, you need to write a customized letter for each opportunity you wish to pursue.)

Sample Cover Letter

Your address
Your city, state, and zip code
Current date

Name of addressee
Job title
Company name
Company address
City, state, and zip code

Dear Mr./Mrs./Miss/Ms. (as appropriate) Last name:

I am writing to inquire about the advertised position for (give the job title) with your company. Please see the enclosed résumé, which gives details of both my experience and education. I believe these will demonstrate that I meet the requirements set for the position.

My current work (or education) in this field has provided me with opportunities to (list a few accomplishments that are relevant to the job you seek). My supervisor considers me a valuable employee because (give relevant information briefly), which will allow me to be an asset to your company.

I am familiar with your company (name it) and admire (name something you have discovered by researching the company). I would like to contribute my education and skills to meet your company's needs. I would like the opportunity to discuss the position and how I might fit with your company goals. Thank you for considering my interest in working for (name the company).

Sincerely,
(handwrite your signature)
Type your signature

Enclosure: Résumé

---

4. **References**—References or letters of recommendation, can be powerful support for your quest for employment. Before asking someone to write you a letter of recommendation, or to serve as a reference, carefully think about who can best speak for/about you, what information that person might share, and how you should request the recommendation. Keep in mind that you will want to seek reference letters from those who know you (or more specifically, your work) well and who can write effectively about it. Consider creating a fact sheet to give to your reference at the time you make your request. Always give the referee plenty of time to complete their work; you don't want the individual rushing to get something completed! Make it clear that you will not request to see the letter once it is written. Provide a stamped, addressed envelope for a written reference or an email address if the reference letter is to be sent electronically. Once the task is complete, be sure to send a note expressing your appreciation for the assistance. You may need to ask for an additional reference at another time, so it is important to show your appreciation for the help you are receiving. Always let the reference know whether your application was successful or not.

5. **Electronic portfolio**—An e-portfolio is a collection of documents that record your abilities, skills, accomplishments, and goals for the future. It can also serve as a repository for your documents for career research. The portfolio can show your growth over time, as well. You will want to include your college work that demonstrates your mastery, such as your written papers, research projects and results, and artwork, including photography or film records, as well as video capture of presentations and performances. The contents of your e-portfolio should showcase the depth and breadth of your experiences and preparation for work.

   In addition to the examples of your work preparation, your e-portfolio could also expand to include job performance evaluations along with your résumé and letters of commendation or recommendation. Keep the portfolio as an electronic record or create a web presence to which you can refer your potential employers.

Personal Reflection

Review your work to date and consider what you might have available to include in a portfolio.

What work have you done that contributes to your future career goals? Consider the following categories as you think back through your work and nonwork experiences.

Academic accomplishments (papers, research projects, presentations, etc.):

_____

_____

_____

Career accomplishments and awards (key work events/accomplishments/ recognition):

_____

_____

_____

Volunteer positions or internship work:

_____

_____

Professional memberships

_____

_____

Special skills and accomplishments (list ones related to the job opportunities you will be seeking):

_____

_____

_____

6. **Interview preparation and follow-though**

There are two types of interviews for which you should prepare yourself. The first would be considered an information interview and is used to collect information about a career or position that you believe you may be interested in pursuing. For this interview, you are the primary questioner. Think carefully about what you wish to learn about this career or opportunity, and write questions that can tease out the details you are lacking. Be sure to take careful note of the information your interviewee is sharing, and be careful to give opportunity for the interviewee to provide information about the work that you had not considered previously. Always promptly follow up the information interview with a thank-you note. If appropriate, you might ask to shadow your interviewee at his/her work to gain further information on the day-to-day operation of the work.

The second type of interview is the interview for employment. There are some basic steps to ensure your best results from the interview. Let's look at some of those next.

An interview is a way to give an in-person impression to the employer, who may have only seen your résumé. It is important to put your best foot forward, so to speak, to continue the momentum toward hiring that you accomplished with your cover letter and résumé. There are steps you can take before you arrive for the interview that can enhance your chance of being hired. First, learn all you can about the company or organization. This can begin with a web search. See what you can learn about the company's successes, management style, leadership, and culture. You may find articles in the newspaper or magazines that can further inform you about the company.

Think ahead about the questions you will be asked and rehearse your responses. You should be able to give a succinct recital of the salient details of your work history, as well as why you are interested in employment with the company in question. Be prepared for questions about your qualifications, how they fit the company, and what your goals and aspirations are for the future.

When it is time for the interview, be sure to dress appropriately in business attire. If you believe this may be too formal, do a little advance scouting to see what employees are wearing, so you can be dressed appropriately. Be on time for the interview by ensuring that you have additional time to overcome any traffic or parking obstacles you may encounter.

When you meet the interviewer or his/her receptionist, make sure to give a firm handshake, with good eye contact. A smile can indicate your interest and enthusiasm for the job and the interview. When given the opportunity, ask any questions you have prepared about the company or the specifics of the job. This can show that you have thought ahead about details you would like to know about the potential work.

When your interview draws to a close, ask what you might expect of the hiring process: when you might hear something further, how long the decision process takes, and so on. This is not the time to ask about benefits or salary. Thank the interviewer for his/her time. Follow up the interview quickly with a thank-you note to the interviewer, reiterating your interest in the position. Consider mentioning the particular aspects of the work that you would enjoy and which you could contribute to. This can show that you are not only polite, but also a potential team player for the company.

Take Advantage of the Services of the Career Center

The following information gives you a first-hand account of the assistance available to you through the Career Center. Counselor Tracey Good describes her experiences as both a student and a Liberty University Career Counselor. Read on to see the advice she has for you.

After waiting 20 years to go back for my master's degree, I wasn't sure what my next steps should be. That is when I first realized that Liberty University had a Career Center. Due to my uncertainties, I set an appointment with a Career Counselor to discuss my options. Through this meeting, I learned of some counseling opportunities as well as adjunct positions. I'm glad to report that today I am both a Career Counselor and an Adjunct Instructor.

As a Career Counselor, I have the opportunity to meet with students from all over the globe, both by phone and in person. It's important to begin this journey toward professional development earlier in your academic career so that some action steps can be taken right from the start. The Career Center provides many different FREE services just for you!

As you begin this process, one of the first steps is to understand your options. The Career Center provides the Focus 2 Assessment, which tests you on your Interests, Personality, Skills, and Values to show you where your strengths lie. You may also want to set a follow-up appointment to examine your results with a Career Counselor. Career Counseling is a service that offers you the opportunity to discuss your career options and to improve your professional development skills.

Keeping in mind that Networking is still the number one way to achieve your career of interest, there are important steps to consider in setting your strategy. The Career Center can help you with your social media presence as well as ideas to gain essential experience through volunteering. I have personally witnessed many students land a position due to their active involvement as an unpaid worker. This is another solid way to network while proving your worth and work ethic.

Once you are aware of your career direction, the Career Center can assist you with your Internship and Job Search through a database called LU Network. This includes positions that are both national and global, specifically for Liberty students and alumni. When employers want to recruit Liberty talent outside of LU Network, they will also visit Liberty's campus for evening informational sessions or attend major specific Career Fairs. If you're within driving distance, we would love to see you here on campus. You'll want to RSVP before attending.

As soon as you've found some positions of interest, you'll be ready to write your resume. Make sure to always use the job description and tweak your information for each new position. The Career Center will review your **Résumé**. Please be mindful of the high volume received daily. You'll want to plan ahead and make sure not to submit last minute. Most employers will only first glance at your resume for 6–15 seconds, so you'll be given tips to help yours stand out to entice a longer evaluation.

A strong résumé will increase the possibility of gaining an interview. The Career Center provides customized practice through a Mock Interview, by becoming your company of interest and asking pertinent questions for the intended position. The feedback received is that the questions asked by our Career Counselors are usually more difficult than the actual interview!

If you are considering Graduate School, the Career Center can discuss your differing options as well as help with the timeline, encouraging the importance of knowing the various deadlines within the process.

I'm so grateful and blessed to work as a Career Counselor in the Liberty University Career Center. I search for ways to assist students and alumni in setting their career plans, but more importantly I spend time praying with them for the Lord's guidance and direction. For more details concerning these services, please go to www.liberty.edu/careers. May the Lord bless you in your career endeavors!

The work that you do completing your preparation for a new position can provide the important final step to gaining the position you want. Be sure to create your documents carefully, and then review them with your Career Counselor for best results. The time you spend preparing documents, gathering a portfolio, and polishing your presentation will pay off when you apply for and receive a wonderful position.

BUILDING BLOCKS

In Chapter 1, we mentioned that Dr. Falwell, the founder of Liberty University, set "big, hairy, audacious goals" from the time he was a young man up until the day he died. What career goals do you have in place now? Are they ones you feel God is leading you to pursue, or are they ones that originated with you? At times, it seems that God is calling us to tasks that are bigger than we are or are ones we are not capable of achieving. Are you familiar with the story of how God called Moses? We read the story in Exodus in the Bible's *Old Testament*. Moses, a son of Hebrew parents, was raised in the palace of the Egyptian pharaoh. He ran away from Egypt and spent 40 years away, tending his father-in-law's sheep. One day, God called Moses to a special job in a very dramatic way . . . He spoke to him from a burning bush! Imagine that! Do you suppose Moses set off right away to follow God's direction? Not quite, for Moses insisted to God that he was unprepared for the task of leading God's people out of Egypt, where they had been for 400 years. Rather than go straightaway and relay God's message to the Egyptian leader, Moses responded with a "Who, me?" attitude! Eventually, Moses came around and followed God's direction. He became the leader of the exiles who left Egypt to go to the land God had promised their ancestors. From a humble shepherd to a leader of hundreds of thousands, Moses followed where God called him. Have you heard the expression, "God does not call the equipped, He equips the called"? Think on the story of Moses' call and reflect on how that "equipping" might play out in your life.

What tasks stand between you and completion of the career goals you have set? Do you have both a short-term plan and a long-term plan for the future? What steps will be required to move from where you are now to live out your plans? What obstacles do you see in your path? Are your plans not only God-honoring but also God-inspired? In Mark 3:35, Jesus says, "Whoever does God's will is my brother and sister and mother" (NIV). That is an exciting prospect. What does "doing God's will" look like for you? How does it reflect in your career plan? Are the characteristics you possess, along with your skills, relevant to the career choice you are pursuing? Are you able to connect your personality, skills, education, and drive to achieve the career goals you have set for yourself?

Photo courtesy of Dave Moquin.

Construction workers expand the top level of Williams Stadium, making it the beautiful, state-of-the-art facility it is today!

TOOL BOX

Alumni Relations

Get involved early with the Liberty Alumni Association. The alumni site has listings of physical and virtual groups from around the globe. You can utilize these groups to connect and network with other Liberty alum who know just what it takes to be successful after graduation.

Portfolios

- **Cloud-based storage**—When developing a portfolio, consider the use of cloud-based storage options. These are free sites that store your files on the Internet and allow you to access them from anywhere in the world. You can use this space as a personal storage drive, but most will also allow you to share documents and folders with outside users, which is perfect for creating an online portfolio. Once you register, you will be able to download a small software program that lets you use your cloud drive just like you would use any other storage folder on your computer. When it comes time to share your work, you can make a document, or an entire folder, public so that anyone can view it, or you can limit who you share with by entering specific email addresses. Check out the Breaking Ground website to see some of the options that are available to you.

- **Websites**—Another option for creating an online portfolio is to create a website. This can be a bit more complex than managing a cloud drive, but it also affords you the ability to create an aesthetically pleasing interface, which could be more appealing to prospective employers. Google Sites and WordPress are great free options for creating your first site. There is a learning curve, but these sites also offer tutorials to help you learn your way.

Resume Building

- **Course selection**—Put your elective credits to good use by considering what skills may be beneficial in your future career and taking courses that will help you develop those skills. Do you need computer skills? Consider signing up for a class on computing basics, or advance your skills by mastering a new program. Would additional language skills benefit you as you work toward a position as an inner-city teacher? Try registering for one of Liberty's many conversational language courses.

- **Syllabi**—Besides selecting courses that will broaden your skill set and appeal, you can also use the syllabi for those classes to help craft your resume. Each of the measurable learning outcomes in the course syllabus represents a skill that you may potentially acquire. Why not copy these into a working résumé for later use?

Letters of Reference

- **Faculty**—An often-overlooked concept for online students is the power of a good letter of reference from an instructor. Develop a relationship with your professors and let them know who you are. Consider asking them if they teach classes other than the ones you are currently taking. If you develop a good relationship, it is likely they will remember you, increasing the chances that they would be willing to write a letter of reference for you.

Additional resources and links to specific sites, worksheets, and apps can be located by accessing the Breaking Ground website:

www.breakinggroundlu.com

References

Clarke, M. (2009). Plodders, pragmatists, visionaries and opportunists: Career patterns and employability. *Career Development International, 14*(1), 8–28.

Falwell, J. (1997). *Falwell: An autobiography*. Lynchburg, VA: Liberty House Publishers.

Falwell, J. (2014). *Press quotes*. Retrieved from http://www.liberty.edu/about liberty/index.cfm?PID = 26726.

Korotov, K., Khapova, S. N., & Arthur, M. B. (2011). Career entrepreneurship. *Organizational Dynamics, 40*(2), 127–135. DOI:10.1016/j.orgdyn.2011.01.007.

McKay, Dominique. (2009). *Dr. Elmer Towns speaks at convocation*. Retrieved from http://www.liberty.edu/news/index.cfm?PID = 18495&MID = 5840.

Networking. (n.d.). In *Merriam Webster Online*, Retrieved February 6, 2015, from http://www.merriam-webster.com/dictionary/networking

Occupational Outlook Quarterly, (2012, Spring). *56*(1), 2–42.

Quast, L. (2013, October). Mmm Mmm Good: A Q and A with Campbell Soup Company Executives. *Forbes*.

Sommers, D. (2012). Getting started. *Occupational Outlook Quarterly, 55*(4), 2–5.

Chapter 11

Your Degree: The Key

KEY CONCEPTS

In this chapter, you will:

- Reevaluate present and future goals.
- Reflect on your experiences within the course.
- Project new scholastic experiences.
- Identify keys that will make you successful.

THE KEY

When the builder finishes the building project and the client settles the debt, the builder presents the client with the key to the completed building. That key opens the door to the finished building, beautiful, fresh, and new. With the key in hand, the client can make this building his or her own by adding furnishings and personal effects. Getting your degree is just like the transfer of the key; once you have your degree, doors will open for you that would have otherwise been closed. Look forward to the day you receive your degree, and you can celebrate as Paul does in II Timothy 4:7–8, having "fought the good fight" and "kept the faith" (NIV).

© 2013 by by Marie C Fields. Used under license of Shutterstock, Inc.

II Timothy 4:7–8,
"I have fought the good fight, I have finished the race, I have kept the faith. Now there is in store for me the crown of righteousness, which the Lord, the righteous Judge, will award to me on that day—and not only to me, but also to all who have longed for his appearing" (NIV).

THE CORNERSTONE: TRADITIONS

I Peter 5:2–7, "Be shepherds of God's flock that is under your care, watching over them—not because you must, but because you are willing, as God wants you to be; not pursuing dishonest gain, but eager to serve; not lording it over those entrusted to you, but being examples to the flock. And when the Chief Shepherd appears, you will receive the crown of glory that will never fade away. In the same way, you who are younger, submit yourselves to your elders. All of you, clothe yourselves with humility toward one another, because, 'God opposes the proud but shows favor to the humble.' Humble yourselves, therefore, under God's mighty hand, that he may lift you up in due time. Cast all your anxiety on him because he cares for you" (NIV).

As you pursue your degree and once you complete it, you will gain more and more responsibilities (at home, at school, and at work). With these responsibilities come opportunities to serve others by caring for them and living by example. John E. Johnson, Sr., one of the first graduates of Lynchburg Baptist College, tells the story of his graduation; his story evidences examples of the kind of servant leadership in Liberty University's founders that I Peter 5:2–7 describes.

Photo courtesy of Liberty University.

In 1973, Lynchburg Baptist College (now LU) held its first graduating ceremony (pictured here). One of the first graduates, John E. Johnson, shares his story of that first graduation; in the picture, he is located fourth from the left.

"Merriam-Webster's online dictionary states that tradition is 'a way of thinking, behaving, or doing something that has been used by the people in a particular group, family, society, etc., for a long time' (Merriam-Webster.com, 2013). Liberty University has several traditions, one of which I was inadvertently complicit in starting.

In the late 60s, I attended various universities and colleges before landing in Lynchburg, Virginia, in the summer of 1972 for my senior year at the small, Baptist college that Jerry Falwell had founded just the year before, called Lynchburg Baptist College. The thing that drew me and other enthusiastic young people to the school in those early years was not the facilities. We lived in cabins and barracks on Treasure Island in the middle of the James River; the church youth camp converted to house us as we attended classes in the Sunday school rooms at Thomas Road Baptist Church. We were transported back and forth in old rickety school buses and were offered bologna and peanut butter and jelly sandwiches as our meal plan. What attracted these early pioneers to LBC was the fact that where other schools were teaching students things that they could apply once they graduated and went out into the world, at LBC we were doing it through various opportunities to work in media, public speaking, performance, ministry, and hospitality.

Jerry was reaching the world with the gospel through the weekly televised broadcast of the "Old Time Gospel Hour," which was seen in every major city in North America. On the days when Jerry wasn't preaching from the pulpit of TRBC, he, along with gospel soloist Doug Oldham, the LBC Chorale, and a host of others would board the converted DC-3 or the Convair 580 and fly around the country, holding events and promoting the school. The students were enthusiastic and eager to be a part of the dream of becoming the largest Christian university in the world and in doing so, reaching the world for Christ.

That year went fast, and on the last Sunday of the school year, Jerry announced that the first class of LBC graduates would be graduating that evening and that all graduating seniors needed to meet at the front of the sanctuary at 4 o'clock for rehearsal. (We would actually receive our Certificates of Completion since LBC was not able to confer degrees until 1974.) Well, as a graduating senior, that was the first I heard about it! However, I didn't think it unusual since a lot of things happened fast and at the last moment back then. So, at 4 o'clock I walked in and sat on the front pew and watched eight students dressed in black robes complete with caps assemble on the platform.

The co-founder of the school, Dr. Elmer Towns, was directing the rehearsal, when he noticed me sitting on the front pew and asked, "John, what are you doing here?"

I said, "I came to graduate."

With an astonished look on his face, he responded, "Really!" I explained that this was my fifth year in school, and I was sure that I had more than enough credits to graduate.

He said, "Well, there is only one way to find out." He left the graduates to practice on their own while he and I raced up the hill to his office where he opened the lower right hand drawer of his desk and pulled my file out of the folder that held all of the student's files. He began adding all the credits from the transcripts of the four various schools that I had attended (Ohio University, University of Hawaii, Cedarville College, and now LBC), all the while apologizing that I had somehow fallen through the cracks, and he had somehow missed me in the process. In the end, he declared I had more than enough credits to graduate. He threw the file back in the drawer, and he and I raced back to join the others.

When we got back, it dawned on him, "You don't have a gown!" Whereupon, Vernon Brewer, a good friend of mine, who was also graduating, jumped up and exclaimed, "Hold on! I've got an idea!" He bolted through the door at the back of the platform and before long returned clutching Jerry's *baptismal robe in his hand, waved it above his head, and told me to try it on. It was a little long for me, so Vernon and I switched. Elmer said, "You must have a cap," so he offered me his. He said it would be okay if he went without one. I put it on my head, and I was ready to go!*

About that time, Jerry entered from his room in the back, dressed in his robe, cap, and stole. He noticed right away that Elmer wasn't wearing his cap and said "Elmer, where's your cap?" Elmer told him what had happened. Jerry immediately took off his cap, flung it across the platform, and said, "Well, Elmer, if you're not gonna wear one, neither am I!" It was a good excuse not to have to wear the old mortarboard, and he didn't. From that first graduation ceremony in May of 1973, at every graduation until his final commencement service in 2006, Chancellor Falwell went without his cap.

I often attend the commencement services at Liberty University, and whenever I do and notice President Jerry Falwell without his cap, it takes me back to that first ceremony in 1973. I can still see Jerry, Sr. flinging his cap across the platform and saying, "Well, Elmer, if you're not going to wear one neither am I!" Is it a tradition? I don't know . . . but it continues!"

Co-founders of Liberty University, Dr. Jerry Falwell, Sr. and Dr. Elmer Towns, made a small decision that day in 1973 that impacted the lives of one of their graduates forever. By allowing a young man to wear a borrowed cap and robe so he could graduate in proper attire, they humbled themselves and showed camaraderie with each other by declining to don the graduation cap. This may have seemed like a small decision to these leaders, but to John, it became a lasting memory that he will cherish. Not only did these men teach the students how to be "young champions for Christ," they also lived it through their actions, "because they were willing, as God wanted them to be; not pursuing dishonest gain, but eager to serve; not lording it over those entrusted to them, but being examples to the flock" (I Peter 5:2–3, NIV). This tradition has transcended generations as President Jerry Falwell continues to lead the school with handpicked faculty unified to serve others in the vision of Liberty University. Take this tradition of service to heart everywhere you go as you touch the lives of others as a "champion for Christ!"

Photo courtesy of Liberty University; photographer: Les Schofer.

At Liberty University's 2003 commencement, Chancellor Jerry Falwell challenged graduates with an encouraging message.

Photo courtesy of Liberty University; photographer: Les Schofer.

John E. Johnson and his wife, Paula, are pictured here with Jerry and his wife, Macel, at the opening of the Jerry Falwell museum. John and Paula met while attending school at LBC (now LU). Both John and Paula loved to share their stories of LU's foundational years with others. In 2014, John went to be with his Lord and Savior, Jesus Christ, after having served in ministry since graduating from LU. Paula presently serves as the Curator of the Jerry Falwell Museum and continues to share these precious memories with students, parents, visitors, and friends of LU.

Reevaluate Present and Future Goals

Philippians 3:12–14,

"Not that I have already obtained all this, or have already arrived at my goal, but I press on to take hold of that for which Christ Jesus took hold of me. Brothers and sisters, I do not consider myself yet to have taken hold of it. But one thing I do: forgetting what is behind and straining toward what is ahead, I press on toward the goal to win the prize for which God has called me heavenward in Christ Jesus" (NIV).

Terry

Q: *Did you commit to your education one term at a time, or did you go all in from the beginning?*

A: "All-in from the beginning."

Q: *How did you feel when you earned your degree?*

A: "Relieved, not only had I accomplished something of significance, but also my family helped me, and that made it even sweeter."

In Chapter 5: Academic Goals: The Foundation, we discussed the importance of determining a set of goals to direct you as you complete your courses (and ultimately, your degree). Take a minute to evaluate your progress by filling out the chart below, listing your original goals, noting what you have accomplished, and the steps it took to accomplish that goal. Identify the goals that are still outstanding and what needs to be done to achieve those goals.

Personal Reflection

Fill out the following charts and answer the questions that follow each chart.

Original Goal	Was this a short-term or long-term goal?	Have you accomplished this goal? How?	Is this goal still outstanding? Why?	If not already met, how can you reach this target?

Original Goal	Was this a short-term or long-term goal?	Have you accomplished this goal? How?	Is this goal still outstanding? Why?	If not already met, how can you reach this target?

Kristy Motte

"Don't forget the goals that you're seeking to attain through this degree—write them down. When things get tough, looking back on those goals will help you persevere and finish the race!"

Roger

Q: *How did you feel when you earned your degree?*

A: "Of all the schools I attended, this is the first time I really wanted to attend graduation and walk with my classmates. I was both very proud of my accomplishments and humbled that the Lord allowed me the opportunity to have a world-class education."

Dr. Harold Willmington

"We don't know what the future holds, but we know who holds the future" (Laird, 2012).

After completing this activity, reflect on what you have recorded. Then answer the following questions:

1. Did you notice patterns that have developed that help you master your objectives?

_____

_____

_____

_____

2. Did you notice patterns of obstacles that interfere with your goals?

_____

_____

_____

_____

3. Are your goals still worthwhile? If they are no longer worthwhile, how have they changed?

_____

_____

_____

_____

4. Take a minute to revise and make new goals as you look toward the future.

New Goal	Is this a short-term or long-term goal?	What do you need to do to accomplish this goal? How?	What potential obstacles may interfere with this goal?	How can you overcome the obstacles? *(This could be a practical suggestion or a motivating verse of scripture.)*

New Goal	Is this a short-term or long-term goal?	What do you need to do to accomplish this goal? How?	What potential obstacles may interfere with this goal?	How can you overcome the obstacles? (This could be a practical suggestion or a motivating verse of scripture.)

Roger

Q: *After earning your degree, what do you wish you had done differently?*

A: "I wish I hadn't accrued so much school debt."

Dr. Jerry Falwell, Sr.

"There are far more valleys than mountain tops in the Christian life. God sends us two bad days for every good day in order to keep us looking towards Him" (Falwell, 1997, p. 471).

Cheryl

"As an adult learner, I am GRATEFUL I was able to complete my undergrad in a non-traditional format . . . one that afforded me the opportunity to attend from home."

5. How do these new goals fit in with your time management plan that you established?

_____

_____

_____

_____

_____

Through this activity, you may have noticed that while you have achieved some goals, other goals went neglected or you determined that they were not necessary. In working through this, you may also have realized that you have new goals worth setting. Take a moment to celebrate the goals you have accomplished and the decisions you have made toward tweaking or setting new goals. Celebrate the strategies that you have put into place to conquer any obstacles that stand in your way and remember these words of encouragement from our founder, Dr. Jerry Falwell, "It is not the boulders ahead of us which wear us down. It is often the grain of sand in our shoe. God never puts more on us than He puts in us to bear up every burden" (*Falwell,* 1997, p. 427).

© 2015 by Neonci. Used under license of Shutterstock, Inc.

"It is not the boulders ahead of us which wear us down. It is often the grain of sand in our shoe. God never puts more on us than He puts in us to bear up every burden" (Falwell, 1997, p. 427).

Reflect on Your Experiences Within the Course

Proverbs 1:5,
"Let the wise listen and add to their learning . . . and let the discerning get guidance" (NIV).

Throughout this book you have been exposed to a variety of information regarding:

- Your responsibilities as a learner,
- Study strategies,
- Goal setting and time management strategies,
- Andragogy—learning as an adult,
- Learning theories—learning as an individual,
- Information literacy, and
- Scholarly writing.

As you have applied the various techniques and information to different assignments in this course, you have done as Proverbs 1:5 advocates; you have added to your learning and you have received guidance! Reflect on the guidance you have received and learning you have absorbed while working through this book. What different techniques/information did you embrace naturally? What techniques/information will you use in the future? Analyze and chart these in the table provided. Also, consider revisiting the chart once you have completed the technique you planned to try out and record the results of your trial.

Terry

Q: *What was your scariest time in online college?*

A: "The scariest time was the initial class, fear of the unknown; once I settled down, everything was a breeze after that."

Photo courtesy of Aaron Traphagen.

"Reflect on the guidance and learning you have absorbed while working through this book."

Personal Reflection

In the following chart, document the different information from this textbook that you have learned and the strategies you have tried. Answer each of the questions, as well.

LEARNING OBJECTIVE	What do you naturally do?	What new strategy will you try?	How did that new strategy work for you?
Adult Learning			
Time Management			
Goal Setting			
Learning Preferences			
Study Strategies			
Information Literacy			
Scholarly Writing			
Career Planning			

Terry

Q: *Who provided support for you as you studied?*

A: "My lovely wife and our newborn baby (what a great motivator she was even then)."

Shannon Bream, Liberty alumna and American journalist for Fox News in her address to Liberty graduates at the 40th commencement ceremony

"There will be joyous successes and beautiful families. There will be challenges and times when your burdens feel unbearable . . . But we know nothing is a surprise to the Lord. He has already woven a stunning tapestry of your life, but it's one you'll only get to experience a single thread at a time. It will require trust and patience and walking very close to Him. That is what we are called to do" (Menard, 2013).

Project New Scholastic Experiences

KEY CONCEPT

Proverbs 16:3,
"Commit to the Lord whatever you do, and He will establish your plans" (NIV).

As you make plans for your academic future, what do you want to achieve? A degree, right? Or, is it more than that? Is it also the ability to qualify for a new job, advancement, or a raise? Is it the opportunity to be the first person from your family to graduate from college? Is it to set an example for the younger generation in your family, so that they see the importance of education at any age? Is it to follow your true calling? Whatever your reasons for pursuing a college education, commit your plans to the Lord and cover them in prayer, believing that he will do as Proverbs 16:3 promises. As you plan and pray, you must also prepare for the new scholastic experiences that will come your way.

In preparation for your future academic endeavors, consider the factors that will contribute to your success: goal setting, time management, and course selection and sequencing. Prayerfully consider the questions that correspond with each factor because your answers will drive the direction you take toward degree completion.

Photo courtesy of Aaron Traphagen.

"As you make plans for your academic future, what do you want to achieve?" Reflect on the answers to that question and begin setting realistic goals.

Personal Reflection

Consider the factors (goal setting, time management, and course selection and sequencing) that will contribute to your success and answer the following questions.

Set Realistic Goals

When do you want to complete your degree?

_____

_____

_____

_____

Alissa Keith

"No one cares more about your education than you do, so take the reigns and plan your own degree completion plan and complete what you started. Also, beware of those pesky pre-requisites."

Tim

Q: *Who provided support for you as you studied?*

A: *"The best support I had while taking college courses was from my wife. She helped me in every way possible, from submitting my papers while I was away to reminding me of work that I needed to complete. This is why I love her so much, of course."*

T. Marcus Christian

"Think of degree completion as a race. Sometimes they are long with many hills, but there is always a finish line. Strive for that line, you will be glad you did."

Is this goal realistic when compared to the responsibilities you currently have in your life?

_____

_____

_____

Do your finances allow for you to complete your degree within this timeline?

_____

_____

_____

Time Management

What time do you have to devote to your degree?

_____

_____

_____

How many courses can you reasonably take during a term without overloading yourself?

_____

_____

_____

If your degree is a priority, what might you have to sacrifice in order to complete it?

_____

_____

_____

Course Selection and Sequencing

What courses are relevant to your degree?

_____

_____

_____

_____

_____

In what order should you take the courses that are required for your degree?

_____

_____

_____

What other factors need to be considered to ensure that you meet your degree deadline: certification timelines or internships, for example?

_____

_____

When making academic decisions regarding your course load for future terms, keep the above factors in mind. Communicate your ideas with your academic advisor, so he or she can help you make the best decision given the context of your situation. Also, share these concerns with your family and friends, so they can support you through your academic career. As poet John Donne wrote, "No man is an island." You do not have to go through this experience alone; your family, friends, advisors, and professors will be your cheerleaders, if you invite them to the game. When you graduate, it will be a shared victory—the sweetest kind, "And let us consider how to stir up one another to love and good works, not neglecting to meet together, as is the habit of some, but encouraging one another, and all the more as you see the Day drawing near" (Hebrews 10:24–25, ESV).

Photo by Rachel Dugan © Liberty University.

As poet John Donne wrote, "No man is an island." You do not have to go through this experience alone; your family, friends, advisors, and professors will be your cheerleaders, if you invite them to the game. When you graduate, it will be a shared victory—the sweetest kind." (Pictured here: Liberty University Commencement 2014)

Nathaniel Valle

"If you spend time planning out your degree, you'll find it incredibly helpful—knowing what courses remain for your degree will lessen the chance that you sign up for an unnecessary course or miss a requirement. Most of you also have the freedom to take multiple electives, so planning your schedule ahead of time allows you to take courses outside of your major that interest you. Who knows? Maybe you will find English courses addictive!"

Jenny Walter

"Once you have decided on a course of study, become familiar with your Degree Completion Plan (DCP) or the lists of courses required for your chosen major. Not only will your DCP keep you on track by helping your plan your course order, the DCP will keep you from taking unnecessary classes."

Identify Keys that Will Make You Successful

Joshua 1:7–9,

"Be strong and very courageous. Be careful to obey all the law my servant Moses gave you; do not turn from it to the right or to the left, that you may be successful wherever you go. Keep this Book of the Law always on your lips; meditate on it day and night, so that you may be careful to do everything written in it. Then you will be prosperous and successful. Have I not commanded you? Be strong and courageous. Do not be afraid; do not be discouraged, for the Lord your God will be with you wherever you go" (NIV).

As Joshua 1:7–9 says, obeying the Lord's guidance in your life will lead to success. The Lord's guidance can be found in scripture, in prayer, in daily devotionals, in church involvement and attendance, and in fellowship and relationships with other believers through wise council. Which of these have you already adopted as part of your walk with Christ? Which of these suggestions will you try? Recently, Willie Robertson, successful business-man and star of the hit TV show, "Duck Dynasty," came to Liberty University's convocation. He shared this advice with the student body, "When you are moving toward God, you are moving in the right direction. . . . My challenge to you is to not let the world's measuring stick show you what is successful. . . . Our family views success (as being) able to go around the country and share the message of the Lord and to talk about our faith" (Skinner, M. & Liberty University News Service, 2013). As you read further in the chapter, you will discover many other practical tips that will bring you success in your college experiences; in your reading, look for things that you can incorporate into your routine that will help you grow and develop. Most importantly, just as Willie Robertson and Joshua 1:7–9 suggest, focus on the tips/keys that will put you on the path to a stronger relationship with Jesus and a strengthening of your faith because this will lead to a successful life.

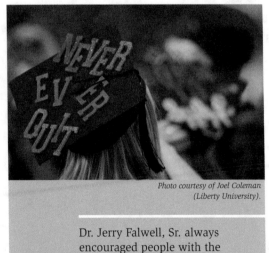

Photo courtesy of Joel Coleman (Liberty University).

Dr. Jerry Falwell, Sr. always encouraged people with the message, "Never Quit!" These words continue to inspire successful graduates.

Successful Beliefs

Stephen Covey's book *The Seven Habits of Highly Effective People* has been described as one of the most influential books of the 20th century.

In 2004, he released a new book called *The 8th Habit: From Effectiveness to Greatness.*

These habits are based on beliefs that lead to success.

1. **Be proactive.**

   Being proactive means accepting responsibility for your life. Covey uses the word "response-ability" for the ability to choose responses. The quality of your life is based on the decisions and responses that you make. Proactive people make things happen through responsibility and initiative. They do not blame circumstances or conditions for their behavior.

2. **Begin with the end in mind.**

   Know what is important and what you wish to accomplish in your life. To be able to do this, you will need to know your values and goals in life. You will need a clear vision of what you want your life to be and where you are headed.

3. **Put first things first.**

   Once you have established your goals and vision for the future, you will need to manage yourself to do what is important first. Set priorities so that you can accomplish the tasks that are important to you.

4. **Think win-win.**

   In human interactions, seek solutions that benefit everyone. Focus on cooperation rather than competition. If everyone feels good about the decision, there is cooperation and harmony. If one person wins and the other loses, the loser becomes angry and resentful and sabotages the outcome.

5. **First seek to understand, then to be understood.**

   Too often in our personal communications, we try to talk first and listen later. Often we don't really listen: we use this time to think of our reply. It is best to listen and understand before speaking. Effective communication is one of the most important skills in life.

6. **Synergize.**

   A simple definition of synergy is that the whole is greater than the sum of its parts. If people can cooperate and have good communication, they can work together as a team to accomplish more than each individual could do separately. Synergy is also part of the creative process.

(continues)

President Jerry Falwell

"Our ultimate purpose for our graduates is to know Christ and make Him known. We are now poised to carry out that mission in unparalleled ways" (Falwell, 2014).

Roger

"Success is obeying the Lord and submitting oneself to His control. I desire to let Him guide and direct my life and future. He has the authority and right to allow me to teach or to take that position away. I will strive to keep Him in the position of first place in my life. He must be before school, job, and family."

Katie Robinson

"James 1:12 states, 'Blessed is the man who perseveres under trial, because when he has stood the test, he will receive the crown of life that God has promised to those who love him' (NIV). So often, academics isn't about who has entered the classroom with the most knowledge or the most gifts. Instead, those who persevere through the many obstacles—and they will come—meet their educational goals. Anything that is worth having takes hard work."

Terry

Q: *How has receiving a degree at Liberty impacted your life?*

A: "Too many ways to list, but financially and work-happiness are the two most impacted areas."

Q: *What have been the keys to success in your life throughout your time at LU and beyond?*

A: "Much the same keys that made me successful in school: perseverance, determination, and the willingness to push forward when others would not."

Dr. Jerry Falwell, Sr.

"There are some things money will do; there are some things human effort will do; there are some things human ingenuity will do; but there are some things only God can do" (Falwell, 1997, p. 266).

Cheryl

"I know I can! This phrase has become more a philosophy than just a statement. My degree was hard. There were times I wanted to walk away! But, I didn't give up!

Situations in life can be over-whelming (like taking my child to urgent care in the middle of the night, when I'm amazing crazy sick with the flu; or calling the ambulance to take my mother to the ER, every week for a year; or dealing with stage two cancer, wondering if it will crop up again; or trying to figure how I'm going to pay for my daughter's $2700 braces). But I remember that I not only kept moving forward with my undergraduate degree, but went on to earn straight A's in a master's degree program, as well."

7. **Sharpen the saw.**

Covey shares the story of a man who was trying to cut down a tree with a dull saw. As he struggled to cut the tree, someone suggested that he stop and sharpen the saw. The man said that he did not have time to sharpen the saw, so he continued to struggle. Covey suggests that we need to take time to stop and sharpen the saw. We need to stop working and invest some time in ourselves by staying healthy physically, mentally, spiritually, and socially. We need to take time for self-renewal.

8. **Find your voice, and inspire others to find theirs.**

Believe that you can make a positive difference in the world and inspire others to do the same. Covey says that leaders "deal with people in a way that will communicate to them their worth and potential so clearly that they will come to see it in themselves." Accomplishing this ideal begins with developing one's own voice or "unique personal significance."

From *College and Career Success*, 5/e by Marsha Fralick. Copyright © 2011 by Kendall Hunt Publishing Company. Reprinted by permission.

Brad Burgess, Liberty University Professor and Department Chair for the College of General Studies, has worked with students and faculty alike, training them for success through a variety of tried and true techniques. In the following article, Brad offers tips for success, specifically in the areas of time management, accountability, diligence, and goal setting.

Tips for Success

Technology has created the opportunity to pursue a degree without ever having to physically attend a classroom. This flexible format helps to meet the needs of adults who may have busy lives with families, careers, and church obligations. Although the online classroom creates a great venue for learning, the online student needs to recognize that there can be pitfalls. Below are some basic tips for success for online students to consider as they pursue their degrees.

Time Management

The most important tip for success when pursuing a degree online is understanding the role of time management. One of the general pitfalls with time management is that a student will underestimate the time needed each week to successfully complete their studies. This can be a common problem, and students need to make sure that there is significant time available on a weekly basis to commit to homework, reading, writing papers, and taking tests. Education has to be a priority, and our priorities help dictate how time should be spent.

Action Plan

1. Closely examine your schedule and block out intervals of time throughout each week that can be committed to your studies.

2. Treat these allotted times as sacred and avoid the tendency to break these time commitments.

3. Set artificial deadlines for assignments at least 48 hours ahead of the actual due date. This will naturally build in some extra time just in case it is needed.

Accountability

Unlike a residential class, online classes do not have specific times to meet during a given week. Most students appreciate the flexibility the online environment offers, but this can also create a hardship because it may become easy to put off their studies. Knowing this, it is important to develop accountability within a student's weekly schedule. In many cases, it may be recruiting a spouse, family member, or friend that the student can interact with and be accountable to regarding his or her studies. The lack of a face-to-face environment can create a feeling of isolation, but successful students recognize that having individuals involved who hold them accountable will increase their opportunity for success.

Action Plan

1. Recruit one or two people who can be involved in your educational pursuits and keep you accountable.

2. Develop an extensive weekly plan that builds in time for school work and make this known to the individuals who are holding you accountable.

3. Give your accountability partners permission to hold you accountable, and make sure that you are on task with your studies. Allow them to exercise "tough love" as needed.

Diligence

A great quality to enhance the opportunity to obtain a degree is diligence. The book of Proverbs has much to say about the importance of diligence,

Dr. Elmer Towns

"See a vision, own a vision and share a vision. See what God wants you to do and then own it. I don't want you to just have a dream. I want you to become a dream" (McKay, 2009).

Cheryl

Q: *How did you feel when you earned your degree?*

A: "I felt like I won an incredibly long and challenging marathon. I felt: euphoric, accomplished, and proud that I hadn't given up. I DID IT!"

President Jerry Falwell

"The common theme is always how many of them (our graduates) never could have obtained a college degree if not for Liberty University Online" (Menard, 2013).

Tim

"The best advice that I can give any military personnel is to take your time. Do not try to rush through courses and set up a full load of course work. Sometimes, the courses can require a lot from you, the best thing to do is to take one or two at a time and work slowly. This will also help when it comes to field duty because you will not have as much work to catch-up on when you get back. I understand that you just want to get through college and get it over with. Slow and steady WILL win this race."

Dr. John Hugo, composer of Liberty's theme song

"Champions arise and seek the prize of knowledge aflame!" (Hugo, 2014).

Tim

"Tips for military personnel:

- Constantly remind your chain of command that you are taking college courses and that you have course work that must be completed.

- Take your assignments to work with you. There are many times when you are just standing around, taking a two-hour lunch, etc. Do your homework during this time.

Find someone who is also taking college courses and build a support group; the encouragement that comes from friends and family helps."

and this certainly applies to the online classroom. Proverbs 21:5 states, "The plans of the diligent lead surely to abundance, but everyone who is hasty comes only to poverty" (ESV). There can be a tendency to wait until the last minute and try to complete a week's worth of work in one day. This approach creates unneeded stress and is often a recipe for failure. A diligent person will review the weekly assignments early and make sure that he or she fully understands the instructions. In addition, the student will allow plenty of time to complete the work and will divide it up into achievable segments throughout the week.

Action Plan

1. Review weekly assignments early in the week to ensure that you understand what is expected and that you clearly comprehend the instructions.

2. Contact the instructor earlier in the week to clarify any issues. This will allow ample time for a response and make sure that you can easily submit assignments on time.

3. When you submit your work, always go back and verify that it has been submitted properly according to the instructions.

4. Recognize that diligence is a spiritual characteristic that demonstrates honor to God.

Long- and Short-Term Goals

Pursuing a degree is a long and sometimes tedious process. As with most things in life, when someone begins pursuing a degree, there is a tremendous amount of excitement and energy because it is new. Over time the newness wears off and the student can become discouraged. One of the ways to overcome this challenge is goal setting. In the case of online learning, it is important to have short- and long-term goals. The long-term goal is to earn a degree that will enhance one's vocation or ministry. The challenge with long-term goals is that they are "LONG" term. In this particular case, it is good to periodically stop and remind yourself of the ultimate goal and how it will enhance the future.

Short-term goals work a little differently. In these cases, a student is developing a shorter benchmark as the student works toward the long-term goal. It may be a short celebration or reward at the conclusion of each class. These are designed to recognize that a short-term goal has been accomplished, and although there may still be a long way to go, everything is moving in the right direction.

Action Plan

1. Periodically remind yourself of the ultimate goal of earning a degree and enhancing opportunities you may have in your vocation or ministry.

2. Regularly review your degree completion plan so that you can see that you are making progress.

3. Plan short-term celebrations when certain goals are accomplished. For example, you may decide to take an overnight trip with your family once you have completed four classes. This can be a nice motivation and helps remind you that you are accomplishing your short-term goals as you work toward the long-term goal.

The pursuit of a degree is a tremendous undertaking, which will require sacrifices of time and finances, but can also create a bright future with more opportunities. Students who succeed with an online degree recognize the commitment early on and work hard to achieve this lofty goal. My hope is that these tips for success will serve as a guide to help you earn a degree.

Dr. Jerry Falwell, Sr.

"If God's people will see nothing but the goal line, will accept nothing but victory, will pay any price, will suffer any hurt and hardship, will refuse to be discouraged or disheartened, we cannot help but win; because we are charged with the power of God's Holy Spirit" (Falwell, 1997, p. 236).

Terry Conner

"There is a saying on Mt. Everest, that when you reach the summit, you're only half-way done with the journey (understanding that you are only safe when you're back at base camp). Degree completion is like summiting, you've completed a tremendous feat, but you must then take the knowledge and skills you've attained and go fulfill God's purpose for you in your chosen profession."

Just as Brad has offered some practical tips for success, Lisa Stephens Taylor, Instructor and Instructional Mentor for the College of General Studies, has identified areas that can direct your spiritual walk as you balance a myriad of responsibilities, along with the pursuit of a college degree. Read her article regarding "Tips for Spiritual Balance" and take note of the areas that you want to become a permanent part of your routine.

Tips for Spiritual Balance

Finding the right balance between your studies, your personal life, and your spiritual development can be a tremendous challenge. During your studies, put forth effort to grow in the spiritual disciplines. Focusing on the following inward and outward disciplines can help you become stronger in your walk with Christ while also completing your studies here at Liberty University.

1. **Pray.**

   The scriptures call believers to pray without ceasing (1 Thessalonians 5:17). Meeting with the Lord in an

© 2013 by Edward Lara. Used under license of Shutterstock, Inc.

II Timothy 3:16-17, "All Scripture is God-breathed and is useful for teaching, rebuking, correcting and training in righteousness, so that the servant of God may be thoroughly equipped for every good work" (NIV).

Shannon Bream

"You are heading out into the world with your ambitions and hopes and dreams at a critical time . . . There is a lot of uncertainty, there is fear, and those who would like to create chaos and take innocent lives. . . . You will need to be strong, principled, and brave. And having earned an education that emphasizes not only facts and figures, but also absolute truths—I know you are ready" (Menard, 2013).

Terry

Q: *After earning your degree, what do you wish you had done differently?*

A: "While it was great completing the program quickly, I wish I had spent some more time on certain subjects. So, I would suggest smaller course loads to help retain the information."

Dr. Jerry Falwell, Sr.

"God has a vision for you. Don't settle for second best. Don't ever retire. Don't ever quit. Let your vision become an obsessive reality" (Falwell, 1997, p. 479).

ongoing basis day-by-day opens the line of communication between yourself and Christ. Taking the time to pray will enable you to take your concerns to God, while also taking the time to listen to His response.

2. **Read the Bible Daily.**
   The Bible is our God-breathed book (2 Timothy 3:16). It is our sole guide for conduct, behavior, and belief. So much spiritual nourishment comes directly from time spent in individual, small-group, and large-group Bible study. Learn to spend time each day with God through daily study of the Bible.

3. **Meet With the Lord.**
   Too often, people believe that reading the Bible automatically equates with spending time with God. This is not necessarily the case. Find a quiet, uninterrupted place in order to spend one-on-one time with God through Bible study, prayer, and meditation on the Bible's truths. Through these, you come to have a true connection with God, and you can hear His voice as you meditate on the truth of His Holy Word.

4. **Submit to the Word.**
   The Bible is true, and it provides us with guidance for right living, right relationships with one another, and a right relationship with God. In addition to reading the Bible, seek to live by its precepts. Doing so will provide you with guidance in how to manage your life and its challenges.

5. **Serve God and Others.**
   Christians are not only called to study the Bible, worship together, and pray. They are also called to serve. Giving is not only limited to financial giving, but also giving of our time and our abilities. Although you are busy as a student, do not forget to be actively involved in your local church, using your gifts to serve God, to serve the church, and to serve those who desperately need you in their lives.

6. **Integrate Your Faith Into Your Studies.**
   At Liberty, we encourage you to integrate your faith into your studies, just as your professors integrate their faith into how they teach you. Your academic studies should come alongside the growth of your faith and fuse together. History is full of men and women whose faith in Christ led to great learning, and whose learning led to achievements that have changed the world for the better. You are coming along in that great tradition. Use your faith and God's word as lenses for understanding all of the lessons before you. They will put the courses that you are studying in their proper context.

BUILDING BLOCKS

If you have read this far in the textbook, you probably understand that you are at a pivotal point in your education. Having come this far, you have had times of great success, perhaps some times of struggle, and perhaps even a few times that you did not make an attempt to struggle to build your success. Some of you will have had a hot and cold relationship with your coursework. You may have begun strong, but quickly burned out when the assignments were not to your liking or did not seem to be leading where you wished to go. Now is a good time to evaluate your work as you reflect on how you conducted your work this important term, as this course is the groundwork for so much that will come after it as you work toward your college degree.

Think back to the YOU who began the course. What do you see that has remained the same over the weeks you have been taking this course, and what has changed? Are the changes ones of attitude, work habits, or time management? These are the critical elements that will allow you to continue to build your success or that will drag you far from it. This chapter is the "key" chapter, but there are really multiple keys to your success. As you reflect on the YOU who is now completing the textbook, what lies ahead for you? Have you planned your next term's courses and are you eager to get them underway? In the New Testament book of Matthew, in Chapter 13, we read what is called the parable of the sower. It says:

> A farmer was sowing grain in his fields. As he scattered the seed across the ground, some fell beside a path, and the birds came and ate it. And some fell on rocky soil, where there was little depth of earth; the plants sprang up quickly enough in the shallow soil, but the hot sun soon scorched them and they withered and died, for they had so little root. Other seeds fell among thorns, and the thorns choked out the tender blades. But some fell on good soil, and produced a crop that was thirty, sixty, and even a hundred times as much as he had planted. If you have ears, listen!"
>
> (Matthew 13:3b-9, The Living Bible)

As you read that passage and evaluate yourself as a student, what sort of ground do you think you are? The title of this book is *Breaking Ground* because this is a course designed to help you lay the groundwork of online education in a way that will lead you to success. Have you "produced a crop," as the Bible passage puts it, with your work in this introductory course? Has your work been its best, leading you to ultimate academic success? We pray it has!

TOOL BOX

Accountability—As mentioned in the chapter, having an accountability partner can be a major factor in staying on task. Recruiting friends or family members who are close to you is a good idea, but you might also consider an online accountability partner who is going through the same experiences that you are.

Was there another student, or group of students, who you made a connection with while in this class? Consider the idea of working together to keep yourselves moving forward toward your goals. This will not only benefit your time management but will also help to establish a sense of community.

Syllabus and Course Schedule—As you enter each new class, be sure to navigate to the Syllabus and Assignment Instructions folder in the Course Content area and download the syllabus and course schedule. These documents explain, in detail, what the learning objectives are for your class, how they will be attained and assessed, and what work will need to be accomplished each week. Reviewing these documents as you begin each of your next classes will help you to connect activities to learning outcomes and will allow you to plan an appropriate amount of time in your schedule each week.

Degree Completion Plan (DCP) Audit—You reviewed your DCP Audit earlier in the course, but don't let this be a one-time event. Log into your DCP Audit before the start of each new term. Watching your degree completion plan fill up, as you progress through your degree, can be a huge motivational factor, and it can also save you time, money, and frustration.

By checking your audit before each term, you can confirm that you are taking classes that will count toward your degree. This means you will avoid accidentally taking a class, only to find out that it was not one of your degree requirements. Always verify your findings with your Academic Advisor. Your time and money are too valuable to waste.

End of Course Surveys—At the end of each class, Liberty University will ask you to complete a brief survey related to your experience with your professors and the course materials. Some students do not fill these out because they believe that professors will be able to see their comments and hold their comments against them when the time comes to assign final grades. Rest assured, Liberty takes your privacy and your feedback very seriously.

Prior to final grade submission, your professors are able to view a list of who has or has not completed the survey, but they are not able to see your comments. This is used primarily so your professors can encourage those who have not completed the survey to do so. After final grades have been assigned, usually about two weeks after the course has ended, Liberty will release the survey results to your professors and their supervisors. This list does not contain any names, and there is no way for anyone to see who wrote what. All that is visible is the individual questions followed by a listing of anonymous responses.

Your professors and their supervisors will review the feedback of your entire class and utilize that information to make any necessary adjustments to the curriculum. This is your opportunity to help shape the future of your university. Take full advantage of it and offer your feedback at the end of each class.

Additional resources and links to specific sites, worksheets, and apps can be located by accessing the Breaking Ground website:

www.breakinggroundlu.com

THE ULTIMATE CORNERSTONE

Psalm 118:21–23, "I will give you thanks, for you answered me; you have become my salvation. The stone the builders rejected has become the cornerstone; the Lord has done this, and it is marvelous in our eyes" (NIV).

Throughout this textbook and this course, we have shared a lot of information with you to equip you for a successful academic career. As we conclude our time together, we want to share the most important message of all, which is the cornerstone of our faith—our forgiveness and salvation through Jesus Christ. Mark Tinsley, Army Chaplain (retired) and Associate Dean of the College of General Studies, elaborates in the story that follows, "Our Altitude & Our Salvation."

Our Altitude & Our Salvation

I started flying airplanes when I was only 15 years old. In fact, I could fly solo in an airplane before I was legally allowed to drive a car in my home state of Virginia. As paradoxical as it sounds, my parents would drive me to the airport so I could fly alone in a plane. The situation with its waist-deep irony was quite humorous, even for a teenager. Still, it provided for some great stories among family and friends—stories that we still share with one another today, some 20–25 years later.

Regrettably, not all of my aviation experiences are so lighthearted in nature. I have been involved in several close calls around the country and one crash on the runway of the Raleigh-Durham Airport in North Carolina. Fortunately, the crash involved no injuries and was, when compared to other aviation accidents, rather minor. One of the close calls, though, was quite serious, and I avoided certain injury or death by only minutes.

A fellow pilot and I were flying from the Shenandoah Valley Airport in Weyers Cave, Virginia, en route to the Winchester Airport in Winchester, Virginia. The weather that day was cold and cloudy, so we had filed what is called an instrument (IFR) flight plan—a flight plan that allows properly trained pilots to fly in bad weather.

Photo courtesy of Cali Lowdermilk (Liberty University).

Dr. Jerry Falwell, Sr.: "God has a vision for you. Don't settle for second best. Don't ever retire. Don't ever quit. Let your vision become an obsessive reality" (*Falwell, 1997, p. 479*).

Sometime soon after takeoff from Weyers Cave, we entered the clouds and began flying solely by reference to the cockpit instruments. Everything went well until we got closer to Winchester. During our flight north through Virginia, the weather had deteriorated significantly, and the temperature at our altitude had fallen well below freezing. Consequently, our wings started to accumulate ice—and lots of it. For those who are unaware, airplanes and ice do not mix. If a plane's wings accumulate too much ice during flight, then the airplane can become unstable and crash. After a few minutes of rapid ice buildup, the co-pilot and I realized we were in serious trouble.

We had two choices at that point in the flight. We could encourage the ice to melt by either climbing above the clouds where the sun was shining or descending to a lower altitude where the temperatures were most likely warmer. Since the route between Weyers Cave and Winchester is extremely mountainous, we would have preferred to climb to a higher altitude. Unfortunately, we had accumulated so much ice that the aircraft was too heavy to safely execute this option. We were left with only the descent. After obtaining approval from air traffic control to move to a lower altitude, we did so, praying all the while that temperatures would be high enough to melt the ice and that our controllers would safely guide us through the dangerous mountains of Northwestern Virginia.

Happily, the temperatures were indeed warmer, and the controllers did not disappoint in their ability to provide safe passage. After a few minutes at the lower altitude, we noticed ice starting to slough off of the wings and struts, and soon the plane was completely free of its burden. What is more, air traffic control maintained positive communication with us throughout the ordeal and constantly adjusted our heading, speed, and altitude to place us on final approach to the Winchester Airport within the shortest timeframe possible. When the wheels touched down on the runway, the co-pilot and I breathed a sigh of relief, thus concluding a one-hour flight that made us feel about 20 years older.

As I look back on this experience today, I realize just how fortunate we were. Had we decided to continue flying at our original altitude, our plane would have gathered excessive ice, causing it to become unstable. A crash would have likely ensued. Likewise, had we tried to climb to a higher altitude, the increased weight on the airframe would have prevented our ascent, and, again, we would have likely crashed. However, we made the right decision and descended to a lower altitude. Indeed, ours was the only safe and wise decision to make.

At the same time, I am reminded that neither my co-pilot nor I melted the ice that day. We simply made the decision to descend to a lower altitude. It was the natural laws of physics and thermodynamics that melted the ice. In other words, we decided to fly the plane at an altitude where the air was warmer, but it was the warm air—not the efforts of the co-pilot or me—that melted the ice. One might say that the "promises" of science were what saved us that day, even though our decision to move out of danger is what placed us in the right posture for positive change to occur.

When I read God's Word, I am amazed at how well this anecdote applies to the biblical concept of salvation. As sinners, we are flying at a dangerous altitude. The world around us is cold, and the icy burdens of life accumulate rapidly on our wings. We are seemingly helpless. We know we can't stay where we are, or we will surely die in our wretchedness and sin (Rom. 6:23); we are unable to climb by our own power to a higher altitude and, thus, save ourselves (Eph. 2:8–10); and we realize there are treacherous mountains below and, to go that direction means the assumption of considerable risk. So, what do we do? Where do we go?

In his grace and mercy, God does not leave us to wonder. Romans 5:8 reads, "But God shows his love for us in that while we were still sinners, Christ died for us" (ESV). Through his death on the cross at Calvary, Christ provides the warm air below. His sacrifice and atonement make staying at our present altitude a foolish choice and render futile any attempt at some sort of cavalier, self-directed climb. Christ alone is our Savior! In John 14:6, Jesus proclaims, "I am the way and the truth and the life. No one comes to the Father except through me" (ESV). The decision is singular and clear, and it is one that only we can make. We must power back and descend in order to place ourselves in the warmth below. If we do so, Christ promises to take away our icy-cold burdens. Romans 10:9, 13 states, "Because, if you confess with your mouth that Jesus is Lord and believe in your heart that God raised him from the dead, you will be saved. . . . For 'everyone who calls on the name of the Lord will be saved'" (ESV). That is to say, if we trust in Christ and give our lives over to him in full submission and obedience, we are promised ultimate deliverance from the trials and tribulations of this world. Indeed, as John 3:16 tells us, our faith is rewarded with eternal life.

Of course, trusting in God is not easy. Descending means coming in close proximity to the treacherous terrain of life. A life of faith is always wrought with rugged, dangerous peaks, deep, dark valleys, and raging rivers of temptation and worldly desire. What we have to remember, though, is that God has complete and perfect knowledge of this terrain. He is our air traffic controller, and He will guide us along a path that will bring us safely to our destination (i.e., eternal life with Him). Hebrews 13:5 quotes Deuteronomy 31:6 and records God's promise, "I will never leave you nor forsake you" (ESV). God is our trustworthy guide through all of life's dangers.

If you do not know Christ as your personal Lord and Savior today, the ice is building up on your wings, the air is cold, and you are in danger. You cannot stay where you are, nor can you climb out of the danger yourself. However, you do have an option. All you have to do is reach for the throttle, power back, and descend. Make a decision for Christ; warm air awaits you.

Dr. Jerry Falwell, Sr.

"I believe in ignoring the walls that people build. Behind the facades that separate us, we are all alike. We all need to know that God loves us. We all need to know that in Christ God has forgiven our sins and our failures. We all need to know that through Christ we can begin again" (Falwell, 2008, p. 43).

• •

As Mark explained, making a decision to serve Jesus Christ is the most important decision of your life! If you have decided to make this decision, please let your professor know. He or she will take delight in this incredibly awesome news! Your professor can also put you in touch with campus pastors, who can help disciple you or put you in contact with someone in your area who can. As Psalm 118: 21–24 states, this is a cause for much rejoicing, "I will give you thanks, for You answered me; You have become my salvation. The stone the builders rejected has become the cornerstone; the Lord has done this, and it is marvelous in our eyes. The Lord has done it this very day; let us rejoice today and be glad" (NIV). Let the world know that you are now a true "champion for Christ!"

Photo courtesy of Joel Coleman (Liberty University).

"Let the world know that you are now a true 'champion for Christ!'"

References

Falwell, J. (1997). *Falwell: An autobiography*. Lynchburg, VA: Liberty House Publishers.

Falwell, J. (2014). *Press quotes*. Retrieved from http://www.liberty.edu/aboutliberty/index.cfm?PID = 26726.

Falwell, M. (2008). *Jerry Falwell: His life and legacy*. New York, NY: Howard Books.

Fralick, M. (2011). *College and career success*. Dubuque, IA: Kendall Hunt Publishing Company.

Hugo, J. (2014). *Registrar: Liberty University Alma Mater*. Retrieved from http://www.liberty.edu/academics/registrar/?PID = 5648

Laird, B. (2012). *80 years dedicated to God*. Retrieved from http://www.liberty.edu/champion/2012/04/eighty-years-dedicated-to-god/comment-page-1/.

McKay, D. (2009). *Dr. Elmer Towns speaks at convocation*. Retrieved from http://www.liberty.edu/news/index.cfm?PID = 18495&MID = 5840.

Menard, D. (2013). *40th Commencement: Celebrating historic accomplishments, continuous growth*. Retrieved from http://www.liberty.edu/aboutliberty/index.cfm?PID = 24995&MID = 91512.

Skinner, M. & Liberty University News Service. (2013, September 27). *'Duck Dynasty' star Willie Robertson calls students to be successful*. Retrieved from http://www.liberty.edu/news/index.cfm?PID = 18495&MID = 100031.

Tradition. (n.d.). In *Merriam-Webster.com*. Retrieved from http://www.merriam-webster. com/dictionary/tradition.

GLOSSARY

abstract—A concise summary of a source's content, usually appearing at the beginning of an article, which can help you to decide quickly whether the source is relevant to your research topic.

academic accommodations—*Educational* practices, systems, and support mechanisms designed to accommodate functional challenges posed by an individual's disability.

academic integrity—Avoiding the unethical practice of stealing the ideas of others, whether they are the ideas of peers (e.g., cheating on exams) or the words and ideas of authorities that have been used in a written paper (plagiarism).

academic misconduct—Any action or attempted action that may result in creating an unfair academic advantage for oneself or an unfair academic advantage or disadvantage for any other member or members of the academic community.

academic standing—A measure of the student's academic achievement relative to his/her degree requirements, and determines his/her eligibility to be admitted to and/or proceed in his/her academic plan and to qualify for graduation.

active engagement—the efforts a student puts in to read, write, and think about what he/she is learning."

active reading—Reading something with a determination to understand and evaluate it for its relevance to your needs.

andragogy—The art and science of helping adults learn.

APA style—Standing for the American Psychological Association—the citation style most commonly used in the social and natural sciences (e.g., sociology and anthropology).

attendance—In an online course, signing in and completing an assignment for credit. Merely signing in to the course does not count as attendance for federal financial aid reporting purposes.

biblical worldview—Absorbing information through God's truth (found in the Bible), and it also involves your actions towards others.

body paragraphs—Three or more paragraphs (depending on the assignment requirements) that follow the sequence outlined in the thesis statement; each body paragraph should begin with a topic sentence, include an explanation of the item(s) brought up in the topic sentence, and end with a concluding sentence that wraps up the main points of the paragraph and transitions into the next paragraph.

catalog—A library database containing information about what information sources the library owns and where they are located, or a written (or online) compendium of information on a college's policies, programs, and courses.

cheating—A dishonest or an unfair act in order to gain an advantage.

Christian worldview—An overall concept of the world and our part in it, grounded on God's authority, which He reveals to us through the Bible.

citation—A reference to an information source (e.g., book, article, Web page) that provides enough information to allow the reader to retrieve the source.

conclusion paragraph—The final paragraph in a piece of writing; it should include a review of the main points addressed within the writing and provide a final, convincing application.

Course Requirements Checklist (CRC)—This brief checklist ensures that students are aware of some basic expectations and is the tool we use to record initial attendance.

course schedule—A chart that specifies what reading and study assignments are to be done for each module/week of the term.

credible—One of the criteria used to evaluate the quality of academic sources, specifically related to determining if the source was written by an authority or expert in the related field.

current—One of the criteria used to evaluate the quality of academic sources, specifically related to ensuring that the source was published recently enough to keep up with the pace of research being generated in the field.

database—A collection of data (information) that has been organized to make the information easily accessible and retrievable.

descriptor—A keyword or key phrase in the index of a database (card or catalog) that describes the subjects or content areas found within it, enabling you to quickly locate sources relevant to your research topic; a.k.a. subject heading.

discussion board—A form of online, ongoing (over a few days) conversation that allows students to "meet" each other to discuss an academic topic. Students learn from the experiences and ideas shared in the forum.

documentation—References that support or confirm your conclusions.

editing—A stage of writing in which the author evaluates his/her work to ensure there are no misspelled words or grammatical errors.

falsification—To make (something) false or to change (something) in order to make people believe something that is not true.

FN—A grade indicating failure for nonattendance.

fundamental attribution error—"When we see someone doing something, we tend to think it relates to their personality rather than the situation the person might be in" (Sherman, 2014).

index—An alphabetical listing of topics contained in a database.

information literacy—The ability to search for, locate, and evaluate information for relevance and accuracy.

introduction paragraph—The first paragraph of an essay; it should always include an attention getter, explanatory transition sentences, and a comprehensive thesis statement.

keyword—A word used to search multiple databases by matching the search word to items found in different databases. Keywords are very specific.

learning outcomes—Statements that describe significant and essential learning that learners have achieved, and can reliably demonstrate at the end of a course or program.

metacognition—Thinking about thinking.

MLA style—Standing for the Modern Language Association—the citation style commonly used in the humanities and fine arts (e.g., English and theatre arts).

netiquette—The rules of etiquette that apply when communicating over computer networks, especially the Internet. It requires that responses be respectful, using polite language to agree or disagree with the thoughts shared by others.

objective—Not influenced by personal feelings, interpretations, or prejudice; based on facts; unbiased.

overlearning—a study strategy in which you rehearse the study material past the point of mastery as a method to defeat test anxiety."

pedagogy—The art and science of teaching children.

plagiarism—A violation of academic integrity that involves intentional or unintentional use of someone else's work without acknowledging it, giving the reader the impression that it's the writer's original work.

prerequisite courses—Courses that a student must pass before enrolling in the actual or advanced course. Equivalent skills or prior experience may also be accepted.

primary sources—Firsthand information or original documents (e.g., research experiments or novels).

randomized—Make random in order or arrangement; employ random selection or sampling in (an experiment or procedure).

registrar's office—the official custodian of all academic records for the university.

revision—According to Sommers (as cited in Witte, 1980) as "a sequence of changes in a composition, in which ideas, words, and phrases are added, deleted, moved, or changed throughout the writing of the work" (2013).

rubric—A tool that professors use to evaluate and grade submitted assignments.

scaffolding—a learning method in which one concept is build upon a previous one.

scholarly—One of the criteria used to evaluate the quality of academic sources, specifically related to sources that have been reviewed by a panel or board of impartial experts in the field before being published.

search engine—A computer-run program that allows you to search for information across the Internet or at a particular website.

search thesaurus—A list of words or phrases with similar meaning, allowing you to identify which of these words or phrases could be used as keywords, descriptors, or subject headings in the database.

secondary sources—Publications that rely on or respond to primary sources (e.g., a textbook or a newspaper article that critically reviews a novel or movie).

self-reflection—Careful thought about your own behaviors and beliefs.

subscription database—A database that can only be accessed through a paid subscription.

success—Achievement of an objective or goal.

syllabi—Plural form of syllabus; see syllabus.

syllabus—A document that includes a description of the course content, rationale, prerequisite courses, required course materials, and expected learning outcomes. Basic expectations for required assignments, evaluation and grading, and late work policies are included.

teachable moment—An unplanned opportunity that arises where a teacher has an ideal chance to offer insight to his or her students. It is not something that you can plan for; rather, it is a fleeting opportunity that must be sensed and seized by the teacher.

thesis statement—One sentence that establishes the main topic(s) and point/direction of a piece of writing.

transcript—A concise display of the courses you have taken and the grades you earned.

Turabian style—Named for the original author, Kate L. Turabian, and very similar to Chicago Style—the citation style commonly used in religion courses here at Liberty.

URL (Uniform Resource Locator)—An Internet address consisting of a series of letters and/or numbers that pinpoints the exact location of an information resource (e.g., www.breakinggroundlu.com).

widgets—small computer application.

wildcard—A symbol, such as an asterisk (*), question mark (?), or exclamation point (!), that may be used to substitute different letters into a search word or phrase, so that an electronic search will be performed on all variations of the word represented by the symbol.

worldview—"A particular philosophy of life or conception of the world" (Merriam-Webster.com, 2015).

INDEX

Career planning, 293–315
    action steps for career growth, 301–303
    documents to use in future job search, 304–312
    exploration and development, 297–300
Catalog, 221
Center for Curriculum Development, 21
Center for Writing and Languages (CWL), 38, 39
Chaining, for memorization, 67
Chambers, Oswald, 101–102
Character traits, goal-setting, 141–146
Cheating, 33, 228, 232
Christian worldview. *See* Biblical worldview
Citation Software, 239
Civil Rights Movement, 100
Cloud-based storage, 314
Code of Honor, 33
Communication, interpersonal, 31–32, 45–46, 333
Comprehension, reading, 53, 56, 75
Concept mapping, 62–63, 197
Cornell note-taking, 62, 63
Course
    guides, 29–30, 151, 181
    reflecting experiences within, 327–328
    schedule, 29, 45, 340
    sequencing, 151
    syllabus, 29–30, 45, 151, 165, 181, 182, 251, 315, 340
Course requirements checklist (CRC), 29, 45
Coursework, time spent on, 51–52, 128
Cover letter, 306–307
Covey, Stephen, 206–207, 333–334
Cramming, 68, 137
Credits, 181–182
Critical thinking, 41, 225
Crystallizers of intelligence, 202

D

Daily planning, in time management, 134
Dantes Subject Standardized tests (DSSTs), 181
Database
    definition of, 221
    subscription database, 222–223

Deadlines, assignment, 30, 32, 45, 128
Degree Completion Plan (DCP) Audit, 151, 152, 166, 340
Descriptor, definition of, 222
Determination, 143
Diligence, 143, 335–336
Disabilities, students with, 38–39
Discussion boards, 30–31, 45, 204, 211–212
Distractions, dealing with, 53, 135–137
Doctrinal Statement, 16, 33, 93–94
Documents for job search, 304–312
During-reading strategies, 55–65
During-viewing strategies (lecture presentations), 59

E

Editing, in academic writing, 272–277
E-learning strategies, 204
Electronic portfolio, 308–309
Elim Home for Alcoholics, 13
Employment interview, 309–310
Encyclopedia of Careers and Vocational Guidance, 16th ed., 300
End of course surveys, 340–341
Environment, learning, 189–190, 196, 210
Equivalency credit, 181
Essay questions, 70–71
Ethical behavior, 31, 33, 45
Evernote (software), 75
Exam, credit by, 181
Excelsior exams, 181
Existential intelligence, 201
Experimenter bias, 225
Externship experiences, 302–303

F

Failure, nonattendance (FN) grade, 30
Faithfulness, 101–102, 117–118, 144–145
    success as, 118
Falsification, 33, 232
Falwell, Jerry, 7, 10–12, 14–15
Falwell, Jerry, Sr., 3–13, 141, 145, 187, 321

Final draft (academic writing), 278–284
Financial Aid Office, 35, 40
Flashcards, 67, 75, 197, 199, 200
Focus 2 software, 35, 151
Forbearance, 100
Foreign language learning, 38
Frankl, Viktor, 205, 206
Fundamental attribution error, 145–146

G

Gardner, Howard, 201
General education, 166
Generosity, and plagiarism, 230
Goals, 111–152
    defining success, 116–118
    establishing priorities, 132–140
    present/ future, reevaluating, 322–326
    setting, 336–337
        character traits, 141–146
        educational goals, 119–127
    time management, 128–131
        plan, 132–140
Godwin, Ronald S., 11
Goodness, 101
Google Sites, 314
Grading expectations, 251–253
Graham, Billy, 98
Graphic organizer, for pre-writing, 255–256
Gratitude, and plagiarism, 230

H

Honesty, 142, 145
    and plagiarism, 231
Humility, and plagiarism, 231

I

Illative sense, 167
Index, definition of, 222
Industriousness, and plagiarism, 231
Information interview, 309–310

Information literacy, 215–240
    definition and importance of, 219
    identifying and avoiding plagiarism, 228–236
    research strategy, 220–227
Information Technology department, 21–22
Institutional Challenge Exam (ICE), 181
Integrity, 101–102, 142
    academic, 228, 230–232, 235
    citing sources with, 232–236
    and plagiarism, 231
Intelligence
    definition of, 201
    multiple intelligences, 201–202
Internet, 220, 224, 234, 256
Internships, 35, 303, 311
Interpersonal communication, 31–32, 45–46, 333
Interview
    Mock Interview, 312
    preparation, 309–310
IQ test, 201
IT Help Desk, 35–36
IT Marketplace, 35–36

J

Jerry Falwell Library, 9, 14, 36, 239
Jerry Falwell Museum, 8
Job search, documents to use in, 304–312
Job shadowing, 302
Joy, 98–99

K

Keyword, definition of, 222
Kindness, 100–101
Kinesthetic learning, 193
    strategies, 199–200
King, Dr. Martin Luther, Jr., 100
Knowledge, 166–167

L

L'Abri, 102
Law-ruled paper, for note-taking, 62

True/False questions, 68, 69
Turabian referencing style, 235
Tutor.com, 40, 57, 181, 278

U

URL (uniform resource locator), 223
U.S. Department of Labor
   Occupation Exploration website, 300
   O*NET OnLine, 300

V

Values of Liberty University, 92–94
Variety of reference citations, 226–227
Visual learning, 192
   strategies, 196–197, 200
Volunteer work, 303, 311

W

Websites
   for academic writing, 290
   for online portfolios, 314
Weekly assignments
   deadlines, 32, 45
   timely submission of, 30
Weekly planning (time management), 133–134
Wildcard, 223
Wisdom, 141–142
WordPress, 314
Word processing software, 289
Worldview, definition of, 82. *See also* Biblical
   worldview
Writer's block, 288
Writing. *See* Academic writing